Ilan Pappé is Director of the European Centre for Palestine Studies and a fellow of the Institute for Arab and Islamic Studies at the University of Exeter. He is also Co-director of The Exeter Centre for Ethno-Political Studies. He is the author of various books, including *The Making of the Arab–Israeli Conflict* (I.B.Tauris).

Jamil Hilal is a sociologist associated with Birzeit University and has lectured at several UK universities. He has held senior associate research fellowships at the University of Oxford and SOAS, and in 2008 he was a visiting scholar at Carnegie Middle East Center.

Across the
WALL

Narratives of Israeli–Palestinian History

Edited by
Ilan Pappé and Jamil Hilal

I.B. TAURIS
LONDON · NEW YORK

Published in 2010 by I.B.Tauris & Co Ltd
6 Salem Road, London W2 4BU
175 Fifth Avenue, New York NY 10010
www.ibtauris.com

Distributed in the United States and Canada
Exclusively by Palgrave Macmillan
175 Fifth Avenue, New York NY 10010

Library of Modern Middle East Studies: 88

ISBN: 978 1 84885 345 4

A full CIP record for this book is available from the British Library
A full CIP record is available from the Library of Congress

Library of Congress Catalog Card Number: available

Printed and bound in the UK by CPI Antony Rowe, Chippenham, Wiltshire
from camera-ready copy edited and supplied by
the editors with the assistance of
Pardes Publishing House, Haifa

Contents

PALISAD

Palestinian and Israeli Academics in Dialogue

Jamil Hilal and Ilan Pappé

Introduction

As this volume goes to the press, Israel is rapidly completing the Wall it is illegally constructing deep into the West Bank. When finished, its 670km-long serpentine route of 8m-high concrete slabs, barbed wire and guarded watchtowers will result in Israel effectively occupying over 90 per cent of historical Palestine, leaving a mere 10 per cent for the Palestinians to build their state in. This makes a mockery of all peace efforts towards a two-state solution and again shows Israel's utter disregard of international law.[1] But, of course, the Apartheid Wall is only the physical counterpart of the ideological wall Zionist settlers first introduced into Palestine when they began arriving in the 1880s. And it is with this wall and how to tear it down that the people in this volume are concerned.

---

1 In the ruling it published on 9 July 2004, the International Court of Justice in The Hague stated: 'Israel is under an obligation to terminate its breaches of international law; it is under an obligation to cease forthwith the works of construction of the Wall being built in Occupied Palestinian Territory, including in and around Jerusalem, to dismantle forthwith the structure therein situated, and to repeal or render ineffective forthwith all legislative and regulatory acts relating thereto.' That the Wall runs more than twice the length of the 315km-long 'Green Line' (the June 1967 border) further points up the hypocrisy of the 'security' argument Israel puts forward as the reason for erecting it.

In the spring of 1997 a number of Palestinian and Israeli academics met to discuss the possibility of together studying and researching the history of Israel and Palestine. What prompted us was a shared sense of urgency in the wake of the deadlock in the so-called peace process and a common dissatisfaction with the nature of the Oslo Accords. At the time, we all felt that the whole process would at best result in workable political and military arrangements but could never lead to any genuine national and cultural reconciliation. But more important perhaps than the *political* solidarity enveloping our group was the strong common *academic* ground that brought us together. All of us shared the belief that what was needed was an alternative historical perspective on the conflict, one capable of bridging over the two national meta-narratives and their ethnocentric and segregationist orientations. These meta-narratives, rather than bringing the two sides together, spelled the defeat of all chances for reconciliation between our two peoples.

We called ourselves PALISAD, Palestinian-Israeli Academic Dialogue, and began meeting on a monthly basis in either Ramallah or Jerusalem. Each time one of us, with Palestinians and Israelis alternating, would present a paper for discussion on subjects of immediate concern and benefit to both sides. This quickly produced an intriguing dialogue about the connection between national narratives, historical research and collective identities. Looking in Gramscian terms at the 'unity of the historical process' of which we are part helped us steer away from the nationalist dichotomy we had been brought up with. Where this proved impossible we set out to deconstruct the two conflicting meta-narratives and re-write them as two less antagonistic perspectives that, instead of inevitably leading to confrontation, could offer a potential basis for co-operation. There were, of course, other attempts at creating a dialogue between the two nations in the wake of the Oslo Accords, some even quite popular. But none of these adopted the critical view on national identity our group embraced as one of its central tenets, though we never severed ourselves completely from the national perspectives so dominant in both societies.

Naturally, a wide range of general theoretical subjects came up for discussion, especially on historiography and nationalism, but topics of an outspokenly concrete nature were equally central, such as '1948', the Israeli occupation, Palestinian democracy, and so on. With the benefit of hindsight, we now know that our joint efforts did not produce the overarching meta-narrative we wanted to come up with. But we are in fact no longer convinced that that is necessary. Our dialogue produced something more valuable: a dynamic and dialectical bridging narrative that, by accentuating areas of agreement and highlighting gaps of dissent, has succeeded in pulling together our different points of view and opening up vistas towards a common future. The process we are engaged in is a volatile one and needs to be nurtured not just for the sake of academic dialogue, but to help foster future reconciliation between, and within, our two societies. In the following pages we will briefly seek to conceptualize this bridging narrative that we have been building and outline how it cements together the articles that make up this volume.

Bridging Narratives

The scholarly literature provides little by way of theoretical references to the concept of 'bridging narratives'; it shows up mainly in the analyses of fictional plots. Bridging narratives are usually intercalary chapters, short pieces that help connect the so-called 'plot' chapters. In Classical Greek plays they are the sections where a narrator, in the form of the chorus, helps bridge over parts of the drama's action. This narrator appears as an omniscient presence guiding the audience through the dialogues and events on and, even more, off stage. Our PALISAD group in a way functions as such a narrator in the reconstruction of the historical plot for which we are pleading—a version of past events that bears significant relevance for our present reality and creates common space for the future. At the same time, the authors who make up this volume, much like our group as a whole, seek to build a bridge not only between the two antagonistic national meta-narratives, but also between their own position and the national narrative that happens to be 'theirs'. This became clearer as we moved on, making the dialectical process incremental as well. What follows is an outline of the various stages we covered and of how they are reflected in the structure of the volume.

The concept of bridging narratives as we employ it extends beyond the historian's 'presence' in the emplotment of the historical narrative. It calls for our intrusion in the orientation of the reconstruction we have undertaken to be more blunt. And, of course, the very idea of bringing together academics interested in past history for the sake of the present and propelled by a vision of the future is by itself actively 'interventionist'.

As no clear conceptualization presents itself, we need at least a working definition, one that can serve not only the case study of Palestine presented here, but hopefully also historiographical efforts within other nations at war or societies torn by historical conflicts in our contemporary world. A bridging narrative thus becomes a conscious historiographical effort undertaken by historians in societies wrought by long internal and/or external conflicts, to create a transitional structure spanning narratives and historiographies that are antagonistic. Embarked upon in this spirit, such a historiographical enterprise becomes part and parcel of the overall reconciliation effort that is to bring an end to the conflict. It also means that what inspires their navigation in the plots of the past is the historians' inner drive to have some impact on the events of the present. Together with a good sense of historiographical contexualism, this requires our active 'presence' through the critical approach we adopt towards hegemonic ideologies. In this volume Israelis and Palestinians are doing exactly that as they choose to deconstruct the national narratives of the past and challenge the common interpretation of the present.

This recognition, that the contemporary political reality we live in has to be present in our scholarly work, entails a 'soft relativist' approach to writing history within a context of national conflict. 'Soft relativist', because the sea of facts exposed to the historians' eyes will be absorbed in as wide a spectrum as possible. While, much as in any positivist historical enterprise, empirical evidence will be gathered, the emplotment of the mass of evidence brought out into the open no longer strives to be the 'neutral', 'objective' business positivists claim to be involved in, particularly not when we are dealing with a conflict that continues to rage on while we, partisan historians, are trying to write its history.

Bridging-narrative projects undertaken elsewhere came to naught exactly because, besides their ideological inhibitions, they were hampered by the purely positivist nature of professional historiography. As the historiosophical debates moved on, practicing history became less elitist, more interdisciplinary, and historians more aware of the dialectics between power and knowledge that underpins hegemonic structures. Allowing contemporary agendas to become part and parcel of the historical enterprise is no longer a heresy. In other words, historical reconstruction becomes a joint historiographical effort involving individuals who seek to absolve themselves from their given national and positional identities (in our case, invaders vs. invaded, colonizers vs. colonized, occupiers vs. occupied, etc.). It entails also a fresh recognition of the way history is always contexualized and, more importantly, of the way power structures seek to determine the nature of the dialogue between present and past. And we witness how shifts in power relations outside the scholarly world bring about changes within the research paradigms. The catch phrase, of course, is positionality, i.e., the conscious impact of one's own politics of identity on the historical research one is involved in.

In this collection, positionality becomes the critical cement for the bridging narrative we set out to construct. This is immediately evident in our choice of topics. Some of us decided to divert from the agenda we had initially set and instead took up challenges that happened to arise within the group to throw light on a particularly formative chapter or analyze an area of obvious contention. Others felt liberated within the context of the group to expand on their own personal extractions from the historical lessons we were drawing and to experiment with issues that lie on the dim borderline between politics and academia. The result is a collection that obeys an intriguing historical mode of selection: it encompasses only issues of the past that haunt the present and are sure to affect the future. Periods or issues that seemed to us meaningless or irrelevant we simply ignored.

It was not long into our dialogue that we reached our first and perhaps most fundamental 'bridge', the one that enabled us as a group to ditch the 'paradigm of parity'.

Ditching the 'Paradigm of Parity'

With hindsight, what proved to be the main facilitator for our group to embark on our common journey as a collective of scholars was the severe critique we all shared of the 'paradigm of parity', still the one prism through which the western world insists on viewing the 'Arab-Israeli' conflict. The paradigm of parity posits that there are two warring parties in Palestine who each carry equal responsibility for both the outbreak of and the solution to the conflict. It is behind the abortive peace efforts typical of the second half of the twentieth century and, despite its proven track record of failure on all accounts to advance the chances of peace on the ground, continues to prevail today.

The paradigm of parity has spelled and will always spell total failure because the reality in Palestine is the exact opposite—the conflict is one of disparity and inequality on all fronts. It was that already in 1882, when colonizer—a European Zionist settler movement—first confronted the colonized—the indigenous Palestinian population—and again in 1948, when nationalist Jewish settler forces drove most of that indigenous population out of Palestine. The paradigm of parity is also totally inadequate when it comes to describing the reality between occupier and occupied in the West Bank and the Gaza Strip since 1967, not to mention the inequality in rights and status the Jewish state has forced upon its Palestinian minority over the past 57 years.

The paradigm of parity was adopted by the Americans, the main peace brokers since 1967, and by the Quartet—the UN, the US, Russia and the EU—that recently joined the mediation efforts. All mediators seem oblivious to, or have decided to ignore, two basic hard facts: that when Israel was created it took over 80 per cent of Palestine, and that UN Resolution 194, of 11 December 1948, enshrines the right of all Palestinians the Zionists have expelled since 1948 to return home.

In the field of knowledge production, again especially in the West, the situation is even more perplexing. Here the two sides are often portrayed as *not* equally responsible or accountable for the conflict, but what is stressed then is intransigence not on the part of the Zionists but of the Palestinians. The corollary of this was that for decades academic efforts by Palestinians were ridiculed as sheer propaganda, while those produced by the Israeli academic establishment passed for scholarly and professional representations of the local reality.

PALISAD is part of a wider academic effort to redress this particular imbalance. The shift we witnessed in the late 1980s in the power structures that underpin knowledge production meant that the official historiography of Palestine turned more in favour of the Palestinians. It is true that so far this has had very little impact on the overall political (im)balance, but that is a general phenomenon anyone involved in post-colonial, ethnic minorities and women's studies will be familiar with: any shift in the production of knowledge tilting their way seldom reflects an immediate change in the fields of politics or economy. But the combined political protest of all these deprived groups has proven successful enough to generate a change. In our own case, it was powerful enough to persuade academics worldwide that the version of the victim is no less—and possibly more—valid than that produced by the hegemonic party in its account. A by-product of this development, as we see clearly in the case of Palestine, is a gradual erosion of the international (and even local) status of the stronger party's knowledge producers.

More specifically, the impact of the first Intifada of 1987 was strong enough to legitimize—in the eyes of the international scholarly community—the Palestinian historical version and de-legitimize, to a large extent, the Israeli-Zionist one. This change was part of a more comprehensive shift in attitudes towards non-Western historical perspectives, to which the Palestinian intellectual, Edward Said, contributed more than anyone else. This legitimization means accepting as professionally valid (parts of) the Palestinian version, while at the same time exposing (parts of) the Israeli historiography as ideological and polemicist in nature.

The present volume clearly reflects this change both in structure and style. Most of the articles are critical of the Zionist narrative, and the nature of the critique levelled at the actions and policies of the victimizer differs in tone and content from that directed at those of the victims. All critiques, nonetheless, jointly produce a pluralist atmosphere that enables all contributors to present an historical narrative that is nowhere to be found in the two hegemonic historiographies and that forcefully challenges the way political elites have manipulated history for their own interests.

The positionality and contexuality that are at the heart of our joint journey into the past ensure a multi-perspectival approach whose importance for tracing areas of agreement and approaching sites of disagreement cannot be overstated. This bridge—the recognition of the all-pervasive reality of disparity—was put in place through a dialectical process. The first step, in fact the pre-condition, for that process to take off was the unique political atmosphere heralded by the signing of the Oslo Accords in 1993. The diplomatic efforts that gave us Oslo produced a rare—and as we now know, all too brief—period of academic openness in Israel (one of our contributors argues that it set in following the outbreak of the first Intifada in December 1987 but was then terminated by the murder of Yitzhak Rabin in November 1995, but most of us would point to the years 1993–2000). The more critical segments within the Israeli academic community began deconstructing some of the foundational myths of the Jewish state and disputing the common Zionist narrative of the country's history. This was a professional challenge from within the Israeli academia that, the more it distanced itself from the hegemonic Zionist narrative, began revealing an historical picture of Zionism and Israel that was closer to the one portrayed through the years by the Palestinian narrative.[2]

It was, of course, this new trend that eventually fostered the dialogue between Palestinian and Israeli academics that became PALISAD. But initially these Israeli challengers—labelled 'new historians' or 'post-Zionist' scholars—denied their work bore any relation to the counter narrative of Palestinian academics. Unlike our group in Ramallah, Israel's 'new historians' never sought a parallel dialogue with Palestinians working on similar issues. Most of them, however critical, remained insulated because of their insistence that only new evidence extracted from mainly Israeli archives had prompted them to publish their

---

2   Ilan Pappé, 'Critique and Agenda: The Post-Zionist Scholars in Israel', *History and Memory* 7/1 (Spring/Summer 1995), pp. 66-91.

changed views, refusing to recognize, much less accept, any impact the Palestinian narrative might have had on their research.

No wonder then that this so-called 'new history' was cold-shouldered by Palestinian historians: that only Israeli historiography and archives could serve as the gate to the past was a thought they naturally found insulting, one that struck them as arrogant and betraying a neo-colonialist approach. Palestinian historians had hoped for—and were entitled to expect—a more constructive dialogue with their 'critical' Israeli counterparts.

To what extent Israeli scholars were lagging behind came to the fore in May 1998, when *Le Monde Diplomatique* hosted exactly such an attempt at dialogue in Paris. The initiative failed possibly because it was set up not as a closed workshop but took place in public. But the obvious non-starter was the insistence of most of the Israeli historians taking part that empirical data retrieved from Israeli archives was all that was needed to arrive at the 'truth' about the past. In the face of such a blatant positivist approach, the Palestinian participants asked for, but did not receive, an explanation as to what may motivate 'cool-headed objective Israeli historians' to choose *their* catastrophe as subject matter. When the Israelis in response said the Palestinians did not have the required historical documents to write their own history nor were they likely to ever obtain the necessary expertise, Edward Said, one of the driving forces behind the meeting, threw up his arms in disgust, exclaiming that not only had the Israelis perpetrated the Nakba, they now also tried to confiscate its historiography.[3]

By then, a different, more genuine dialectical process of common historiographical work was underway in Ramallah and Jerusalem, one that totally embraced the Palestinian point of view, not just in the various papers people presented to our joint group, but in the principle it upheld: the legitimization for a scholar's historiographical approach to go hand in hand with his or her ideological viewpoint.

3   For a report on this debate, see Edward Said in 'New History, Old Ideas', *Al-Ahram Weekly*, 21-27 May 1998.

First Stage: The Emergence of an Internal Israeli Critique

As the first imperative of a bridged outlook on the present had now been met, the way was open for ditching the paradigm of parity once and for all by recognizing that there was no room to demand parallel critical journeys into the past or equally critical approaches towards hegemonic narratives and discourses. Our journey's first destination, so to speak, was to deconstruct the representational means through which Israel as occupier, colonizer and expeller had monopolized the field.

The volume opens with three articles representing this deconstruction of the hegemonic Israeli scholarly narrative of the past and the present. Ehud Adiv sees historiography as an effort within the history of political thought. Through this prism he analyzes the development over time of the Israeli historiographical enterprise and is thus able to show it up for the nationalist project it largely is. As we shall see, the critical theoretical approach to nationalism informs most, if not all, of the contributions in this volume. Put differently, critique of nationalism forms part of the scholarly scaffolding for our PALISAD project.

Adiv's article is followed by Dan Rabinowitz's review of the early Israeli anthropological studies on 'Palestinians'. This survey, too, emanates from a critical approach to nationalist knowledge production. Like Adiv, Rabinowitz exposes the fabrication and manipulation embedded in the Zionist scholarly representation of 'reality' in Palestine and Israel. The leading names in the field of Israeli anthropology are scrutinized here, through their works, as representatives of the admixture of colonialism and nationalism that is typical of the Israeli anthropological establishment as a whole, itself a crucial element within the overall Israeli Orientalist establishment.

Moshe Zuckermann, the third article in this part, exposes the instrumentalization of the Holocaust memory in Israel and concludes that 'the memory of the Holocaust still remains to be liberated from the ideological chains of its instrumentalization'. These chains were effective not only because of the power of nationalism, i.e., Zionism, to keep them in place, but also because of much deeper layers of guilt and fear that inform the Holocaust memory in the Israeli Jewish society.

All three articles explore the matrix of power, knowledge and ideology that through the years has shaped the historiographical discourse and enterprise in Israel and, beyond it, in the West. Each of the three contributors is concurrently an observer of and participant in the new critique inside the Israeli academia.

Second Stage: Palestinian Re-appraisal of 1948

By the way it focussed on 1948, the 'new' Israeli historiography prompted Palestinians to produce a number of intriguing works on the same period. The dialectical process at work here was clear. Walid Khalidi was among the first Palestinian historians to significantly sketch the picture for us in the 1980s. This was then expanded by the new history in Israel—jolted by fresh archival material—and propelled further by Palestinian historians who in their works combined to great advantage Khalidi's commitment and the opportunities access to new archival material gave them. Two such works make up the second part of this volume. Salim Tamari explores the chronicles of the Palestinian community of Jerusalem in 1948 and beyond, an area of inquiry totally neglected by other historians. Tamari offers us a historical survey that explores the nature of refugee-hood in the Jerusalem context, both as a historical chronicle and as a basis for claims in a future settlement. The rights of the Palestinian Jerusalemites are no different from those of other refugees, but the discourse of the 'peace accords' and that of the Israeli government potentially threaten to exclude them from global attention and concern. Hopefully this article, and Tamari's collection bearing a similar title, will help prevent such an injustice from ever taking place in the future.

Nur Masalha expands the notion of the Nakba—the Palestinian catastrophe created by Israel—beyond 1948, well into the late 1950s. The article integrates the Israeli policy towards the question of the Palestinian refugees within the concept of the Nakba. Israel's denial of the Nakba, on the one hand, and its attempts to resettle the refugees in the Arab world, on the other, are additional layers in the catastrophe. The Israeli government's abortive resettlement plans were accompanied by a concerted effort also to expel the Palestinian citizens of Israel.

Israel's ethnic cleansing policy—never abandoned after 1948—is examined here as part of the overall Israeli drive to erase the refugee issue from the world's consciousness.

Both articles highlight the contemporary relevance of the Nakba's historiography—Tamari by providing us with a clear idea of the scope and value of the Palestinian loss in Jerusalem and Masalha by underscoring the connection between the Israeli policies towards the refugee problem and the way the issue could 'vanish', for so many years, from the international agenda.

Third Stage: General Critique on Nationalism

The basic consent within our group about the Nakba's centrality in any bridging narrative—and, of course, in any future solution—opened the way to critical approaches on the Palestinian side that echoed but also amplified similar tendencies in the Israeli academic challenge. This third stage provoked some compelling critiques on nationalism in the local context of Palestine.

Part Three opens with a historical review by Ilan Pappé of the peace efforts we have seen come and go in the Palestine conflict and of why they failed. Pappé focusses his examination on colonialism and nationalism as core sentiments that have fed and deepened the mutual alienation and fear, sentiments totally ignored by the various peace brokers in the genuine but also cynical attempts they have made to help solve the conflict. What ought to come first, as Pappé pleads, is reconciliation between the Zionist victimizer and the Palestinian victim, not 'peace' between two national movements.

In the second article here, Jamil Hilal takes on the two political projects, Zionism and Palestinian nationalism, by viewing them through the same scholarly prism and not as two sacred epic stories of success and failure respectively. The 'failure' of the Palestinians is not brought here as a narrative of sorrow, but rather explained as the result of circumstances shaped by internal as well as external balances of power. Similarly, the 'success' of the Zionists Hilal portrays here as the outcome of efficiently employed colonialist and expulsionist policies.

This is followed by Issam Nassar applying critical theoretical approaches to nationalism to the Palestinian case study, one of the first attempts of this kind. Doing so while the struggle for national liberation still rages on requires delicate navigation skills from any observer of the Palestine reality, let alone from a Palestinian scholar. Nassar's article marks the onset of a debate that is bound to inform Palestinian scholarship well into the future.

The de-nationalization of the narratives highlights the history of groups that never belonged to, nor ever benefited from, the national, and at times nationalist, agenda. The most obvious of these groups are women. Rema Hammami's is unfortunately the only representative article in this growing field of historical inquiry that we include here. We are keenly aware that there is much work in progress on the subject and we expect our group in the future adequately to reflect this essential perspective on past and present realities. Hammami fuses the two main interests that have come to the fore so far in the volume: the history of the Nakba and the power of the national narrative. Hers is the first attempt to trace the presence and absence of women within the national narrative of the Nakba. She does so by looking at a project of memory narration that was sponsored by the semi-official Palestinian media in the late 1990s. Like other contributors to this volume, it is again the theoretical critique on nationalism that inspires her deconstruction, here augmented by the vast critical feminist literature she brings to bear on her subject.

Delving deeper into gender history will make the connection between women and Palestinians as subaltern groups more explicit, as already manifested in this volume by the methodological approach some of us adopt here. The reconstruction of refugee lives and women's chronicles requires a re-definition of what passes for 'legitimate' primary sources for historical reconstruction. This means that oral histories, vital for both women's history and that of the Nakba, have to be legitimized and given equal standing with the elitist political material from official archives—as they have been accorded, for example, in Holocaust studies—so as to allow a truer understanding of Palestine's past.

The critique on nationalism within Israeli society is provided here by Oren Yiftachel, who in his analysis of past and present defines the Jews as an ethnic group. For Yiftachel, the 'Judaization' of Palestine is an ethnic project. Relying on a wide theoretical framework and comparative background, he portrays Israel as a settler society where colonialism and nationalism converge. The disentanglement of this admixture underpins his future vision. With the particular stress we find here on 1948 as the turning point in Palestine's history, the article further corroborates our volume's overall orientation. The paradigm of ethnicity enables Yiftachel to touch upon a subject that so far has been missing in the project, i.e., the Mizrachi/Ashkenazi divide within Israeli society. As Ella Shohat before him,[4] Yiftachel introduces the dichotomy of 'first world' versus 'third world' that applies not only to the Arab-Jewish cleavage in Israel but also to the one within that country's Jewish society. His major conclusion, that Israel does not comply with the basic requirements of democracy, brings us to the scrutiny of democracy in both societies.

Fourth Stage: The Fate and Future of Democracy

Part Four includes Musa Budeiri's historical trajectory of the concept of democracy within Palestinian society up to the Oslo period, juxtaposed with Lev Grinberg's assessment of how democracy fared in Israel in the wake of Oslo.

For Budeiri, democracy is closely linked to liberal struggles over rights and liberties (as separate from formal democracy, where human and civil rights can be systematically violated under majoritarian rule). The Palestinian case is akin to democracies trying to emerge through their struggle to throw off colonialist rule. In the case of the Palestinians the balance sheet of this struggle was informed by the unique conditions in which the Palestine Liberation Organization (PLO) operated ever since it appeared on the scene. Peace, as envisaged by Oslo, did not necessarily benefit the prospects of democracy in Palestine, one

---

4   Cf., e.g., Ella Shohat, 'Sepharadim in Israel: Zionism from the Standpoint of its Jewish Victims,' *Social Text* (1988) 19/20, and idem, 'The Invention of the Mizrahim,' *Journal of Palestine Studies* 29/1 (Autumn 1999), pp. 5-10.

gathers from Budieri's concluding remarks, but this is left open for future research.

Lev Grinberg, on the other hand, concludes that the failure of democracy in Israel was the failure of peace, and that both the democracy and the peace process ended with the assassination of Yitzhak Rabin in November 1995 by one of his own people. Employing political sociological tools for his analysis of democratization processes similar to those brought into play by Jamil Hillal, Grinberg highlights the intricacies of peace processes and the chances they offer for democracy in general and in the case of Israel in particular.

As we mentioned above, others in this volume also refer to the Oslo years as a period of opportunities either lost or never really exhausted. For others, again, Oslo never meant to give the Palestinians a chance. Said saw that early on: 'The tragedy [of Oslo] is not that peace was achieved but that it was not.'[5] The grim reality that has been unfolding on the ground after, in September 2000, Israel's continuing oppression let to the outbreak of the second Intifada makes it difficult to look towards the future with some hope that a long-term peaceful solution must be possible after all. Here, the disparity that permeates our social and political reality comes trenchantly to the fore.

Fifth Stage: Quo Vadis Israel?

When we look ahead and try to imagine a post-conflictual Palestine, the major problem lying in front of us—in this we all concur—is Israel, that is, what becomes of the 'Jewish state', how does one define the Jewish polity and society in that new utopian-like reality. Because it is clear to us that no one can question, let alone take away, the rights and status of the indigenous Palestinian population in their own land.

5   Edward Said, *Peace and Its Discontents* (London: Vintage, 1995), p. xx; 'For the first time in the twentieth century an anti-colonial movement had not only discarded its own considerable achievements but had made an agreement to cooperate with a military occupation before that occupation had ended' (p. xxv).

Uri Davis deals with the question of collective Jewish identity from within an anti-Zionist critique. Accepting as departure point the definition of Judaism as a 'divine religion, not a man-made political programme', he calls for a wider perspective that should be based on 'an international humanist world of values'. Davis's search is for an a-national or de-segregationist definition of the inhabitants of a future unitary democratic state in Palestine, liberated from colonization, occupation and Apartheid.

Similarly, our concluding article, by Ilan Pappé, is a personal journey into the past and the future in search of an adequate political structure that is capable of containing, and thus guaranteeing, the welfare and well-being of Palestinians as well as Israeli Jews. Therefore, it is only natural for Pappé to adopt the one-state paradigm as his departure point. Pappé reminds us that Palestine was a unitary political unit throughout nearly all of its modern history, and argues that, for any solution to be equitable and durable, it should again become so in the future. While not necessarily reflecting the position of the group as a whole, Pappé's conclusion stakes out future projects the group might be interested in exploring, now that we have solidly put behind us the 'paradigm of parity', successfully challenged nationalist prisms and clearly defined the parameters of both a bridging narrative of the past and a humane solution for the future.

En/closure

As the final stages of producing this book came to a close, the world around our intimate group invaded with full force. The invasion appeared in more than one way, but we want to highlight two issues that almost inevitably will impact the group's future orientation, if not existence.

The first interruption was physical. One of the main locations where we would come together was the office of MIFTAH, the Palestinian NGO headed by Hanan Ashrawi, near the ar-Ram checkpoint in East Jerusalem. In the course of 2005, Israel's Segregation Wall had been approaching this location as well. Apart from being a constant reminder of the reality that was closing in on Palestine as a whole, the scheduled completion of the Wall in April-May 2006 would make all future meetings there impossible. Therefore, when we met in the beginning of March 2006 we knew this would be the last time we could get together as PALISAD, at least in its present form.

We parted with the strong sense that a continued dialogue on 'bridging narratives' or, for that matter, any other academic issue is a luxury while Israel's machinery of destruction is inexorably bent on strangulating the Palestinian people in the Occupied Territories. The ar-Ram checkpoint most forcefully imprints on the retina the four methods the Israeli army uses to cleanse the Palestinians out of what Israel's political consensus considers 'Greater Jerusalem': an area that stretches all the way from south of Beit Lehem to south of Ramallah, and from west of Jericho to Eastern Jerusalem. The first method is the monstrosity of the Segregation Wall itself, the second are newly and illegally built Jewish settlements that completely encircle and choke Palestinian urban and rural centres, the third is an extensive system of roads for the exclusive use by Jewish vehicles, and finally there is the network of military camps that allows Israel to clamp down on the Palestinian population whenever and wherever it wants.

Then, in 2004, there came the call to the outside world from the Palestinian civil society in the Occupied Territories for cultural sanctions to be imposed against Israel, including a boycott of the Israeli academia. In essence, this was a call to intensify the struggle against Israel's occupation by non-violent means. It found quick support from similar initiatives worldwide, the most notable of which was the decision, in April 2005, of the British Association of University Teachers (AUT) to boycott two Israeli universities (before being retracted under heavy Israeli-organized pressure). Other initiatives directed against Israeli cultural and economic interests are underway.

The Palestinian call and the outside initiatives that reinforced it triggered an intriguing debate in the group whose sad overtones, however, are hard to ignore. Almost all of the Palestinian members of the group and three of its Israeli members came out unswervingly in support of the boycott effort—the other Israeli PALISAD members all rejected it. Of course, the very concept of PALISAD itself might have formed an interesting case study for the boycotters. But then the Palestinian initiative from within the Occupied Territories made a clear distinction between boycotting institutions, which it endorses, and boycotting individuals, which it rejects. And thus, despite the disappointment among our Palestinian colleagues at the refusal of most of the Israelis in our group to join the boycott call and continue the struggle against Israel's occupation also in this way, PALISAD continued to meet. Until the Wall caught up with us.

Why do we then after all publish our efforts? We see this volume as a compelling reflection of what our grass-roots Palestinian-Israeli Academic Dialogue has been able to achieve so far. Today it is clear that only international pressure can force Israel to take down the physical Wall it has cut into the heart of Palestine and shame it into abolishing the system of Apartheid it enforces there. But, at the same time, it is up to us to continue working on the inside towards tearing down the ideological wall that is at the heart of Zionism and feeds Israel's segregation policies.

Only time will tell whether the discord in our group prompted by the boycott issue will fatally undermine the future of our Palestinian-Israeli Academic Dialogue. Should that happen, other groups in different formations may well spring up and take its place. Meanwhile, the mind boggles at the dark irony that Berlin and South Africa should be our beacons here.

Some of the articles included here have appeared elsewhere, either in English, Arabic or Hebrew. But they derive their main impact of course from being read in the context for which they were originally created. Thus, we are truly grateful to Iradj Bagherzade, from I.B. Tauris Publishers, who embraced the idea of PALISAD early on and whose encouragement has been so instrumental in making this volume become a reality. We also want to thank Dick Bruggeman for the way he helped us edit the texts that we are publishing here. *Across the Wall* appeared, with a slightly different configuration of articles, in 2004 in Italian as *Parlare con il nemico. Narrazioni palestinesi e israeliane a confronto*, translated by Maria Nadotti and Paola Radelli (Turin: Bollati Boringhieri). It was awarded the *Minimum Prize 2004* by Cittadellarte, Fondazione Pistoletto (Biella).

Politics and Identity
A Critical Analysis of Israeli Historiography and Political Thought

Ehud Adiv

This paper aims at presenting a critical perspective on Israeli historiography and political thought. I wish to suggest that, historically and
conceptually, both Israeli historiography and political thought move
between two poles: on the one hand, a strict adherence to the ideological discourse and practices of nineteenth-century East European
Jewish nationalism—i.e., Zionism—and, on the other, a critical political analysis that considers the nature of the Israeli-Palestinian conflict as the only adequate historical context for a definition of Zionist-
Israeli identity. I will therefore first try to locate Israeli historiographical, sociological and political studies on the continuum between
these two poles in terms of to what extent they embrace or reject the
Jewish-nationalist orientation I outline. I will then turn to examine
more closely Israeli scholars who interpreted the formation of the
Zionist-Israeli body politic in the Middle East in terms of nineteenth-
century East European Jewish nationalism. Striking here is how most
of them continue to explain a modern body politic in terms of Jewish
ethnic identity. But, to put my own cards on the table from the start,
collective identities of course 'are like shirts rather than skin', as Eric
Hobsbawm has it, meaning 'they are, in theory at least, optional, not
inescapable'.[1] In other words, they will always be invented and in-

---

1   E. Hobsbawm, 'Identity Politics and the Left', *New Left Review* 271 (1996), p. 41.

terpreted in specific political circumstances. To paraphrase E.H. Carr, our question is not, 'What really is Zionist-Israeli history?' but 'How has this history been re-constructed by Israeli historiography and political thought?'

My theoretical context, then, is the question of nationalism. I will examine Israeli historiographical and political studies in the light of the two ideal types of nationalism I briefly hinted at above. The first type is what Gellner and Hobsbawm have called 'political nationalism'. That is, nationalism is a modern political principle that corresponds closely with industrial-bourgeois society, i.e., the nation-state that emerged at the turn of the eighteenth century. Hobsbawm, again, phrases it quite explicitly:

> I do not regard the 'nation' as a primary nor as an unchanging social entity. It belongs exclusively to a particular and historical period. It is a social entity only insofar as it relates to a certain kind of modern territorial state, the nation-state, and it is pointless to discuss nation and nationality except insofar as both relate to it.[2]

Gellner, in characteristic fashion, is perhaps even more blunt:

> Nations as a natural, God-given way of classifying men, as an inherent though long-delayed political destiny, are a myth; nationalism, which sometimes takes pre-existing cultures and turns them into nations, sometimes invents them, and often obliterates pre-existing cultures, *that* is a reality.[3]

In other words, nationalism belongs to the age of republicanism—that is, the state by the people and for the people, as first introduced by the French Revolution. Gellner and Hobsbawm argue mainly against 'ethnic ideologies' (Eriksen's term) that define nationalism in terms of a given ethnic and/or cultural identity. As Eriksen writes: 'In terms of genetics, this is an arbitrary distinction; in terms of culture, it is

2   E. Hobsbawm, *Nations and Nationalism since 1789* (Cambridge: Cambridge University Press, 1989), p. 9.
3   E. Gellner, *Nations and Nationalism* (Oxford: Blackwell, 1983), pp. 48-49 (emphasis in original).

probably even more so, and the example is interesting in indicating how biology and "race" are culturally constructed.' [4]

The distinction we find here is that between an a-historical, metaphysical, idealistic approach and an historical, rational (what the old Marxist used to call 'materialistic') one. Paraphrasing Gellner, in the case of France it was not the French nation that gave us France and French nationalism but the other way round. This meant, as Brubaker has it, that French political nationhood was understood as state-centred and assimilationist, and therefore emancipatory.[5]

The second type I want to briefly outline here is 'romantic' or, as Hans Kohn has called it, 'organic nationalism'. This first arose in Germany precisely as a reaction to the dual challenge of the industrial revolution in Britain and the democratic emancipatory vision of the French Revolution. In contrast to 'people-made' French political nationalism, the driving force behind German nationalism in the early nineteenth century was mainly an ethnic ideology that highlighted the mythological past and the 'authentic' cultural-biological identity of the German *Volk*. As Marx put it, in the reactionary circumstances of Germany at the time, it was an imaginary nationalism substituting—and/or compensating—for the absence of a truly popular republican movement. In the words of Karl August von Hardenberg, one of the reformers at the court of Prussia's Frederick William III, 'What France did from below, we should do from above.'[6]

Historically, the German nation-state was indeed implemented in the end from above, i.e., with the help of the Prussian army, rather than, as in France, voluntarily from below. Moreover, in the 1920s, following Germany's defeat in the first world war, its *Volk*-centred nationhood gradually transformed itself into Nazism, a populist ideology that was invented and put to work precisely so as to prevent the emergence of any truly popular republican movement from below.

4   T.H. Eriksen, *Ethnicity and Nationalism* (London: Pluto Press, 1993), p. 65.
5   R. Brubaker, *Citizenship and Nationhood in France and Germany* (Beverly Hills: Sage Publications, 1992).
6   D. Thomson, *Europe since Napoleon* (London: Penguin Books, 1978), p. 120

Concludes Hobsbawm: '[E]xclusive identity politics do not come naturally to people. It is more likely to be forced upon them from outside.'[7] In the case of the 'German people', the *Volk*-centred nationhood they had imposed upon them was therefore reactionary from the very beginning.

In what follows I set out to analyze the underlying assumptions and terms of reference of Israeli scholars who in their works apply the theoretical tools of either of these two ideal types. My principal hypothesis is that mainstream Israeli historiographical and political studies have placed the Zionist *Yishuv*[8] and the state of Israel within the context of German—and Russian—organic nationalism, rather than that of the political nationalism as it emerged in France.

Historical Background

Zionism emerged as a Jewish national response to the wave of anti-Semitic pogroms that swept across southern Russia and Ukraine following the assassination of Czar Alexander II in 1881. It was then that a 'small group of Jewish intelligentsia'[9] established the first Zionist organization, *Hovevei Zion* ('Lovers of Zion'). This small group of Jewish intellectuals, quite similar in nature to German nationalists at the time, soon gave up their Russian Enlightenment ideals for the idea of Jewish 'auto-emancipation'. Obviously, this was a Jewish version of Russian organic nationalism,[10] i.e., an attempt to force upon East European Jewry a new collective identity.

7　Hobsbawm, 'Identity Politics and the Left', p. 41.
8　Literally, Hebrew for 'settlement'; in Zionist discourse *yishuv* is made to stand for the pre-state Jewish colony in Palestine thus allowing the Zionist settlement that started in the 1880s to portray itself as the continuation of the ancient Jewish community that throughout history was an integral part of Palestine.
9　The term is Yoav Peled's; cf. his *Class and Ethnicity in the Pale: The Political Economy of Jewish Workers' Nationalism in Late Imperial Russia* (New York: Macmillan, 1989), p. 18
10　Defining Zionism, 'both ideological and social', as a synthesis of four components—(i) the Jewish religion, (ii) a variety of socialist ideals, (iii) secular nationalism, and (iv) classic liberalism—Kimmerling analyzes the contribution of

Following the establishment of *Hovevei Zion,* a new type of Zionist immigration began to trickle into Ottoman Palestine and settled there between 1880 and 1910. It arrived in two waves, in Zionist-Israeli discourse called 'First' and 'Second *Aliya*'.[11] These two *aliyot* inevitably changed the East-European *Volk*-centred nationhood of *Hovevei Zion.* Moreover, during the first Zionist Congress in 1897, Theodor Herzl, as the founder-leader of political Zionism, made his European colo nialist orientation explicit regarding his vision of a Jewish state in Palestine. He reports having told the Ottoman sultan in Istanbul: 'If his Majesty the Sultan will give us Palestine, we shall, in return, settle Turkey's financial affairs. For Europe we shall be there part of the wall against Asia. We shall be the pioneers of civilization against barbarism.'[12] That is, rather than in the East European Jewish nationalist terms of *Hovevei Zion,* Herzl—a well-known Austrian writer and journalist at the time—viewed Zionism more in European colonialist terms. And it was into a colonial settler movement that Zionism then gradually transformed itself after Britain—having already officially recognized the Jewish national movement in the 1917 Balfour Dec-

each of these components to the Jewish national movement and its collective identity. Thus, he explains, 'Jewish nationalism, that is Zionism, moved from the particularistic orientation that developed within the religious components and the universalistic orientations that flourished in the other components'; cf. B. Kimmerling, 'Between the Primordial and the Civil Definition of the Collective Identity: Eretz Israel Or the State of Israel?', in E. Cohen, M. Lissak and U. Almagor (eds.), *Comparative Social Dynamics* (Westview, Boulder CO, 1985). Kimmerling commences with a deconstruction of Zionism, yet fails to mention that Zionism was first constructed in the historical and ideological context of East European nationalism. Ze'ev Sternhell, in *Binyan Ha'uma o Hevra Hadasha?* ('House of the Nation or A New Society?', Tel Aviv: 1995), quite clearly portrays Zionism as an explicit case of East European organic nationalism.

11 The literary translation of the Hebrew *aliya* is 'going up [to Zion]', 'ascendance', or 'pilgrimage'. Historically, this was the religious term for Jewish migration to *Eretz-Israel,* the 'Land of Israel', i.e., Palestine. In the Zionist context it has been used to idealize, and consequently to legitimize the Zionist settlement project in Palestine, in a typical case of what Moshe Zuckermann has called 'ideological instrumentalization' of Jewish traditional terms for the sake of modern Zionist purposes; see, e.g., Zuckermann's article in this volume.
12 T. Herzl, *Herzl-Worte* (Berlin: Welt-Verlag, 1921), p. 32.

laration—had wrested Palestine from the now defunct Ottoman Empire. Under the British Mandate, in the 1920s and 1930s the trickle of Jewish immigrants broadened into a constant stream, reinforcing the Zionist *Yishuv*. For example, during the first six years of British rule, while Herbert Samuel was high commissioner, the Zionist *Yishuv* in Palestine doubled in size—from 55,000 settlers in 1919 to 108,000 in 1925—and the number of Jewish agricultural settlements rose over more or less the same period from only forty-four to one hundred. The British were quick to accord recognition to the representative bodies of the *Yishuv* and Hebrew became one of the three official languages of the country, this while Jews made up less than 10 per cent of the total population when the British took over.[13] Farm machinery and animals Jews imported into Palestine were exempted from customs duty, as was equipment for educational and charitable institutions. The Hebrew University of Jerusalem opened its doors on 1 April 1925.

By then the indigenous Palestinian population began deepening its opposition to the Zionist project that was unfolding in their midst. Thus, the history of the three decades of the British rule in Palestine is already the history of a national struggle—pitting the Palestine national movement against the Zionist *Yishuv* and its British protector. With their defeat of the Palestinians in 1948 the Zionist forces expelled the majority of the more than 1.2 million indigenous Palestinians, so as to 'ensure' Israel could be established as their 'Jewish state'—by May 1948 the Jewish population stood at 650,000 and the Palestinian population that had survived the ethnic cleansing within the borders the new state of Israel had carved out for itself by October 1948 over 78 per cent of Mandatory Palestine, numbered 156,000.

---

13 According to the British census of 1922, the figure had risen to 12.9 per cent; see *A Survey of Palestine. Prepared in December 1945 and January 1946 for the Information of the Anglo-American Committee of Inquiry* (Washington DC: Institute for Palestine Studies, 1991 [originally published Jerusalem (?): Government Printer, 1946-1947]), 3 vols., vol. 1, p. 140.

Writers of the First and Second Generation

The paradox we now encounter is that a movement that took over and settled on another people's land—that of the people of Palestine—and has been oppressing that people for more than half a century, defined itself in the emancipatory terms of *Hovevei Zion*. In other words, early Israeli writers interpreted and reinterpreted former East-European Jewish nationalism ignoring the evidence of the colonialist conditions that pertained in Ottoman and Mandatory Palestine. As Gellner would have it, they 'manipulated the past for current political purpose.'[14] In the following, therefore, I will argue for the approach that places Zionism in the context of the geo-political structure of Mandatory Palestine rather than in terms of its East-European Jewish national origins.

Mainstream second-generation Zionist historians, sociologists and political scientists appear to analyze the Zionist *Yishuv* using the intellectual frames of reference of their individual disciplines. Still, they too adhere to the organic national type elaborated by the scholars of the first generation. That is, they ignore the Mandatory political perspective because they view the Zionist *Yishuv* in what Kimmerling has called 'a sociological vacuum', i.e., as an organic Jewish *Volk* somehow existing independently of the British Mandatory state. For example, when Dan Horowitz and Moshe Lissak—two of the prominent sociologists of the second generation of Israeli scholars—define the 'socio-political structure of the *Yishuv*', they use the then prevailing structuralist-functionalist approach to explain the Zionist *Yishuv* as a modern functional structure that succeeded in keeping its autonomous

---

14 A characteristic case of manipulation of Jewish history for current Israeli purposes is a decision by the Haifa District Court from January 1949: an Arab resident of Shfa'amer claimed in court that according to the Partition Plan he had committed his offence outside the borders of the state of Israel. Moshe Etzioni, the district judge at the time, argued against this that 'the State of Israel is based on the natural and historical right of People of Israel and therefore the borders of the UN decision are not the actual borders of the state'; cf. *Ha'aretz*, 10 January 49, quoted in T. Segev, *Haisraelim Harishonim* (Tel Aviv: Domino, 1984), p. 16

interrelationship against internal and external 'disturbances'. For them, 'the Jewish national structure' and the 'political structure' of the Mandate government existed alongside each other:

> We refer to the *Yishuv* as a political structure in itself and not as a sub-structure of the Mandatory structure [because] the first loyalty of the population was inspired by the *Yishiv*'s sphere of influence and not that of the Mandate [...] This form of analysis has guided us in the definition of the borders of the political structure of the Jewish *Yishuv* in the land of Israel.[15]

According to Horowitz and Lissak, the Zionist *Yishuv* at the time was an independent *political* structure, enabling them to define the borders of the Zionist *Yishuv* independently of the political structure of the Mandate state as those of the 'Jewish *Yishuv*'. They seem to explain, in rational terms, the political characteristics of the Zionist *Yishuv*, but their subject matter is always the 'Jewish *Yishuv*'—an organic national entity. In other words, mainstream Israeli sociologists, as well as historians, view the Zionist *Yishuv* in terms of Jewish organic nationalism, always separate from its concrete political interconnections. Hence, what Max Weber has called 'the totality of social conditions'[16] they define in terms of a duality, i.e., of two apparently organic national entities and of the conflict that 'inevitably' arose between them.

This Jewish national orientation of mainstream historians of Zionism created a void that was then filled by Israeli Orientalists (Hebrew: *mizrahanim*) who did look beyond the borders of the Zionist *Yishuv* and consequently sought to locate it in a Palestinian and Middle-Eastern context. From the outset, these mainstream Zionist-Israeli Orientalists had an important function in the Zionist-Israeli body politic: it was their job to construct an exclusive Jewish national identity in Mandatory Palestine. First, personally they frequently served the Zionist-Israeli

---

15 D. Horowitz and M. Lissak, *Miyeshuv Limedinah: Yehudei Eretz-Israel bitkufat Hamandat Habriti Kekihila Politit* (Tel Aviv: Am Oved, 1977), p. 9

16 M. Weber, *The Protestant Ethic and the Spirit of Capitalism* (London: Routledge, 1992), p. 183.

establishment as so-called advisors on 'Arab affairs' and/or represented it vis-à-vis Palestinian and Arab public figures. Second, ideologically they fulfilled the Orientalist task that entailed deconstructing the Palestinian discourse and re-configuring it within a purely Zionist context.[17]

Writers of the Third Generation

In the early 1970s research emerges that is more critical in tone and content, produced mainly by relatively young scholars at Tel-Aviv University and the Hebrew University, such as the historians Anita Shapira, Yosef Gorny, Yigal Eilam, Israel Kolatt, Shmuel Almog and

---

17 In 1979, Gabriel Baer, one of the more prominent representatives of the second generation of Israeli Orientalists, summarized the development of Israeli Orientalism as follows: 'Thirty years ago Orientalist studies in Israel went through a quantitative and qualitative transformation. The establishment of the State of Israel created a great need for officials, administrators, journalists, teachers, translators and scholars who knew the language and the culture of the Oriental countries. Thus, during a period when the *Yishuv* increased five fold, the Orientalist staff in the academic institutes increased twenty times. No less important was the transformation of the centre of gravity of research and teaching from classical Islamic culture to the modern age. The Orientalists of the 1920s and 1930s were motivated by a cultural attraction, as a complement to their classic and Jewish education, whereas the younger generation of Orientalists after the 1940s tried to find in Orientalism answers to the Middle Eastern reality that surrounded them'; G. Baer, 'Hamizrahanim Bi'israel bishloshim ha-Shanim Ha'ahronot' ('The Orientalists in Israel over the last Thirty Years'), *Hamizrah Hehadash* 25 (1979), p. 179. Baer never seemed to have noticed the negative side of this 'quantitative and qualitative revolution' of Israeli Orientalism, namely, the lack of academic freedom it entailed and the narrow militaristic and diplomatic outlook to which it was confined. Cf. Elias Zureik, in the introduction he wrote to Shukri Abed's *Israeli Arabs: The Latest Incarnation of Orientalism* (International Center for Research and Public Policy, 1986): 'It is clear that the Orientalists shape, filter and "frame" the Arab image in the Israeli public eye.' By looking 'à la Mannheim' for the socio-political circumstances within which it was produced and analyzing Israeli Orientalists within the theoretical matrix of Mannheim, Foucault and Said, Zureik aptly brings out the monolithic perspective of Israeli Orientalism and the political and ideological function it plays in the Israeli power structure.

Israel Bartal and the sociologists Jonathan Shapiro, Hanna Herzog and Baruch Kimmerling. Representative of the third generation of Zionist immigration, they had been brought up and educated in the more democratic—less ideologically monolithic—circumstances of the State of Israel. Thus, they turned their focus on the Zionist *Yishuv* itself rather than on the East-European Jewish nationalist origins of Zionism. For most of them, the various practices of the Zionist *Yishuv* as it established itself in Ottoman and Mandatory Palestine were their main concern.[18] In the words of Israel Kolatt:

> Surely, the Zionist point of departure was not the reality of the land of Israel as such, but rather the Jewish problem and Judaism and the consciousness of the attachment to the land [...] In recent years there has been a growing interest among both the public and the academy [in Israel] in the question of Jewish-Arab relations. As far as Zionist history is concerned the transformation of the focus from the 'Jewish problem' to the question of Jewish-Arab relations is very significant. It means a shift in discourse from Jewish history and Jewish distress into the chain of relations in the Middle East. This transformation has changed the proportions the Zionist historical view was used to.[19]

18 Though it means moving ahead a bit of my story, I want to quote here Anita Shapira's 'Politics and Collective Memory: The Debate over the New Historians in Israel' (*History and Memory* 7/1 [1997], p. 16), where she writes: 'These Jewish historical circumstances are utterly rejected by most of the New Historians. They are not concerned with the processes that occurred in Europe in the nineteenth and early twentieth centuries that led to the emergence of Zionism. In their eyes, the problem of Palestine is isolated from the wider European-Jewish context and stands on a different plane, that of the Middle-East.' In her polemic with the New Historians Shapira defends the Zionist ideological assumptions of the older generations. Paradoxically, even a cursory reading of her studies reveals that she, too, is 'not concerned with the process that occurred in Europe', but with what occurred in Mandatory Palestine as most of Shapira's work, rather than with the East European 'Jewish Problem', deals with the 'Arab Question'.

19 I. Kolatt, 'Hatnuah ha-Tzionit veha-'Aravim', in S. Etinger (ed.), *Ha-Tzionut veha-She'ela ha-'Aravit* (Jerusalem: Zalman Shazar, 1979), pp. 9-10

Kolatt's new perspective is typical of most writers of his generation who, unlike the older generations, recognized the 'reality of the land of Israel'. And yet, at the same time, when they view the Palestinian reality, Kolatt and his peers continue to use Zionist ideology as their frame of reference. Kolatt's point of departure is the existence of 'the old and new Jewish *Yishuv* in the Land of Israel', rather than the 'historical block' (Gramsci) of Ottoman and Mandatory Palestine. Only Kimmerling, as the more radical among the sociologists of his generation, appears interested in examining the Zionist *Yishuv* in its true political context, i.e., that of the Mandatory state. Kimmerling focusses in his works on the conflict between what he calls 'two sub-structures under a general structure of an external power'.[20] However, though admittedly he views the land as a principal factor, Kimmerling, too, talks of a 'conflict management' between two rival national groups.

As such, the studies of the third generation have generally been a mixture of the rational, capitalist-oriented paradigm—Gellner's 'educationally dominant path'[21]—and the subjective, value-oriented elements of what Chomsky calls 'the state doctrine'.[22] Thus, even the relatively critical writers of the third generation still define the Zionist *Yishuv* in Ottoman and Mandatory Palestine in the meta-historical ideological term used by old-guard Zionist leaders.[23] In other words, the subject matter in most of the historiographical and sociological studies during the 1970s and 80s remains the Zionist *Yishuv* as an 'organic nation', a collective Jewish entity that existed independently of the political structure of the Mandate state.[24]

20 B. Kimmerling, *Zionism and Territory* (Berkeley: Institute of International Studies, 1983), p. 17
21 E. Gellner, *Culture, Identity and Politics* (Cambridge: Cambridge University Press, 1987), p. 9
22 N. Chomsky, *Language and Responsibility* (New York: Pantheon Books, 1979), p. 38.
23 In 1992 the Department of Jewish studies at the Hebrew University of Jerusalem published a monumental collection of articles, entitled *The History of the Jewish Yishuv in the Land of Israel*, whose editors and main contributors exclusively represent mainstream Israeli historians and sociologists.
24 For example, The Institute for the Study of Zionism that Anita Shapira, Yosef Gorny and their colleagues at Tel Aviv University established in the 1970s, whose activities ostensibly centre on Zionism as an independent historical subject, forms an integral part of the University's Department of Jewish History.

Writers of the third generation did recognize Kolatt's 'chain of relations in the Middle East', namely the Zionist-Palestinian conflict.
Unlike the previous generation, Shapira, Gorny and Kolatt do write
about the conflicting circumstances of the Zionist *Yishuv* in Mandatory
Palestine. But, like their earlier peers, they viewed these colonial circumstances of Ottoman and Mandatory Palestine as an 'unavoidable
conflict between two peoples with national aspirations'—i.e., of Arab
nationalism pitted against Jewish nationalism. As Kollat put it, 'the
Arab opposition raised the principal question of the relation between
Jews and Arabs as two peoples with national aspiration.'[25] In the article
she penned against Israel's so-called 'new historians' Shapira takes recourse to similar terms: 'They do not see two nations caught in a tragic
situation which led to an unavoidable clash between them.'[26] When he
wrote his doctoral dissertation, Kimmerling too spoke of 'the development of the Jewish-Arab struggle over Palestine's land'.[27]

The most prominent representative of the third generation of Israeli
Orientalists is Yehoshua Porath of the Hebrew University. He was the
first Israeli scholar to 'rediscover' modern Palestinian nationalism after
the June 1967 war. Porath defines Palestinian nationalism as a modern
political movement that emerged during the Mandate era through the
dual conflict it encountered with Zionism and British rule. However,
like the Zionist Arabists of previous generations, Porath basically
adopts the Israeli perspective of the Palestinian people as the 'other'
national movement on the 'Land of *Israel*' and systematically speaks of
'the Arabs of the Land of *Israel*', which is why he called his study 'The
Emergence of the Palestinian-*Arab* national movement' (emphases
added). By placing Palestinian nationalism in the general context of
Arab nationalism Porath focusses on the Arab-Islamic identity as a
major driving force of Palestinian national struggle:

---

25 I. Kolatt, 'The Zionist Movement and the Arabs', in *Studies in Zionism* 5 (1982),
    p. 129
26 Shapira, 'Politics and Collective Memory', p. 17
27 B. Kimmerling, 'The Impact of the Land and Territorial Components of the
    Jewish-Arab Conflict on the Building of the Jewish Society in Palestine' (PhD
    thesis, the Hebrew University of Jerusalem, 1974), Preface.

Social differences, the strange cultures, habits and way of life of the *Yishuv*, played a major role in Palestinian opposition to Zionism. Zionism threatened the Arab character of Palestine. For the masses ethnic and cultural differences were the source of their hostility to Zionism.[28]

In his more recent articles Porath shifted his focus to Arab nationalism as the propelling force behind the Palestinian national movement. 'I do not believe,' he says, 'that it is possible to find a compromise between two conflicting national ideologies that view the world in ethnocentric eyes.'[29]

Israeli historiography of Palestinian nationalism during the 1970s and 80s became increasingly interested in what Israeli sociologists and orientalists insisted on calling 'the Arabs in Israel'. Sami Smooha, of Haifa University, in 1986 found a definite trend of increasing productivity in terms of the numbers of scientific publication on 'Arabs in Israel', with a range varying from zero for several years in the 1950s to a maximum of 44 in 1976.[30] For Smooha, it was obvious that this increase in the volume of publication pointed to the level of interest Israel's scholarly community was now showing in Palestinian issues. Yet, Smooha, as well as the other Orientalists of the third generation, still viewed the 'Palestinian issue' within the overall domain of Israeli research matter. Thus, they reduced the study of Palestinian political nationalism to that of 'the Arab minority in Israeli society', thereby at the same time revealing what prompted their growing interest in the 'Palestinian issue'.

---

28 Y. Porath, *Tzmihat ha-Tnuah ha-Le'umit ha-'Aravit-Palestinit, 1918-1929* (Tel-Aviv: Am Oved, 1976), p. 48.

29 Y. Porath, 'Ha-Gvul ha-Mizrahi, ha-Pitaron ha-Yardeni: Yitronot, Migbalot', in *Ha-Derekh Shelanu le-Shalom* (Ha-Shomer Ha-Tsa'ir, 1982), p. 35.

30 S. Smooha, *Social Research on the Arabs in Israel* (Haifa: Haifa University Press, 1986), p. 14.

Communist Interpretations

Historically, the only ones to suggest a Palestinian-oriented interpretation of Zionist history were Palestinian—and later Israeli—
Communist writers. As Shmuel Mikunis, one of the historical leaders
of the Palestine Communist Party (PCP), put it, 'Jewish-Arab relations
are the key to the national question of this country.'[31] One could say
that the Palestinian orientation reflects the history of the PCP itself, as
even a cursory reading of early Communist writings bears out.[32] In
Kimmerling's terms (see below), unlike the early Zionist writers
Communist writers focussed on the 'consequences' of Zionism and less
on its 'intentions'. Thus, rather than providing the solution of the East-
European 'Jewish question', Zionist settlement in Palestine was first of
all responsible for the creation of the 'Palestinian problem'.

Unlike the Zionist parties, the PCP was established in Palestine by a
small group of people belonging to *Poalei Zion* who were aware of and
argued against the impact Zionist settlement had on the lives of the
indigenous Palestinian population. In other words, these were radical
socialist Zionists who defined themselves as Palestinian communists
because they had succeeded in replacing their East-European Jewish
national perspective with a local Palestinian national orientation. Significantly, during the Mandate period the PCP basically adopted the
Palestinian national position and argued on behalf of the country's
Arab workers and *fellahin* (peasant farmers) against the colonialist nature of the Zionist *Yishuv.*

After 1948, the Israeli Communist Party (MAKI), made up of both
Jews and Palestinians, continued to adhere to the Palestinian orientation of the PCP. However, given the 'changed' geo-political circumstances wrought by the making of the Jewish state, MAKI could
soon no longer ignore the question of Jewish national identity. In the

31 Shmuel Mikunis, *Stirot Umaskanot* ('Contradictions and Conclusions'; Tel-Aviv,
    1976), p. 4.
32 For this, see, e.g., Musa Budeiri, *The Palestinian Communist Party, 1919-1948*
    (London: Ithaca, 1979), and Joel Beinin, *Was the Red Flag Flying There?* (Ber-
    keley: University of California Press, 1990).

Communist interpretation, the state of Israel had its legal basis in the Partition Plan—as laid down in UN Resolution 181 of 29 November 1947—and should not be understood as the political outcome of Zionist settlement. As Israeli Communist writers saw it, the 'unity' of the Zionist-Israeli entity was transformed into a 'duality' with the State of Israel as the country of 'Jewish-Arab brotherhood'.[33]

As an anti-Zionist party, MAKI continued to argue against the imperialist consequences of 'international Zionism'. Moreover, unlike Israeli writers belonging to the mainstream, Communist writers supported the right of the Palestinian people to self-determination. But simultaneously, like their mainstream counterparts, they recognized the self-determination of the 'Jewish people'. According to Mikunis, 'One ought to acknowledge that the Zionist idea contributed to the creation of a Jewish nation in the Land of Israel following the anti-Hitler war.'[34] This may also help explain why Meir Wilner saw no reason to hesitate when he appended his signature to Israel's 'Declaration of Independence' on behalf of MAKI because that declaration stated that the state of Israel was established by and for the 'Jewish people', rather than by and for the Zionist settlers. In the end, however, notwithstanding their Palestinian orientation, Communist writers, too, failed to propose a viable alternative political interpretation of the Zionist-Israeli identity.

New Historians and Post-Zionists

Starting in the 1980s a number of studies appeared that proved seminal for the qualitative shift in Israeli historiography they represented and for the impetus they gave to a change in Israeli ideological discourse. These were the works of the 'New Historians,' as they were soon

33 On how MAKI emerged as the leading political force in the Arab community, fully supporting the right of the Palestinian people to self-determination, see Beinin, *Was the Red Flag Flying There?*
34 Mikunis, *Stirot Vemaskanot,* p. 6.

dubbed, mainly Israeli-born writers, a generation more critically aware and less ideologically oriented than their predecessors. Among them rank Tom Segev with *1949—The First Israelis* (1984), Benny Morris with *The Birth of the Palestinian Refugees Problem* (1988), Avi Shlaim and *Collusion Across The Jordan: King Abdallah, the Zionist Movement and the Partition of Palestine* (1988), and Ilan Pappé with *Britain and the Arab-Israeli Conflict* (1988) and *The Making of the Arab-Israeli Conflict* (1992). All of these studies locate Zionism and what it meant for the fate of the local Palestinian people squarely within the historical context of Mandatory Palestine. In his 'The Eighteenth Brumaire' Marx writes at one point: 'Such periods of revolutionary crisis anxiously conjure up the spirits of the past to their service and borrow from them names, battle-cries and costumes in order to present the new scene of world history in this time-honoured disguise and this borrowed language.'[35] One could say that until the 1980s mainstream Israeli historiography used to conjure up the spirit of a Jewish historical past in order to present the new Zionist *Yishuv*. The New Historians then portray the Zionist *Yishuv* without recalling the Jewish past. They deal with the Zionist *Yishuv* a posteriori.

Works of the New Historians appeared alongside the works of 'post-Zionist' sociologists and political scientists who suggested a critical analysis and/or deconstruction of the old ideological discourse. This 'critical sociology' (Uri Ram's term) offers a socio-politically oriented analysis of Zionism and Israeli society. Main works here are studies by Baruch Kimmerling, *Zionism and Territory: The Social-Territorial Dimension of Zionist Politics* (1983), Shlomo Swirski's *Israel, the Oriental Minority* (1989), Avishai Ehrlich's 'Israel, Conflict, War and Social Change' (1987), Gershon Shafir, *Land, Labor and the Origins of the Israeli-Palestinian Conflict, 1882–1914* (1989), Uri Ram, *The Changing Agenda of Israeli Society* (1995) and Oren Yiftachel, 'Nation-Building and the Division of Space: Ashkenazi Domination in the Israeli Ethnocracy' (1998). As I outline below, my own critical work should be

---

35   K. Marx, 'The Eighteenth Brumaire of Louis Bonaparte', in Marx, Engels, *Selected Works* (Moscow: Progress Publishers, 1986), p. 96

viewed mainly in the light of the writings of Kimmerling, Pappé, Ram, Ehrlich and Yiftachel.

With his critical interpretation of the Zionist-Israeli identity Kimmerling today is regarded as among the most outspoken of the 'post-Zionist' sociologists. In a critical analysis of 'Zionist historiography' he argues—quoting Hobsbawm—that the old guard of Israeli historians never left their Zionist convictions behind when 'entering the library or the study'. Despite the various interpretations their works arrive at and the semblance of academic autonomy they carry, Kimmerling claims, 'two presumptions are common to all the variations: (1) the unequivocal right of the Jewish people to the Land of Israel; and (2) the ultimate and the only correct "solution" to the so-called "Jewish problem".' This ideologically biased historiography, he argues, can be defined in terms of its 'seven main methods': (1) applying ideologically tinted Zionist concepts—e.g., 'aliya', 'Eretz-Israel', 'disturbances', etc.—to the reality of Zionist settlement in Ottoman and Mandatory Palestine; (2) determining a periodization of the history of Zionist settlement according to categories that are, similarly, Zionist ideological; (3) positing teleological explanations for historical events, e.g., a European history that 'ineluctably leads to the statist "Zionist solution" of the "Jewish question"'; (4) arguing 'for the historical exceptionality and uniqueness of the Jewish and Israeli case'; (5) drawing the boundaries of the Zionist *Yishuv* 'as an almost exclusive "Jewish bubble"'; (6) offering a meta-historical orientation to explain modern Zionist practice in terms of an ancient Jewish past; and (7) stressing the intentions rather than the consequences of the Zionist settlers in Palestine.[36]

As the problem with Israeli historiography and sociography is their Zionist ideology, Kimmerling concludes that the solution for Israeli historians is to 'take a broader look at the nature of [their] vocation and discipline'.

It is easy to agree with much of Kimmerling's analysis of mainstream Israeli historiography and sociography. However, when he suggests this

36 B. Kimmerling, 'Academic History Caught in the Cross-Fire', *History and Memory* 7 (1995), p. 42.

'broader' approach—which he sees as value-free and purely academic—as an alternative to the seven methods he outlined as typical of hegemonic Israeli historiography, Kimmerling seems not to notice that these seven methods all are equally manifestations of what I have called the Jewish national orientation of Israeli historiography and political thought. In other words, what we need—and what I am after in this paper—is an alternative historiographical interpretation that differs not only in *method* but also in *substance*. That is, what we are after is not just to deconstruct Zionist historiography and sociology, but also to try to reconstruct an interpretation based on the theoretical ramifications we are offered by the first of the two ideal types of nationalism I outlined at the beginning, i.e., political nationalism.

In recent years the historian Ilan Pappé has been in the forefront of the critique of Zionist historiography. Using the value oriented and relativistic historiographical theories of E.H. Carr, E.P. Thompson, Charles Beard and Carl Becker, Pappé constructs an ideal type of the Israeli 'new historian' and the relativistic paradigm he or she is likely to employ. Unlike the 'old' historians, who seek to portray Zionist history as it 'really was'—Ranke's 'wie es eigentlich gewesen'—the 'new' historians view it in the light of the present. That is, they explicitly suggest their own critical interpretation of Zionist history. New historians do not believe Jewish history is unique *qua* history and they view Zionism in comparative terms, as a historical phenomenon rather than as the manifestation of a meta-historical spiritual Judaism.

The problem with most Israeli historians, Pappé explains, has not been their Zionist ideological orientation—given his own relativistic paradigm, it is the right and duty of the historian to present her/his own ideological perspective. Rather, the main drawback of mainstream Israeli historians has been their claim to objectivity. That is, they are unaware of—or refuse to acknowledge—the subjectivity of their Zionist perspective and consequently present their own ideological interpretation as if it were Zionist history 'itself.[37]

37   Ilan Pappé, 'A New History of the War of 1948,' *Theory and Criticism* 3 (1993), pp. 99-144 (Hebrew).

Obviously I follow Pappé in most of the critical claims he makes. But even Pappé's point of departure remains more methodologically oriented than aiming at shifting the substance of Zionist history itself. As Gramsci observed, 'Widespread mass ideology must be distinguished from the scientific works and the great philosophical syntheses, which are its real cornerstones. It is the latter that must be overcome, either negatively, by demonstrating that they are without foundation, or positively, by opposing to them philosophical syntheses of greater importance and significance.'[38] As I see it, Pappé sets out the inevitable relativistic nature of Zionist historiographical studies, but the main thing is to 'overcome' these studies by historiographical works 'of greater importance and significance'.

In 1995 Uri Ram published his *The Changing Agenda of Israeli Sociology: Theory, Ideology and Identity* in which he offers a 'critical sociology' of 'the established sociology' that dominated Israeli universities until the 1980s. Following Thomas S. Kuhn, Ram recognizes three stages in the development of the Israeli sociological paradigm. The first stage—from 1948 until 1973—finds its representation in the works of Shmuel N. Eisenstadt. Eisenstadt reflected the hegemonic power of Israel's Labour Movement mainly because he presented Israeli society as a functional homogenous structure, i.e., as a horizontal Jewish 'comradeship'. The second stage, following the political earthquake of the October War in 1973, was an attempt by Eisenstadt's disciples to reconstruct the hegemony of the old monolithic paradigm. Dan Horowitz and Moshe Lissak in particular suggested a revised functional model for Israeli society, though still viewing the latter in the monolithic—i.e., Jewish national—terms of the old hegemonic ideology. The third stage reflects the '*mahapakh*' (Hebrew for 'upheaval', 'turnabout') brought on by the elections of 1977 that, after more than forty years, took away the political power from the Labour Movement. The established sociologists explained the *mahapakh* still in the mon-

---

38 A. Gramsci, *Selections from the Prison Notebooks* (London: Lawrence and Wishart, 1991), p. 433

olithic terms of the 'centre', i.e., as a victory for the periphery of
Mizrahi immigrants over the centre of the early East-European Ashkenazi settlers. Against the old structuralist-functionalist paradigm,
Ram sees five critical sociological approaches developing—Elitist,
Marxist, Pluralist, Feminist and Colonialist—and he defines Israeli
sociology today within the context of these critical sociological paradigms.

Ram, basically, applied the same relativistic paradigm also suggested
by Pappé, and thus with him, too, it remains difficult to see the wood
for the trees. That is, Ram's five paradigms. I wish to suggest, should be
analyzed further and deconstructed in terms of political nationalism.

The sociologist Avishai Ehrlich, in a 1987 article entitled 'Israel:
Conflict, War and Social Change', explicitly criticizes Israeli sociology
for its failure to discuss the significance of the Israeli-Arab conflict.
'Despite its centrality in everyday life,' Ehrlich argued, 'the Israeli-Arab
conflict is still a neglected marginal area of research in mainstream
Israeli sociology.'[39] Ehrlich suggests 'a typology' of Israeli sociology in
terms of its attitude to what he called 'all three components' of Israeli
society. He found five ideal types. The first, dominating Israeli sociology until the 1980s, viewed Israeli society as an 'Israeli-Jewish social
structure' and consequently 'overlooked' the Arabs: 'The Arabs and the
conflict are thus viewed as external to the structure and process of
Israeli society.'[40] The second, the Orientalist approach, filled what
Kimmerling called 'the sociological vacuum' and saw Arabs as an underdeveloped Asian element in the general context of modern Israeli
society: 'The terminology creates an analytical analogy between separate phenomena and thus shifts the discursive grid away from the
context of the colonial-settler type societies to the general context of
underdevelopment.'[41] A third type of political Orientalism viewed Is-

39 A. Ehrlich, 'Israel: Conflict, War and Social change', in C. Crighton and M.
    Shaw (eds.), *The Sociology of War and Peace* (London: Macmillan, 1987), p. 121
40 Ibid.
41 Ibid.

raeli Arabs in the general context of the Israeli-Arab conflict—the Arabs are seen as an alien and therefore hostile people and continued to be studied separately from Israeli-Jewish society. The fourth and more recent category focussed on war and its effects on Israeli society. Here the problem is that 'it concentrates on the bigger wars and does not take into account the indirect effect of a continuous guerrilla war, and the modes of conflict which are not armed struggle.'[42] Although it produced quite novel critical observations, the approach still saw Israeli society as 'committed to the national consensus of Jewish exclusivity'. The fifth, and most recent, approach integrated Israeli-Jewish society and Israel's Arab citizens into 'one analytical framework, namely: the settler-colonial model'.

Ehrlich, quite clearly, comes out in favour of the latter type, which he calls the 'integrative approach'. He applies E.P. Thompson's definition of 'class'—not as a 'thing' but rather as an 'inter-relationship'—as a major explanatory category of Israeli-Palestinian reality. 'The *Yishuv* and Palestine's society', Ehrlich argues, 'are not independent "categories" or "structures" to be studied separately and then brought together, but should be seen as forming and reshaping each other through the historical process of the conflict.'[43] Ehrlich thus is able to criticize the other four types of studies, such as those of Smooha and Swirski, who, however critical, still define the Israeli society they look at in and by itself, i.e., separately from the general context of the Israeli-Palestinian conflict. That is to say, they still accept the basic assumptions of the hegemonic ideology regarding the history and the sociology of Zionist *Yishuv* and the State of Israel. And their studies start with the 'deus-ex-machina' establishment of Israeli society and thus ignore the wholesale destruction of Palestinian society Israel started in 1948. Israeli society, Ehrlich concludes, should be analyzed in terms of what above, following Weber, we have called the totality of the Israeli-Palestinian circumstances.

As an example of his 'integrative approach', Ehrlich analyzes the question of land ownership and types of Israeli settlement. Before

42 Ibid.
43 Ibid.

1948, Ehrlich explains, the Jewish settlers, without the power of a state mechanism, could only buy land by means of private and 'national' funds and so, by 1948, had managed to acquire 7 per cent of Mandatory Palestine. When, during the 1948 war, the Zionists expelled the majority of the indigenous population and conquered close to 80 per cent of Mandatory Palestine, the new state of Israel confiscated this Palestinian land and turned it over to a special authority that was prevented by law from selling any agricultural land to Arabs. In this way, the vast bulk of the land was concentrated in 'Jewish hands'. Moreover, Ehrlish explains, the 'nationalized' water resources were also used as a tool to limit the agricultural production of the country's Palestinian citizens.

The situation in the Palestinian territories that Israel occupied in 1967 is quite similar—all of the state's mechanisms and its legal system are mobilized to confiscate Palestinian-owned land, which is then distributed to the Israeli army and to Israeli settlements there.

The three types of traditional Zionist settlement—*moshava, kibbutz* and *moshav*—should also be examined in terms of the conflict. The first type, the *moshava,* Ehrlich explains, was the dominant agricultural settlement at the turn of the twentieth century and was based on the hired labour of indigenous Palestinians. The *kibbutz,* based as it was on the collective labour of its members, came to the fore as the main development type in the turbulent circumstances of the Mandate period—it simultaneously served the economic no less than the military and political expansionist purposes of the Zionist *Yishuv.* The *moshav* became the dominant type in the wake of the establishment of the State when it was used to absorb the mass of impoverished Jewish immigrants that arrived during those years, and to settle the vast areas of land and property from which the indigenous Palestinians had been cleansed. By helping to consolidate the borders of the new state the *moshavim* played a similar military and political role to that of the *kibbutzim.*

Ehrlich lists all the other types of settlement that were developed before and after the 1967 war and shows to what extent these settlements were determined by the conflict. He concludes:

Ideally, one would want to show how all major aspects of Israeli society have been structured by the conflict [...] The development of the research into the effects of the conflict calls for a critique of existing approaches dominant in the social sciences in Israel, and of the dividing lines between fields of study and the basic premises, which have been influenced by political commitment to the existing order. The price exacted by the conflict on Israeli society can only be comprehended by making the conflict itself an independent and integrated field research.[44]

Ehrlich thus succeeds in analyzing Israeli sociological studies clearly in terms of their approach to the Israeli-Palestinian conflict. Yet, his typology of Israeli sociography looks too schematic because it lacks the historical and conceptual perspectives that could have helped shed more light on the ideological assumptions of mainstream Israeli sociology. For example, Ehrlich typifies Israeli sociology in negative terms, i.e., according to its failure to deal with the Palestinian factor. But Israeli sociology did recognize the conflict implicitly when it projected an image of the Zionist *Yishuv* and Israeli society within the reality of Ottoman and Mandatory Palestine. Then, too, the conflict with the Palestinians is also here being interpreted in the ideological terms of East-European Jewish organic nationalism. Furthermore, Ehrlich uncritically defines Zionist-Israeli identity in Jewish national terms, i.e., the ideological terms used by the sociologists of the mainstream. Consequently, and *pace* Ehrlich's protestations to the contrary, the '*Jewish-Arab*' conflict', as an ethno-national conflict, for him too is made up of 'two sides' rather than embodying an 'interrelationship'. However, I fully adopt Ehrlich's critical hypothesis that Israeli sociology should be defined in terms of what Walter Benjamin has called 'the sphere of actuality', i.e., the actuality of the Israeli-Palestinian conflict, rather than in the framework of an ideology, i.e., Zionism.

Oren Yiftachel, a geographer at Ben-Gurion University and an outspoken critic of the Zionist approach to social geography, seeks to

44 Ibid, p. 141

undermine the underlying assumptions of the old structuralist paradigm of Eisenstadt and his disciples. In a 1998 article, Yiftachel suggests that Israeli 'nation-building' is based on the uneven division of
Israeli space.[45] He calls these areas

> 'alien' within the collective's boundaries into which the core attempts
> to expand, penetrate, and increase its control. Activities associated
> with internal frontiers may include the dissemination of national
> culture, the settlement of minority regions, or the modernization of
> 'backward' regions, all in the name of 'the national interest'. The
> social construction and promotion of frontier regions has formed a
> central pillar of identity-building projects in most settler societies,
> such as the United States, Australia, Israel and Canada.[46]

However, he argues, in the Israeli case the core of the old European
elite used the state apparatus to settle the poor and less educated
'oriental' (Mizrahi) immigrant population in such 'frontier' regions, in
this case the very same regions from which it had first cleansed the
indigenous Palestinian population in 1948. 'Ashkenazi domination'
was both manifested and reinforced by this uneven division of the
Israeli space. 'In broad terms,' Yiftachel affirms, 'settler societies
combine three major social groupings: a powerful "charter group", later
immigrants, who are incorporated by the charter group, and a weak
indigenous group, which is often excluded from the "nation".' Israel is,
therefore, an obvious case of a 'settler society' as it combines the following three social groups: the dominant Ashkenazi group of the old
immigrants; the later Jewish 'oriental' immigrants who were brought in
from Arab countries and settled in the frontiers regions and the peripheries of the big cities, 'all in the name of the national interest'; and a
weak Palestinian group, which is 'excluded from the nation'.

Given his social geography framework, Yiftachel is able to view
Israeli identity in its Palestinian context, eschewing the old Zionist

45 Oren Yiftachel, 'Nation-Building and the Division of Space: Ashkenazi Domi-
    nation in the Israeli Ethnocracy', *Space and Polity* 1/2 (1998), pp. 149-169.
46 Ibid.

ideological terms. At the same time, however, Yiftachel continues to employ the East-European national model: 'The term "nation" is defined here in its narrow East-European connotation, meaning a group aspiring for, or exercising, ethno-territorial sovereignty.' In the light of these 'East-European connotations' Yiftachel views Israeli nation-building as a 'deliberate effort to construct an over-arching collective political identity based on belief in common culture, ethnic origin and homeland.' In other words, the dominant power of the Israeli elite Yiftachel defines as 'Ashkenazi domination'. That is to say, he defines 'domination' in ethnic-cultural terms, rather than in the light of the state-oriented nationhood of my first ideal type, i.e., political nationalism. Yiftachel seems to move between two explanatory models, one offered by socio-geography and the other by East-European ethnic-oriented nationhood. Hence, in the end, when he defines Israel simultaneously as a 'settler society' and as an 'ethnocracy', it remains unclear what—or why—Israel really is. The question arises whether 'Ashkenazi domination' is a manifestation of the 'uneven division of space' and/or a code name for economic domination and cultural hegemony, or the other way round. Furthermore, in the light of the East-European ideal type, Yiftachel distinguishes between the 'oriental' immigrants and the indigenous Palestinian population. Unlike the latter, 'oriental' immigrants were included in the Israeli nation-building project and, whether they wanted to or not, played an active part in the 'Judaization of the Israeli-Palestinian space'. At the same time, using socio-geographic and economic terminology, Yiftachel explains that the Israeli settler project was directed against both, i.e., Palestinians as well as 'oriental' immigrants. Third, like Ehrlich, Yiftachel uncritically applies the ideological term 'Judaization', the very term that incorporates the 'oriental' (Jewish) group. But he then explains that it is an invented term and that actually these immigrants were excluded from the 'nation'. Yet again, it remains unclear whether the oriental immigrants were included in the Israeli nation-building project or, like the Palestinians, became its victims. Fourth, with Yiftachel the 'Jewish-Arab' conflict appears in the past tense and the present Ashkenazi domination is based on the 'uneven division' of the (empty) Israeli space, i.e., on the exploitation and manipulation of the 'oriental' group. But, of course, today more than ever before, it is clear that *Israel's anti-Palestinian drive* remains the primary force behind, and the ultimate aim of, the Israeli-Zionist nation-building project: the development of the frontier regions should be seen as a means and not as an end in itself. For that reason it is also problematic to compare the case of Zionism-Israel with that of the United States and Australia where the indigenous peoples have been annihilated as an autonomous political entity. In 'Israel/Palestine' the Palestinian nation is very much in existence and the Palestinian people continue to claim their national rights.

However, Yiftachel's social-geographic approach offers us an explicit case of what I called modern political nationhood. Unlike Israeli mainstream academics, Yiftachel sets his definition of Zionist-Israeli identity in the Palestinian and Middle Eastern contexts in which it belongs and nowhere views it as a 'primary' nor as an 'unchanging social entity'. As such his analysis becomes one of the important reference points for my own work, which I see as an extension and elaboration of Ehrlich's and Yiftachel's attempt to put the Israeli-Palestinian conflict at the heart of Israeli sociological and historiographical discourse.

Oriental Othering and National Identity

A Review of Early Israeli Anthropological Studies of Palestinians

Dan Rabinowitz

The September 11 attacks in 2001 on the World Trade Center in New York and the Pentagon in Washington revealed degrees of anti-American animosity and resolve few Westerners ever imagined could exist. Perplexed, the Western mainstream rediscovered the grand theory of a historic, apocalyptic war between civilizations[1] whereby the harbingers of death assault life itself and barbarians attempt to take away the West's most cherished prizes—freedom and progress. Other, less widely accepted interpretations suggest the attacks were revenge on the part of the poor and politically weak for the injustices incurred by American globalization. Others still see Osama Bin-Laden and al-Qa'ida in the context of Saudi-Arabian real-politik—an opposition front that uses staunch Wahhabist ideology of 'infidel-free Arabia' to destabilize the house of Saud in the hope of taking over the state. Whichever theories

Author's note: I am indebted to the Centre of Israeli Arab Studies for a grant that enabled me to do the initial research that led to this article. Thanks are also due to the editors of *Identities: Global Studies in Culture and Power*, in which this article was first published in 2002 (9:305-324), and to the journal's anonymous reviewers for their insights and suggestions.
1   Significantly, Samuel Huntington, who coined the phrase and popularized it as a means to analyze the relationship between the West and Islam (Huntington 1993), proved reluctant to replicate it on electronic media interviews in September and October 2001.

prove persuasive in public discourse, the overriding sense across the West is that Islam in general, and Arabs in particular, present an alien force that is inherently irreconcilable with what many see as the fundamental tenets of Western civilization.

This review focusses on what at first glance seems somewhat removed from the current divide between the (American) West and the (Arabian) Rest. Highlighting early Israeli anthropology, it looks at the role of representations of Palestinians and Arabness at large in the construction of identity in the first decades of Israeli statehood. This inquiry is particularly meaningful given the significance of this formative period in the history of Zionism. Its theoretical import stems from Israel's peculiar borderline position between Europe and the Arab east, both geographically and in terms of the identity dilemma engendered by Jewish and regional histories.

The uses, abuses, invention and construction of culture within national narratives has been deliberated within the social sciences, including anthropology, for the best part of two decades (see, for example, Anderson 1983, Gellner 1983, Hobsbawm and Ranger 1983). Appadurai (1996:1–23) enhances the debate by moving it from the realm of nations to that of states. He does this through the introduction of the notion of culturalism: an active, often conscious attempt by formal and informal state agencies to establish composite notions of 'culture'. The emergence of state hegemonies as politically motivated brokers of culture suggests a keen realization on their part of the potential that lies in the construction and manipulation of notions of culture for strengthening solidarity and mobilizing support. At the same time, an analysis of the dynamics of culturalism highlights the ethno-national contradictions inherent in so many modern states, including those that fondly see themselves as liberal and benevolent to all constituents. Ostensibly egalitarian and even-handed in the treatment of all citizens, most states, including those of the West, are built around exclusionary ethno-territorial nuclei: dominant groups purporting ancient linkages to the territory and the symbolic capital engendered by their primordial role as guardians of the 'authentic' nationally defined cultural core. The implications of this entitlement on the marginalization of non-affiliates are clear.

Israeli culturalism was defined by the attempt of Zionism and, later, of the state, to fabricate a new, essentially secular and highly modernized identity (Zrubavel 1995:2–35). The aim was to pluck Jewish immigrants originating in a variety of histories, territories, cultural milieus and socio-economic backgrounds from their previous co-ordinates, and mobilize them into a new space whereby the Nation was rapidly being engraved into the land (Dolev-Gandelman 1987, Ben-David 1988), society (Eisenstatdt 1985) and the state. This effort, which produced a rich inventory of positive 'Israeli' cultural signifiers (Katriel 1986, 1987, 1988/9), was largely premised on the dual negation of the Jewish diaspora (cf. Raz-Krakotzkin 1993, Boyarin and Boyarin 1994) and of anything and everything remotely associated with the Arab East.

This ethno-territorial self-assertion, so often couched in culturalist jargon, becomes particularly stressed in the political spaces that lie between states and indigenous or immigrant minorities within them. The concepts of culture selected to signify, reify and glorify the state are easily manipulated, and can be stretched almost at will to include some groups and shrunk to exclude others. The flexibility and inherent ambiguity of these concepts enable the powers that be to promote inherently exclusive mental spaces such as a lingua franca (normally the one used by the dominant group), canons of high culture and at times religion to buttress domination, control political arenas and legitimize unequal resource allocation.

Kimmerling (1993) asserts that unlike religion—a realm in which the Israeli state displays a compulsive need to officiate and clarify individual affiliations—social identity has always been a theatre where the Israeli hegemony remained relatively indifferent, leaving sub-groups and constituencies largely to their own devices. While this is partly valid as far as official intervention by formal state institutions is concerned, it overlooks the energetic operation of hegemonic Israeli forces in the realm of culture. The construction and reification of an effigy of Arabs generally and Palestinians in particular is a case in point.

The review that follows of early Israeli anthropological writing about the Palestinians reveals an interesting reverse correlation. Traits which Israeli writers single out as defining Arab culture are often diametric oppositions of features many Israelis see as typical of their own identity. This does not imply that the ethnographic validity of the texts reviewed is necessarily compromised. Neither does it suggest that early Israeli anthropology worked as a concerted conscious effort, with unified intent or an agreed agenda. Rather, what I am out to demonstrate is how the political climate that prevailed when early Israeli anthropology was consolidated shaped *what* ethnographers were interested in, *where* they looked for it and *how* they tried to prove it.

Haidar (1985) notes a division of labour that characterized Israeli social science until the 1980s. It had sociologists studying Jewish Israeli society, leaving Arab society in general and Palestinians in particular to scholars trained in Middle Eastern studies, many of whom had been previously employed by the state's security establishment. Israeli anthropology was not directly employed in the system of control-through-knowledge of Arabs and Palestinians indicated in Haidar's scheme. Its first generation—people who came of academic age in the 1960s and 1970s—displayed considerable interest in Arabs and in Palestinians without complying to either the regional or the sociological paradigm. Their contributions to the national project were made in other, subtler ways.

Early Israeli Anthropology and the Arabs

The first generation of Israeli anthropologists, some of whom are active in Israeli academic life to date, consisted of approximately twenty scholars, mostly male.[2] Roughly half arrived in Israel from English speaking countries in the 1950s and 1960s, equipped with doctoral degrees obtained at anthropology departments in North America and

---

2   Two Jewish anthropologists, Erich Brauer and Raphael Patai, operated in pre-1948 Palestine. They were not accepted by the academic establishment, which in those days consisted of the Hebrew University alone, and both emigrated in the 1940s. Patai made an academic career for himself in the United States (see, e.g., Patai 1949, 1958). Both men remained largely irrelevant to Israeli anthropology in subsequent decades.

Britain. Others were born in Mandatory Palestine or had arrived at an early age from east and central Europe, and were socialized and educated in the Jewish proto-state in Palestine. A cohort from amongst the latter obtained their doctoral degrees at Manchester in the early 1960s and were incorporated into the Bernstein Project of Research of Israeli Society under the leadership of Max Gluckman.

Many of the early Israeli anthropologists were naturally preoccupied with the massive new arrival in Israel of Jewish immigrants from Africa and Asia, to whom they applied Manchester school field methods, analysis and theory (Van Teeflen 1977). A proportion of them, however, developed an interest in Bedouin and 'Arabs' (the term they most frequently applied to people I prefer to call 'the Palestinian citizens of Israel'[3]).

Some amongst the first cohort of Israeli anthropology carried over an interest in local Palestinians from previous careers. Emmanuel Marx and Yosef Ginat, for example, began their respective professional trajectories as Arabists in the state-security sense of the word.[4] Prior to turning to academia they were both employed by a security outfit entrusted with gathering intelligence about the Palestinian citizens as part of the state's surveillance and control apparatus.[5] Abner Cohen, who had arrived from Iraq as a youngster, was in the early 1950s a school inspector in Palestinian villages near the Jordanian border. Like Marx and Ginat, he too crossed over to full-time research, carried out fieldwork in border villages (Cohen 1965), and eventually became an academic in Britain.

This shift from civil service jobs associated with state control of Palestinians to academic life was not unique to anthropologists. Israeli officers who relinquish jobs with the security establishment to pursue a career in university departments and research centres—particularly

3   For a detailed exposition of my preference for the term 'Palestinian citizens of Israel', see Rabinowitz 1993.
4   Marx and Ginat both elected to study the communities with which they had been previously engaged as government officials (see below).
5   For an early analysis of Israel as a system of control of its Palestinian citizens, see Lustick 1980.

ones that specialize in Middle Eastern studies—are a common feature of Israeli academia today (Eyal 1993).

But one did not have to be a professional Arabist to develop ethnographic interest in the Palestinian citizens of Israel. Henry Rosenfeld, whose only involvement with Israeli state security could have been as a target for surveillance,[6] wrote extensively about the Palestinian citizens of Israel (Rosenfeld 1958, 1964a, 1964b, 1968, 1988). Gideon Kressel published studies of Bedouin groups (Kressel 1976, 1982); Eric Cohen carried out research on Palestinians in the early stages of his academic life (Cohen 1969a, 1969b, 1971); Moshe Shokeid and Alex Weingrod began research into urban concentrations of Palestinians in the more advanced stages of their respective careers (Shokeid 1980, 1982a, 1982b; Weingrod and Roman 1991), as did Don Handelman, whose interest in the status of the Palestinian citizens of Israel developed concomitantly with his preoccupation with ethnicity and nationalism in contemporary states (Handelman 1994).

A closer examination of some of the early work produced by members of this cohort yields some interesting common features.

Marginalizing Gazes

Emmanuel Marx began his ethnographic pursuits in 1955, when he spent three months of intensive fieldwork with the Bedouin in the hills of Arad in the north-eastern corner of the Negev, not far from the border with the West Bank, then under Jordanian rule. A more elaborate fieldwork project followed in the early 1960s, as Marx prepared his doctoral thesis in anthropology at Manchester University, which he subsequently published as a monograph (Marx 1967). Counting from

---

6 Rosenfeld's political inclinations excluded him from the Israeli mainstream. In fact, his affinity and contact with Palestinians at a time when they were under military rule was probably enough to raise the suspicion of Israel's Security Services, although I am not aware any action or investigation was ever initiated against him.

Marx's initial research steps in 1955, this was probably the first comprehensive project conducted by an Israeli in the established tradition of classical anthropology—complete with extended fieldwork amongst a remote tribe, writing up at a well-known university, and the eventual publication of a monograph at an academic press. The later Hebrew version of the monograph (Marx 1974) became a milestone in the way many Israelis would come to perceive Bedouin life and anthropology generally.

Marx's work identifies the internal heterogeneity of the Negev Bedouin, many of whom are descendants of landless *fellahin* (peasant farmers) from Gaza and the West Bank (Marx 1967:57–71). It provides useful insight into the interface between Bedouin and *fellahin* in and around historic Palestine (cf. Rabinowitz 1994; Abu-Rabi'a 1995) and is cognizant of the crucial role played by Israel in shaping the social and economic reality of Bedouin life since 1948. Marx acknowledges that in the early 1950s most Bedouin now living in the north-east Negev were forcibly removed by Israel from homelands further south. It also indicates their economic, administrative and political dependence on the state, thus dispelling the aura of spatial isolation so typical of anthropological writing of that period.[7] It demonstrates how pastoralists, who are often forced into marginal desert landscapes when they fail to become integrated into neighbouring metropolitan economies, are doomed to poverty and want. With few alternatives at their disposal, they tend to oscillate between a rudimentary existence at the margins and a miserable life at the lowest occupational levels of neighbouring market economies (cf. Rabinowitz 1985; Lavie 1990).

Marx describes a peculiar and exotic Bedouin culture. The group that he researched, the Abu Jway'id clan of the D'ulam tribe (part of the Tiaha federation), was one of two dozen clans and lineages that the Israeli authorities recognized as 'tribes' (Marx 1974:19). His study of the Abu Juway'ids is thus in many ways a classic specimen of British

---

7   For critiques of the tendency of traditional anthropological interpretations of pastoral nomadism and marginal peasants in the Middle East to obfuscate economic marginality, see Rosenfeld 1966, Asad 1975.

functionalism. Beginning with an account of desert ecology, the monograph depicts the grazing and cereal cultivation techniques developed to adapt to the environment. Pastoral nomadism is thus established as the defining feature of most societal and cultural patterns, including cycles of transhumance, segmentary social structure, marriage patterns, kinship and corporative action.

The geographical location of this group of Negev Bedouin, in a remote and relatively empty region near the lightly policed frontier with Jordan, is significant. Corrigan and Sayer (1985), in their discussion of the growth of the English state, identify modern capitalism and the cultural revolution that came with it as the main catalysts fuelling the emergence of the nation state. At the same time, however, they recognize another element contributing to the ascendance of the state, namely the ever-present tension with aliens at the frontier. Kearney's discussion of borders in the colonial context likewise points out the predication of modern empires on a distinct spatial separation between them and their colonies: 'a structural feature [...] which provides the basis for the cognitive distinction between the colonizer and the colonized' (1991:53). Capitalism, in other words, creates a spatial differentiation between developed, underdeveloped and de-developed regions. Within this context, the modern nation state emerges as a supreme unit of order, 'a social, cultural and political form which, as Anderson shows, is distinctive in having absolute geopolitical and social boundaries inscribed on territory and on persons, demarcating space and those who are members from those who are not' (Kearny 1991:54).

Marx's work on the Bedouin was prepared at a time when Israel was struggling to define its own geopolitical separateness from its Arab others, a period when zones along state borders were sites in which identity was being etched (Kemp 2000). Marx's ethnography was thus much more than a study in tribal culture. It was also a semi-conscious essay on the symbolic limits of Israeli state and society.

The significance of this ethnography for Israeli readers was its ability to lock the Negev Bedouin into their consciousness as a community of essentialized, if by and large benevolent, Other. The clan, the shepherd, the kidnapped bride, the sacrificial sheep and other elements of Bedouin 'culture' became emblematic markers of the cultural boundaries of modernism, the Israeli state and Jewish ethno-territorialism. A similar exercise was repeated after the 1967 war, in which more Bedouin[8] were incorporated into the Israeli system of control. A volume edited by Marx with Avshalom Shmueli (Marx and Shmueli 1984) offers a comprehensive overview of life at the margin and the process of modernization that brings an era to an end.

The complexion of Marx's ethnography was almost predetermined. 'His' orientalized Bedouin inhabited a remote frontier region, thus lending themselves to be framed, in the vogue of anthropological writing of the time, as a distant, romanticized group. To an extent, however, his work became a prototype of ways the Arab Other would be studied—and read—by Israelis later.

Eric Cohen's study of Palestinian youths in Acre (Cohen 1969a, 1969b, 1971) is in many ways quite different from Marx's study in the Negev. Acre is an ancient urban centre where Palestinian life and heritage has little resemblance to that of desert Bedouin. The aspirations of urban Palestinians are not like those of Bedouin, and their uneasy co-existence with the Israeli state has a divergent history. These notwithstanding, a deeper analysis of the discursive means employed by Cohen reveals a strategy of Othering that is in many ways akin to Marx's.

Cohen conducted intensive fieldwork in Acre, an old walled Palestinian fishing town, in 1966. When Israel's army captured the town in May 1948, many of Acre's original Palestinian residents were expelled and fled, mostly to Lebanon. Those who stayed were soon joined by internal Palestinian refugees from Haifa and from destroyed villages in the Western Galilee (cf. Morris 1991:150–154, Rabinowitz and Abu-Baker 2002). Once the war was over, Jewish immigrants from East Europe and North Africa came to settle, mainly in new residential neighbourhoods constructed outside the walls. The physical and

---

8   Particularly those belonging to the hills east of Hebron and Bethlehem (which Israelis know as the hills of Judea).

demographic contours of the town rapidly expanded, soon rendering the Palestinians, who were largely confined at the time to the old walled city, a minority (see Rubin 1974, Torstrick 2000).

Cohen, who was the first ethnographer to focus on an urban Palestinian community in Israel, reflects a sound awareness of the structural predicament characterizing Palestinian life in Israel. No less significant, however, is his choice of subject matter for his published works on Acre. One article is on the consumption and distribution of hashish and opium in the old city (Cohen 1969a). Another is on Palestinian youngsters courting European women tourists (Cohen 1971). A third deals with mixed marriages between Palestinian men and Jewish women (Cohen 1969b).

The pursuit of foreign women, Cohen argues (1971), is not merely an attempt by Palestinian youngsters to achieve sexual gratification. Rather, it reflects an identity crisis. The younger generation of Palestinians, he asserts, were caught between their parents' generation, dishonoured by defeat in 1948 and isolated by modernizing Israel as anachronistic and archaic, and modernizing social movements in the Arab world, largely unattainable for anybody under Israeli rule. Some Palestinian youngsters solve this identity gap by joining the Communist Party, which Cohen labels 'an extremist nationalist movement'. Others dream of emigrating in pursuit of a better life, a strategy they hope to expedite through romance with European women. Wooing tourists thus emerges as an ideal remedy for self-respect: it builds a masculine self-image that compensates for an inherently inferior standing vis-à-vis Israeli men.[9] Europe thus emerges as a last resort: a locus suggesting immediate gratification as well as a sense, however dubious, of identification and potential belonging.

Another article on Acre deals with small-scale drug trafficking and consumption (Cohen 1969a). At the time the piece was written, and to an extent today as well, doing drugs is widely seen in mainstream Israel

---

9   A similar argument would later be made by Glenn Bowman in his account of sexual exploits of Palestinian shopkeepers with European women in the market of the Old City in Jerusalem during the Intifada (Bowman 1989).

as an escapist solution elected by passive, juvenile and deviant individuals. Chasing European tourist women is likewise offered as a Gluckmanian carnival solution—a temporary suspension of daily reality tolerated as a safety valve that ventilates pressures and allows the system to function in a balanced fashion. Mixed marriages (Cohen 1969b) are similarly portrayed as a sociological dead-end, a last resort for both the Palestinian men and their Jewish Israeli wives, who come almost exclusively from lower socio-economic Mizrahi backgrounds.

The depiction of Palestinian life in Acre around the practices of drug abuse, ephemeral sex with tourists and marriage with Jewish Israeli women thus suggests a certain correlation between being Palestinian and engaging in marginal and sometimes morally suspect behaviour, strongly associated with flight and exit. Drug escapism, the contemplation of unthinkably 'radical' (thus hopeless) political outfits and courting ephemeral women so as to break away from the culture and possibly the country are options that ostensibly stand in stark contrast to rationality, practicality, and attachment to the homeland.

Marx's patrol along the physical and international frontier, constructed partly through the encounter with ultimate Bedouin Others, is thus replicated in Acre through a gaze at Otherness engendered by moral marginality. The modernizing Israeli mainstream inadvertently defined in Marx's work by the contours of the pre-modern margins of the state is replaced in Cohen's work by an implicit notion of 'proper' (i.e., Israeli) society, propped against precarious elements of Palestinian life at the socio-cultural margins of Israeli 'normalcy'.

Kinship as Temporalization

A second trajectory in early Israeli ethnography of Palestinians focusses on the socio-cultural and political centrality of the agnatic kin group. Henry Rosenfeld, who immigrated to Israel from the United States in the early 1950s, conducted fieldwork later that decade in Tur'an, a village halfway between Nazareth and Tiberias in Lower Galilee. The early corpus of his work dealt mainly with material aspects of marriage patterns. He prepared a census of all marriages in the village four and five generations back (Rosenfeld 1964b:93), described the mechanics of the extended patriarchal family (*'a'ila*), distinguished it from wider structures such as the patrilineage (*hamula*) and the lineage (*'ayal*), and analyzed the occurrences and logic of marriage patterns on a continuum from weddings involving parallel cousins to marriage unions with brides and grooms external to the village altogether. He looks at bride-wealth and bride exchanges (Rosenfeld 1964b:119), at polygamy and divorce (1964:137–145), and at the economic implications of residence patterns in tri-generational households (Rosenfeld 1958).

Rosenfeld emerges from these studies as a staunch materialist. He treats kin-based relationships as a theatre where culture, politics and conflicting intergenerational and gender interest combine to create a somewhat barren environment—a structural-functionalist perspective in which feelings, personal agency and choice are hardly present. However, this did not prevent him from producing contextualized and convincing accounts of Palestinian life in Israel.

In subsequent decades, as Rosenfeld's analytical preoccupation gravitated more and more towards political economy and the proletarization of Palestinian villagers (Rosenfeld 1964a, 1964b), his work became much more explicitly critical of Zionism, Israel and state practices vis-à-vis the Palestinian citizens. Unlike Israeli scholars who decades on were still prepared to blame Palestinian culture and 'disposition' for the dire circumstances of the community,[10] he consistently returns to the macro picture, highlighting the devastating structural damage that befell the Palestinians in 1948, and the consequences of being ruled by Israel.

But critical of Zionism and of Israel as he was, Rosenfeld was still an anthropologist writing in and for his times. Many parts of his text exoticize rural Palestinians with accounts of calculated marriage strategies guided by rigid and ascriptive social hierarchies, devoid of personal choice and feeling, guided by inter-generational strife. This came at a time when the residual Palestinian community, the survivors of the

---

10 For examples of this inclination, see Landau 1969:130, Stendel 1992, Rekhes 1989:166-9, R. Cohen 1990:108-112, Layish 1989:8-9.

Nakba, living under Israeli Military Governorate, was struggling to find a place in a society that emphasized modernity and commitment to perpetual progress. Rosenfeld's choice of subject matter thus reified an image of the Palestinian citizens of Israel as people who reside across a cultural divide, a community that Israelis could hardly count as 'PLU' (People Like Us, cf. Rabinowitz 1997). In this respect his work was somewhat similar to that of a contemporary anthropologist whose work he vehemently criticized (see Rosenfeld 1966), Abner Cohen.

Abner Cohen came to Israel from Iraq as a youngster in the early 1950s. A native Arabic speaker, he became a school inspector in Palestinian villages east of Tel-Aviv, next to the border with another part of the (then) Jordanian ruled West Bank. In 1956–7 he conducted fieldwork in one of the villages that had been in his educational jurisdiction, Kufr Qassem.[11]

Cohen claims the 1950s brought drastic changes to the village, which was quickly integrated into Israel's economy. The strategy of the villagers, he argues, was to handle this dramatic change by resurrecting their traditional social structure—the patrilineal clan known as *hamula* (Cohen 1965:1–2). From this point on Cohen's work is more or less linear, emphasizing the relationship between this old-new social structure and a variety of socio-cultural institutions and phenomena—another classic study of structural functionalism.

Written with a clear diachronic awareness, the book traces the shifting roles of local hamulas from the late Ottoman period through the British mandate to 1950s Israel. It shows how endogamy is reasserted in the ethnographic presence, and how the oligarchy strengthened its controlling grip in the process. We learn of the return of inter-hamula blood feuds, and witness how hamula chiefs are co-opted by the Zionist establishment to act as vote brokers on behalf of mainstream Jewish parties.

The social portrait of the Palestinian village which emerges is that of a community that tackles modernity by digging its heels deeper into its

11 In his monograph Cohen (1965) pseudo-names Kufr Qassem 'Bint al-Hdud' ('Daughter of the Borders').

past. Rich as it is in ethnographic detail, the text ends up further separating Palestinians, particularly villagers, from the Israeli mainstream. Talal Asad's critique of Cohen's monograph (Asad 1975) in fact argues that Cohen's history of the village and its hamulas is ideological, hence grossly inaccurate. The problem, Asad argues, is not so much with Cohen personally as it is with British anthropology in general. By focusing on traditional structures—in this case the hamula—the anthropologist obscures political issues he is reluctant to address, namely the political definition of the Palestinian citizens of Israel. The anthropological lens, which looks at the community in terms of cultural ethnicity and 'tradition', silences the more politicized discourses of class, nationalism and dispossession Asad would have clearly preferred to read. He is convinced that in the case of Palestinians as elsewhere, anthropological promotion of 'soft' notions, including culturally bound ethnicity, serves the metropolitan ideology of which the discipline is a hostage (Asad 1973), thus betraying the objects of inquiry on the ground.

A third example of this approach to Palestinian ethnography by early Israeli anthropologists is the research conducted in the 1960s and 1970s by Gidon Kressel in Ju'arish, a Palestinian neighbourhood outside Ramla (Kressel 1976). Established in the 1950s by the government to provide housing for Bedouin of Libyan descent who had co-operated with the Jewish settlers of the southern coastal plain prior to 1948, Ju'arish soon attracted a variety of immigrants. By and by it became home to internal Palestinian refugees from neighbouring villages destroyed in 1948, to Negev Bedouin who immigrated northwards after the termination of military rule in 1966, and, after 1967, to Bedouin from North Sinai and Palestinians from the West Bank and from Gaza seeking employment and sojourn inside Israel. The village grew until it became a neighbourhood of Ramla, a Palestinian town that after 1948 was predominantly populated by Jews.

The main part of Kressel's ethnography of Ju'arish (Kressel 1976) focusses on the relationship between economy, culture and behaviour. Faithful to concurrent anthropological preoccupations with social structure, Kressel concentrates on endogamy and parallel cousin marriage. His argument is that the primary function of endogamy (i.e., marriages between blood relatives) is to protect lineage unity and purity and re-establish class-based hierarchies whereby dominant lineages continue to take women from weaker ones rather than the other way round.

Kressel's second monograph about the Ju'arish is dedicated to blood feuds (Kressel 1982). Following a theoretical introduction to the origins of warfare in humankind, it unfolds a painstakingly detailed account of violent eruptions, concomitant civil and police inquiries, trials, reconciliation ceremonies and recurrent violence.[12] The main conclusion offered is that blood feuds have histories and tend to be carried over from one locality to another. Rather than remaining in the desert, where traditional alliances supposedly began, feuds feature in towns and cities throughout the Middle East, including Ramla. They persist in urban centres in the region despite professionalization and the contractual relations that typify modernity. Elsewhere Kressel surveys some twenty cases of 'honour killings'—murders of women by their agnatic kin related to alleged incidents of improper sexual conduct (Kressel 1980). His conclusion there is consistent with his earlier work: the social context of each particular case is crucial. Maintenance of inter-lineage hierarchy is often more important for the resolution of a case than the actual act committed or imagined.

In his essay on time and ethnographic writing, Johannes Fabian identifies how lexicon, syntax and style employed by the ethnographer 'temporalizes' the objects of anthropological inquiry (Fabian 1983:71–80). Implicit as they are, these three discursive means tend to isolate the objects of inquiry in temporal, moral and political universes that the reader is led to assume must be radically different from the

---

12 The community of Ju'arish became infamous in the 1990s for drug-related crime and violence, including a series of inter-lineage murders. The situation changed somewhat in 1998 when the Israeli authorities, aided by Palestinian politicians acting as intermediaries, forced one of the warring lineages to leave Ramla and resettle in other locations.

Euro-centre. Kinship, Fabian argues (1983:76) is a particularly effective vehicle for such temporalization. On one level, it is a technical—and universal—tool of the ethnographic trade, denoting how groups living today are linked to their primordial pasts. A more critical inquiry into the use of kinship lexicology, augmented with an appraisal of the syntax and style of prose that go with it, reveals that kinship studies often produce powerful demarcation lines between those whose kinship web is being studied and the modern world. The significance of these observations for anthropological studies conducted by Israelis on Palestinians such as those reviewed is clear. The gazing Israeli anthropologist, after all, is looking at his objects from across a political line that, in Fabian terms, is very much a temporalizing one. The kinship prism thus becomes a means of political distantiation at last as much as it is a tool for social-scientific inquiry.

The Prism of Gender

Moshe Shokeid's research in Jaffa in the late 1970s focussed on attempts by young Palestinian activists to break away from a corrupt, co-opted older leadership engaged in selling off the property of Muslim Waqf (religious endowment) to Israeli real-estate development (Shokeid 1980, 1982a, 1982b). One article (Shokeid 1982a), which touches on the status of Palestinian women in Jaffa, seeks an answer to a phenomenon presented as a paradox: how is it that Palestinian men who are exposed to modern Israel and Israelis, and who openly aspire to renewal and reform in public life, remain so rigidly attached to tradition when it comes to the status and role of women in their own society.

Shokeid attributes this traditionalism to the inter-ethnic strife characterizing Palestinian life in Israel, interpreting subscription to traditional codes as a symbolic act against the Israeli state. Palestinian men are quoted as saying that Jewish men may have won the 1948 war, but have since been losers on their home fronts. For them, the independence displayed by Israeli women reflects a failure on the part of Israeli masculinity. The control Palestinian men have on 'their' women, on the other hand, is depicted as compensation for the loss of national honour in the 1948 and 1967 defeats.

Elsewhere, Shokeid documents political mobilization on the part of young Palestinians who seek to counteract the corrupt practices of older local Palestinian representatives (Shokeid 1982b). The activists demonstrate, win media support, are partly recognized by the establishment, but finally allow Jewish municipal officials to co-opt them. Manipulated and eventually divided, their motivation and ability to effect real change is spent.

Shokeid's argument, modelled on earlier anthropological work and explicitly indebted to Schneider (1980, 1984), places the Palestinians firmly within 'the Mediterranean culture of honor and shame' (Peristiany 1976). Traditional masculine behaviour, he argues, blurs the boundary between personal gain and wider public interest. Individual success at whatever level is sought primarily so as to glorify the actor, not to further any common cause. The dubious expressions of personal status that the reformists-turned-collaborators attain intoxicate them, boosting their masculine self-esteem, somewhat repairing the sense of failure stemming from the 1948 defeat. Morally impaired as this preference of individual interest over public utility may be, the article interprets it as an act of political resistance.

This blend of cultural determinism and sensitivity to local politics and history breeds a tacit distinction between an Israeli Euro-centre, ostensibly a seat of modernizing rationality and honest politics, and Palestinian society. Physical proximity to Tel-Aviv notwithstanding, the older generation of corrupt politicians finally has its (moral) way. The young reformists, now exposed as old-style misogynists, use the honour and shame conundrum to justify their own betrayal of collective goals.

Yosef Ginat spent some five years (1969–1974) conducting fieldwork on the status of women in the four Palestinian hamlets of Yamma, Bir al-Sika, Ibtan and Marja, all on the Israeli side of the Green Line north of the West Bank town of Tulkarem. Born in Palestine in the 1930s, Ginat had worked at the Prime Minister's office since 1964, where he reached the rank of deputy advisor to the Prime Minister on Arab

Affairs.[13] It was at that time that he became acquainted with the four hamlets, all of which are daughter settlements of the older village Dir al-Ghusun in the West Bank. Later, when he made the move from the civil service to academia, he chose to conduct his study with a population he had previously been in control of. More or less aware of the budding discussion within anthropology of the encounter with colonialism (e.g., Asad 1973), Ginat is evidently mindful of the awkward situation created by this choice of field. Reluctantly engaging the point, he realizes that the colonial overtones engendered by the security regime he was part of might infiltrate his ethnographic project (Ginat 1982:9–10).[14] The early sections of the volume, which trace the history and economic background of the four rural communities in recent decades, lead to two substantive chapters dealing with patterns of marriage and the status of women. The data concerning agnatic endogamy are in line with earlier finds of Palestinian marriage strategies. Parallel cousin marriage emerges as the option of choice; marriage within the agnatic hamula lineage comes as a close second (cf. Granqvist 1935; Rosenfeld 1958, 1964; Kressel 1976). The text shows how changes in political and economic circumstances in the previous decades influenced people's choice of marriage partners (1982:86–130).

13 In the 1980s Ginat—by then a Professor at Haifa University—was called back to the civil service and served as the Prime Minister's Advisor for Arab affairs for some three years.

14 Ginat acknowledges that while his prior knowledge of the villages gave him a head start in terms of distinguishing significant from insignificant details, his obvious identification with the state could have stood in the way of receiving openness and trust amongst the villagers. He attempts to resolve this with the optimistic but rather naive assertion that the villagers understood his choice of research topic as a sign of intellectual interest in their community that had been triggered while he worked there for the government (Ginat 1982:9). He brings ethnographic vignettes to buttress this assumption, including confessions made by informants of petty crimes and misdemeanours such as using unlicensed firearms for hunting (ibid:10). He also explains that despite his contacts with officialdom, he repeatedly refused to intervene with the authorities on the villagers' behalf, a policy, he claims, that was received by the villagers with equal understanding.

The 1930s and 1940s, shortly following the establishment of the four villages as half-way settlements between the hills and Jaffa, saw the villagers preferring marriage bonds with partners from outside the village and the area, with special preference for partners from the mother village of Dir al-Ghusun. The period between 1948 and 1956, however, saw the newly delineated border between Israel and the West Bank under Jordan (the 'Green Line') officially sealed, and a considerable reduction of daily contact with Jaffa and the coastal plain, now emptied almost entirely of its indigenous Palestinian population. The result of this forced isolation was a resurgence of familial and village endogamy. Later, with the opening of the border following the occupation by Israel of the West Bank in the 1967 war, contact with the mother village Dir al-Ghusun was renewed, boosting inter-village marriage again, particularly between relatives.

The last section of the book deals with the status of women, leading to a discussion of the murder of women by male kin. The text suggests that European stereotypes portraying Arab women as totally powerless are overstated. Women are shown to have considerable freedom in running households and owning assets. They collect and control vital information and, not least, often control the choice of marriage partners for sons, daughters, nieces and nephews. In certain places they are even involved in local politics (Ginat 1982:203–207).

Ginat's argument regarding murder of women by male kin—a topic that would reappear in his work in subsequent years—is that the crucial factor is not necessarily the realities of deviant sexual behaviour, but to what extent it is publicly known. If a woman suspected of adultery is a member of a respected family, her deviance is likely to remain concealed and thus contained. Women of lesser families, however, are considerably more vulnerable. Effectively lacking social protection, their real or alleged misdemeanours are more likely to become public knowledge and to be punished.

Shokeid and Ginat both use gender-related issues to make more general statements about Palestinian culture, society and politics. Shokeid (1982a, 1982b) demonstrates how the culture of honour and shame, of which the Palestinians are ostensibly a part, is responsible for the chronic inability of male political actors to co-operate effectively and honestly for the good of the community. Ginat's work on the murder of women by kin (Ginat 1982) implies a rigid and discriminatory class system in which women belonging to stronger families get away with 'crimes' those of humbler origins could be killed for. He also stresses that the penal code for women gives priority to exposure and disclosure over actual fact, implying a culture in which reality is second to appearances and rhetoric.

Discussion

This review examined some fifteen works on Palestinians written by seven members of Israel's first generation of anthropologists over a span of some twenty-five years. The works were divided into three sub-sets, although some could fit in more than one. The first subset, consisting of works by Marx (1967, 1974) and E. Cohen, (1969a, 1969b, 1971), which could also include parts of Rosenfeld's early work (1958, 1964) and some of Kressel's (1976), looks at the distantiation of the Palestinians through discourses of cultural, spatial and moral margins (Marx 1967, E. Cohen 1969a, 1969b). The second, citing works by Rosenfeld (1958, 1964a, 1964b, 1968), A. Cohen (1965) and Kressel (1976, 1980), and which could also encompass certain elements of Marx's (1967) and Ginat's (1982) work, is a good example of how ethnographic discourses of kinship and social structure can separate the objects of anthropological inquiry from the Euro-centre that investigates them. The third subset, which looks at works by Shokeid (1982a, 1982b) and by Ginat (1982, 1987), shows how gender issues are used to elicit more general statements about Palestinian Otherness.

An interesting feature of this corpus of research emerges when we take representations of Arab culture featured in it and invert them. Marx highlights the extent to which the Negev Bedouin are geographically marginal and politically dependent—the opposite of being metropolitan and self-reliant. E. Cohen characterizes Palestinian youths as escapist and easily uprooted—the reverse of being resilient, industrious and rationally committed to pragmatic politics. The ascriptive and unequal kinship system described by Rosenfeld can be contrasted with depictions of 'modern' families, where personal choice and autonomy reign. A. Cohen's characterization of a society dominated by traditionalism and primordial structures is the opposite of a society that emphasizes transactionalism, meritocracy, free will and individual preference. Kressel's emphasis on traditional stability and resistance to change is the opposite of dynamic social innovation. Shokeid's account of the culture of honour and shame contrasts with depictions of elected representatives as servants of their voters. Ginat's focus on differentiated treatment of offenders according to their social standing is the opposite of absolute equality before the law; his allusion to the preference of rhetoric over factuality is the antithesis of the notion of ideal fit between theory and practice. A graphic summary of these binary opposites is given in Fig. 1.

Fig. 1 *Features of Palestinian Society and Culture and their Opposites as reflected by Early Israeli Anthropology*

Features of Palestinian society and culture...	... and their opposites
Peripheral, dependent	Metropolitan, independent
Traditional family, based on material logic, no individual freedom	Modern family, based on personal choice
Traditional structures dominate social life	Transactionalism and meritocracy, social innovation
Escapism, unrealistic politics, uprootedness	Resilience, rootedness, common sense and pragmatism
Subordination of public life to the culture of honour and shame and to self-promoting individuals	Political leaders are committed to serve communities
Traditionalism, stability of ancient structures and customs	Dynamism, social innovation, willingness to change
Inequality before the law, misfit between rhetoric and action	All are equal before the law, practice and theory are one

Significantly, the right-hand column includes many elements that in the early decades of Israel were fabricated by formal and informal institutions, and genuinely experienced by many Israelis, as the essential ingredients of Israeliness. Such traits include personal and communal autonomy and self-reliance; a brave and new approach to family life; dynamic social innovation and experimentation; rootedness in and faithfulness towards the newly found homeland; common sense; pragmatic realism; solidarity, co-operation and responsibility; equality before the law and a strong alignment between theory and practice. The underlying emphasis of all these features on modernization, hope and vision is implicitly strengthened by the depiction of the ultimate Other as possessing diametrically opposed characteristics.

Early Zionism was replete with fear of and alienation from the Arab East—the dark side of Orientalist infatuation with the sensuous wonders of the Levant (Said 1978). Segev (1999, chapter 7) demonstrates this with a series of telling quotes by Zionism's patriarchs. At the turn of the twentieth century, Theodor Herzl, the prophet of Zionism, asserted that the movement should provide the vanguard of (European) culture against (eastern) barbarism (Segev 1999:125). Max Nordau likewise told the Zionist congress that Zionism must attempt to do to Western Asia what the British did to India, 'coming to the land of Israel as envoys of culture, with the aim of widening the moral boundaries of Europe as far as the Euphrates.' Mordechay Hacohen, writing in the first decade of the twentieth century, described the Arabs and the Bedouin as savages 'yet to be reached by world culture'. He was adamant that Zionists must neither imitate the Arabs nor become integrated with them (Segev 1999:126). Aharon Kabak thought that Yemenite Jews, like other natives of the east, have a tendency to daydreaming, sloppiness, slowness, physical fatigue and weakness of the nerves. Zeev Jabotinsky, the charismatic leader of Revisionist Zionism before the first world war, was crystal clear about the need to distance Jews and Zionists from Arab culture:

> We Jews have nothing in common with what is called 'The East',
> and so much for the better. To the extent that our uneducated
> masses have ancient spiritual traditions and laws reminiscent of 'The
> East' we must wean them—as indeed we do in every decent school
> and as, in fact, is happening successfully in daily life itself. We go to

the Land of Israel first and foremost for our national convenience, and secondly [...] to finally sweep from the Land of Israel [...] all traces of the 'Eastern soul'. As for the Arabs who are in the Land of Israel—that is their matter. But if there is one favour we can extend to them, it is to help them liberate themselves from 'The East' (quoted in Bielsky Ben-Hur 1988:173 and in Segev 1999:126; my translation).

Zionist culturalism emerged as an attempt to prop a new identity against a negated ultimate Other, personified in Palestinians. The features cited in the formative Zionist musings about the East are thus politically and historically significant. For one thing, they identify rural Palestine, its rudimentary technology and marginal economy, as the epitome of Arabness. In the process they completely overlook Palestinian urban culture, ignoring Arab contributions to science, learning, progress and modernity.

Members of the first generation of Israeli anthropologists, people of moderately diverse political and ideological inclinations, were not mobilized in the service of the nation in the same ways that were evident in Israeli Oriental studies (see Haidar 1985, Saadi 1992), sociology (see Ram 1993) or history. As anthropologists, they were 'professionally empathetic' towards the Palestinians they wrote about, staying clear from scholarly traditions that sought to merge Arabness with backwardness and malice.[15] Like most Israelis of their generation and their socio-political rank, their Zionism was mostly taken for granted, as was their willingness to reproduce its rationalizations almost unquestioningly. Most of them thus did not have to be consciously in touch with formal ideology. The two emancipatory movements in which they were involved—Jewish ethno-territorialism and academic research of the ultimate Other—incarcerated Palestinians as perpetual candidates for corrective reform. Based on deep conviction and unencumbered by critical inquiry—which at the time was only budding

15 For examples of this tendency, see Landau 1969, Rekhes 1976, Stendel 1992; cf. n. 10, above.

within anthropology—the project they were part of allowed Israel to preserve its clean self-image as a progressive agent of advent. Their contribution to the construction of a new 'theodeological space', where theory and ideology fuse, was as effective as it was tacit.

The concern of many first-generation Israeli anthropologists with what they perceived, often innocently, as merely 'cultural', and their implicit adherence to certain segments of Zionism ideology and rationalization, had a profound political and intellectual impact. It prevented them from using their empathy and first-hand acquaintance with Palestinians, their insight into the hardships of Palestinian daily life and their comprehension of the stress associated with being a Palestinian inside Israel to produce a meaningful critique of Israeli sociology—let alone of Zionism generally. In fact, when a critique of Israeli sociology finally emerged in the late 1980s (see Ram 1993, Kimmerling 1993), anthropologists did not easily fit in as objects or as critics.

Simmons (1995, after Trinh 1989 and Spivak 1990) shows how colonialist anthropology used terms such as 'culture', 'cultural characteristics' and the idiom of cultural relativism as markers separating 'primitivism' from modernity. Rosaldo (1988) and Appadurai (1990) likewise demonstrate how traditional anthropology isolates the primitive native, establishes strong barriers between the essentially European discipline and its non-European objects of inquiry, and so tacitly reduces the feasibility of joint membership in a universal humankind. The dichotomy between 'primitive' and 'modern', inspired by nineteenth-century sociology and perfected by twentieth-century anthropology, may have been freed of its more blatantly racist connotations. But in many parts, including Israel, it served forces identified with modernization and reform as justification for the rescue—and control—of groups in deserts and in jungles.

The current bewilderment triggered in the West by the events of 9/11, 2001, and particularly by the tide of anger that seems to have created them in the Middle East, was anticipated more than a decade earlier in essays such as Bernard Lewis' *The Political Language of Islam* (1991) and Samuel Huntington's 'Clash of Civilizations' (1993). Edward Said recently exclaimed that Lewis and Huntington both overlooked the fact that cultures see and interpret each other is ways that often reflect internal needs and tensions. This seems to have been the case with the ways Israelis, amongst them anthropologists, made use of Palestinians and their image in their quest for the crystallization of 'Israeliness'. The walk I offered here along the envelope of Israeli identity thus seems to teach us at least as much about Israel and Israeliness as it does about Palestinian culture and society.

References

Abu-Rabi'a, 'Aref. 1995. *The Negev Bedouin and Livestock Rearing: Social, Economic and Political Aspects* (London: Berg).

Anderson, Benedict. 1983. *Imagined Communities* (London: Verso).

Appadurai, Arjun. 1990. 'Disjuncture and Difference in the Global Culture and Economy', *Public Culture* 2/2:1–24.

Appadurai, Arjun. 1996. *Modernity at Large* (Minneapolis: Minnesota University Press).

Asad, Talal (ed.). 1973. *Anthropology and the Colonial Encounter* (New York, NY: Prometheus Books).

Asad, Talal. 1975. 'Anthropological Texts and Ideological Problems: An analysis of Cohen on Arab villages in Israel', *Economy and Society* 4:251–281.

Ben-David, Orit. 1988. *Nature and Society in the Society for the Protection of Nature,.* M.A thesis, Deptartment of Sociology and Anthropology, Tel-Aviv University (Hebrew).

Bielsky-Ben-Hur, Raphaela. 1988. *Every Individual a King: The Social and Political Thought of Zeev Jabotinsky* (Tel-Aviv: Dvir).

Bowman, Glenn. 1989. 'Fucking Tourists: Sexual Relations and Tourism in Jerusalem's Old City', *Critique of Anthropology* 9/2:71–93.

Boyarin, Daniel, and Jonathan Boyarin. 1994. 'The People of Israel has no Motherland', *Theory and Criticism* 5:79–104 (Hebrew).

Cohen, Abner. 1965. *Arab Border Villages in Israel* (Manchester: Manchester University Press).

Cohen, Erik. 1969a. 'Hashish and Hashishniks in Acre', *Crime and Society* 3/1:34–39 (Hebrew).

Cohen, Erik. 1969b. 'Mixed Marriage in an Israeli Town', *Jewish Journal of Sociology* 11/1:41–50.

Cohen, Erik. 1971. 'Arab Boys and Tourist Girls in a Mixed Jewish Arab Community', *International Journal of Comparative Sociology* 12/4:217–233.

Cohen, Ra'anan. 1990. *Complexity of Loyalties: Society and Politics in the Arab Sector in Israel* (Tel-Aviv: Am-Oved) (Hebrew).

Corrigan, P., and D. Sawyer. 1985. *The Great Arch: English State Formation as Cultural Revolution* (Oxford, New-York: Basil Blackwell).

Dolev-Gandelman, T. 1987. 'Symbolic Inscription of Zionist Ideology in the Space of Eretz-Israel: Why the Native Israeli is Called Tsabar', in H. Goldberg (ed.), *Judaism Viewed From Within and From Without* (Albany: SUNY Press).

Eisenstadt, Shmuel. 1985. *The Transformation of Israeli Society: An Essay in Interpretation* (London: Weidenfeld and Nicholson).

Eyal, Gil. 1993. 'Between East and West: The Discourse on "The Arab Village" in Israel', *Theory and Criticism* 3:39–56 (Hebrew).

Fabian, Johannes. (1983). *Time and the Other* (New York: Columbia University Press).

Gellner, Ernest. 1983. *Nations and Nationalism* (Oxford: Basil Blackwell).

Ginat, Yosef. 1982. *Women in Muslim Rural Society—Status and Role in Family and Community* (New Brunswick: Transaction Books).

Ginat, Yosef. 1987. *Blood Disputes among Bedouin and Rural Arabs in Israel: Revenge, Mediation, Outcasting, and Family Honor* (University of Pittsburgh Press and Jerusalem Institute for Israel Studies).

Granqvist, Hilma. 1935. *Marriage Conditions in a Palestinian Village* (Helsingfors: Akademische Buchhandlung).

Haidar, Aziz. 1985. 'The Contribution of Research in Israel to Additional Knowledge about Arab Societies', in Aluf Hareven (ed.), *To Become Acquainted with Neighbouring Nations: How Israelis Learn about Arabs and their Culture* (Jerusalem: The Van-Leer Jerusalem Foundation) (Hebrew).

Handelman, Don. 1994. 'Contradictions Between Citizenship and Nationality: Their Consequences for Ethnicity and Inequality in Israel', *International Journal of Politics, Culture and Society* 7/3:441–459.

Hobsbawm, Eric, and Terence Ranger. 1983. *The Invention of Tradition* (Cambridge: Cambridge University Press).

Huntington, Samuel. 1993. 'The Clash of Civilizations?', *Foreign Affairs* 72/3:22–49.

Katriel, Tamar. 1986. *Talking Straight: 'Dugri' Speech in Israeli Sabra Culture* (Cambridge: Cambridge University Press).

Katriel, Tamar. 1987. "'Bexibudim!": Ritualized Sharing Among Israeli Children',
Language in Society 16:305–320.

Katriel, Tamar. 1988/9. '*Hahlafot:* Rules and Strategies in Children's Swapping
Exchanges', *Research on Language and Social Interaction* 22:157–178.

Kearney, Michael. 1991. 'Boundaries of State and Self at the End of Empire',
Journal of Historical Sociology 4/1:52–74.

Kemp, Adriana. 2000. 'Borders, Space and National Identity in Israel', *Theory and
Criticism* 16:3–44 (Hebrew).

Kimmerling, Baruch. 1992. 'Sociology, Ideology and Nation-building: The
Palestinians and their Meaning in Israeli Sociology', *American Sociological
Review* 57:1–15.

Kimmerling, Baruch. 1993. 'State–Society Relations in Israel', in Uri Ram (ed.),
Israeli Society: Critical Aspects (Tel-Aviv: Breirot), pp. 328–350 (Hebrew).

Kressel, Gideon. 1976. *Individuality Versus Tribalism: Dynamics of Bedouin in the
Process of Urbanization* (Tel-Aviv: Hakibbutz Hameuhad) (Hebrew).

Kressel, Gideon. 1982. *Blood Feuds amongst Urban Bedouin* (Tel-Aviv: Hakibbutz
Hameuhad) (Hebrew).

Landau, Jacob. 1969. *The Arabs in Israel: A Political Study* (London: Oxford
University Press).

Lavie, Smadar. 1990. *The Poetics of Military Occupation* (Berkeley: University of
California Press).

Layish, Aharon. 1989. 'The Arabs of Israel—A Crisis of Identity', *Hamizrah
Hehadash* 23:1–9 (Hebrew).

Lewis, Bernard. 1991. *The Political Language of Islam* (Chicago: Chicago
University Press).

Lustick, Ian. 1980. *Arabs in the Jewish State* (Austin: University of Texas Press).

Marx, Emanuel. 1967. *Bedouin of the Negev* (Manchester: Manchester University
Press).

Marx, Emanuel. 1974. *Bedouin Society in the Negev* (Tel-Aviv: Reshafim)
(Hebrew).

Morris, Benny. 1991. *The Birth of the Palestinian Refugee Problem, 1947–1949*
(Tel-Aviv: Am Oved) (Hebrew).

Patai, Raphael. 1949. 'Musha'a Tenure and Co-operation in Palestine', *American
Anthropologist* 51:436–445.

Patai, Raphael. 1958. *Sex and Family in the Bible and the Middle East* (New York:
Doubleday).

Peristiany, John. 1976. *Kinship and Modernization in Mediterranean Society* (Rome: Center for Mediterranean Studies).

Rabinowitz, Dan. 1985. 'Themes in the Economy of Sinai Bedouin in the 19th and 20th Centuries', *International Journal of Middle Eastern Studies* 17:211–228.

Rabinowitz, Dan. 1993. 'Oriental Nostalgia: How the Palestinians became "Israel's Arabs"', *Theory and Criticism* 4:41–152 (Hebrew).

Rabinowitz, Dan (ed.). 1994. *Five Voices: Arab Youths in Israel Speak About their Lives and Culture* (Tel-Aviv: Centre for Educational Technology) (Hebrew).

Rabinowitz, Dan. 1997. *Overlooking Nazareth: The Ethnography of Exclusion in a Mixed Town in Galilee* (Cambridge: Cambridge University Press).

Rabinowitz, Dan, and Khawla Abu-Baker. 2002. *The Stand-Tall Generation: The Palestinian Citizens of Israel following Intifadat al-Aqsa* (Jerusalem: Keter) (Hebrew).

Ram, Uri (ed.). 1993. *Israeli Society: Critical Aspects* (Tel-Aviv: Breirot) (Hebrew).

Raz-Krakotzkin, Amnon. 1993. 'Exile Within Sovereignty: Toward a Critique of the "Negation of Exile" in Israeli Culture', *Theory and Criticism* 4:23–56 (Hebrew).

Rekhes, Elie. 1976. *Israel's Arabs after 1967: Accentuation of the Orientation Problem* (Tel-Aviv: Shiloah Centre) (Hebrew).

Rekhes, Elie. 1989. 'Israeli Arabs and the Arabs of the West Bank and Gaza Strip: Political Ties and National Identification', *Hamizrah Hehadash* 23:165–191 (Hebrew).

Rosaldo, Renato. 1988. 'Ideology, Place and People Without Culture', *Cultural Anthropology* 3/1:77–87.

Rosenfeld, Henry. 1958. 'Processes of Structural Change within the Arab Village Family', *American Anthropologist* 66/6:1127–1139.

Rosenfeld, Henry. 1964a. 'From Peasantry to Wage Labor and Residual Peasantry: The Transformation of an Arab Village', in R. Manners (ed.), *Process and Pattern in Culture* (Chicago: Aldine), pp. 211–234.

Rosenfeld, Henry. 1964b. *They Were Fellahin* (Tel-Aviv: Hakibbutz Hameuhad) (Hebrew).

Rosenfeld, Henry. 1966. Review of A. Cohen's (1965) *Arab Border Villages in Israel*, in *Man (n.s.)* 1:272–273

Rosenfeld, Henry. 1968. 'The Contradictions between Property, Kinship and Power, as Reflected in the Marriage System of an Arab Village', in J.G. Peristiany (ed.), *Contributions to Mediterranean Sociology* (Paris: Mouton).

Rosenfeld, Henry. 1988. 'Nazareth and Upper Nazareth in the Political Economy of Israel', in J. Hofman, *Arab–Jewish Relations in Israel* (Bristol, Indiana: Wyndham Hall Press).

Rubin, Morton. 1974. *The Walls of Acre: Intergroup Relations and Urban Development in Israel* (New York: Holt, Rinehart and Winston).

Said, Edward. 1978. *Orientalism* (New York: Pantheon).

Sa'adi, Ahmad. 1992. 'Between State Ideology and Minority National Identity: Palestinians in Israel and in Israeli Social Science Research', *Review of Middle East Studies* 5:110–30.

Schneider, David. 1980. *American Kinship: a Cultural Account* (Chicago: University of Chicago Press).

Schneider, David. 1984. *A Critique of the Study of Kinship* (Ann-Arbor: University of Michigan Press).

Segev, Tom. 1999. *Palestine under the British* (Jerusalem: Keter).

Shokeid, Moshe. 1980. 'Political Parties and the Arab Electorate in an Israeli City', in E. Marx (ed.), *A Composite Portrait of Israel* (London: Academic Press).

Shokeid, Moshe. 1982a. 'Ethnicity and the Cultural Code among Arabs in a Mixed Town: Women's Modesty and Men's Honor at Stake', in M. Shokeid and S. Deshen (eds.), *Distant Relations* (New York: Praeger).

Shokeid, Moshe. 1982b. 'The Ordeal of Honor: Local Politics among Urban Arabs', in M. Shokeid and S. Deshen (eds.), *Distant Relations* (New York: Praeger).

Simmons, Jon. 1995. 'The Feminist Coalition in the Border Zones', *Theory and Criticism* 7:20–30 (Hebrew).

Spivak, Gayatri Chakravorty. 1990. *The Post-Colonial Critic* (London: Routledge).

Stendel, Ori. 1992. *The Arabs in Israel: Between Hammer and Anvil* (Jerusalem: Academon) (Hebrew).

Trinh, T. Minh-ha. 1989. *Woman, Native, Other* (New York: Routledge).

Van Teefelen, Toine. 1977. *Anthropologists in Israel: A Case Study in the Sociology of Knowledge*, Papers on European and Mediterranean Societies 9 (Amsterdam: Anthropologisch-Sociologisch Centrum, Universiteit van Amsterdam).

Weingrod, Alex, and Michael Roman. 1991. *Living Together Separately: Arabs and Jews in Contemporary Jerusalem* (Albany: State University of New York Press).

Zrubavel, Yael. 1995. *Recovered Roots: Collective Memory and the Making of Israeli National Tradition* (Chicago: University of Chicago Press).

The Shoah on Trial
Aspects of the Holocaust in Israeli Political Culture

Moshe Zuckermann

The insight that the historical past of a collective is always instrumentalized by that collective has almost become a commonplace by now: while talking about or debating the past, people usually say something about themselves—i.e., about their actual feelings, needs, and interests—'here and now'. This does not mean that the instrumentalization itself is a mere result of malice or deceitful manipulation, but rather points up a matter of inescapable necessity: as inevitably only parts of the past are remembered, and even these memorized selectively, the past as an imagined 'whole' is always codified and—even more important in our context—widely furnished with particularistic meanings and values. One may say that it is exactly this necessarily partial perception of the historical that is bound to constitute its ideological character: the 'what has been' and the 'there' of the collective are not only codified, but their mode of codification is subordinated to current views and orientations. Suffice it to say that while these views and orientations themselves are historically pre-structured, it is the ongoing monopolization of these very historical evolvements by the 'here and now'—the incessant process of their actualization and permanent adaptation to current interests and needs—that eventually may result in an essentially *heteronomous* reception of the past, or, if you will, in a more or less estranged, if not alienated, dealing with it.

This goes especially for a memory organized and cultivated by the state and its political institutions. The relation of the modern nation-state to the historical past of its society has always been somehow

precarious: on the one hand, it had to 'break' with the past and distinguish itself from its former social, political and cultural structures,
particularly so in the revolutionary cases of the so-called 'birth of the
nation'; on the other hand, the newly born state needed this very past
in order to suggest some organic continuity and consensual development of its own nation-body. It is truly fascinating to observe the
variety of historiographic strategies and ideological convolutions that
are sometimes adopted to achieve this double-fold purpose.

The case of Israel was/is especially peculiar in this respect: its acknowledged major ideology—Zionism—relied on the basic postulate of
the 'negation of the Diaspora', i.e., on emancipating itself from an
ongoing historic reality of persecution. Yet, in order to do so, it needed
to 'import' so-to-say the subjects of this very Diaspora into its newly
established territory. This confrontation between those who were absorbing, yet negating, and those who were to be emancipated by negation had far-reaching implications, all the more so as a massive portion
of the immigrants to the newly founded 'Jewish' state were Holocaust
survivors. Not only had the Palestinian people to pay an inordinate price
for this modern *Völkerwanderung* and the sufferings of its subjects; not
only did the Holocaust become the raison d'être for the establishment of
the state of Israel, ideologizing, thus, the Jewish nation-state as the
ultimate telos of the industrial mass extermination, but this very past
had to be politicized according to the current interests and needs of the
new state, shaping thereby main patterns of Israeli political culture and
its major attitudes towards the 'past' and the 'Other'. This I would like
to elaborate on, with special attention to one particular factor of this
political culture: its ideologized facets of 'hatred'.

The stronger the impetus gained by the process of the so-called
'normalization' of the relationship between Israel and Germany since the
1950s, the more it became a reified pattern of incompatibility with the
attitude of many Israelis towards Germany. Normalization—pertaining to
what Jürgen Habermas has called the 'dialectic of normalization'—does
not at all mean 'back to normality',[1] but rather the contrary, i.e., the

1   Jürgen Habermas, *Vergangenheit als Zukunft* (Zürich: Pendo Verlag 1991), pp. 41f.

conservation of the essentially abnormal precisely by the formal, yet ultimately heteronomous 'normalization' of what cannot be easily normalized. Admittedly, the intensive official political, economic, and cultural relations established between the two countries has generally helped to dismantle the bulwarks between them, and institutional expressions of anti-German emotions have gradually been eliminated from the sphere of governmental public life (the ban against any public performance of Wagner's music is desperately preserved as a last symbol of the public manifestation of such emotions). Still, we find that the intense feeling of resentment towards Germany is not at all vanishing, but rather—and since the mid-1980s accompanying a newly launched examination of the Holocaust under changed conditions—that it is increasing.

It is no accident, then, that a young and highly popular Israeli writer could maintain, less than fifteen years ago: 'Fifty years after what happened, today's Germany is not removed from Nazi Germany, just as today's Israelis are not removed from the victims of the Nazis. Under these conditions, the *hatred* for the Germans is a kind of monument one should respect.'[2] She even asserted that a theory referring to 'infected genes' of the German people was as reasonable in her eyes as any other economic or sociological explanation. One assumes that she is not alone in holding this view: though most Israeli writers and publicists would probably oppose the almost biologically racist tenor of her remarks, many, if not most, of them would certainly agree with her overall anti-German tone of resentment. Even more symptomatic, though, is the following. Asked whether she did not think that her viewpoint was somehow racist, she answered: 'No, of course not. Racism [...] pertains, by definition, to the ability to harm others. The emotion of the weak towards the strong can never be racist.'[3] Now, this is an extremely well-known pattern in Israel: the instrumentalization of the ideologically appropriated 'weakness' as a latent matrix of legitimation for one's own repressive practices. Grotesque as the present

2 Irith Linor, 'I-ne'imut ktana' ('A Little Unpleasantness'), *Ha'aretz Magazine*, 19 August 1994, p. 110.
3 Zohara Ron, 'Lama Anahnu son'im Germanim' ('Why do We Hate Germans'), *Ha'ir*, 12 August 1994, p. 63.

'weakness' of a young Israeli vis-à-vis the historical Nazis may seem—and even more so vis-à-vis today's sweepingly 'Nazified' Germans—it exactly reflects the political line of manipulative argumentation and rationalization adopted by many Israelis against real as well as imagined (Arab) enemies.

The fact that this Israeli writer is considered part of what is called the Israeli left—people we may describe as holding to progressive liberal views, critical about conventions and readily inclined to use blunt language—is all the more telling. Seen from a general Zionist viewpoint, there is no essential distinction between right and left in the ideological instrumentalization of the Holocaust as a whole, and especially of its most popular derivative, the 'hatred' for the Germans. By calling it 'ideological' I do not mean to question the authenticity of the experienced emotion, but rather to highlight its heteronomous function within broader politico-cultural structures and the exchangeable character of its occasional aims. By way of example, I would like to elaborate on another striking incident of ideologized 'hatred'.

Some years ago, in the daily newspaper *Ha'aretz*, the Israeli historian and publicist, Tom Segev, wrote about his impressions following a journey he had made to the extermination camps in Poland with 'third-generation' Israeli-Jewish pupils, organized by the Israeli Ministry of Education. He described the undertaking as 'a pilgrimage towards the Diaspora' as part of 'a cult, wholly saturated with emotions and symbols, a bizarre glorification of memory, death and Kitsch.'[4] To prepare them for the demanding and difficult journey, the Ministry of Education had equipped all pupils taking part with an article by the Israeli historian Shabtai Tevet, the inner logic of which may be summed up in the assertion that the Polish people have emerged from recent history as 'victor', viz., 'they have got away with Jewish property and have inherited [the Jewish people's] suffering and catastrophe as well.'[5] Segev

4   Tom Segev, 'Ma Lamadta be-Treblinka hayom?' ('What did You Learn in Treblinka today?'), *Ha'aretz*, 2 November 1990: B2.
5   Shabtai Tevet, 'Tzilume-rega: Russia, Polin' ('Snapshots: Russia, Poland'), *Ha'aretz*, 31 August 1990, p. B4.

reported that the pupils read the article with great approval, all the more so as many of them 'identify the Holocaust with today's Poland'; they looked everywhere for swastikas, some of them seeming to have 'an internal need to actually find some'. As one of the youths declared emphatically, 'Somebody has to be blamed for the Holocaust; we have to hate somebody, but we have already made our reconciliation with the Germans.'

This is, no doubt, an amazing confession. It depicts one of the most conspicuous paradoxes of the reception of the Holocaust in Israeli political culture. On the one hand, the pupil fully expresses the natural need to grasp the Holocaust in terms of *guilt* (and *recrimination*): because the vast dimensions of the monstrosity prevent one from perceiving the victims of the catastrophe as individuals, they are co-dified into the slogan of 'six million'. The focus of attention may now be shifted to what seems easier to understand—the originators of the horror. In fact, this is not surprising: Israeli political culture has never been able to openly confront—let alone empathetically identify with—the true situation of the Holocaust victim, that is, a situation of total helplessness. At best, it simply denied the situation; in its less pleasant moments, it manifested open contempt for it from the condescending heights of the ruling ideology, based on the doctrine of 'the negation of the Diaspora'.

On the other hand—and as a necessary consequence of the guilt paradigm—the pupil expresses the need to *hate*: because the Israeli-Jewish collective memory never went through any real process of grieving, the collective recoils from remembering the Holocaust in terms of its having been the catastrophe of its victims—both the slain and the survivors—and even more from recalling it in its universal significance as a symbol of the cataclysms of general human history, piling ever higher and higher—'like a heap of rubble reaching to the heavens', in Walter Benjamin's words—namely, as a meta-Jewish paradigm that preserves the memory of the Jewish victims as victims by transforming them into a warning sign against the oppression of *any* human being. Indeed, since the memory has been structured around the principle of *guilt* (and the self-image of 'eternal victim' that Israeli political culture has embraced does not rest on the memory of the

historical   victims—thus   'redeeming   them'—but   rather   in-
strumentalizes memory ideologically), 'hatred' is a fitting manifestation
of this construction of memory.

But it is at this point that historical reality suddenly appears, 'sensibly'
outwitting the ideology of memory, so to say: the willingness to hate is
there, but the object of hate has become blurred and ambiguous! We
are talking here about one of the central patterns in the reception of the
Holocaust in Israeli political culture: the incessant disconnection between the public and private spheres in all that pertains to the contents
of memory and their mechanisms of employment. While in the private
sphere, a whole spectrum of responses and behaviour towards Germany
and Germans has developed, in the public sphere—as I mentioned
before—all expressions of resentment to Germany, at least since the
1960s, have been excised from institutional discourse, except for occasional public outburst of private hostility of one sort or another. The
reason for this is clear *ab initio*: what the pupil calls 'reconciliation' is
nothing but the formal normalization of something that cannot be
normalized by force, and certainly not by decree, as was the rather early
established system of relations between Germany and Israel, based as it
was from the very beginning on both the instrumentalization of the
Holocaust (on the part of Israel) and the complementary materialization of the atonement (on the part of Germany).

And thus the pupil, an evident victim of Israel's collective memory,
finds himself vulnerable to the anguish of ambivalence: he is asked to
confront the Holocaust in a baffling period, after the formal
'reconciliation' of Israel with the Germans, those who perpetrated the
genocide. And because, as we have said, the collective memory has not
taught him real '*Trauerarbeit*' (i.e., working through a true process of
mourning), and he thus does not know how to remember the Holocaust without invoking the terminology of recriminating 'guilt',
'hatred' is a necessity for him. He is therefore forced to produce a new
'guilty party' as a certified replacement for the original object of hate
which he slowly but steadily lost on the road to 'normalization', paved
as it was with payments of compensation and other forms of mate-
rialized atonement. He responds to the 'internal need' bubbling up

inside him by engaging in a Manichean act of shifting the 'guilt' and directing the hatred onto 'someone' else: the Poles, for example. Shabtai Tevet's article seems to have been tailor-made for him.

Suffice it to say that this mechanism of 'guilt' shifting can also be aimed in other directions. In the same article Tom Segev reports how Holocaust survivors were recruited for the trip to the death-camps in Poland and appeared before the pupils as 'living witnesses' who, because they had been 'there', served to justify the projection of fear and hatred onto the *contemporary* enemies of the State of Israel and to entrench the all-encompassing ideological dread of the Arabs and fortify the hostility towards *them*. Not for nothing did Segev conclude his article by saying that the main thing the pupils learned was that it is necessary to love the state [of Israel] and to defend it. They did not learn that the right of self-determination is a universal right belonging to all peoples. On the contrary, the booklet that the Ministry of Education distributed to the participants asserts that Poland supports Arab terrorist organizations and the Palestinian's right to self-determination, as if the two things were equivalent. He added:

> The pupils were repeatedly taught that the Holocaust imposes a duty on them to remain in Israel. They were not taught that it imposes a duty on them to strengthen democracy, to fight against racism, to defend minorities and human rights, to refrain from obeying unlawful orders.[6]

Israeli political (but not only political) culture abounds in mechanisms of exchange of certain elements in the ideological reception of the Holocaust for others, heteronomous in their essence. And just as the memory of the slain is liable to be 'translated' into the present diplomatic, economic, and military demands of Israel; just as it is possible to transform *all* the Germans as Germans into 'Nazis' when the need arises; and just as the Germans, the perpetrators of the historic genocide, can be replaced by the Poles ('there') or the Arabs ('here and now')—so too can all sorts of emergency situations, real and imagined,

6   Segev, 'Ma Lamadta.'

be cast in the mold of the experience of the historical Holocaust.[7] There is no small measure of irony in the fact that precisely in Israel, where the uniqueness of the Holocaust has become a political-ideo-logical slogan in every mouth, the archetype of the 'Holocaust' is projected at every available opportunity.

All this should be properly understood: whether the emotional ex-clamation of a pupil on the journey to the extermination camps or the assertions of a popular writer, such items are paradigmatic. Viewed in themselves—however highly or lowly evaluated—they are of no great consequence. They gain their immense relevance only because they sharply mirror the mental matrix of a whole political culture: they are, then, the generic product of something already existing, but at the same time they serve as a mechanism of its ideological perpetuation and reinforcement.

It is in this respect that 'hatred' for Germany and the Germans, as well as the sudden vanishing of this very 'hatred' (because of the formally proclaimed reconciliation with Germany), are basically ideological. It is ideological because 'Germany' is not viewed and perceived in its cur-rent complexity, its heterogenous facets, its different life-worlds and developing political culture, but rather seen as a mere projection screen, a convenient platform on which to live through one's own aporetic contradictions, to self-righteously 'eat one's cake and have it'. It is ideological because it does not reflect at all upon Israeli reality: neither on the irreversible fact that the materialization of atonement produces a reification of the moral claim itself, thus transforming 'hatred' into a fetish, nor on the fact that the mere exchangeability of the 'hate' object—the easily performed transformation of the Nazi into a Pole, a Palestinian, or anybody else—indeed reveals the essentially vengeful and thus oppressive nature of the politically structured Israeli collective memory. But it is first and foremost ideological because the 'hate' paradigm itself is not at all 'a kind of monument', as the young Israeli

7   Cf. Moshe Zuckermann, *Shoah be-Cheder he-Atum* (Shoah in the Sealed Room) (Tel-Aviv; Hamechaver Publications, 1993).

writer would have it, but rather quite the opposite: a way of bypassing the true memory of the victims qua victims by chanelling its emotional and cognitive energy to the level of 'hatred' for their persecutors, all the more so as this 'hatred' turns out to be instrumental for the achievement and satisfaction of heteronomous goals and purposes, at times even the rhetorical legitimization of policies and ideologies that are clearly bound to produce an ever growing oppression and to result in more and more victims. It is in this particular sense, then, that the ideologically fetishized 'hatred' is doing wrong—not only towards those who do not deserve the hatred, but also towards those in whose name this 'hatred' is being conducted and perpetuated.

But there is yet another aspect to all of this. From the outset the ideological discourse—dividing the structures of memory into Israeli public and private spheres, on the one hand, and linking the psychological codes of 'guilt' and 'hatred', on the other—at the officially institutionalized level of the *state* took the only shape a state could bestow: the concrete form of legality. This became manifest quite early on, not only in the complex relationship with the newly founded West-German state—resulting in the reparation agreements of 1952 and the establishment of full diplomatic relations in 1965—but also within the inner-Israeli discourse, especially with regard to the two major trials pertaining to Israel's confrontation with the Holocaust: the Eichmann and the Demianjuk trials. I do not mention them in order to discuss any *legal* right the State of Israel had or had not in taking either Eichmann or Demianjuk to court. Rather, I would like to pose the question: What kind of (collective) memory is promoted by dealing with the world historic catastrophe, the *Zivilisationsbruch* (i.e., the collapse or cataclysm of civilization), within the paradigm of judicial recrimination, i.e., by *formally* codifying the murderer and his victim, turning them into ideological 'character masks' rather than accepting them as authentic protagonists of the historic event. Already as early as 1960 Max Horkheimer commented on the Israeli assertion that the Eichmann trial was intended to enlighten 'the youth in their own land and the peoples outside' about the true nature of the Third Reich. He said that if 'such an insight cannot be mediated through the extensive literature, available in scientific as well as in generally approachable works in all civilized languages, but is to gain its appropriate meaning, as perceived by current and future generations, only in the form of new trial reports and international sensations, it looks quite bad for such an insight.'[8]

From this perspective the only true confrontation possible between the horrors of the Holocaust (personified by Eichmann) and the survivor may well have been the collapse of Katzetnik, one of the witnesses, in the witness stand, when he came face to face with the mass murderer—the definitive representative for him of what he referred to, at that time, as 'the other planet'—and had to remember what had happened 'there'. The inability to bear the confrontation under the given conditions (organized by the state) paradoxically represented the true essence of what had happened there: the total powerlessness of the historical victim in view of his historical murderer. The trial—a rational procedure for 'achieving justice' coupled with the formal satisfaction of the need for 'vengeance'—could not bring about any true confrontation. Retrospectively, it seems that many Israelis 'respected' the collapsing witness, and probably even felt a deep compassion for him, but more than anything else they were estranged and alienated from him. To be more precise, his psychical state of being embarrassed them: his breakdown did not 'fit', so to speak, the advanced collective 'upright posture', the newly evolved national Israeli pride. The 'Diasporic' reality/mentality of the witness was harnessed as an useful factor in extrapolating the need for the establishment and existence of the State of Israel, but not as the embodiment of a still unassimilated dimension of this very existence. People perceived this particular shocking moment in the Eichmann trial not through the survivor's agony but through their own ideologized preoccupations as citizens of the young state. In the Zionist *memento*, the historical reality—on account of which the witness broke down—has undergone an incessant metamorphosis, until it ceremoniously established itself officially as the 'Remembrance Day of the Holocaust and *Heroism.*'

8 Max Horkheimer, 'Zur Ergreifung Eichmanns (1960/1967)', in idem, *Gesammelte Schriften* (Frankfurt/M: Fischer Taschenbuchen Verlag, 1985), vol. 8, pp. 156ff.

Many years later, the Demianjuk trial, from the outset perceived as an 'educational' event, turned out to have to deal first and foremost with the issue whether the accused was actually the presumed criminal, whom the State of Israel made every effort to sentence in order to perform, so to speak, a last symbolic act 'for the benefit' of the 'memory' of the Holocaust. In view of the fact that the generation of both the murderers and the survivors is about to perish, the ceremony was imbued with a documentary meaning and given the status of a memorial. But many Israelis became confused about its essence: an Israeli lawyer was vigorously fighting to prove the defendant's innocence, who—so he claimed—was *not* 'Ivan the Terrible', the criminal from Treblinka. In doing so—in addition to presenting the Soviets as the true forces of evil—he incessantly doubted the credibility of the survivors' memory, leading the trial into various academic debates all of which aimed at proving that it was hard, if not completely impossible to establish—after over forty years—a sufficient identity between the person of the murderer, as preserved in the memory of the survivors, and the person of the defendant. Thus, the intended memorial became—by the very event initiated by the state, though, most likely, not by intent—a huge monument for the *disintegration* of memory: even before the final verdict was given, it became quite clear that—whatever the outcome of the Demianjuk trial—nobody in Israel could ever be sure whether the State of Israel had convicted or, alternatively, released the real murderer, Ivan from Treblinka. In paradoxical contrast to the original intention, the very formal act performed by the state played into the hands of those who try to undermine the status of the Holocaust code in the collective memory. Not without reason a well-known Israeli publicist claimed that the Demianjuk trial 'has contributed, so far, more to the denigration of the Shoah [memory] than have one thousand of those in the West who deal in the falsification of history.'[9]

9   Rubik Rosental, 'Mutar lehitvakeah al Masa'oth ha-No'ar' ('One is Entitled to Argue about the Trips of our Youth [to Poland]'), *Hadashoth*, 18 September 1992, p. 14.

The debacle of the Demianjuk trial is symptomatic for the state of reception of the Holocaust in Israeli society. Though new discourses evolved in recent years, critically examining the modes of impact of the Holocaust on Israeli political culture, it can be maintained that the reception as a whole is still very much ideologized. Whether this can be changed depends mainly on the development of other repressive moments and forces structuring Israeli reality. In a way, the memory of the Holocaust still remains to be *liberated* from the ideological chains of its instrumentalization. This is all the more urgent, as those who remain of the generation of survivors will not be with us for very much longer.

Jerusalem 1948
The Phantom City

Salim Tamari

Talbiya, Baq'a, Qatamon, 'Ayn Karim, Lifta and most of the other Arab villages and neighbourhoods in and around Western Jerusalem that were uprooted and destroyed in 1948 seem to have been over-looked by history. Virtually all of them were occupied by the Zionist forces and then after, or already during, the war re-settled with Jewish immigrants. Later still, 'Ayn Karim, Lifta and Talbiya were 'gentrified' by well-to-do Israelis.

'Western Jerusalem' is, of course, a post-1948 term, delineating the boundaries defined by the Armistice Agreement of 1949 that separated the now Israeli-occupied part of Jerusalem from its 'eastern' half which became part of the West Bank under Jordanian rule (1948–1967). But even before 1948, differences in topography and commercial sig-nificance meant that villages in the west and the east of the city had their own distinctive features. The western villages had two main at-tributes that set them apart: proximity to the Jaffa-Tel Aviv highway, and integration into the western expansion of Jerusalem's middle-class neighbourhoods. Moreover, rich soil, a high annual rate of rainfall and

Author's note: This article is an expanded version of the 'Introduction' to Salim Tamari (ed.), *Jerusalem 1948. The Arab Neighbourhoods and their Fate in the War* (Jerusalem: The Institute of Jersusalem Studies, and Bethlehem: Badil Resource Center, 1999; 2nd ed. 2002).

lush foliage are typical of the western slopes of the Judean hills. The region has a number of perennial streams and the terrain gradually slopes in the direction of Lydda, Ramleh and the coastal plains. The eastern slopes, on the other hand, are arid and semi-arid and fall sharply towards the Jordan Valley, the soil here is poor and the steepness of the slopes makes terracing difficult to maintain. The result is—was—a higher population density and concentration of villages in the Western Jerusalem district—the area that Israel occupied in 1948.

For sixty-one years now the memory of these destroyed villages and neighbourhoods has been kept alive by the thousands of Palestinians Israel uprooted from their ancestral communities and expelled across the armistice lines as refugees. Many of Jerusalem's refugees subsequently made their way to Amman, Beirut, and Damascus or moved on to more distant Arab and foreign diasporas. Striking is how, except for the village of Bayt Safafa, the Jewish military forces went about and succeeded in totally cleansing Jerusalem's western suburbs and villages from their indigenous Arab Palestinian population. John Rose, an Anglo-Armenian Jerusalemite who managed for a while to stay on in Baq'a, has left us a unique eye-witness account of what happened to these neighbourhoods and of the fate of the few non-Jewish families who, like him, had managed to stay put (mostly because they were affiliated with the various churches and convents there):

> By the end of 1948 all unoccupied houses in the Arab suburbs had been totally vandalized and nothing was left in the way of worthwhile loot. Nerves were frayed and, as one observer said, we were living 'as if it were in a concentration camp on the edge of a battlefield.'[1]

Rose continued to live in Baq'a for another four years but then, in 1952, crossed over to what was now 'East' Jerusalem, in Jordanian territory. As the small Jewish community that had inhabited the Old City was relocated to the western city during the war, the armistice

---

1   John Rose, *Armenians of Jerusalem: Memories of Life in Palestine* (London, Radcliffe Press, 1993).

lines that now cut the city into two also became the lines of an ethnic/
national divide.[2]

Current debates on Jerusalem have been so mythologized by the
nature of ideological claims put forward by Israelis, Palestinians and the
world community that we easily forget that before the war of 1948
there was an 'ordinary' city called Jerusalem, made up of various
communities and neighbourhoods divided along historical lines of
ethnicity (of various nationalities), as well as by class. Similarly, the
religious identity and sacred geography of the city have so permeated
our idea of 'Jerusalem' that it has almost become impossible for us to
grasp how cosmopolitan Jerusalem had become during those pre-1948
decades. Today, we inevitably think of Jerusalem in terms of 'East' and
'West', a city divided into two by the 1948 war and then 'united' again
in June 1967 by the military might of Israel. We now tend to draw this
division retroactively when we seek to define the contours of the city
before the cataclysm of the 1948 war, and even when we want to
transcend them in an act of historical re-creation we find we have little
choice but to use them as analytical categories.

The New City Expands

When we attempt to re-construct the displacement and expulsion that
befell Palestine's indigenous population in 1948 and trace the fate of
the Arab Palestinians who not only had their property and homes taken
from them but were robbed of a whole world and culture that had been

---

2 Cf. Nathan Krystall, 'The Fall of the New City, 1947-1950', in Tamari (ed.),
   Jerusalem 1948: 'On 2 February 1949, the Israeli government declared that it no
   longer considered West Jerusalem occupied territory and abolished military rule
   there. Negotiations over Jerusalem—and the rest of the territory bordering the
   Israeli-Jordanian front lines—began the same month. Addallah al-Tal represented
   the Transjordanians and Moshe Dayan the Israelis. The division of Jerusalem
   between Transjordan and Israel, without Palestinian Arabs having a say in the
   matter, was a foregone conclusion' (126, quoting Stuart Perowne, *The One Remains* [New York: E.P. Dutton & Co., 1955]).

theirs for centuries, the pre-1948 Jerusalem that emerges is fundamentally unrecognizable to us today. What we find is a city of considerable social mobility and ethnic diversity, where communal conflict
was kept at bay by a fair amount of mutual dependence and local
solidarities. This particular combination of ethnic hybridity is tellingly
exemplified in the way traditional, messianic, and secular trends co-
existed side by side and lent the city the cosmopolitan character it
acquired under British colonial rule.

Nowhere is this cosmopolitan culture more evident than in the social
and intellectual milieu of West Jerusalem life as narrated in the diaries
of the Qatamon essayist, Khalil Sakakini.[3] The picture one gleans from
such accounts of contemporary life in the 1930s and 40s (including
those of John Rose, Hala Sakakini, Edward Said, and others) and from
later ethnographic contributions is one of a rapidly evolving and vibrant city whose life was then abruptly cut short. As Rochelle Davis
writes:

> When the British occupied Jerusalem at the end of 1917, they found
> a city wasted by the hardships and deprivations of World War I.
> When they left the city in the spring of 1948, they relinquished what
> had become a vibrant and cosmopolitan city to be ravaged and
> divided in the 1948 war over Palestine.[4]

As she describes the development of the New City pre-1948, Davis
explains how, as the majority of the land outside the city walls was
owned by Arab villagers, churches or urban landowners,

> those Arabs, Armenians and Greeks who had the economic means
> were encouraged by the general growth to build or rent outside the
> walls. The spacious new Arab suburbs in the New City were an
> indicator of social/class mobility, as at least moderate amounts of

---

3   Khalil Sakakini, *Kadha Ana Ya Dunya: Yawmiyyat* ('Such Am I, Oh World: A
      Diary'), (Jerusalem: al-Matba'a al-Tujariyya, 1955).
4   Rochelle Davis, 'The Growth of the Western Communities, 1917-1948', in
      Tamari, *Jerusalem 1948*. p. 32.

capital were required to build or rent in the Arab neighbourhoods outside the walls.[5]

She adds that, in both ways, the Arab expansion of the New City contrasted with that of the Jews, as the latter 'had a more difficult time buying land in the city, and Jews living in the New City represented a variety of different classes, not just the middle and upper class.' As she further outlines, 'these suburban living areas were part of the expressions of a rising middle class and a new "modern" value system' that emphasized 'education and public life.'[6]

The dynamism of these communities in the west contrasted visibly with the growth of the New City towards the north and southwest that dates back to the late Ottoman period, with Palestinian Arab notables and *ashraf*[7] establishing manorial residencies in Shaykh Jarrah and Wadi al-Joz before the turn of the twentieth century. The British Mandate economy gave rise to a new class of professionals, merchants and, of course, government civil servants. In the late 1920s, the Arab middle classes, whose households benefited from the creation of a new bureaucratic apparatus in the capital, began to move from the congestion of the Old City to the rapidly emerging bourgeois suburbs in the west of Qatamon, Talbiya and Baq'a.

These new Arab communities displayed several patterns of expansion depending on family networks and links with neighbouring village communities that here, too, went back to Ottoman times. Three elements combined to propel these moves: government allocation of state land (*iqta*), family *awqaf* (s. *waqf*, religious endowment) and institutional *awqaf* (mostly Orthodox Christian property) transferred to individual members of the various denominations. The resulting family-based housing schemes grew simultaneously with the Christian mo-

---

5   Ibid., p. 33.
6   Ibid.
7   *Ashraf*, s. *sharif*: the term given to people who claim their families are descendant from the family of the Prophet Muhammad.

nastic, Jewish, and Templar (German) communities that began establishing themselves in the Western hills.

One of the earlier documented cases of Arab family neighbourhoods was the emergence of the Nammari and Wa'ri quarters (*ahya'*) in, respectively, upper and lower Baq'a. While traditional Palestinian families, such as the Hussaynis, the Nashashibis and the Khatibs, built their residencies in the northern neighbourhoods, the Nammari family had acquired land in the 1870s from villagers in Malha and Bayt Jala.[8] The Wa'ris meanwhile had prevailed on the Ottoman governor of Jerusalem to transfer to them state land in lower Baq'a, both families registering their lands as family *waqf*.[9] By the late 1920s the area had its own market (Suq an-Nammari) which handled the wholesale trade for the surrounding villages and the retail trade for the local region.

Religious endowments and church properties engendered a second wave of suburbanization from the Old City, much of it involving Greek and Russian Orthodox properties in Musrara, the Russian Compound, Talbiya and Qatamon. Here we have a combination of families registering their own properties as church *waqf* (a way of protecting them against the state) and long-term leases and grants that religious endowments extended to their followers.

By the early 1940s already most of these suburbs were encroaching on the village properties of the Jerusalem hinterland, bringing them into daily contact with two previously separate communities: the suburbanized and expanding indigenous villages of Lifta, Malha, Deir Yassin, and 'Ayn Karim, and the mushrooming immigrant Zionist settlements, such as Bikur Hayim, Yamin Moshe, Mea She'arim and Rehavia. The village economy was absorbed into the urban fabric of Jerusalem through the growing demand for skilled builders (stone masons and cutters), and because of the outlying quarries that produced the famous Jerusalem stone. Village produce was now pouring

8   Taher an-Nammari, 'The Nammari Quarter in Baq'a', unpublished manuscript (Jerusalem, November 1995).
9   Ibid.

into the city as improved road systems facilitated transportation: the Jaffa Jerusalem railroad (which went through Battir), new bus lines, and asphalt roads.

Significantly, in the 'seam' of these communities (the areas bordering and within Musrara, Romeima, and Talbiya) we can clearly detect the beginning of shared or 'mixed' communities where economic inter-dependence re-enforced social co-existence between Arabs and Jews. Hadawi's fascinating property map outlining the ethnic mix of real estate holdings in these seam areas in 1946 keenly reflects this emerging reality. That is, property ownership still shows how the city was still largely divided along confessional and ethnic lines (it is too early to use the word 'national' in this context), but that new mixed living areas were definitely emerging, all the more if we take into consideration that much of the living space in Jerusalem was rented, quite frequently from owners belonging to other ethnic groups.

While secular Arab historians, such as 'Arif el-'Arif and Muhammad al-Amiry, tend to create a portrait of exaggerated harmony between Arabs and Jews for the pre-48 period, Zionist historiography wants us to see the conflict as perennial and to believe that under Ottoman and other Islamic rules Jews were, at best, accorded the status of a protected (*zhimmi*) community. Everyday relations at the turn of the twentieth century between the two communities, as we find them reflected in contemporary testimonies, tally with neither version. Broadly speaking, we can say that patterns of employment, investment and public spending by the British Mandate authorities created new arenas of integrated social domains. Cultural modernities, and the globalization of a European life style they represented, also bear witness to the emergence of 'mixed' Arab-Jewish communities in middle-class neighbourhoods in Jaffa and Haifa, and in Jerusalem in such areas as Romeima, Shamma', Shaykh Badr, and Musrara. Militating against these trends, however, were the increasing diffusion of Zionist ideology among Jewish immigrants to Palestine, and the concomitant rising tide of Arab nationalist sentiments among the indigenous Palestinians, which worked to undermine the confessional boundaries between Palestinian Christians and Muslims, while reinforcing the ethnic boundaries between Arabs and Jews. Unlike their co-religionists in Hebron (al-Khalil) and Tiberias, few Jerusalem Jews were Arabic speakers—an additional factor crucially setting the two communities apart.

At the heart of the contestation over territory in Jerusalem during the British Mandate period stood 'zoning politics', i.e., zoning laws and the delineation of the municipal boundaries. While in 1947 Palestinian Arabs constituted a majority of the population in the overall Jerusalem District, Jews predominated within the city's municipal boundaries (99,000 Jews vs. 65,100 Arabs).[10] Reviewing the literature on the 'selective' demographics of Mandate Jerusalem, British historian Michael Dumper suggests two main reasons for these population discrepancies: one was the inclusion of Jewish migrants who had arrived before 1946 in Jerusalem and later moved to Tel Aviv and other localities; and the second was the exclusion of Palestinians who lived in the rural periphery but worked in the city (daytime populations such as the commuting workers from Lifta and Deir Yassin), but counting Jewish residents equally living in the city's periphery but somehow incorporated into the municipal population (e.g. Beit Vegan, Ramat Rahel, Meqor Hayim). Dumper calls this process 'demographic gerrymandering'.[11]

Administrative incorporation within the metropolitan area, however, was not the determining factor that differentiated between Arab and Jewish communities. Organizations of the Jewish *Yishuv* (the pre-48 Zionist settlement in Palestine) chose to establish some of their new Jerusalem suburbs in the western and north-western hinterlands that

10 Walid Mustafa, *Al-Quds, Imran wa-Sukkan* (Jerusalem: Jerusalem Media and Communication Centre [JMCC], 1997).
11 Michael Dumper, *The Politics of Jerusalem* (New York: Columbia University Press, 1997), pp. 61-62. On birth registration, see Justin McCarthy, *The Population of Palestine* (New York: Columbia University Press, 1990), p. 165 (note to table A8-14). Dumper claims that these Jewish neighbourhoods were excluded from the municipal boundaries, but Sami Hadawi includes them as part of the municipal boundaries during the mid-1940s; see S. Hadawi, *Palestinian Rights and Losses in 1948. A Comprehensive Study* (London: Saqi Books, 1988).

were still within the expanded boundaries of the city. The 'garden suburbs' of Talpiot and Rehavia designed by Richard Kaufman are salient examples.[12] In her analysis of how these communities evolved, Rochelle Davis discusses the well-planned and organized character of these Jewish neighbourhoods, so different from the more spontaneously sprawling and family-based nature in which the city's Arab suburbs developed.[13]

The Fall of the New City

There is no shortage of Zionist works narrating the course of the 1948 war. Far fewer works narrate how that war led to the tragedy of displacement and dispossession from a Palestinian Arab perspective. The publication in 1993 of Bahjat Abu Gharbiyyeh's war memoirs formed a beginning, albeit modest, of redressing this imbalance.[14] The studies and documents that make up *Jerusalem 1948* are a further step in this direction.

As I already indicated, when we try to reconstruct the nature of Jerusalem's pre-1948 Arab communities, we inevitably confront the problem of how to avoid using anachronistic—and therefore potentially misleading—terminology. 'West Jerusalem' itself is already problematic since it designates a border delineation that was only created by the 1948 war. The communities that were built west of the Old City in the 1920s and 30s, as in the case of villages such as 'Ayn Karim, Lifta and Malha, had no particular corporate existence outside their relationship with the Jerusalem urban administrative nexus at large and the economic web that further linked Jerusalem to Jaffa,

12　Dan Bahat, *The Illustrated Atlas of Jerusalem* (New York: Simon and Schuster, 1990), pp. 131-132.
13　Davis, 'The Growth of the Western Communities.'
14　Bahjat Abu Gharbiyyeh, *Fi-Khidamm an-Nidal al-Arabi al-Filastini* ('Memoirs of Bahjat Abu Gharbiyyeh 1916-1949') (Beirut: Institute for Palestine Studies, 1993).

Haifa and the rest of the country. But, of course, when reconstructing these lost communities and assessing what happened to the people that lived there and the properties they owned, it has become common to use 'West' Jerusalem according to the current, i.e. post-1967, boundaries of the city.

A similar problem arises with terms of ethnic identification. Significantly, 'Palestinians' in the Mandate period included both Jewish and Arab natives of the city. 'Arab' was a designation that increasingly came to mean Christians and Muslims together, as opposed to 'Jewish' Palestinians (i.e., 'inhabitants of Palestine'), who—especially after the 1936 rebellion and the massive Zionist immigration from Europe—became more and more identified in people's minds, consciously or unconsciously, with the Zionist movement. And, of course, there were the native Arabic-speaking Palestinian Jews—particularly in towns like Tiberias, Safad, Hebron, but also in smaller numbers in Jaffa, Haifa and Jerusalem. Finally, there were also a sizable number of native Jerusalemites who were neither Jews nor Arabs, but definitely Palestinian. These include the Armenians, Greeks, Syriacs and Ethiopians of the Old City, and the German Templars of the New City. In identity if not in citizenship, these people were all Jerusalemites and Palestinians, and it would therefore not do at all to speak of Palestinians in the exclusive contemporary connotation of 'Palestinian Arab'. One could, of course, decide to use the term 'Arab' to mean Christian and Muslim Jerusalemites who were Arabic speaking, together with denominational terms (Orthodox, Catholic, Muslim, Jewish, etc.) when applicable. Since confessional associations played a critical role in the expansion of the Western suburbs of the city, these functional designations do make sense, however politically incorrect they may be in the jargon of today. Admittedly they are approximations, and the main victims of this are the non-Arab Palestinian minorities (such as Greeks and Armenians) who were sometimes subsumed in these ethnic categories.

The fiftieth anniversary, in 1998, of the establishment of a Jewish state in Palestine—Israel—and of the expulsion of the Palestinians from their homeland—the Nakba—gave fresh impetus to the debate about the exiling of the indigenous Palestinian population and how it was carried out. *Jerusalem 1948* forms part of this debate. Its contributions paint in vivid detail the atmosphere that preceded the war, reconstruct how already in the first days of January 1948 the Zionists started expelling Palestinian Arab residents from the Western suburbs and villages, and offer an eye-witness account of how only the last-minute entrance into the fight by Jordanian Amir Abdallah's Arab Legion prevented the Zionists from occupying all of Jerusalem. In the narrative he constructs of the events that sealed the fate of Arab West Jerusalem, Nathan Krystall quotes the British high commissioner, Sir Alan Cunningham, reporting on a strike on 1 December 1947 in reaction to the UN's Partition Resolution of 29 November that had turned violent:

> The initial Arab outbreaks were spontaneous and unorganized and were more demonstrations of displeasure at the UN decision than determined attacks on Jews. The weapons initially employed were sticks and stones and had it not been for Jewish recourse to firearms, it is not impossible that the excitement would have subsided and little loss of life been caused. This is more probably since there is reliable evidence that the Arab Higher Committee as a whole and the Mufti in particular, although pleased at the strong response to the strike call, were not in favour of serious outbreaks.[15]

On 4 January 1948, the Hagana (the main pre-state Zionist militia) bombed the Semiramis Hotel in Qatamon, which killed twenty-six civilians and prompted many people to start evacuating the neighbourhood. Khalil Sakakini's daughter, Hala, described the mayhem that followed:

> All day long you could see people carrying their belongings and moving from their houses to safer ones in Qatamon or another

---

15 Nathan Krystall, 'The Fall of the New City, 1947-1950', in Tamari, *Jerusalem 1948*, p. 96.

quarter altogether. They reminded us of pictures we used to see of European refugees during the war. People were simply panic-stricken. The rumor spread that leaflets had been dropped by the Jews saying they would make out of Qatamon one heap of rubble.[16]

The chilling eye-witness accounts Krystall has collected of the Deir Yassin massacre, on 9 April 1948, again forcefully bring home the point that the slaughter served to terrorize the entire Palestinian Arab population, most immediately those living in and around Jerusalem. Qatamon was at the centre of Zionist military plans to conquer West Jerusalem. The attacks began on 30 April and lasted three days. A Jewish woman Krystall interviewed described the looting of Arab property by Jews that she witnessed:

> I remember the looting in Qatamon very well. I was a first aid nurse stationed at *Beth Havra'a Etzion* (a military convalescence center) in Qatamon [...] located in two large Arab houses. One night a soldier took me out and showed me around the neighborhood. I was stunned by the beauty of the houses. I went into one house—it was beautiful, with a piano, and carpets, and wonderful chandeliers. [...] For days you could see people walking by carrying looted goods. [...] And it was in broad daylight, so everyone could see.[17]

The Siege of the Old City

Constantine X. Mavrides was a Greek who had settled in Jerusalem at an early age and by 1948 had served as interpreter and secretary in the General Consulate of Greece in Jerusalem for 25 years. The diaries he

16 Ibid., p. 101.
17 Ibid., p. 110, Hagit Shlonksy, interviewed on 1 May 1997.

wrote form a unique contemporaneous eye-witness account of the siege of the Old City.[18] At one point he writes:

> Prior to the departure of the High Commissioner [on 14 May 1948], many of the more important buildings in Jerusalem were placed under the protection of the Red Cross, and a special concentration zone was established for the war victims and refugees. Such buildings included the YMCA, the King David Hotel (the area around these two buildings constituted the international area of the Red Cross), the Government House and all the hospitals, as long as they were not used for waging war operations, like the Hadassah and others.
>
> Immediately after midnight on May 14, the Jewish army occupied all these security zones. So they occupied the Greek and German colonies, the Upper Baq'a, the Russian Compounds and the prisons, and later arrived in front of the Old City walls. The next day, they started to pound the Old City gates with bombs, mortar shells and rifle fire, claiming to want to take the city, but with a first priority of rescuing the almost two thousand besieged Jews inside the city, many of whom were from the *Haganah* organization.

Mavrides goes on to describe how, long before 14 May, inhabitants of Jerusalem's Muslim and Christian suburbs had fled to the Old City and taken refuge there, bringing with them what furniture, household utensils and other articles they were able to transport without using

18 'War in the Old City. The Diaries of Constantine Mavrides, May 15–December 30, 1948', translated by John N. Tleel and with an introdcution by Musa Budeiri, in Tamari, *Jerusalem 1948*, pp. 258-278; Constantine X. Mavrides was of Greek Tracian origin. Born in Adrianople in 1890, he had received his early education in his native country and then immigrated to Palestine to continue his studies in Jersualem, where he settled down. He studied at Jerusalem's Greek Orthodox Patriarchate schools and at the then highly regarded Theological School of the Holy Cross. After he graduated Mavrides served in the secretarial department of the Greek Orthodox Patriarchate of Jerusalem for eight years. In 1918, he was employed by the British in various posts in Palestine, Syria and Lebanon. Following the establishment of the British Mandate, Mavrides became interpreter and secretary in the city's General Consulate of Greece (ibid., p. 258).

motor vehicles (damage to the refineries in Haifa and the destruction of the railways and the road network had led to a fuel shortage for already several months). The first attacks continued until 5 p.m. on Monday, 17 May, 'spreading panic and fear. None of the besieged and the refugees got to shut their eyes. We were all walking around seeking safer shelter.'[19] It was only on 19 May that King Abdallah's army, the Arab Legion, entered the Old City.[20] Mavrides describes the growing desperation inside the City before that as follows:

> Around noon of May 17, panic spread: it was rumored that the Jewish army had forced open the New Gate and was threatening to enter the City. It was also said that they had occupied the French buildings, such as the Notre Dame, the [Saint Louis] hospital and Reparatrice Convent situated immediately outside the New Gate. Having the advantage of these buildings, the army was firing at the defenders who were on the Wall.
>
> The panic-stricken inhabitants of the New Gate neighborhoods inside the wall migrated to the inner part of the city. Fueling the panic were the mournful cries of some mothers and sisters accompanying the transport of their dead. On top of all that, the electric power and the municipal water [supply] had been disconnected.[21]

Mavrides' diaries take us through the entire siege, describing how by the end of the first, 4-week long truce, i.e., on Friday, 10 July, the Old City was almost empty as from the 60,000 inhabitants and the nearly 10,000 refugees, 'only five to seven thousand remain. Most of them

---

19   Ibid., pp. 263-64.
20   As Budeiri reminds us in his introduction: 'According to the most authoritative sources on the agreements reached between Prince Abdullah and the Jewish Agency [before hostilities broke out], both parties undertook not to interfere with each other's plans. Abullah would not allow his army to enter the area allocated [by the UN Partition Resultion of 29 November 1947] to the Jewish State, while the Jews undertook not to thwart his occupation of the Arab parts of Palestine. There was, however, no agreement over Jerusalem. There is no doubt that both Ben Gurion and Abdullah coveted Jersualem', ibid., p. 259; cf. Avi Shlaim, *Collusion across the Jordan. King Abdullah, the Zionist Movement, and the Partition of Palestine* (Oxford: Clarendon Press 1988), esp. p. 178.
21   'War in the Old City', p. 264.

were very poor, and thus did not have enough money to move away …
Complete desolation.'[22]

Restitution and the Right of Return

Because of the way they deferred the issues of the Palestinian refugees, the
Right of Return, settlements and Jerusalem to 'final status' negotiations,
the Oslo Accords, of 3 September 1993, pushed into the foreground the
pressing need to start documenting all Arab properties in West Jerusalem
prior to the 1948 war. On 11 December 1948, nearly a year after the
Zionists had expelled the first Palestinian Arab citizens from their homes in
Jerusalem, the UN General Assembly adopted Resolution 194, enshrining
the Right of Return for all refugees. Paragraph 11 outlines how

> Refugees wishing to return to their homes and live at peace with their
> neighbors should be permitted to do so at the earliest practicable date
> [while] compensation should be paid for the property of those
> choosing not to return and for loss or damage to property which,
> under principles of international law or in equity, should be made
> good by the Governments or authorities responsible.[23]

UN Resolution 194 also established a Palestine Conciliation Committee (PCC) that was to facilitate the carrying out of the Resolution's
specific functions and directives, among them safeguarding the rights
and properties of the refugees.[24] Dalia Habash and Terry Rempel ad-

---

22 Ibid., p. 268.
23 Quoted in Dalia Habash and Terry Rempel, 'Assessing Palestinian Property in
    West Jerusalem', in Tamari, *Jerusalem 1948*, pp. 154-188.
24 In the spring of 1949, the PCC presented several proposals to that effect to the
    Lausanne Conference, which brought together delegations from Israel, Egypt,
    Jordan, Syria and Lebanon, and a delegate from the Arab Higher Committee
    representing the Palestinians. On this first peace conference, and why it failed, see
    Ilan Pappé, *The Making of the Arab-Israeli Conflict, 1947-1951* (London & New
    York: I.B. Tauris, 1992), pp. 203-243; Pappé (p. 240) quotes Abba Eban on
    Israel's standpoint: 'There's no need to run after peace. The armistice is enough
    for us. If we pursue peace, the Arabs will demand a price of us—borders or
    refugees, or both. Let us wait a few years.'

dress the question of land loss and property claims in light of the findings of the PCC.[25] Many problems haunt any attempt at a systematic assessment of these property claims. West Jerusalem's land titles were only partly recorded in the land registry since they were not all included in the land settlement survey the Ottomans initiated in 1858 and that the British Mandate authorities later continued but never completed. But there are, of course, the land tax records that can help authenticate land claims where such *tapu* (land title) records are missing or unobtainable. In his meticulous research on these records, Salman Abu Sitta provides a preliminary tabulation of these properties.[26] More difficult, of course, is the process of tracing the fate of Jerusalem refugees and where they can be found today. The UNRWA registry has records for all Palestine refugees eligible for relief services and who sought shelter in one of the five UNRWA field areas (West Bank, Gaza, Jordan, Lebanon, and Syria). But since a substantial number of West Jerusalem exiles were middle-class refugees, few of them appear in these records.

The Unified Registration System (URS), UNRWA's vast data base of refugee registration, utilizes four categories of urban Jerusalem refugees, and a fifth category of Jerusalem district refugees, by village.[27] The urban categories are: 'New City Refugees', 'Jerusalem General' (i.e. unspecified), 'Jerusalem Poor', and 'Jerusalem Old City'. The final two categories list Jerusalem residents whose livelihood had been affected by the war, but who had not been displaced from territories occupied by the new Jewish state. When trying to trace the fate of Jerusalem refugees, the first two categories are the most crucial, as Table 1 illustrates.

25 'Assessing Palestinian Property in West Jerusalem'; in 'Dispossession and Restitution in 1948 Jerusalem,' also in Tamari, *Jerusalem 1948* (pp. 190-235), Terry Rempel further examines the implications of international law and Israeli practice concerning restitution for Palestinian refugees from the Western neighbourhoods and villages of Jerusalem.

26 Salman Abu Sitta, *Palestinian Property in West Jerusalem* (forthcoming).

27 UNRWA Registration Manual (Codes); 95.10 Place of Origin in Palestine/Jerusalem Subdistrict. The manual contains listing for 'Towns', 'Villages', and 'Tribes' (Amman: UNWRA Amman HQ [n.d.]).

Table 1 *Jerusalem City (West) Urban Refugees from the 1948 War in UNRWA Records By Host Region, 1997*

Current place of refuge	Born <Jan. 1948	Born >Dec.1947	Total
West Bank	12,427	41,226	53,653
Gaza	296	515	811
Lebanon	707	703	1,410
Jordan	8,420	18,077	26,497
Syria	978	919	1,897
Total			84,268

Source: Data derived from UNRWA, Relief and Social Services Department, URS (UNRWA Amman HQ, Jordan), 22 May 1997. The figures include refugees living today and their descendants.

URS data, with all its limitations, shows that the bulk of urban refugees from Jerusalem ended up living in the West Bank, with most of them having taken up residence in East Jerusalem and its suburbs, and in Ramallah and Bethlehem.[28] Jordan contains the second large number of urban refugees—almost half the figure for the West Bank, with Gaza, Syria and Lebanon containing very few concentrations. These patterns are drastically reversed for *rural* refugees: while the global figure for UNRWA registered Jerusalem rural refugees (and their off-spring) is 110,439 (URS; May 1997), more than two-thirds (73,908 refugees) are today living in Jordan, and only 36,130 in the West Bank.[29]

28 URS, UNRWA Amman HQ, Jordan, 22 May 1997. I have excluded from these figures the two categories of 'Jerusalem Poor' and 'Jerusalem Old City', so that the data corresponds to urban refugees actually expelled from Israeli-occupied territory.

29 Ibid.; for a discussion of these figures, see Tamari, 'The City and its Rural Hinterland', in idem, *Jerusalem 1948*. I have excluded all data for Jerusalem villages that were not held by Israel after the war of 1948, but included refugees from Abu Ghosh and Beir Naquba.

What does this tell us? First, it means that the bulk of all UNRWA-registered Jerusalem refugees stayed within the vicinity of the homes they had been expelled from. Most urban refugees, who tended to be better off and had substantial documentation for their lost property, even ended up living within sight of their confiscated West Jerusalem properties.[30] Second, it indicates that the poorer refugees from villages in the western hinterlands of Jerusalem—most of whom live in camps—followed UNRWA services to Jordan *before* 1967, when prospects for employment were higher in Amman, Irbid and Zarqa, and *after* the war of 1967, when many Jerusalem refugees realized UNRWA services would no longer be available in the West Bank that was now occupied by Israel.

For the implications they have for future claims by Jerusalem refugees over their properties that Israel has confiscated in Jerusalem's Western suburbs and villages, the relevance and significance of these figures cannot be overstated. Since many exiles continue to live either in the Eastern part of the city that Israel—unlawfully—annexed in 1967 or in its immediate vicinity, their claims for the return of their property (and residence) are particularly poignant since Israel has already established (and expanded several folds) Jewish private residencies in the Old City (Jewish Quarter), in Silwan, Ras al-Amud, Neve Ya'coub, Atarot, Abu Tor, etc.—all areas in which some Jews had property and residence claims *before 1948*—but then also in over a dozen newly built settlements in areas where no Jewish claims existed before. Palestinian claims to their properties in the Western city and its rural hinterland are fully substantiated, both in records derived from the land registry (whether in *tapu* or in land tax records), as well as in the above-mentioned files of the PCC. That Israel continues to claim the City of Jerusalem as

---

30 For data on East Jerusalem residents who are refugees from West Jerusalem and other areas occupied by Israel in 1948, see Israel Central Bureau of Statistics, *Census of Population and Housing 1967*, 'East Jerusalem' (Jerusalem, 1968), Tables 17 and 18 ('Population Aged 15+, by Place of Personal Residence before the 1948 War').

'united and indivisible', subject to the same administrative laws of the state, makes the validity of these Palestinian claims all the more obvious—and their denial equally ludicrous.

Final-status negotiations over the future of Jerusalem, or rather the US-backed Israeli dictates into which they have deteriorated, make it ever more pressing that these historical rights of Arab Jerusalemites are put centre stage. As most of these internal exiles are still alive, or have immediate offspring who are alive, their patrimony is as truly actual today as it is historically valid. As for the Right of Return: Zionist forces demolished nearly all of the 41 Arab villages in that part of the Jerusalem district they conquered and expelled 60,000 Palestinian Arabs from West Jerusalem and its surroundings.[31] And while today it is beyond doubt that the Zionists worked according to a central blueprint for the take-over of Palestine when they expelled the country's indigenous Arab population,[32] perhaps the best evidence of their true intentions is that Israel continues to refuse to allow the refugees to return: to this day, not one Palestinian Arab refugee has been able to make it back to his or her home in West Jerusalem.

31 Krystall, whom I quote here ('The Fall of the New City', p. 134), relies on Bashir Nijim and Beshara Muammar, *Toward the de-Arabization of Palestine/Israel 1945-1977* (Kendal/Hunt, Iowa: Jerusalem Fund for Education and Community Development, 1984).

32 A seminal study here remains, of course, Walid Khalidi's 'Plan Dalet: Master Plan for the Conquest of Palestine,' *Journal of Palestine Studies* 18/1 (Autumn 1988), pp. 5-50, which also contains a full translation from the Hebrew taken from *Sefer Toldot Hahaganah* ('History of the Haganah'), vol. 3 (ed. Yehuda Slutsky), (Tel Aviv: Zionist Library, 1972). In a recent assessment (*A History of Modern Palestine. One Land, Two Peoples* [Cambridge 2004]), Ilan Pappé writes (pp. 129-30): 'In March 1948, the military campaign began in earnest. It was driven by Plan D [which] had two very clear objectives, the first being to take swiftly and systematically any installations, military or civilian, evacuated by the British. [...] The second, and far more important, objective of the plan was to cleanse the future Jewish state of as many Palestinians possible.'

'Dis/Solving' the Palestinian Refugee Problem

Israeli 'Resettlement' Plans in the First Decade of the State (1948–1958)

Nur Masalha

Introduction

In 1948 close to 900,000 Palestinians were dispossessed and expelled from their homes, villages and towns. As Jewish settlers of the new state of Israel moved in and occupied their land, Palestinian refugees found themselves thrown together in crowded refugee camps in neighbouring Arab countries. Israel has consistently denied any moral responsibility for having created the Palestinian 'refugee problem', shifting the blame instead onto the Arab countries that therefore, so it argues, also ought to solve it. At the same time, Israel itself has never been short on plans to encourage the resettlement of the refugees in the Arab countries. Except for one limited—and quickly retracted—offer in mid-1949 to take back '100,000' of the refugees it would then re-settle in places of its own choosing, Israel has never come forward with a proposal that would allow any of the 1948 refugees to repatriate. All along, Israel has insisted that, rather than being repatriated and/or given compensation, Palestinian refugees should all be resettled and rehabilitated in the Arab states. Thus, we find Israel through the years fielding a number of proposals and plans all geared exclusively to the resettlement of the Palestinian refugees in the Arab host states. Between 1948 and the late 1980s around twenty such plans were officially put forward to deal with, first, the Palestinians Israel had expelled in 1948 and later those it had driven out in 1967. From 1967 to 1987—the start of the first

Intifada, the Palestinian uprising in the Occupied Territories against Israeli oppression—Israeli officials came up with no less than a dozen proposals and schemes aimed at the refugee camps in the West Bank and the Gaza Strip.[1]

In this essay I want to set out and analyze Israeli policies towards the Palestinian refugees as these evolved between 1948 and 1957, i.e., from as early as the Nakba, the 1948 catastrophe, until the 1956–57 occupation by Israel of the Gaza Strip, and to discuss each of the various Israeli resettlement schemes within their historical context.

The resettlement proposals Israel put forward and the actual schemes it tried to implement in the 1950s were motivated by political, diplomatic, military and psychological considerations that reflect a consistent policy aimed at:

—preventing Palestinian refugee from returning to their homes;

—'dis/solving' the refugee question so as to remove it from the heart of the Arab-Israeli conflict;

—reducing UN and Western diplomatic as well as international humanitarian pressures on Israel;

—breaking up the collective identification of the refugees as Palestinians and pre-empting the threat of militancy they were perceived to herald;[2]

—dismantling the Palestinian refugee camps in the Gaza Strip, West Bank and neighbouring Arab countries. These camp were—still are today—a highly visible and hugely symbolic reminder of the ethnic cleansing and dispossession of the Palestinians by Israel in 1948 and thus constituted a thorny problem for official Israeli bodies, in par-

---

1   Elia Zureik, *Palestinian Refugees and the Peace Process* (Washington DC: Institute for Palestine Studies, 1996), p. 68; Nawaf Al-Zaru, 'Israeli Plans to Liquidate the Palestinian Camps', *Samid al-Iqtisadi* 83 (1991), pp. 134-142 (Arabic).

2   Norma Masriyeh Hazboun, *Israeli Resettlement Schemes for Palestinian Refugees in the West Bank and Gaza Strip since 1967* (Ramallah, Palestine: Shamle—Palestinian Diaspora and Refugee Centre, 1996) at http://www.shaml.org/publications/monos/mono4.htm (accessed on 1 December 2001).

ticular for the Israeli Foreign Ministry and its propaganda (Hebrew: *hasbara,* 'explanation') campaigns in the West.

Admittedly, two Arab regimes briefly considered resettlement plans at one point: in 1949 the Syrian dictator Husni al-Za'im accepted a plan to resettle 300,000 refugees in the al-Jazira region of northeast Syria;[3] and in 1954, against the background of escalating Israeli 'retaliatory' attacks against the Gaza Strip, the Egyptian government—fearing a potentially explosive situation in the Strip and the consequences of provoking the Israelis into a war for which Egypt still was unprepared—considered a US–UNRWA sponsored plan to resettle the Gaza refugees in the Sinai. Husni al-Za'im's military dictatorship lasted no more than four and a half months, and the Egyptians were forced to abandon the Sinai scheme when details of it were leaked and protests by the refugees culminated in two days of demonstrations and rioting in Gaza in which Egyptian government buildings came under siege and Egyptian vehicles were torched.[4] Both offers were made half-heartedly. It was Israel that was the most persistent advocate and practitioner of refugee resettlement schemes—not for humanitarian reasons but so as to never allow the refugees to return home and remove the entire Palestine refugee problem from the heart of Arab-Israeli conflict.

In the official Israeli position there could be no returning ever of the refugees to Israeli territories—the only solution of the problem was for them to be resettled in the Arab states or even elsewhere. After 1949, all Israeli governments have consistently refused to discuss any possible

3   Avi Shlaim, 'Husni Zaim and the Plan to Resettle Palestinian Refugees in Syria', *Middle East Focus* 9/2 (Fall 1986), pp. 26-31. The al-Jazira plan was also enthusiastically supported by George McGhee, special assistant to the US Secretary of State. For an extensive discussion of Zionist proposals to 'transfer' Palestinians to the al-Jazira region in the late 1930s and early 1940s, see Nur Masalha, *Expulsion of the Palestinians: The Concept of 'Transfer' in Zionist Political Thought, 1882-1948* (Washington DC: Institute for Palestine Studies, 1992), pp. 130-141.

4   Michael Palumbo, *Imperial Israel: The History of the Occupation of the West Bank and Gaza* (London: Bloomsbury, updated edition, 1992), p. 28; Paul Cossali and Clive Robson, *Stateless in Gaza* (London: Zed Books, 1986), pp. 13-15.

return of Palestinian refugees to within the pre-1967 borders. Israel made sure to reiterate its rigid positions on the Palestinian refugee issue regularly throughout the early 1950s, Zionist spokespersons repeating the official Israeli claim that the Palestinians had been urged to leave by their leaders and that Arab governments were to blame for keeping the refugee issue alive by refusing to dismantle the camps and resettle the refugees. The Israeli propaganda machine continues until today to regurgitate the myth that in 1948 the Palestinians had fled their villages and towns spurred on by calls from their leaders—an allegation that many scholars, including Walid Khalidi, Erskine Childers, Benny Morris, Tom Segev, Simha Flapan, Avi Shlaim and Ilan Pappé, have shown to be totally baseless.[5] Moreover, in the official view, the Palestinian refugees 'made up for' the number of Jews who had left Arab countries for Israel.

In the 1950s, a key slogan coined by senior Israeli Foreign Ministry officials was: 'If you can't solve the problem—dissolve it!' (Hebrew: '*im enkha yakhol liftor et habe'aya—moses otah*'),[6] whereby they meant: if you cannot find a political solution to the Palestinian refugee problem, try to disperse the refugees by economic means and employment projects, i.e., make them disappear and so 'dissolve' the problem. In other words, the problem of the Palestine refugees should, but also could be solved by adopting an economic approach: have them integrate into the economies of their current countries of residence and/ or make sure they are dispersed throughout the Arab world.

5   This and several other Israeli allegations have been examined and discredited as being part of an Israeli dis-information campaign; see article in *The Spectator*, 12 May 1961; Morris, *The Birth of the Palestinian Refugee Problem*; Simha Flapan, *The Birth of Israel: Myths and Realities* (New York: Pantheon Books, 1987); Tom Segev, *1949: The First Israelis* (New York: The Free Press, 1986); Ilan Pappé, *The Making of the Arab-Israeli Conflict, 1947-1951* (London: I.B. Tauris, 1992); Nur Masalha, *Expulsion of the Palestinians*, 173-199; idem, *The Politics of Denial: Israel and the Palestinian Refugee Problem* (London: Pluto Press, 2003).

6   See 'Ezra Danin, *Tzioni bekhol Tnai* (A Zionist No Matter What), Vol. 1 (Jerusalem: Kiddum, 1987), p. 317.

Significantly, in the 1950s proponents of the active approach to resettlement schemes included both hawkish and dovish members of the Israeli establishment. Thus, we find Foreign Minister Moshe Sharett (a man with clearly a dovish reputation: it was Sharett who, under intense American pressure, had agreed in 1949 to allow the return of 100,000 refugees as part of an overall settlement of the Arab-Israeli conflict, though he soon again changed his mind and retracted the offer[7]) and his senior Foreign Ministry officials agreeing with such hawkish Jewish National Fund executives as Yosef Weitz and Yosef Nahmani. This may well be because in those years the Palestinian refugee problem was still a major 'diplomatic headache' for the Israeli Foreign Ministry, particularly vis-à-vis US and UN officials. The United States had supported the UN General Assembly Resolution 194 (III) of 11 December 1948 that calls for the repatriation of and/or compensation to the refugees. The United States had also suggested, in 1949, that Israel allow the return of one third of the refugees (assumed to be some 250,000) while the United States would cover the costs of resettling the other two thirds in Arab states.[8] Thus it was mainly diplomatic and political but undeniably also public relations reasons that early on prompted senior Israeli Foreign Ministry officials to actively pursue secret resettlement schemes and so eliminate the refugee problem as one of the core elements of the Arab-Israeli conflict. One of these schemes was the so-called 'Libyan Operation', a secret plan to transfer Palestinians from refugee camps in Jordan (including the West Bank), the Gaza Strip and Lebanon and permanently resettle them in Libya and other parts of North Africa, as remote as possible from Israel and the 1949 cease-fire lines (see below).

7   For further discussion of the '100,000' offer, see Varda Schiffer, 'The 1949 Israeli Offer to Repatriate 100,000 Palestinian Refugees', *Middle East Focus* 9/2 (1986), pp. 14-20; Morris, *The Birth of the Palestinian Refugee Problem*, pp. 275-285; Muhammad Abu-Masara, 'Be'ayat Haplitim Bamdiniyut Hayisraelit Bashanim 1948-49' (The Refugee Problem in Israeli Policy in 1948-49), *International Problems, Society and Politics* 28/53 (1989), pp. 48-53.

8   S. Gazit, *The Palestinian Refugee Problem* (Tel Aviv: Jaffa Center for Strategic Studies, 1995), p. 11.

Palestinian refugees themselves have all along continued to demand repatriation—their legal right in international law—and to refuse re-settlement outside their homeland. For Palestinians the word refugee is synonymous with 'returnee' (*'aaid*). That they will return to Palestine is a strongly held belief and feelings about the 'dream of return' are intense. The yearning for Palestine runs through the whole refugee community and enfolds especially the younger refugees for whom 'home' exists only in the imagination. The Palestinians' Right of Re-turn is enshrined in UN Resolution 194, reaffirmed almost yearly by the General Assembly, which states that 'the refugees wishing to return to their homes and live at peace with their neighbours should be permitted to do so at the earliest practicable date.'

In the early 1950s, the refugees themselves knew no better than that sooner or later they *would* be able to return to their homes and villages, even if their part of Palestine was now Israel. Moreover, many of the refugees camped either along or within a short distance from Israel's borders, in southern Lebanon, in the West Bank and the Gaza Strip. At times they would attempt to get back to their villages and homes to retrieve possessions they had been forced to leave behind or to try to harvest part of their abandoned crops. Israel treated these people as 'illegal infiltrators'. No reliable estimate exists of the number of such returnees. That Israel called them 'infiltrators' highlights again both the refusal of the authorities to allow their return and their marked anxiety that increasing numbers of Palestinians might somehow succeed in returning to now Israeli-held territories—this may well have led them to exaggerate the numbers of those who actually did so.[9] In the Gaza Strip, moreover, the population trebled from 80,000 in 1947 to nearly 240,000 at the end of the 1948 war, creating a massive humanitarian problem of tens of thousands of destitute refugees crammed into a tiny area. In 1956, of the then 300,000 inhabitants of the Gaza Strip, 215,000 were listed as refugees, occupying eight vast camps. In other

9   Charles S. Kamen, 'After the Catastrophe I: The Arabs in Israel, 1948-51', *Middle Eastern Studies* 23/4 (October 1987), pp. 462-463.

words, the Strip held nearly 25 per cent of the total of about 900,000 refugees from historic Palestine.

Between 1949 and 1956, refugees continued to cross the armistice lines, trying to make it back to their villages to collect possessions or save what they could from their crops at harvest time or, increasingly, to carry out raids on Israeli settlements adjacent to Gaza and the West Bank.[10] To combat this persistent 'infiltration' by refugees,[11] the Israelis began carrying out 'retaliatory' attacks against Palestinian civilian targets in general and refugee camps in the Gaza Strip in particular. These attacks resulted in many civilian deaths. According to the Israeli historian Benny Morris,

> Israel's defensive anti-infiltration measures resulted in the death of several thousand mostly unarmed Arabs during 1949–56, the vast majority between 1949 and 1952 ... Thus, upward of 2,700 Arab infiltrators, and perhaps as many as 5,000, were killed by the IDF, police and civilians along Israel's borders between 1949 and 1956. To judge from the available documentation, the vast majority of those killed were unarmed 'economic' and social infiltrators.[12]

For former Israeli journalist Livia Rokach, one major reason for the insistence with which Israel prosecuted its 'retaliatory' policy during these days was the constant pressure the Zionist ruling establishment wanted to exert on the Arab states to move the Palestinian refugees from the 1948 war away from the armistice lines and to disperse them throughout the interior of the Arab world. It had little to do, in the early 1950s, with military considerations.[13] Thus, in the early years of its existence, the state of Israel expelled thousands of Palestinian refugees who had somehow managed to return to their villages and homes back across the border.

---

10 On Arab refugee 'infiltration', see Benny Morris, *Israel's Border Wars, 1949-1956* (Oxford: Clarendon Press, 1993), pp. 28-68.
11 Segev, *1949: The First Israelis*, p. 52.
12 Morris, *Israel's Border Wars*, pp. 135-137.
13 Livia Rokach, 'Israel State Terrorism: An Analysis of the Sharett Diaries', *Journal of Palestine Studies* 9/3 (Spring 1980), p. 21.

Early Proposals (1948–1950)

The Transfer Committee

In late August 1948, the Israeli Cabinet formally appointed an official 'Transfer Committee' that was to plan the organized resettlement of Palestinian refugees in the Arab states. It was composed of three people: 'Ezra Danin, a former (1936–1948) senior officer of the Hagana's (the main pre-state Zionist militia) Intelligence Service (Shai), Zalman Lifschitz, a senior Foreign Ministry Advisor on Arab Affairs (since July 1948) who was a prominent cartographer and the Prime Minister's Advisor on Land Matters, and, as head of the committee, Yosef Weitz (1889–1972), head of the Jewish National Fund (JNF)'s Land Settlement Department. Their brief was to do everything possible to reduce the Arab population in Israel, and by October 1948 Weitz and his colleagues on the Transfer Committee had a 5–point proposal ready for the demographic 'transformation' of Palestine that aimed at:

(1) preventing Palestinian refugees from returning to their homes and villages;
(2) the physical destruction of Arab villages in Israel;
(3) the settlement of Jews in Arab villages and towns and the distribution of Arab lands among Jewish settlements;
(4) 'the extrication of the Jews of Iraq and Syria';
(5) ensuring the Palestinian refugees would be absorbed in Arab countries—Syria, Iraq, Lebanon, and Transjordan—and launching a propaganda campaign to discourage repatriation.

Apparently Prime Minister David Ben-Gurion approved of these proposals, even though he much rather saw all Palestinian refugees resettled in one Arab state, preferably Iraq, rather than have them dispersed among the neighbouring states. Thus, he was also set against refugee resettlement in neighbouring Transjordan.[14]

---

14 Benny Morris, 'Yosef Weitz and the Transfer Committees, 1948-49', *Middle Eastern Studies* 22/4 (October 1986), pp. 549-550.

Resettlement in Monarchical Iraq

The Transfer Committee soon invited Dr. Joseph Schechtman to join its efforts. Schechtman was a right-wing Zionist Revisionist leader and an expert on 'population transfer' who had contributed an entry on the issue to *Encyclopaedia Britannica*. Schechtman, who for three decades had been a close associate of Vladimir Jabotinsky (the founder of the Zionist Revisionist Movement) and who had written a book called *European Population Transfers, 1939–1945* (published in 1946 by Oxford University Press), would soon after 1948 become the single most influential propagator of the Zionist myth of the 'voluntary' exodus of the Palestinians in 1948.[15] Having settled in New York in 1941, he had served as a research fellow in the Institute of Jewish Affairs, 1941–43, as Director of the Research Bureau on Population Movements, which he had helped to establish, and as consultant on population movements for the US Office of Strategic Services in Washington DC, 1944–45. During a visit he made to Israel in September 1948 the Transfer Committee enlisted Schechtman to carry out research and advise them how to go about resettling the Palestinian refugees in Arab states.

In August 1948, the Zionist Actions Committee elected the New York-based Schechtman as a Revisionist representative on the Executive of the Jewish Agency and the World Zionist Organisation (WZO), which thus for the first time included all Zionist parties. More importantly, sometime in early 1948 Schechtman had already worked out a plan of his own, entitled 'The Case for Arab-Jewish Exchange of Population', which he submitted in 1948 to Eliyahu Epstein (Elath), Israel's ambassador to Washington. Epstein later forwarded Schechtman's 'study' to the Israeli Cabinet Secretary, Zeev Sharef, and to the head of the Transfer Committee, Yosef Weitz.[16]

15 Flapan, *The Birth of Israel: Myths and Realities*, p. 107; Joseph Schechtman, *The Arab Refugee Problem* (New York: Philosophical Library, 1952); idem, *European Population Transfers 1939-1945* (New York: Oxford University Press, 1946); idem, *Population Transfers in Asia* (New York: Hallsby Press, 1949); idem, *Post-War Population Transfers in Europe, 1945-1955* (Liverpool, Charles Birchall and Sons, 1962).

16 I first came across the manuscript of Schechtman's 'study' in Weitz's Papers, at the Institute for Settlement Studies, Rehovot, Israel, in 1989. In 1993 I spotted a copy of the same manuscript in Weitz's Papers, in the Central Zionist Archives in Jerusalem.

Schechtman wanted the Israeli government formally to acknowledge the research he was carrying out for the Israeli Cabinet's Transfer Committee and in mid-October 1948 asked Arthur Lourie, of the Israeli UN Office in New York, whether Foreign Minister Sharett could send him (Schechtman) a note stating that 'you [Sharett] are glad to learn that he has been in touch with friends in Israel who are interested in this matter of resettlement of Arabs, particularly in Iraq, and that you would be pleased if he could continue with his investigations.' On the basis of such a letter, Schechtman would approach men like former US President Herbert Hoover with a view of interesting them further in the endeavour.[17] Two weeks later, on 27 October 1948, Schechtman received a cable from Cabinet Secretary Sharef: 'Approve your proposal collect material discussed. Danin [and] Lifschitz will refund expenses five hundred dollars.'[18] The urgent assignment Schechtman was given on behalf of the Israeli government and its Transfer Committee included the collection of material and the carrying out of further 'study' on the resettlement of Palestinians in Iraq. On 17 December Sharett himself wrote to Schechtman from Paris telling him how 'glad' he was to hear that Schechtman was pursuing his 'studies with regard to the resettlement possibilities' of Palestinian Arab refugees: 'Now that Mr [Zalman] Lifshitz [*sic*] is in the United States I am sure that you two got together and pooled your knowledge on the subject.'[19]

Schechtman believed 'that many important conclusions for the future can and must be drawn from the experience of past transfer and that the underlying idea of any transfer scheme is basically a preventive one.' Thus, Schechtman explained that his 'study'—'The Case for

17 From Arthur Lourie, Consulate General of Israel, New York, to Moshe Shertok (later Sharett), Foreign Minister, letter dated 15 October 1948, in Israel State Archives (ISA), Foreign Ministry, 2402/15.

18 From Joseph B. Schechtman to 'Ezra Danin, Israeli Ministry of Foreign Affairs, letter dated 7 December 1948, in Jabotinsky Institute, Schechtman's Papers, file F. 2/10/227.

19 Moshe Shertok, Paris, to Dr. Schechtman, New York, letter dated 17 December 1948, ISA, Foreign Ministry, 2402/15.

Arab-Jewish Exchange of Population'—should not be seen as merely a descriptive and historical explanation of the facts. If a problem of an ethnic minority cannot be solved within the existing territorial frame, then 'timely recourse must be taken to the essentially preventive devise of transfer'. As he put it, 'the case of Palestine seems to offer a classic case for quick, decisive transfer action as the only constructive possibility of breaking the present deadlock' and 'no constructive solution can be arrived at without a large-scale [Arab] transfer.'[20] 'The only workable solution is an organized exchange of population between Palestine and the Arab states mainly to Iraq of Palestine Arabs', and the parallel transfer to Israel of the Jewish communities in Arab countries.[21]

Schechtman's scheme called for the 'compulsory' transfer of Palestinian refugees and non-refugees to, and their resettlement in, Iraq. He was able to rely on a plan by another New York-based Zionist Revisionist publicist and close associate of Vladimir Jabotinsky, Eliahu Ben-Horin.[22] Advisor to the American Zionist Emergency Council, in late 1943 Ben-Horin had met Herbert Hoover, the former US President and a Zionist sympathiser, who agreed to join the Zionist campaign in support of Ben-Horin's transfer plan. Both men appealed to the US administration to support the Zionist drive and 'dictate' Palestinian evacuation to and resettlement in Iraq. Two years later, on 19 November 1945, the so-called 'Hoover-plan'—in fact, a repackaging of Ben-Horin's initiative—was launched in the *New York World-Telegram.*[23] This was the plan that served Schechtman as inspiration for his early 1948 scheme, to which he now added that in the refugee exodus of the spring of 1948 he saw 'unmistakable indications to the effect

20 Joseph Schechtman, 'The Case for Arab-Jewish Exchange of Population', manuscript (in Weitz's Papers, Institute for Settlement Study, Rehovot), pp. 75-76.
21 Ibid., p. 103.
22 For further discussion of Ben-Horin's plan of transfer to Iraq, 1943-1948, see Masalha, *Expulsion of the Palestinians*, pp. 161-165; Eliahu Ben-Horin, *The Middle East: Crossroads of History* (New York: W. W. Norton & Company, 1943), pp. 224-237.
23 Masalha, *Expulsion of the Palestinians*, pp. 162-164.

that the Israeli Government begins earnestly to weigh an Arab-Jewish exchange of population as the most thorough and constructive means of solving the problem of an Arab minority in the Jewish state.' As evidence of transfer discussions in Israeli government circles he quoted Arthur Lourie, the head of the Israeli UN Office and the representative at the Lake Success talks in New York, who had been interviewed by *The New York Times* of 20 July 1948.[24] Writing to Israel's ambassador to Washington, Eliyahu Epstein, Schechtman said that the Arab population flow out of the territory of the Jewish state 'only strengthens the case for the organized Arab transfer' to Iraq.[25]

Schechtman was aware that the Palestinian Arab leaders would never agree to any plan of this kind, 'which provoked on their part limitless indignation'.[26] But he was convinced that '*once uprooted*, they [the Arabs] would probably be responsive to any plan of their resettlement in Iraq, with full compensation by the state of Israel for their property left behind.'[27] The transfer/resettlement scheme would be underpinned by an inter-state treaty between the governments of Israel and Iraq and possibly other Arab states. These treaties 'would provide a compulsory, but not all-inclusive, ethnic sorting out. As a rule, every Arab in the Jewish State and every Jew in Iraq would be subject to transfer; no specific option to this effect would be necessary.'[28] For Schechtman 'the equality of numbers on both sides' of the so-called exchange of population 'in this particular case was of no importance whatsoever, since the prospective Palestine Arab transferees in Iraq' would be resettled 'not on land vacated by the Jewish evacuees', but on land provided by the Iraqi state. In other words, 'the amount of land … would be sufficient in Palestine where millions of dunams[29] would be left behind by the departing Arabs.'[30]

24 Schechtman, 'The Case for Arab-Jewish Exchange of Population', p. 156.
25 Joseph Schechtman, New York, to Eliyahu Epstein, Washington D.C., letter dated 20 May 1948, in Jabotinsky Institute, Schechtman's Papers, F. 2/10/227.
26 Schechtman, 'The Case for Arab-Jewish Exchange of Population', pp. 103-104.
27 Ibid., p. 158 (emphasis added).
28 Ibid., pp.160-161.
29 One *dunam* equals 1,000 square metre.
30 Schechtman, 'The Case for Arab-Jewish Exchange of Population', p. 163.

In December 1948 Zalman Lifschitz travelled to the United States to lobby for the Israeli drive to resettle the Palestinian refugees in Iraq. Soon after his arrival, Israel's ambassador, Eliyahu Epstein, called together a meeting in his office in Washington in which, besides himself, took part Schechtman, Lifschitz, Edward Norman—a New York-based Jewish millionaire who had devoted much of his fortune to supporting the Jewish *Yishuv* in Palestine and had been secretly lobbying for a plan of his own to transfer the Palestinians to Iraq between 1934 and 1948[31]—and Elisha Friedman, a New York economics consultant and member of the Ben-Horin-Hoover team which remained active until the late 1940s in their attempt to remove the Palestinians to Iraq. Epstein had been in close contact with Schechtman throughout 1948 and had received a manuscript copy of Schechtman's plan in early May 1948. On 18 May, four days after the proclamation of the State of Israel, Epstein had written to Schechtman that he had read the manuscript 'with great interest and found it to be an important and constructive contribution to the subject of Jewish-Arab exchange of population.' He added:

> The events in Palestine are developing meanwhile in such a way that if not your conjectures, at least certain of your conclusions will have to be modified in view of the Arab flow out of the area of our State. Certain problems, however, in the exchange of population will remain, especially in view of the necessity of a transfer within possibly a very short time of the Jews living in the Arab countries to Israel.[32]

In mid-June 1948, Epstein had already met Schechtman in New York to discuss the subject. In mid-December 1948 Lifschitz told the

---

31 For further discussion of Norman's plan, see Masalha, *Expulsion of the Palestinians*, p.141-155; Moshe Shertok, Paris, to Edward Norman, letter dated 17 December 1948, ISA, Foreign Ministry, 2402/15.

32 Epstein to Schechtman, letter dated 18 May 1948, in Jabotinsky Institute, Schechtman's Papers, F. 1/10/227.

gathering in the Israeli ambassador's office in Washington about the activities of the Transfer Committee and suggested that Schechtman, Norman and Friedman could be of great help in this matter, in two directions in particular: (1) in the presentation of ideas and supporting data as the basis for a plan to be adopted by the Government of Israel; and (2) in mobilising 'the leaders of public opinion in this country to speak out in support of such a plan as soon as the Government of Israel would make public announcement of it.' Writing to Moshe Sharett, Edward Norman reported: 'It was agreed that the three of us who were present who are American citizens would be considered a sort of advisory committee, with myself as chairman, working in close co-operation with Mr Epstein. It is our purpose now to produce a more or less detailed plan, which presumably will be forwarded to you [Sharett] for your consideration and possible presentation eventually to your government.'[33]

Like Eliahu Ben-Horin, former US President Hoover and New York millionaire Edward Norman, Schechtman appealed to the US administration and the White House to support the Israeli drive and 'dictate' Palestinian resettlement in Iraq. A revised version of his 1948 'study', in which he outlined the transfer of virtually all Palestinians to Iraq, appeared in Chapter 3 of his *Population Transfers in Asia*, published in New York in March 1949.[34] Three years later Schechtman came out with his propagandistic work *The Arab Refugee Problem* (1952), largely based on the actual research he had carried out on behalf of the Israeli government and its Transfer Committee in late 1948 and early 1949.[35] In a letter to Hoover dated 9 April 1949 Schechtman wrote:

I take the liberty of sending you the enclosed copy of my study 'Population Transfers in Asia' whose chapter on the Arab-Jewish

33 Edward Norman, to Foreign Minister Moshe Shertok, letter dated 24 December 1948, ISA, Foreign Ministry, 2402/15.

34 Joseph Schechtman, *Population Transfers in Asia*, pp. 84-145.

35 New York: Philosophical Library, 1952.

population transfer owes so much to the inspiration provided by your plan for the resettlement of Arabs from Palestine in Iraq, published in 1945. [...] Recent events in the Middle East have pushed this idea into the foreground of public attention, and have impelled me to publish this study of the transfer issue against the background of similar transfer movements elsewhere in Asia. [...] As one of the world's elder statesmen who helped originate the transfer idea as a way out of the Palestine conflict, and from whom the public hopes to receive further wise guidance in this issue, you will—I sincerely hope—be interested in this book of mine.[36]

In the event, however, only a small proportion of the Palestinian refugees—about 3,000—ended up in Iraq, and then partly because of the participation of the Iraqi army in the 1948 Arab-Israeli war. This was especially so with some residents from the Jenin area, where the Iraqi army had helped to defend Palestine, and, similarly, many residents from the al-Karmel villages of Ijzim, Jaba' and 'Ayn al-Ghazal.[37] By 1996, the total number of Palestinian refugees in Iraq—mostly living in and around the capital Baghdad—was estimated at no more than 45,000,[38] a tiny figure when compared with other Palestinian communities living outside historic Palestine—in Jordan, Syria and Lebanon—and in the Occupied Palestinian Territories.

The 1949 '100,000 Offer' and the Gaza Plan

In early 1949 the Israeli Foreign Ministry sent 'Ezra Danin, the senior Foreign Ministry official in charge of the refugee resettlement issue and a member of the official Transfer Committee, to England to lobby

---

36 Schechtman's letter to Hoover, dated 9 April 1949, in Jabotinsky Institute, Schechtman's Papers, file F. 1/11/227.

37 Labib Qudsiyyah, *Al-Lajiun al-Filastiniyun fi al-'Iraq* (*The Palestinian Refugees in Iraq*), Monograph No.7 (Ramallah, Palestine: Shamle—Palestinian Diaspora and Refugee Centre, 1997) at: http://www.shaml.org/arabic/publications/monos/ a_m007.htm (accessed on 1 December 2001).

38 Ibid.

discreetly for 'initiatives that would assist as many refugees as possible to be absorbed and strike roots in various Arab countries'.[39] Before his departure to England Danin told Weitz, on 23 January 1949, in Jerusalem that he thought 'a propaganda [campaign] must be conducted among the Arabs [refugees] that they demand their resettlement in the Arab states.'[40] Here, too, the main motive for Danin, Weitz and other colleagues to promote refugee resettlement projects outside Palestine was fear of possible refugee return. From London, on 6 May 1949, Danin wrote back to Cabinet Secretary Sharef that Weitz had complained about the lack of 'planning and direction' on the question of refugee resettlement: 'At times [Weitz] sees a nightmarish picture of long convoys of returning refugees and there is no one to help.'[41]

Less than two months later, on 27 July, Foreign Minister Sharett informed members of the Transfer Committee (Weitz, Danin and Lifschitz) that the US government was putting strong pressure on Israel to agree to the return of a quarter of a million refugees. The Israeli government was considering putting forward a counter proposal to allow '100,000' refugees back, including those 30,000 refugees who (according to Israel) had already 'infiltrated' back to their villages, on condition that the Arab states agreed to full peace with Israel and to resettle the remainder of the refugees. Weitz replied that he saw these proposals as a 'big disaster'.[42] A document distributed to Israeli ministries in May 1953 estimated that '23,000 infiltrators' who had succeeded in returning without permission to Israeli territories had been allowed to remain. Given the anxiety of the Israeli leadership vis-à-vis the possibility of increasing numbers of Palestinian refugees returning to their homes and villages, this estimate may well have been inflated.[43]

39 Danin, *Tzioni bekhol Tnai*, Vol. 1, p. 317.
40 Yosef Weitz, *Yomani Veigrotai Labanim* (My Diary and Letters to my Sons) (Tel Aviv: Massada, 1965), Vol. 4, entry for 23 January 1949, p. 7.
41 Danin, *Tzioni bekhol Tnai*, Vol. 1, p. 319; Benny Morris, *1948 and After: Israel and the Palestinians* (Oxford: Clarendon Press, 1990), p. 138, quoting Danin's letter to Weitz from London dated 26 April 1949.
42 Weitz, *Yomani Veigrotai Labanim*, Vol. 4, entry for 27 July 1949, p. 42.
43 Quoted in Kamen, 'After the Catastrophe I', p. 462.

Weitz had also expressed his extreme apprehensions to Sharett in a letter dated 28 May 1949:

> Infiltration of the refugees across all the borders, from the north, the south and the east, is no longer an isolated phenomenon but a common occurrence which is increasing all the time. *Every day our people meet acquaintances who were formerly absent* now walking about in complete freedom and also returning step by step to their villages. I fear that by the time you will have finished discussing the subject of the refugees in Lausanne and elsewhere the problem will have solved itself to some degree. Refugees are returning! Nor does our government offer any policy to prevent the infiltration. There appears to be no authority, neither civil nor military. The reins have been slackened, and the Arab in his cunning has already sensed this and knows to draw the conclusion he wishes.[44]

Weitz need not have feared: the Israeli government soon retracted the '100,000' offer.[45]

In early-mid-1949 Israel also put forward another plan to the Americans and British: the Gaza Strip—the small coastal strip of southern Palestine, occupied by the Egyptian army since May 1948—would be transferred to Israeli sovereignty along with its indigenous population of 100,000 and the 200–250,000 refugees who had fled there. Initially Israel's relatively moderate foreign minister, Moshe Sharett, though mindful of the price, thought that Israel would gain a 'strategic peace of real estate' and could 'portray the absorption of 100,000 refugees as a major contribution [...] to the solution of the refugee problem as a whole' and so free itself once and for all of UN pressure in this regard.[46] But in 1949 most Israeli leaders were primarily thinking in terms of

---

44 Ibid., p. 463 (italics added).
45 V. Schiffer, 'The 1949 Israeli Offer to Repatriate 100,000 Palestinian Refugees', *Middle East Focus* 9/2 (1986), pp. 14-20; Morris, *The Birth of the Palestinian Refugee Problem*, pp. 275-85; Abu-Masara, 'Be'ayat Haplitim', pp. 48-53.
46 Morris, *The Birth of the Palestinian Refugee Problem*, pp. 266-267.

'more territory' for and 'less Arabs' in the Jewish state and were apprehensive about enlarging Israel's Palestinian minority: judging by the way the Israeli authorities were treating the 'internally displaced persons', it is highly doubtful they would have allowed the refugee population of the Strip to return to their original villages.

Interesting in this respect is that David Ben-Gurion was more open to the Gaza scheme. As he saw it, Gaza offered good agricultural and fishing opportunities and entailed a territorial barrier with Egypt, helping to reduce the threat from Transjordan.[47] Sharett remained hesitant, however; he opposed having to 'swallow [an additional] 150,000' Arabs into the Jewish state and argued against the incorporation of and joint Israeli-Egyptian condominium over the Strip. If Israel became responsible, the Strip's refugees would have to be allowed to return to their original homes in Israel, he argued.[48] The Transfer Committee's Zalman Lifschitz also opposed Israeli incorporation of the Gaza Strip and instead wanted to annex the West Bank towns of Qalqilya and Tulkarm (then under Transjordanian control), which had 'only 20,000 Arabs'.[49]

In most American and British readings of the 'Gaza plan' the refugees of the Strip, after the take-over by Israel, would be allowed to return to their original homes, villages and towns in Israel. In a revised version of the plan, Israel was expected to give either Egypt or Transjordan (or both) 'territorial compensation' for the Strip, probably in the southern Negev region. Although real hope of its acceptance by Egypt and of any actual implementation was always slim, discussion of the plan continued through the summer, with the Americans and the UN Palestine Conciliation Commission hoping that Israel could be induced to agree to a substantial repatriation and the Arab states would agree to refugee resettlement in the Arab countries. However, given the

---

47 Ben-Gurion's diary, 26 June 1949, cited in Avi Shlaim, *Collusion Across the Jordan, King Abdullah, the Zionist Movement, and the Partition of Palestine* (Oxford: Clarendon Press; Toronto: Columbia University Press, 1988), p. 471.
48 Morris, *The Birth of the Palestinian Refugee Problem*, p. 268.
49 Ibid.

realities of Egyptian-Israeli relations in 1949 and the lack of any positive Egyptian response, the 'Gaza plan' remained a mirage, with little chance of being accepted either by the Egyptians or the residents of the Gaza Strip themselves.[50]

Danin had travelled to England under the cover of fund raising for the United Jewish Appeal, thus putting him in touch with influential Jewish financiers. Like many leading Zionists who argued in the 1930s and 1940s that the indigenous population of Palestine should be treated as an economic problem—to be bought out of their lands, relocated and resettled outside Palestine—Danin acted on the belief that Israel could make the refugees disappear by means of money.[51] 'My main efforts were directed at finding big contracting companies, carrying out various schemes in the Middle East, and seeking ways to persuade them to employ mainly Palestinian refugees,' Danin later recorded.[52] Thus we find Danin seeking partners for the Israeli refugee resettlement projects throughout the spring of 1949. In London he was joined by Teddy Kollek, then an aid to Prime Minister Ben-Gurion.[53] Danin also found a collaborator in Marcus Sieff, a Zionist Jewish businessman, who on behalf of Danin began approaching British firms, construction and oil companies to employ Palestinian refugees.[54] Among the big projects that interested Danin were the Aramco oil pipeline that was to go from Saudi Arabia to Lebanon and the construction of the Latakiya port in Syria that would enable thousands of refugees to find work and subsequently allow them to be integrated into Syria. On the advice of his Jewish partners in Britain, Danin approached Scottish Quakers who were on the board of a large firm involved in the Middle East. To them he put forward the following 'original proposal': for every 10 piastres per day the company would

50   Ibid, pp. 266-270.
51   Danin, *Tzioni bekhol Tnai*, Vol. 1, pp. 317.
52   Ibid.
53   Ibid.
54   Morris, *1948 and After*, pp. 139-140.

pay a worker, the Israelis would be prepared to add 5 piasters provided that the company chose its employees from the refugees.[55] 'It was during these days', he wrote later, 'that we coined the saying about the solution of the Palestinian refugee problem: "If you cannot solve it—dissolve it!"'[56]

So that he could begin promoting these schemes, Danin asked the Israeli government for an initial allocation of 50,000 Israeli lira.[57] In early July 1950 Finance Minister Eli'ezer Kaplan placed the sum of not more than 1,000 Israeli lira at Danin's disposal for a proposal aiming at 'exchanging properties of Jews in Iraq with the properties of present (not absentee) Arabs'. By 'present Arabs' Kaplan meant Israeli Arab citizens, as opposed to 'absentee Arabs', the Israeli term for Palestinian refugees.[58] 'I herein authorize you to begin the implementation of the project of exchanging the property of Arabs present in Israel with the

---

55 Danin, *Tzioni bekhol Tnai*, Vol. 1, p. 317.

56 Ibid.

57 Ibid., p. 318.

58 Four months earlier, in March, Israel had enacted the Absentees' Property Law, which defines 'absentee' as follows:

> (b) 'absentee' means—1. a person who at any time during the period between the 16th of Kislev, 5708 (29 November 1947) and the day on which a declaration is published, under section 9(d) of the Law and Administration Ordinance (5708-1948) that the state of emergency declared by the Provisional Council on the 10th of Iyar, 5708 (19 May 1948) has ceased to exist, was the legal owner of any property situated in the area of Israel or enjoyed or held it, whether by himself of through another, and who at any time during said period—[...] (iii) was a Palestinian citizen and left his ordinary place of residence in Palestine (a) for a place outside Palestine before the 27th of Av, 5708 (1 September 1948); or (b) for a place in Palestine held at the time by forces which sought to prevent the establishment of the State of Israel or which fought against it after its establishment.

In other words, Palestinians within the borders of the new state, i.e., very much present and now Israeli citizens, could still have their property declared 'absentees' property—they became 'present absentees', in the Orwellian term Zionism invented for the purpose. For a complete text of Israel's Absentees' Property Law, see David Kretzmer, *The Legal Status of the Arabs in Israel* (Boulder, Colorado: Westview Press, 1990), pp. 55-60 (for the number of Palestinians in Israel whom the law turned into 'present absentees' Kretzmer gives a figure of 75,000). For further discussion, see Masalha, *The Politics of Denial*, pp. 142-177.

property of Jews from Iraq', Kaplan wrote to Danin on 7 July, suggesting he deduct 2 per cent of the value of the properties exchanged to be set aside as a fund required to carry out these activities.[59]

These initial efforts by Danin ended in failure, according to his account, partly because of the delays he encountered and the financial constraints the Israeli government faced in those days—Ben-Gurion told Danin and his colleagues that he could not spare money for these projects. Furthermore, the talks with the people of Aramco came to nothing and the Arabs refused to discuss his plans.[60] More crucially, however, was the Middle East peace conference the UN Palestine Conciliation Commission had convened in Lausanne, in August 1949, after Israel had rejected Palestinian and Arab demands for a general return of refugees within a political solution of the Arab-Israeli conflict. Palestinian refugees simply demanded to be allowed to return to their homes and villages and showed little interested in Israeli schemes to resettle and employ them in the Arab states.

Resettlement in Sanusi Libya (1950–1958)

In October 1948 senior Israeli diplomats had approached French authorities with the idea of relocating Palestinian refugees from Jordan to North Africa.[61] In March 1950, Foreign Ministry officials raised a proposal of resettling refugees in Libya and Somalia that would involve the Italians. On 24 March, the Director of the Foreign Ministry's International Organisations Division, Ezekiel Gordon, sent a memo to Walter Eytan, the Foreign Ministry's Director General, entitled 'The Resettlement of Arab Refugees in Italian-held Somalia and Libya'. According to Gordon, the Italian representative on the UN Trusteeship Council had said that it was part of his government's policy to en-

---

59 Kaplan's letter dated 7 July 1950, no.1613710/18998, in ISA, Foreign Ministry, 2402/16. A copy of the letter was also sent to Sharett.

60 Danin, *Tzioni bekhol Tnai*, Vol. 1, p. 318.

61 Weitz, *Yomani Veigrotai Labanim*, Vol. 6, appendix 21, p. 526.

courage immigration of Arab farmers to Italian-held Somalia, who
would 'not be foreigners' there. Gordon suggested approaching the
Italians directly to check out the feasibility of resettling Palestinian
refugees in Somalia. 'I would also like to draw your attention to the
possibility of settling Arab refugees in Cyrenaica and Tripoli who could
take the place of the 17,000–18,000 Jews who had emigrated from
there to Israel since its establishment,' Gordon wrote.[62] Referring to
Gordon's memo, Yehoshu'a Palmon, the Prime Minister's Advisor on
Arab Affairs, wrote three weeks later to Eytan that, in his view, Israel
should not pay individual compensation for the properties of the
Palestinian refugees who would be resettled in Libya and Somalia, but
rather a lump sum covering the collective resettlement of those refugees
in Arab countries, including Libya.[63]

The Libyan scheme was twofold: it aimed at resettling Palestinian
refugees in Libya and inducing Palestinians from Israel to emigrate to
Libya—their properties in Israel would be exchanged for those of North
African Jews who would be encouraged to immigrate to Israel. Two points
are relevant here. First, Israeli ministers and officials now increasingly
tended to link the fate of the Palestinian refugees to that of the Jewish
communities in Arab countries. Second, the Israelis wanted to exploit the
fact that the Sanusi monarchy, set up in Libya in 1951, was under indirect
control of and heavily relied on Britain and the United States. Under the
Sanusis, Libya was characterized by great poverty; low-level economic
development was made possible only by payments and loans from various
Western countries. A 1953 Anglo-Libyan treaty allowed Britain to establish military bases in Libya in return for economic subsidies.

The Israeli scheme—'A Combined Proposal for the Resettlement of
Arab Refugees in Libya, the Rescue of Jewish Property [in Libya] and
the Emigration of Arabs from Israel to Libya'—is outlined in a top-
secret letter, dated 13 March 1952, to Foreign Minister Moshe Sharett
by Moshe Sasson, a senior official of the Foreign Ministry's Middle

62 See Gordon's memo, dated 24 March 1950, in ISA, Foreign Ministry, 2402/15.
63 See Palmon's letter, dated 17 April 1950, no.12246/89, in ISA, Foreign Ministry,
    2402/15.

East Department and the son of Israel's ambassador to Turkey at the time, Eliyahu Sasson (Moshe Sasson himself later became Israeli ambassador to Egypt, 1981–1988).[64] Moshe Sasson explained that there were still 3,500 Jews 'lingering' in Libya who seemed in no hurry to immigrate to Israel—a modest estimate of the value of their real estate property Sasson put at £6 million.

Sasson gave the names of two Palestinians, one living in Israel and the other a refugee in Lebanon, who would be willing—though on what ground he claimed this is hard to establish—to collaborate in the scheme and who could help persuade certain circles of Palestinian refugees in neighbouring Arab countries to immigrate to and settle permanently in Libya. In his 1952 proposal, Sasson asserted that 'poor Libya would willingly receive intellectual and technical Arab [human] resources, which have a much higher level than those existing in Libya':

> The success of this small-scale resettlement in Libya depends on [obtaining] the agreement, in principle, of Britain and the local Libyan authorities and ensuring the financial means for it, on the one hand, and advance planning and organisation, on the other. Diplomatic activity at high levels in London [...] and negotiation with UN institutions on the permanent resettlement of the refugees (in order to finance the resettlement of those [refugees] who would emigrate from Arab countries [to Libya])—would ensure one side of the coin, and the JNF (which agrees to be in charge of the exchange of properties between Israeli Arabs and Libyan Jews) would ensure the other side of the coin. The JNF is prepared to undertake the carrying out of this task provided the Foreign Ministry empowers it exclusively to talk to elements concerned in Israel in order to begin implementation.[65]

64 From M. Sasson, Foreign Ministry Middle East Department, to Foreign Minister, Most Secret letter, dated 13 March 1952, in ISA, Foreign Ministry, 2402/5. Copies of the letter were also sent to Foreign Ministry Director General (Walter Eytan), Prime Minister's advisor for Arab affairs (Yehoshu'a Palmon), and Israel's ambassador to Turkey (Eliyahu Sasson).

65 Ibid.

Sasson believed that 'the political and propagandistic reward that will stem from the emigration of Arabs from Israel, after they had been living there and the lesson [this will be] for the refugees, who are still demanding to return, is great.' Sasson suggested that if 'the proposal as a whole, or in part, were to be approved, we [the Foreign Ministry's Middle East Department] could work out a detailed plan to be implemented in stages.' The first stage would aim at having three to four Arabs from Israel emigrate to Libya and a similar number of refugees from neighbouring Arab countries. Prime Minister Ben-Gurion's Advisor for Arab Affairs, Yehoshu'a Palmon, 'approves of the plan and would be prepared to assist in its implementation', Sasson concluded.[66]

Although we do not have Sharett's formal response to this specific proposal from one of his senior officials in the Foreign Ministry, it is most likely he approved of it. At the centre of Israel's foreign diplomacy, Sharett advocated an active approach towards resettling the Palestinian refugees in Arab states. During both his short premiership (1954–1955) and his last six months in office as Foreign Minister (he resigned in June 1956) we find him strongly encouraging his senior officials to pursue the Libyan scheme.

Another person heavily involved in the Libyan plan and other Israeli resettlement schemes in the 1950s was Finance Minister Levi Eshkol. Eshkol had become head of the Land Settlement Department of the Jewish Agency and in this capacity coordinated the settlement of the masses of Jewish immigrants arriving from Arab countries in Israel, who were mostly resettled on land and property belonging to Palestinian refugees. Eshkol also planned the construction of hundreds of new Jewish agricultural settlements throughout the country, most of these on destroyed Palestinian villages. From 1950 to 1952 he served as treasurer of the Jewish Agency. In 1951 he became minister of agriculture and development, and in June of that year finance minister, a post in which he was responsible for the implementation of the reparations agreement Israel concluded in 1952 with West Germany. This agreement obliged Germany to pay to the State of Israel, over a period

66 Ibid.

of 12 to 14 years and in kind, the counter-value of $845 million. Of this amount, $110 million was to be turned over by Israel to the Conference on Jewish Material Claims against Germany, representing 23 Jewish organisations.[67] Eshkol directed most of the reparations funds primarily to help develop Israel's industry.

The Libyan plan was formally approved on 13 May 1954, in a meeting in which took part Prime Minister Sharett, Finance Minister Levi Eshkol, Agriculture Minister Peretz Naftali, Director General of the Finance Ministry Pinhas Sapir, Shmuel Divon, the Prime Minister's Advisor on Arab Affairs, and Yosef Weitz, of the JNF. 'As to the question of exchanging properties of the Arabs here [in Israel] with the properties of Jews in other countries, to which [Arab] farmers would emigrate', the participants gave 'a positive answer', concluding that this was 'the desirable way'.[68] According to Weitz, Sharett, who did not ask many questions, said that 'the matter is respectable and serious and must be carried out'. The participants also approved Weitz's idea that Yoav Tzuckerman, of the JNF, and he himself should travel to 'North Africa to investigate the possibility of exchanging properties of Jews in Tunisia, Algeria, etc.',[69] with those, one assumes, of Palestinian refugees and Israeli Palestinian citizens who might somehow be found ready to accept financial incentives for agreeing to move to North Africa. A second meeting to discuss these proposals in detail, with the participation of Danin, was set for the following Monday—either at this second meeting of mid-May 1954 or shortly after Sharett entrusted Danin with the task of co-ordinating the Libyan scheme.[70]

Like Danin, Weitz was a key player in the Israeli schemes for refugee resettlement in North Africa, which was largely under French and British domination. On 25 October 1954, when he met with Prime

67 *New Encyclopedia of Zionism and Israel*, Vol.1 (London and Toronto: Associated University Presses, 1994), p. 468.
68 Weitz, *Yomani Veigrotai Labanim*, Vol. 4, entry for 13 May 1954, p. 285.
69 Ibid.
70 Danin, *Tzioni bekhol Tnai*, Vol. 1, p. 323.

Minister Sharett to discuss the 'question of the Arab refugees outside Israel', Weitz raised the issue of finding Arab collaborators:

> We have not been assisted [this time] by the means we have generally found to be effective since the return to Zion [i.e., since the onset of Zionist activities in Palestine], namely, recruiting envoys among the Arabs themselves who would then carry out work under our instruction. It is possible [...] that we missed the boat and that the conditions created in recent years in the political world surrounding us have blocked that option for us. However, we are not absolved from checking it out again. The investigation must be carried out by the men of the veteran group [Danin, Tzuckerman, Palmon, etc.] well versed in the customs of negotiating with the Arabs. The purpose is to find out whether there now still is a possibility for that. If it turns out the option still exists, we should work out a detailed plan of action.[71]

Six days later, on the afternoon of 1 November, Sharett called a meeting at his residence in Jerusalem, which was attended by Weitz, Danin, Divon, Teddy Kollek, the Director General of the Prime Minister's Office, and Gideon Raphael, advisor on Middle Eastern Affairs in the Foreign Ministry. Main subject of discussion was a proposal by Weitz and Danin to set up a 'special committee to deal with the Arab refugee affair', whereby Weitz and Danin emphasised that 'only when the subject has been exhaustively investigated would it be possible to know whether there is room for the desired solution'.[72] Weitz later recorded in his diary 'that the special committee would carry out its work in the underground also towards internal people [i.e., Palestinians in Israel]', highlighting the strictly confidential activities that surrounded this and similar Israeli projects in the early 1950s. Finally, Weitz and Danin would present Sharett with a one-page general outline regarding the special committee while Sharett, after consulting other colleagues, would inform Weitz of his reply.[73]

71 Weitz, *Yomani Veigrotai Labanim,* Vol. 4, entry for 25 October 1954, p. 270.
72 Ibid., entry for 1 November 1954, p. 270.
73 Ibid.

Two weeks later, on 13 November, Weitz consulted with Yoav Tzuckerman on the 'special committee for the question of the refugees and the company for the purchase of urban properties from Arabs' in Israel who, one presumes, would simultaneously be encouraged to emigrate to North Africa. Both men also thought they ought to travel to Paris to involve Yehoshu'a Palmon, who at the time was in Europe checking out the possibilities of resettling refugees in Libya.[74]

It took Prime Minister Sharett several months to decide on the appointment of the 'special' or 'refugee committee'. From the meeting he had had with Sharett on the morning of 5 May 1955, Weitz recorded:

> As for my travel [to France and North Africa] it was agreed that Tzuckerman, Palmon and I constitute a committee that would discuss the possibility of finding a solution to the problem of Arab refugees outside the country. The decision to take action must be the responsibility of the three of us, and he [Sharett] should be informed about it. We have to collect material in connection with the exchange of properties of Jews in North Africa with Arab properties here [in Israel], and perhaps there is a possibility of combining these properties with the resettlement of refugees [in North Africa]. He [Sharett] promised to inform Palmon and Sasson [then Israel's ambassador to Italy].[75]

Six days later, on 11 May, Weitz talked to Finance Minister Eshkol, who this time agreed to put at Weitz's disposal 10,000 Israeli lira, as the latter had suggested, so that he could start carrying out initial investigations into the North African-Libyan resettlement scheme.[76]

---

74   Ibid., entry for 13 November 1954, p. 272; Danin, *Tzioni bekhol Tnai*, Vol. 1, p. 323. Two days earlier, on 11 November, two Jews, one a lawyer from Haifa and the other from Tunisia, came to see Weitz and told him that they had brought Finance Minister Eshkol a plan concerning the setting up of a company abroad with the capital of US$0.5 million for the purchase of Jewish properties in Tunisia and Morocco and its exchange with Arab properties in Israel; see ibid., entry for 11 November 1954, p. 271.

75   Weitz, *Yomani Veigrotai Labanim*, Vol. 4, entry for 5 May 1955, p. 294.

76   Ibid., entry for 11 May 1955, p. 295.

On the evening of 25 May 1955 Palmon arrived in Paris from London to meet Weitz and Tzuckerman, who were already in France, and the three talked into the late hours. The next day their discussions turned to the 'means of resettling part of the refugees in the Jordan valley and Sinai and the exchange of [Arab] properties in Israel with properties of Jews in North Africa.' It was also decided that Weitz and Tzuckerman should meet Eliyahu Sasson in Rome before their departure for North Africa.[77]

Weitz and Tzuckerman flew from France to Tunisia on 2 June 1955. Already that same day they talked with some of the local Zionist functionaries and the Jewish Agency envoy about their aim to meet Tunisian Jews who were planning to immigrate to Israel and were 'prepared to exchange their mainly agricultural properties with [Arab] properties in Israel.'[78] In early June Weitz toured the environs of the Tunisian capital, accompanied by two Zionist functionaries, visiting farming estates belonging to Jews. The land was arid and most of the farming was dry, and some of the owners of these properties were prepared to transfer them to the Jewish Agency.[79] Weitz arrived back in Israel on 28 June 1955,[80] having spent nearly five weeks in France, Tunisia and Algeria checking into the feasibility of the combined scheme for resettling Palestinian refugees and Palestinians from Israel in Libya and North Africa, while encouraging North African Jews to immigrate to Israel.

In the afternoon of 6 November 1955, during a meeting of the special refugee committee in Jerusalem, Yehoshu'a Palmon reported that Sharett, then back as Foreign Minister, had recently told US Secretary of State John Foster Dulles that Israel intended to deal directly with the Palestinian refugees and would arrange compensation and resettlement for them if the United States agreed to make available the necessary funds to the Israeli government. According to Palmon, it

---

77 Ibid., appendix 8, entries for 25 and 26 May 1955, p. 375.
78 Ibid., appendix 8, entry for 2 June 1955, p. 377.
79 Ibid., entry for 5 June 1955, p. 377.
80 Ibid., entry for 28 June 1955, p. 295.

sounded as if Dulles had agreed to Sharett's proposal which the two men would further discuss during Sharett's visit to the United States that was to take place within a few days. To prepare himself, Sharett needed data from the special refugee committee on the subject.[81] When Weitz met Sharett on 18 January 1956 in Jerusalem to discuss the project of resettling 'tens of thousands' of refugees in Libya, he explained to Sharett that 'in order to carry out this possibility one million Israeli lira is required as a first step and therefore the government should [firmly] decide: yes or no!' Sharett replied that he 'agrees with this with his heart and soul', but Finance Minister Eshkol's financial reservations had to be overcome first. Sharett told Weitz he wanted Prime Minister Ben-Gurion, Eshkol and members of the special refugee committee to meet and discuss the financial aspects.[82] This meeting took place on the morning of 27 February 1956 in Jerusalem and with Ben-Gurion, Eshkol, Sharett, Weitz, and Palmon participating. Weitz explained that 'it was necessary to set up a fund of five million Israeli lira (£1 million) to be used for the purpose' of resettling refugees permanently. Eshkol suggested that Israel should ask the US administration to increase its foreign aid grant to Israel by $5 million, which would then be allocated exclusively to refugee resettlement schemes. The leading members of the Israeli Cabinet approved the resettlement projects of the special refugee committee in principle and would meet again when the financial details had been worked out.[83]

Two days later the special refugee committee met again, with Palmon, Tzuckerman, Danin and Weitz being present. Palmon reported that Teddy Kollek had told him about the possibility of receiving $5 million from a US government grant or even from Jews abroad to begin practical work on the refugee resettlement project. Foreign Minister Sharett was given the following summary:

81   Ibid., entry for 6 November 1955, pp. 303-304.
82   Ibid., entry for 18 January 1956, p. 311; Sharett, *Yoman Ishi* ('Personal Diary'), Vol. 5, entry for 18 January 1956, p. 1335.
83   Weitz, *Yomani Veigrotai Labanim*, Vol. 4, entry for 27 February 1956, p. 313.

—It is necessary to secure a fund of at least £1 million for the initial action;

—the action must be carried out by a non-governmental committee to be appointed by the Foreign Minister. We propose the four of us [as members], in addition to Teddy Kollek;

—the committee will be authorized to implement actions, after submitting them for approval to the Foreign Minister only;

—we recommend that the committee be subordinate to the JNF and should appear as such to the Arabs and others;

—the first amount [required] for starting the negotiation should be immediately fixed at 50,000 Israeli lira. This amount will be made available by the JNF at the expense of the [government] treasury;

—the action will be carried out in three directions: (a) the rehabilitation of one of the villages of the Hebron mountain [in the West Bank]. We are talking about [the village of] 'Ajur; (b) the purchase of lands from owners who live in villages situated in the Jordanian border region [the West Bank], and whose lands are located in Israel; and (c) the resettlement of one village in Libya.[84]

The resettlement of one village in Libya was supposed to be the start of an operation that aimed to transfer and resettle tens of thousands of Palestinian refugees in that country.

More discussions on the refugee resettlement scheme followed. On the morning of 21 May 1956, Sharett, Eshkol, Weitz, Danin, Palmon, Kollek, Tzuckerman, Divon, and Reuven Shiloah, Israeli Minister Plenipotentiary in Washington, met in the Foreign Ministry in Jerusalem. Sharett started by saying that they had now been discussing the subject already for two years but had as yet to get into action: 'Since the action has been approved by the Prime Minister [Ben-Gurion] and there is money, it is necessary to begin work—which is to investigate what the possibilities are of working with those people who have political and organizational capability among Arab refugees to solve the refugee problem [through resettlement schemes].'[85]

84   Ibid., entry for 29 February 1956, p. 314.
85   Ibid., entry for 21 May 1956, pp. 322-323.

At the same time, Eshkol described the financial situation of the state of Israel as 'catastrophic'—making it very difficult to allocate funds for such resettlement projects. Teddy Kollek suggested again putting pressure on the Americans to increase their grant aid by $5 million, which could then be set aside for refugee resettlement. Sharett thought that Israel should aim at getting half of the amount suggested by Kollek from the Americans. However, when Weitz asked for $1 million to be immediately allocated by the Israeli government to begin work on the project, Eshkol accepted the idea and it was decided to bring the matter before the government for formal approval. The discussion then moved on to what methods the 'new committee' in charge of the refugee resettlement scheme would employ, once it had been officially appointed by the foreign minister (this followed on 30 May).[86] Chaired by Weitz, the committee further included Palmon, Tzuckerman, Danin and Kollek. Sharett also asked Divon to participate in the committee's meetings. In his letter of appointment, Sharett wrote to Weitz that the role of the committee was:

—to investigate practical possibilities regarding liquidating the claims of Arab refugees from Israel, individually and collectively, whether by payment of compensation for their lands, or by arrangement of their resettlement in other countries, or by both means;
—to submit plans for their resettlements; and
—to implement the same plans that the government would approve through the Foreign Ministry.[87]

Weitz, Danin, Tzuckerman, Palmon, Divon, Sasson, and (to some extent) Kollek worked until 1958 to try to bring the Libyan-North African plan to fruition. Their efforts included numerous hours of secret meetings in order to raise money for the purchase of Libyan agricultural lands from Italian colonial settlers who had returned to Italy.[88] Situated in the provinces of Tripoli and Cyrenaica, these lands

86   Ibid.
87   Sharett's letter to Weitz, dated 30 May 1956, no. 27/5/56, in CZA, Weitz's papers, A246/819.
88   In 1939 Libya had been made an integral part of Italy; in the late 1930s about 40,000 colonists had been sent from Italy to the plateau regions of Libya.

were to be offered to Palestinian refugees who had agreed to come and farm it with the help of Libyan workers. In his autobiography Danin later gave the following description:

> The initial investigation I carried out revealed that [the area] in question was sandy land [occupied by former Italian settlers], and it seemed to me that it would be possible to grow on it peanuts on a large scale, and especially at that time since the Chinese had stopped exporting peanuts to Europe and a big shortage of this commodity had been created.[89]

Danin added that he had conceived this project before the discovery of oil in Libya and envisaged the possibility of resettling permanently thousands of refugees within the scheme. A secret agreement had been reached with ministers in the Libyan government to the effect that prospective Palestinian settlers in Libya would be allowed one Palestinian worker with his family for every five Libyan workers they employed. In the initial stage 300 Palestinian agricultural experts and their families would be transferred from Jordan to Libya, all of them refugees who had abandoned properties in Israel. Also according to Danin, a secret tacit agreement was reached with the Jordanian authorities that these Palestinian candidates would be allowed to leave the country via Syria, and through a similar tacit agreement the Lebanese authorities would allow prospective Palestinian settlers to pass through Lebanon and sail through its ports to Libya.[90] Danin writes in his autobiography:

> This whole operation involved enormous efforts to persuade people in Jordan, Libya and Lebanon and obtain their consent. Within the framework of the operation English Jews who did not have Jewish names were persuaded to act for the promotion of the project in Libya. At an advanced stage of the dealings we registered a limited company for development and construction, with the help of a

---

89 Danin, *Tzioni bekhol Tnai*, Vol. 1, p. 323.
90 Ibid., p. 324.

Jewish lawyer from Geneva. The financing was supposed to come from two sources: from the country [Israel] and rich Jews in the USA, including those who had oil business in Libya. We arranged with an insurance company that all the [Palestinian] settlers in Libya would be given life insurance; we would pay the premium, while the company would put at our disposal an advance payment from the amounts to which the insured would be entitled in the future. The candidates for resettlement in Libya undertook to give up their claims for compensation from the government of Israel in the future.[91]

It is hard to establish the truth about these claims of secret tacit agreements with the Jordanian and Lebanese authorities in connection with the Libyan scheme. What is clear, however, is that Danin, Palmon, Weitz, and other colleagues exerted a great deal of effort in promoting this plan. Moreover, from the way Danin explains it, none of the Palestinian refugees in Jordan who had agreed to be candidates for the Libyan scheme seems to have known that the whole project was orchestrated by senior Israeli officials with the assistance of Zionist Jews from England (such as British Zionist author Jon Kimche[92]), Switzerland and other Western countries. On Sunday 17 June 1956, the new refugee committee met in Jerusalem with Danin, Weitz, Kollek, Tzuckerman, and Shmuel Divon taking part, to further discuss the Libyan project. Palmon reported on his dealings with Arab collaborators in London and gave details about his conversation 'with the [Arab?] envoy who will go out there [to Libya] in order to arrange that permission be given to a number of [Palestinian] families [in Libya] to bring relatives and relatives of relatives to settle there, in such a way that they would join 75–100 [Palestinian] clans [expected to settle in

91   Ibid.
92   In his letter to Eliyahu Sasson, dated 17 November 1957, Danin wrote that Jon Kimche had suggested he meet a top man from the Shell Oil company who determined the politics of the company in the Persian Gulf and controlled millions of pounds sterling. Apparently this contact with the man from Shell was in connection with Danin's search for large employment projects for the refugees aimed at economically 'dissolving' the refugee problem; see ibid., p. 253.

Libya].'[93] Palmon reported that it was possible to obtain from the prime minister there [in Libya] permission for four to five Palestinian families, who had settled in Libya and occupied posts in the government, to bring their relatives and the relatives of their relatives to settle there. In this way resettlement of Palestinian Arabs would be established there, which he saw as 'an opening for the development of Palestinian resettlement in Libya'.[94]

On 21 June 1956, shortly before he resigned as foreign minister, Sharett met Finance Minister Eshkol and the head of the refugee committee, Weitz. At this meeting Weitz's proposal to allocate $1 million to the Libyan scheme was approved in principle,[95] although a formal approval by the Israeli government was still required. In early July Golda Meir (a key MAPAI leader later to become Prime Minister) succeeded Sharett as foreign minister and, according to Danin, 'she encouraged us and even obtained the consent of David Ben-Gurion for the continuation of this exceptionally extraordinary and dangerous experiment [the Libyan project], although he [Ben-Gurion] doubted its feasibility.'[96] That is, Ben-Gurion did approve of the Libyan project but remained sceptical—pre-eminently realistic, Ben-Gurion believed that there was a limit to what Israel could do in terms of resettling Palestinian refugees in Arab countries. Furthermore, when four months later, on 4 October 1956, Weitz came to see the Prime Minister and asked him why the government was not doing enough to implement the proposals submitted by the refugee committee, Ben-Gurion—who also acted as Israel's defense minister at the time—replied that much of the government's budget was going to the purchase of weapons, so the money for such a project was simply not available.[97] On 29 October, Britain, France and Israel launched their tripartite attack on Egypt.

93 Undated strictly secret note, signed by Yosef Weitz, in Weitz's papers, III, General A. The Arabs, in the Institute for Settlement Study, Rehovot.
94 Weitz, *Yomani Veigrotai Labanim*, Vol. 4, entry for 17 June 1956, pp. 324-325.
95 Ibid., Vol. 6, appendix 21, p. 528.
96 Danin, *Tzioni bekhol Tnai*, Vol. 1, pp. 324-325; Weitz, *Yomani Veigrotai Labanim*, Vol. 4, entry for 10 July 1956, p. 325.
97 Weitz, *Yomani Veigrotai Labanim*, Vol. 4, entry for 4 October 1956, p. 336.

The prospects for the Libyan scheme to succeed were dimmed by political developments the Middle East witnessed between 1954 and 1958. However, according to Danin, the true reason why the plan in the end was unexpectedly aborted was sudden publicity. This happened in 1958 while Danin and Palmon were in Italy seeking to register the transfer of ownership of the first 100,000 dunam from the former Italian settlers in the Tripoli region into Zionist hands.[98] At that point, the operation—which until then had been kept strictly under wraps—was somehow leaked to an Israeli journalist, who saw it as a journalistic scoop and passed it on to the *Sunday Times* in London, and to *Ma'ariv* and *Lamerhav* in Israel. As a result the whole operation collapsed instantly: 'Our men in Libya were immediately persecuted by the men of the Mufti [Haj Amin al-Husayni], and some of them were detained and tortured.' In summing up his efforts Danin wrote that, although the actual implementation of the project—the transfer of Palestinian refugees from Jordan and their resettlement in Libya—had not been tested, there was no certainty that it would have succeeded even if the whole operation had remained secret.[99] One might add that the success of the scheme also depended on persuading a substantial number of Israeli Palestinians to leave for Libya: that the very few Israeli Arab citizens who had been enticed to move to Libya now insisted on returning to Israel,[100] meant that also from this angle the scheme was doomed to failure.

The collapse of the Libyan project did not bring an end to the efforts of Israeli Foreign Ministry officials to continue to try to 'dissolve' the Palestinian refugee problem and disperse the refugees throughout the interior of the Arab world through economic incentives, employment projects and resettlement schemes. Moreover, the Libyan scheme would re-surface ten years later—following Israel's occupation in June 1967 of the West Bank and the Gaza Strip—in conversations and correspondence between Danin, then retired from the Foreign Min-

98 Danin, *Tzioni bekhol Tnai*, Vol. 1, p. 324;
99 Ibid., p. 325.
100 Ibid.

istry, and Yitzhak Rabin, then Israel's ambassador to Washington. In 1968 Rabin and Danin appear to have discussed the idea of having skilled Palestinians from the West Bank and Gaza—refugees as well as others—'infiltrate' into Libya from where they would then attract Palestinian refugee to emigrate to that country. Both men thought this would help in 'thinning out' the population of the over-crowded refugee camps in the Gaza Strip and the West Bank.[101]

The 1956–57 Occupation of the Gaza Strip and the Sinai

On 29 October 1956, Israel invaded the Gaza Strip and Sinai, as part of the tripartite attack by Israel, France and Britain on Egypt, occupying both areas for four months before strong international, especially US–Soviet, pressure eventually forced them to evacuate them again. Originally, the Israelis had every intention of staying in what their government considered to be an integral part of the 'Land of Israel'—as Golda Meir, Israel's foreign minister at the time, put it at a MAPAI Party rally on 10 November 1956: 'The Gaza Strip is an integral part of Israel.'[102] However, when the Israeli army captured the Gaza Strip in early November 1956, Prime Minister Ben-Gurion was clearly disappointed about the outcome of the war in demographic terms: the vast majority of the refugees and other residents in the Strip had stayed put.[103] That is, of the then 300,000 inhabitants of the Gaza Strip, 215,000 were listed as refugees, spread out over eight vast refugee camps. As we already saw, the Strip held nearly one-fourth of the total of about 900,000 refugees Israel had expelled from historic Palestine. And it was during the 1956–57 occupation of the Gaza Strip that

101 Ibid., pp. 346-47, quoting his letter to Rabin, Israel's ambassador to Washington, dated 20 July 1969.
102 Quoted in *The New York Times*, 11 November 1956.
103 Michael Bar-Zohar, *Mul Hamarah Haakhzarit: Yisrael Berega'a Haemet* (Facing a Cruel Mirror: Israel's Moment of Truth), (Tel Aviv: Yedi'ot Ahronot Books, 1990), p. 27.

Israeli leaders came to realize that, in more than one way, the refugee communities in the region presented the most serious problem. The refugee camps were—and still are—the most overcrowded parts of Gaza and were therefore the most difficult parts for Israel to control. Furthermore, because the refugees refused to accept their sojourn in Gaza as indefinite, Israeli leaders saw a greater long-term challenge coming from the refugees than from the indigenous population. Against this backdrop it was inevitable for Israel to come up with schemes to encourage the emigration and resettlement elsewhere of Palestinian refugees living under occupation.

During the brief occupation of 1956–57 Ben-Gurion set up a secret committee composed of senior Israeli officials and headed by 'Ezra Danin, at the time already deeply involved in the Libyan resettlement scheme, to consider proposals for resettling elsewhere hundreds of thousands of refugees from the Gaza Strip. Little is known about the ideas put forward by this committee. In a letter of 10 December 1956 to Eliyahu Sasson—who as Israel's ambassador to Italy was seeking to purchase the lands of former Italian settlers in Libya for resettlement of Palestinian refugees there (see above)—Danin told him that Finance Minister Levi Eshkol had approved the allocation of financial resources to the work the committee was to carry out, and listed the people involved: Haim Givati (Director-General of the Ministry of Agriculture and later Minister of Agriculture), Yitzhak Levi (Secretary General of the Prime Minister's Office), Yitzhak 'Elam (Director-General of the Ministry of Labour), Shmuel Divon (Ben-Gurion's Advisor on Arab Affairs), and Ra'anan Weitz (son of Yosef Weitz, Director-General of the Jewish Agency's Land Settlement Department).[104] Information remains patchy. It is not clear whether there was any direct link between this committee and Danin's Libyan scheme. On 22 December 1956, Yosef Nahmani, the Jewish National Fund's senior executive in Galilee, wrote to his senior colleague Yosef Weitz: 'You certainly know that a committee headed by 'Ezra Danin is considering proposals to resettle the refugees of Gaza. If Gaza remains in Israeli hands together

104 Danin, *Tzioni bekhol Tnai*, Vol. 1, pp. 328-329.

with its refugees this would put a great burden on the economic development and security of Israel. [...] Your absence [means] the Jewish
National Fund is denied representation on the committee.'[105]

In the official Israeli way of reasoning, if Israel decided to annex the
Gaza Strip, a solution had to be found for the refugee problem. An idea
that surfaced in internal debates was relocating the refugees from the
Strip to the Sinai Peninsula. For instance, on 23 December 1956
Premier Ben-Gurion cut short a cabinet session in Jerusalem in order to
have a lunch meeting with President Yitzhak Ben-Zvi and his wife
Rahel Yanait. The latter was a prominent MAPAI leader, who subsequently joined the Greater-Israel Movement advocating the annexation of the West Bank and the Gaza Strip to Israel. The conversation
that day at the presidential residence in Jerusalem centred on the future
of the Gaza Strip and the Sinai Peninsula and contained the following
exchange between the Prime Minister and Rahel Yanait:

> *Ben-Gurion*: 'We will hold on to Gaza. However, we have no need of
> the 300,000 refugees; it would be better for UNRWA to deal with
> them.'
> *Rahel Yanait*: 'You should propose a constructive settlement.'
> *Ben-Gurion*: 'These things are abstract. Would you suggest the
> resettlement of the refugees of Gaza in Israel?'
> *Rahel Yanait*: 'We would settle them in El 'Arish [in Sinai].'
> *Ben-Gurion*: 'Do you know that in 1920 an expedition went to
> investigate whether or not El 'Arish was suitable for [Jewish]
> settlement and the conclusion was negative. How would we settle
> them in El 'Arish if the land is not suitable?'
> *Rahel Yanait*: 'But things have changed since. Today there are new
> and modern methods for discovering water and improving the soil.'

Rahel Yanait and the president were also trying to persuade Ben-Gurion not to yield to pressure from US President Eisenhower to evacuate
the Sinai Peninsula. An implied threat by the United States of eco-

---

105 Yosef Weitz (ed.), *Yosef Nahmani: Ish Hagalil* (Yosef Nahmani: Man of the
   Galilee), (Ramat Gan: Massada, 1969), p. 139.

nomic sanctions against Israel had already forced Ben-Gurion to agree to withdraw from Sinai when a United Nations force moved into the Suez Canal zone. Ben-Gurion replied to his two interlocutors that Israel could not stand up to two superpowers—the United States and the Soviet Union—and therefore would be forced to evacuate Sinai. But he still regarded Gaza as part of the Jewish 'homeland' and wanted, he said, to hold on to the Gaza Strip.[106] If we look at his past record before and during 1948 and his earlier vigorous advocacy of Palestinian population transfer to Transjordan and Iraq, Ben-Gurion's scepticism vis-à-vis Yanait's argument in favour of relocating the refugees from the Gaza Strip to Sinai may well have had less to do with any fundamental rejection on his part of the idea of resettling Palestinian refugees in Sinai than with *real-politik* in the face of strong American-Soviet pressure.

The same idea of resettling the refugees residing in the Gaza Strip was frequently raised by top officials of the Foreign Ministry, at the time headed by Golda Meir. In his personal diary entry for 20 November 1956, former Foreign Minister Moshe Sharett quoted a cable Walter Eytan (Director General of the Foreign Ministry) had sent from India in which he said that 'the problem of the refugees [in Gaza] is very pressing. [...] There is a need now for more far-reaching actions with the aim of ensuring the future.' An opponent of the occupation of Gaza largely because of the hundreds of thousands of refugees it held but also bitter about having been manoeuvred out of office by Ben-Gurion at this time, Sharett added in amazement: 'What is far-reaching action—the transfer of the refugees to Iraq or their resettlement in Israel? The two solutions are impractical' as neither Iraq nor Israel was prepared to accept them.[107] Eytan had not elaborated on what he meant by 'far-reaching actions', and in Jerusalem Ben-Gurion and Golda Meir

106 Quoted in Yosef Carmel, *Yitzhak Ben-Tzvi: Metokh Yoman Bevet Hanasi* (Diary of Yitzhak Ben-Zvi's body guard) (Ramat Gan: Massada, 1967), p. 92.
107 M. Sharett, *Yoman Ishi* (Personal Diary), Vol.7, entry for 20 November 1956 (Tel Aviv: Sifriyat Ma'ariv, 1978), p. 1866.

seemed determined to keep Sharett in the dark, mainly because of his known opposition to the 1956 war. This, too, may have prompted Sharett's 'amazement'—he clearly felt deceived and humiliated for not having been informed about the impending attack on Egypt.

About the same time, another senior official of the Foreign Ministry and minister plenipotentiary to the Scandinavian countries, Haim Yahil (later to become Director General of the Foreign Ministry, 1960–1964), wrote a secret letter from Stockholm to Walter Eytan, now back in Jerusalem. He strongly advocated the annexation of the Gaza Strip to Israel, but totally rejected a proposal put forward in *Ha'aretz*, on 22 November 1956, by Eli'ezer Livneh, a MAPAI colleague and member of the First and Second Knessets of 1949–1955, calling for the annexation of the Gaza Strip to Israel together with all its Palestinian residents, i.e., including the refugees. Describing Livneh's proposal as totally impractical, Yahil instead suggested that the refugees in the Strip be divided into three groups: the first to be resettled in Sinai, the second in Israel, outside the Gaza Strip; and the third in the Strip itself. Yahil mentions no specific figures as to how many refugees should be included in each category.[108] A month later, he returned to the same proposal in another secret letter to Eytan, dated 26 December. After the annexation of the Gaza Strip to Israel, Yahil explained, Israel would then absorb some of the refugees residing in the Strip 'and the rest of them would be resettled in Sinai or some other Arab country through the payment of compensation on our part.' No less important for Yahil, a solution to the refugee problem is necessary 'not only for political reasons—as our contribution to a resettlement—and humanitarian reasons, but also for [Jewish] settlement reasons. Here the incorporation of Gaza to Israel would be secure and durable only if certain Jewish settlement would be also in this area, and how could we carry out [Jewish] settlement in the area when it is full of refugee camps.'[109]

108 ISA, Foreign Ministry, 3085/16, from Israel's Minister to Stockholm, Haim Yahil, to Foreign Ministry's Director General, Walter Eytan, secret and personal letter no. ST/101, dated 28 November 1956.

109 ISA, Foreign Ministry, 3085/16, from Haim Yahil, Stockholm, to Walter Eytan, secret letter, dated 26 December 1956.

In private and internal discussions, senior officials of the Foreign Ministry and the Prime Minister's Office, including members of the special committee set up to deal with the Palestinian refugees in the occupied Gaza Strip, emerged as the strongest advocates of 'encouraging' the refugees to emigrate from the Gaza Strip to countries overseas. The same officials also realized that neither Egypt nor Syria and Iraq had any intention of opening their borders to let in the quarter of a million refugees from Gaza. There were three men at the centre of these discussions: 'Ezra Danin, Shmuel Divon, a member of the same refugee committee and Ben-Gurion's advisor on Arab affairs; and Ya'acov Herzog, the son of the Chief Rabbi of Israel and a brother of Haim Herzog who later was to become president of Israel (1983–1993).

During the 1956–57 occupation of Gaza, Ya'acov Herzog, in his official capacity as Israel's minister plenipotentiary in Washington, together with officials of the Foreign Ministry in Jerusalem and the Israeli embassy in Washington, actively sought ways to encourage the emigration of refugees from Gaza to countries overseas, including the United States and Latin American countries. It is inconceivable that Herzog's boss in the Washington embassy, Abba Eban (later to become foreign minister), was not privy to these official efforts, which were presided over by Walter Eytan and his boss, Foreign Minister Golda Meir. Gershon Avner, Director of the Foreign Ministry's US Division, wrote a secret letter to Herzog dated 24 January 1957, telling him about 'a new attempt to deal with the problem of the refugees': the 'rehabilitation' of Gaza's refugees through 'the Intergovernmental Committee for European Migration (ICEM)'.[110] Avner had been the director of the Foreign Ministry's West Europe Division between 1948 and 1952 (he later became secretary to the Israeli Cabinet, 1974–1977[111]). In December 1951 the ICEM had been set up on the

110 ISA, Foreign Ministry, 3085/16, G. Avner, to Y. Herzog, Israel's Minister to Washington, secret letter dated 24 January 1957. Abba Eban is also the brother-in-law of Haim Herzog.

111 Avner also served as ambassador to Norway, 1962-1963, and to Canada, 1963-1967; and was President of the University of Haifa, 1977-1981.

initiative of the United States, at a meeting in Brussels in which sixteen nations took part, to be 'responsible for the movement of migrants, including refugees, for whom arrangements could be made with the governments of the countries concerned'. Avner further explained to Herzog that 'Ezra Danin was enthusiastic about this plan 'which fits in with Israel's effort to move a number of refugees to resettle permanently, in the hope that this example would activate others [refugees to emigrate].' Avner added, 'As is known, we are prepared to pay compensation to refugees exploiting this possibility. Assuming that it is possible to reach an agreement with the ICEM, there will be an initial need for a gentle whispering campaign in order to move a number of families to take this road, but it is still early [to know whether this would work].'[112]

The key to success, according to Avner, was to secure the support of the US representative on the ICEM and his government's influence on this organization. He also suggested that the Israeli embassy in Washington should discuss exploiting these ideas to the full.[113] At this stage the Israeli government was still insisting that under no circumstances would it agree to the return of Egypt to the Gaza Strip.

A few weeks later Moshe Bartur, director of the Economic Division of the Foreign Ministry (and later to become ambassador to the UN Europe Bureau), wrote a strictly secret memorandum dated 10 February 1957 (copies were sent to three officials of the Ministry: Y. Herzog; Arthur Lourie, deputy director-general of the Foreign Ministry and a member of the Israeli delegation to the UN General Assembly; and Yosef Teko'ah, later to be ambassador to the UN), suggesting the following:

> Since we are determined to stay in the Strip in one way or another, we have in fact taken responsibility for the 200,000 refugees. It cannot be assumed that we would be able to cause their departure except through an orderly process of resettlement in and outside

112 Avner to Herzog, letter dated 24 January 1957, ibid.
113 Ibid.

Israel. For the sake of that we need the assistance of the UN and USA.[114]

In order to achieve this aim, Bartur went on, the Israeli administration in the Strip should assume joint responsibility with UNRWA for the refugees in Gaza (an Israeli–UN 'condominium', as he called it) and set up an international committee, the composition of which would remain private, to work out a final solution to the problem through resettlement. Bartur did not specify how many refugees would be resettled in the Gaza Strip after its annexation by Israel or how many of them would be resettled overseas.[115]

By March 1957, Israel, under intense international pressure, was preparing to withdraw from Gaza. Reporting to the Knesset on 7 March, Ben-Gurion stressed that under any administration 'the Gaza Strip would be a source of trouble as long as the refugees had not been resettled elsewhere'.[116] By this stage, the United Nations agreed to station an emergency force (UNEF) between Israel and Egypt in the Gaza Strip.

On 12 March 1957, shortly before Israel evacuated the Strip, the US Division of the Foreign Ministry received an undated memorandum addressed to Ya'acov Herzog from Yehuda Harry Levine, a counsellor at the Israeli embassy in Washington who was also in charge of information (and later became director of the Information ('Hasbara') Division of the Israeli Foreign Ministry and ambassador to Denmark), suggesting that Israel undertake a unilateral, practical, and dramatic measure that could demonstrate to the world how the Arab leaders were deliberately preventing a solution to the Palestinian refugee problem. The context here, of course, is the official Israeli claim that the refugee problem had not been created by Israel and that most Arab

114 ISA, Foreign Ministry, 2448/8.
115 Ibid.
116 David Ben-Gurion, *Israel: A Personal History* (New York: Funk & Wagnalls, 1971), p. 534.

countries left the refugees to live in the squalor and misery of the refugee camps on purpose so as to use them as a political and propaganda weapon in their struggle with Israel. The Oxford-educated Levine, who had served as director of the English Propaganda Department of the Jewish National Fund, explained that he had just met the editor of *Harper's* magazine, John Fisher, who had expressed himself in favour of a similar proposal. As Fisher saw it, the refugees in Gaza were now for the first time since 1948 free of pressure from Arab leaders, and consequently as a first step and gesture of goodwill, Israel should offer compensation to a number of refugees in Gaza (he mentioned 5,000) that would enable their relocation to and resettlement in other countries, with the UN's assistance.[117] In May 1949, during the final stage of the Palestinian refugee exodus, *Harper's* magazine had published an article by Eliahu Ben-Horin, the Zionist Revisionist publicist and advocate of Arab population transfer since the early 1940s, entitled 'From Palestine to Israel'. The then editor of *Harper's* had reminded his readers that in an earlier article in the magazine's December 1944 issue, Ben-Horin had advocated a plan that at the time

> looked far-fetched [...] that the Arabs of Palestine be transferred to Iraq and resettled there. Now, with thousands of Arab refugees from Palestine facing a dismal future, the transfer idea appears to be a likely bet. [...] In view of the sound character of Mr. Ben-Horin's earlier judgements and prophecies, we feel we can bank on his word about present-day Israel: 'It works.'[118]

Two days later, on 14 March 1957, another senior Israeli official, Hanan Bar-On (later to become Israeli consul general in Ethiopia), wrote a secret letter to Herzog and Divon suggesting 'the outlines of the plan [we discussed] for encouraging emigration of refugees from the [Gaza] Strip [...] as follows':

117 ISA, Foreign Ministry, 3085/16, from Y. H. Levine, to Y. Herzog, memo no. YHL/114.
118 Central Zionist Archives (CZA) (Jerusalem), A 300/54, Ben-Horin's file.

— The setting up of an organisation in the United States or Latin America, whose aim is to encourage the emigration of refugees to countries of the world, including countries of the American continent, without becoming involved in the political problems of the Middle East.

— The organisation must be based first of all on the leaders of Arab migrants in Latin America and the United States; however, this could also include other elements, such as Christian clergy and perhaps even Jewish factors who are not publicly known as distinguished sympathisers of Israel (Lessing Rosenwald?).[119]

— The organisation should operate on a scale similar to that of the HIAS [the Hebrew Sheltering and Immigrant Aid Society] and the JOINT [American Jewish Joint Distribution Committee] in the years before the Second World War; that is to say, it should not only try to concern itself with the matter of financing emigration as such, but first of all conduct negotiations with governments and various bodies in the world to find absorption places in various countries. The proposed body should operate as a political body based on humanitarian principles, without pretending to represent the refugees or any other Middle Eastern community. In addition to this the body should work in order to bring about the emigration of refugees without religious distinction, in spite of the fact that naturally most of the activists of the organisation would undoubtedly be Christians.

119 Lessing Rosenwald was an American non-Zionist Jewish merchant and philan-thropist. In 1943 he led the foundation of the American Council for Judaism and was its first president. Before 1948 the Council was against the establishment of a Jewish state in Palestine. It is not clear whether Rosenwald would have been interested in co-operating with an Israeli plan of transferring Palestinian refugees from the Gaza Strip to the USA or Latin America. His younger brother William, a financier, served as chairman of the National United Jewish Appeal campaign, and as vice-chairman of the Joint Distribution Committee, American Jewish Committee, and United HIAS Service. Although generally non-Zionists, the Rosenwalds contributed modestly to Jewish educational and agricultural in-stitutions in Palestine.

— Notwithstanding that the financing of the first steps of such an organisation would, undoubtedly, have to come from our own sources, it is possible to assume that it would be possible when the time comes to finance the lion's share of the organizational expenditures with the help of various fund-raising appeals. Clearly this could not include the actual costs of rehabilitating the refugees in their new countries of residence, but perhaps it would be possible to find solutions for this in the framework of UNRWA.

— Despite the fact that the proposed organization should be based first of all on Arab elements, the action of organizing and guidance must, undoubtedly, be made by Israeli and Jewish bodies and personalities jointly, of course with adequate camouflage and concealment.[120]

In summing up the outlines of his proposed plan, Bar-On wrote:

The above are only a few initial thoughts, and it is possible, no doubt, to find impractical flaws in them, but it seems to me that the central idea, that is to say, the setting up of an organization which would attempt by various means to persuade governments to open their borders for emigration, even if limited, is likely to give us not insignificant advantages in the sphere of our dealing with the refugee problem in general and the Arab refugees in particular.[121]

In the same month that Israel was forced to evacuate the Gaza Strip, Danin complained in a letter to David Shaltiel, Israel's ambassador to Brazil, that 'it was possible to operate a great deal in Gaza, but we did not receive permission and money for it'.[122] But it may equally well be

---

120 ISA, Foreign Ministry, 3085/16, Hanan Bar-On, to Ya'acov Herzog and Shmuel Divon, personal and secret letter, dated 14 March 1957. HIAS is the international migration agency of the organized American Jewish community. It assists Jewish migrants and works with various agencies to increase Jewish immigration opportunities.
121 Ibid.
122 Danin, *Tzioni bekhol Tnai*, Vol. 1, p. 251, quoting a letter to Shaltiel dated 21 March 1957.

that because the 1956–57 occupation of Gaza was short-lived and its outcome uncertain, Israel prosecuted its goal of dispersing the refugees under its control through relocation and resettlement schemes less vigorously than it otherwise might have done.

Conclusion

The 'dissolution' of the Palestinian refugee problem, through dispersal and resettlement of the Palestinian refugees, would remain a constant Israeli goal for many years to come. Although the officially (and always secretly) promoted Israeli resettlement schemes of the 1950s ended in failure, they are significant in the sense of showing how determined the Israeli leadership was in seeking to remove the refugee problem from the centre of the Arab-Israeli conflict and block all possibilities of any Palestinian refugee return in the future. The same schemes also constituted a background for other Israeli plans the governments of Levi Eshkol and Golda Meir would harbour and attempt to put into action in the aftermath of Israel's occupation of the West Bank and the Gaza Strip in June 1967. This Israeli preoccupation with the need to 'thin out' the refugee populations in the camps and resettle them stemmed from a variety of reasons, prominent among them the drive to prevent Palestinian refugees from returning and, concomitantly, the determination to remove the refugee problem from the centre of the Arab-Israeli conflict.

In the 1950s the Israeli Foreign Ministry presided over the efforts to 'dissolve' the refugee problem and disperse the refugees through Western-sponsored employment projects and resettlement schemes in neighbouring Arab countries. While the desire among Israeli leaders to see the refugees resettled in the Arab states or elsewhere—blatantly put, to be rid of the 'Palestinian refugee problem'—has remained a constant until the present day, the envisaged modalities of resettlement changed over the years according to circumstance. Diplomatic assessments during the 1950s necessitated strategies and planning that produced a series of specific resettlement schemes, generally involving a number of Arab countries that were subject to Western influences—such as the monarchies of Iraq and Libya—as well as various Latin American countries.

Currently there are more than four million Palestinian refugees—and they claim the right to return home. Theirs is the severest and most enduring refugee problem in the world today. From the outset, Israeli refugee policy has been a classic case of denial: denial of the ethnic cleansing Israel perpetrated in 1948; denial of any wrong-doing it committed or any historical injustice it inflicted; denial of the Palestinians' Right of Return as enshrined in UN Resolution 194; denial of restitution of property and compensation. Finally, Israel's inflexible position that the only solution to the problem is resettlement of the refugees in Arab states or elsewhere underscores Israel's denial of any responsibility or culpability for the creation of the 'refugee problem'. Morally, this is of course a highly questionable position to maintain, one that the victims of the Nakba and their descendants will continue to challenge.

Fear, Victimhood, Self and Other
On the Road to Reconciliation

Ilan Pappé

Fear is no *terra incognita* in the Israeli-Palestinian conflict. It is a country people of both societies visit often. Or rather, Jews and Palestinians alike are more than visitors there: they are its permanent inhabitants. Think of a Luna Park where, out of the many fun and horror sites on offer, people can choose their favourite one. In our case, the most 'popular' site then turns out to be also the basest and ugliest since it leads directly and ruthlessly from the land of fear to that of hatred. This site is called 'Fear of the Other'—the Other construed as the very antithesis of the constituted national self. As in all nationalist conflicts, but particularly in the case of Israel/Palestine, 'otherness' raises pertinent questions about the construction of, in the first place, identity but then also of history and legitimacy.

In this paper I will first provide a brief overview of how the construction of an Israeli national self—and with it the institutionalization of a particular hegemonic discourse in Israel's social and popular culture—rested on the simultaneous constitution of a Palestinian/Arab identity as its demonized Other. The connections between the history of Zionism and the formation of Israeli national identity have been amply discussed elsewhere. Here I will focus on what implications the constitution of this Arab identity as the Other of Israeli national identity is likely to have if we want there to be a chance for reconciliation to emerge in contemporary Israeli society. In particular, I will seek to broaden the debate on victimhood and justice and how they relate to Self and Other in the ongoing conflict. I will also argue that from today's perspective, it is exactly the prevalence and rootedness of this discourse of otherness in Israeli popular culture that forms one of the key obstacles to a just and equitable way out of the conflict.

Nationalism(s)

Beginning in the nineteenth century and well into the 1950s, most of the scholarly literature addressing national identity saw its antecedents in primordial ties: nationalism was viewed as the awakening of an ancient ethnic force that somehow had lain dormant. That is, a pre-existing ethnic identity was said to undergo a modern reworking and so become a nation. This was the view also adopted by the Jewish national movement, i.e., Zionism, as it emerged in Eastern Europe in the late nineteenth century. Until today, Zionism considers Jewish communities around the world as sharing this Jewish national identity with Israel of which it claims they are an integral part. Drawing this kind of linear connection between ethnicity and nationalism enabled Anthony Smith to argue that Zionism was a form of ' Diaspora nationalism' that strove to rekindle its *ethnie* in the territory of the Holy Land.[1]

During the 1960s and 1970s modernization theorists launched a critique of previous theories of nationalism for the way they had associated national identity with primordial roots and set out to reconceptualize 'what is a nation'. For modernists, nationalism was a *novel* phenomenon directly associated with the birth of the modern world in the eighteenth century. Nationalism was now regarded as the inexorable historical expression of 'modernization'. Most of its theorists sought to read the creation of national identity through the prism of elite class politics. That is, nationalism was an instrument in the hands of a political elite and a functional substitute for pre-modern categories. One of the first to think along these lines, Max Weber (1881–1961)

---

1   Anthony Smith, 'Zionism and Diaspora Nationalism', *Israel Affairs* 2/2 (1995), pp. 1-19.

portrayed nationalism as a historical event with a clear beginning and possibly also a predictable end. For Weber, 'nationalism' was an ideology that served the material interests of a particular class and as such became the prerogative of a political and intellectual elite fully cognizant of the artificial conditions of the birth of the 'nation'.[2]

Others were quick to elaborate upon this approach. Crediting elite groups with even more importance than had Weber, Elie Kedourie, for example, saw state formation as more crucial than the construction of a national identity. As the historical cases he chose illustrated, it was the state that gave the nation its identity and significance. By obliterating particularistic identities, state formation enabled societies to establish the new and hegemonic identity that best served their interests. Kedourie's most famous example was the Austro-Hungarian Empire whose primary asset—its strong political structure—was subsequently supplemented with invented Austrian and Hungarian nationalisms as part of a larger strategy of state control. Thus, for Kedourie, nationalism was an elite affair superimposed from above, closely connected to a hegemonic and oppressive modern state apparatus.[3]

Ernest Gellner went further in his critique, re-defining the problematics of nationalism as societal and drawing direct connections between modernization and the formation of national identity: 'Nationalism is not the awakening of nations to self-consciousness: it *invents* nations where they do not exist.' National 'awakening'—a totally fictional interpretation of history in his eyes—was possible only with the progress that came with education and industrialization. Vital for this process was the modernization and systemization of language, the basis for constructing new geopolitical realities from which national movements could spring. Furthermore, modernization was also an effective tool for a new political elite to help it reduce the power structure of the ruling aristocracy.[4] However, the positive link Gellner

2   Max Weber, *Essays in Sociology* (London: Routledge and Kegan Paul, 1948), pp. 171-180.
3   Eli Kedourie, *Nationalism* (London: Hutchinson, 1960).
4   Ernest Gellner, *Nations and Nationalism* (Oxford: Blackwell, 1983).

saw between modernization and nationalism led him to discard an-other, no less critical component of national identity formation: its suppression of *alternative* forms of identity.

It was this latter point that Eric Hobsbawm would cogently argue. Combining a Marxist outlook with Weberian functionalism, Hobs-bawm viewed the nation as the direct outcome of capitalist ambitions in European societies to control units large enough to secure the financial gains of its bourgeois elite. In the process this same elite engaged in the 'human engineering of society' that required complimentary images of the self and degrading images of the other in order to nationalize past and present realities.[5] This, according to Hobsbawm, placed 'emplotment' at the heart of all national historiography, the plot being spun through the selection and re-configuration of past events and symbols as new 'national' traditions are 'invented'.[6]

Perhaps the most forceful critique of the functionalist approach has been that of Benedict Anderson, whose notion of 'imagined communities' steered attention away from the structural and objective constituents of the nation and instead highlighted the discursive forms through which nations imagine themselves into being. For Anderson, nationalism is a product that is sold not as a self-contained unit but as a modular commodity made to fit the different geographical locations and historical periods where it is introduced. But, like all modernists, An-derson insists that disseminating this product, again, was done to serve the few in the name of the many through engineering, manipulation and the invention of historical stories. However, by suggesting that nations, nation-ness and nationalism are 'cultural artifacts of a particular kind', Anderson sought to refute previous objectivist conceptions of the nation, instead highlighting the universality of the phenomenon and stressing the 'irremediable particularity of its concrete manifestation'.[7]

5   Eric Hobsbawm, *Nations and Nationalism Since 1870* (Cambridge: Cambridge University Press, 1990), pp. 14-25.
6   Cf. Hayden White, 'The Historical Text as Literary Artifact', *Clio* 3 (1974), pp. 277-303.
7   Benedict Anderson, *Imagined Communities* (London: Verso 1991).

Finally, this 'constructedness' of national identity has been further probed by Edward Said, Homi Bhabha and members of the school of Subaltern Studies, amongst others, all of whom have questioned not only the 'invented traditions' of national identity but the very systems of cultural representation involved in this process. In varying degrees they have all sought to pinpoint the *exclusionary* practices inherent in the formation of national identity.[8] In the process they have moved the discussion away from the socio-historical and political roots of nationalism to its discursive contours, foregrounding the heterogeneity that nationalism seeks to suppress.

In other words, whether engineered, manipulated or imagined, national identity is a recent human invention borne out of the integration of conflicting ethnic or cultural identities or, of course, the disintegration of such identities. As such, it puts in place a modern axis of inclusion and exclusion that is not organic or natural, but requires the artificial identification of those who belong to a particular nation and—more crucially—of those who are excluded from it. Critical for the formation of the national self is the constituting of an Other to this national identity. This is done by subordinating other identities—communal, religious, ethnic, etc.—so as to set parameters of 'otherness' that then serve to define to what degree that 'otherness' will be constituted as threatening the prevalent or hegemonic identity. As Michel Foucault has argued, in the field of knowledge construed by nationalism the Other—the 'enemy'—occupies exclusively the negative pole of that field.[9]

The 'Enemy' Other

The suppression of difference and the construction of an enemy Other are thus two critical elements when it comes to imposing a hegemonic national identity. How this worked in the particular case of Zionism and

8   Edward Said, *The World, the Text and the Critic* (Cambridge: Harvard University Press, 1983), and Homi Bhabha (ed.), *The Nation and Narration* (London: Routledge, 1990), pp. 1-7. Partha Chatterjee, *Nationalist Thought and the Colonial World: A Derivative Discourse* (London: Zed Books, 1986).
9   Michel Foucault, *Power/Knowledge, Selected Writings* (New York: Pantheon, 1980).

Israel was poignantly exposed already in the early 1950s. Beginning in the nineteenth century, and then far more aggressively following the creation of the state of Israel in 1948, Jewish nationalism came to construe Arab identity as the 'hated Other' of Israeli national identity, making it symbolize everything that Jewish-ness, as the Zionists saw it, was not. However, this juxtaposition of 'Jewish' Self and 'hated Arab' Other ran into trouble already in the early years of the new state when Israel encouraged about one million Arab Jews from North Africa and the Middle East to immigrate and help populate the country, and then made a deliberate effort to de-Arabize them. That is, these Oriental Jews, *Mizrahim* ('Easterners') in Hebrew, were officially taught to treat their mother tongue with contempt, told to reject the Arab culture they had grown up with and prompted to make an all-out effort to 'westernize' themselves.[10]

This approach to identity—of constructing an Other as the negative image of oneself—was reinforced by Israeli historiography in the way, for example, it dealt with Jewish (Zionist) terrorism in the Mandatory period or with the atrocities Jews committed during the 1948 war. Terrorism is a term Israeli Orientalists apply exclusively to actions carried out by Palestinian resistance movements—i.e., only the Other side commits acts of terrorism—and thus can never form part of any analysis of Israel's own acts or be incorporated in chapters describing Israel's own past. One way out of this conundrum was to accredit a particular political Jewish group, preferably an extremist one, with the same attributes as the enemy and so deflect all blame from mainstream national behaviour. In this way, Israeli historians and Israeli society at

---

10 Ella Shohat, 'Mizrahim in Israel: Zionism from the Standpoint of its Jewish Victims', *Theory, Culture and Ideology* 19/20; see also idem, 'Rupture and Return: A Mizrahi Perspective on the Zionist Discourse' (*MIT Electronic Journal of Middle East Studies* 1[2001]), where she writes: '[T]he term Mizrahim came into use in the early 1990s [when] Mizrahi leftist activists [...] felt that previous terms, such as "Sephardim", apart from its imprecision, could be seen as privileging links to Europe while slighting their non-European cultural origins.' Significantly, for Shohat, the term 'Mizrahim', while retaining its implicit opposite, 'Ashkenazim', 'condenses a number of connotations: it celebrates the past in the Eastern world; it affirms the pan-oriental communities [that] developed in Israel itself; and it invokes a future of revived cohabitation with the Arab-Muslim East.'

large were able to acknowledge Deir Yassin, where on 9 April 1948 more than 200 defenseless Palestinian men, women and children were massacred by a right-wing terrorist group, called Irgun, and to deny or cover up the many other massacres carried out by the Hagana, the major Jewish militia that after May 1948 would emerge as the 'Israel Defense Forces' (IDF).[11]

The same dichotomy comes to the fore in the Israeli treatment of victimhood, especially in the light of current events. Acknowledging the Other's victimhood or, beyond that, recognizing yourself as the victimizer of the Other is perhaps the most terrifying ghost train one can decide to embark upon. Most Israeli Jews are unable or simply refuse to contemplate the possibility. As I have argued elsewhere, the first popular attempt at broaching the notion that Jews were not only the ultimate victims of the twentieth century, but also belonged among its main victimizers came in 1998 with the broadcast of the Israeli TV series, *Tekuma,* part of Israel's jubilee year celebrations. Highly timid though the attempt remained—nowhere did the *Tekuma* series deviate in any significant way from the dominant Zionist narrative—the mere suggestion the series made that other narratives of Palestine's history might be possible was enough to cause a massive outcry throughout Jewish Israeli society and from all Jewish Israeli political parties against the programme's editors and its producers.[12]

My contention here is that *acknowledging* the atrocities Jews committed against the people of Palestine when they created their state ought to become a vital and necessary road station in the socialization of the Jews in Israel, no less vital and necessary than the horror destinations which the Israeli Ministry of Education obliges Jewish high-school children to visit in Holocaust Europe.

For Israelis, to recognize the Palestinians as the victims of Israeli actions counts as deeply distressing in at least two ways. As this form of

---

11 Ilan Pappé, 'Post-Zionist Critique. Part I: The Academic Debate', *Journal of Palestine Studies,* 26/2 (Winter 1997), pp. 29–41.

12 Ilan Pappé, 'Israeli Television Fiftieth Anniversary Series *Tekuma*: A Post-Zionist Review?', *Journal of Palestine Studies* 27/4 (Summer 1998), pp. 99–105.

acknowledgement means facing up to the historical injustice in which
Israel is incriminated through the ethnic cleansing of the country's
indigenous people in 1948, it calls into question the very foundational
myths of the state of Israel, pointing up the lie of 'A land without a
people for a people without a land', a slogan Jewish nationalism
adopted as early as 1902. And it raises a host of ethical questions that
have inescapable implications for the future of the state.

Recognizing Palestinian victimhood ties in with deeply rooted psychological fears because it demands Israelis to question their self perceptions of
what 'went on' in 1948. As most Israelis see it—and as mainstream and
popular Israeli historiography keeps telling them—in 1948 Israel was able
to establish itself as an independent nation state on part of Mandate Palestine because early Zionists had succeeded in 'settling an empty land' and
'making the desert bloom'. At play here is another influential Israeli
foundational myth, that of a modern-day little David pitted in a hostile
environment against a contemporary giant Goliath.

The inability of Israelis to acknowledge the trauma the Palestinians
suffered and accept them as a community of suffering stands out even
sharper when set against the way the Palestinian national narrative tells
the story of the Nakba, the catastrophe of 1948, a narrative of destruction, of the loss of lives, homes and villages, a trauma they continue to live until this very day. Had their victimhood been the
'natural' and 'normal' outcome of a long-term and bloody conflict,
Israel's fears to allow the other side to 'become' the victim of the
conflict would not have been so intense—both sides would have been
'victims of the circumstances' (here, the reader may substitute any
other amorphous, non-committal concept that serves human beings,
particularly politicians but of course also historians, to absolve themselves from the moral responsibility they otherwise would carry). But
what the Palestinians are demanding and what in fact for many of
them—excepting the present leadership of the Palestinian Authority[13]—has become a *sine qua non* is that they be recognized as the

---

13   This article was written before the 25 January 2006 elections which gave Hamas
     its landslide victory.

victims of an ongoing evil consciously perpetrated by Israel against them. For Israeli Jews to accept this would naturally mean losing their own status of victimhood. This would have political implications on an international scale, but also—and, as I believe, far more critically—would trigger moral and existential repercussions for the Israeli Jewish psyche: Israeli Jews would have to recognize that they have become the mirror image of their own worst nightmare.

For Palestinians, to recognize the victimhood of Israeli Jews would entail accepting *them* as a community of suffering. The victimization of the Jews by Nazi Europe can, of course, never serve as justification for their own victimizing of the Palestinians, but it may go some way towards explaining a *chain* of victimization and so ought to help reduce the level of Palestinian reluctance to fully acknowledge the Holocaust and the weight it has in the constitution of the Israeli-Jewish national identity. One has to tread carefully here, and I elaborate on this below.

Thus, it is this fear of mutual recognition that we need to confront. Significantly, it is in times of 'peace'— for which such recognition is a pre-requisite—that this fear becomes more acute and is more critically articulated in Israeli public discourse. This we saw happening with the launching of the Oslo 'peace process'. Though commodified and marketed as a process of reconciliation, Oslo was of course little more than, as Noam Chomsky put it, 'a military rearrangement of life concluded by pragmatic political elites'.[14] But the fact that Oslo was presented as a 'peace process' was enough to arouse among Israelis fears associated for them with the victimization of the other and the concomitant deprecation of the self. This will become more evident shortly.

History: Invisible and Indivisible

Inevitably, given the gross imbalance between Palestinian and Israeli realities, being asked to recognize this twin process of other-victim-

14   Noam Chomsky, *Powers and Prospects* (London: Pluto Press 1996), pp. 159-201.

ization and self-deprecation causes the greater fears on the Jewish Israeli side. Palestinians are the victims of deliberate Israeli actions and atrocities and not 'of the circumstances' or of, as one Israeli historian likes to put it, 'à la guerre comme à la guerre'.[15] The latter attitude is part of the kind of 'magnanimous' discourse that Israeli educators, historians, novelists and cultural producers consciously employ to help perpetuate their purposeful misrepresentation of historical processes. In one way or another, all of them have helped to construct and preserve the national narrative, ethos and myths that Israel likes to tell about itself during war(like) times. For the many ways in which this manifests itself in Israeli society—from a person's infancy to adulthood—we don't have to look further than the tales child minders tell their charges on Israel's Independence Day or during the Passover celebration of the 'Exodus from Egypt', the curricula and text books that are taught in elementary and high schools, the ceremonies freshmen undergo and the oath army officers swear at their final induction, the historical narrative the printed and electronic media routinely disseminate as well as the discourse politicians habitually employ in their speeches, the way artists, novelists and poets voluntarily subject their creations to the national imperative, and the historical, social and political research academics in the country's universities tirelessly produce about Israel's 'reality', past and present.[16]

Typical, too, is the posture the 'Peace Now' movement in Israel adopts. For 'Peace Now' members, peace and reconciliation translate into the need for mutual recognition between the Israeli and Palestinian national narrative in such a way that the two will never clash. They achieve this by dividing everything that is *visible*—land, resources and history—into a pre-1967 period, in which 'We, the Jews, were Right and Just', and post-1967 period, in which 'You, the Palestinians, are Right and Just'.[17] In other words, whereas the events and actions by

15 Benny Morris, *Righteous Victims* (New York: Knopf, 1999).
16 Ilan Pappé, 'Post-Zionist Critique: Part III: Popular Culture', *Journal of Palestine Studies*, 26/4 (Summer 1997), pp. 60-69.
17 Ilan Pappé, 'Post-Zionist Critique. Part II: Media', *Journal of Palestine Studies* 26/3 (Spring 1997), pp. 37-43.

the Zionists that preceded and led to the foundation of the state of Israel in Palestine in 1948 not only remain unquestioned but are actually justified, those that followed the June 1967 war, including the conquest and continuing occupation by Israel of the rest of Palestine—the West Bank and the Gaza Strip—are deemed less acceptable. Given this perspective, it then also becomes seemingly possible to divide victimhood in the Israeli-Palestinian conflict into those same two historical periods. In their self-righteous approach to the history of the conflict, the Israeli peace camp sees the Jews as the victims of the earlier and more distant chapters in the history of the conflict, all belonging to the pre-1967 era, and the Palestinians as the victims of its more recent, post-1967 chapters.

This periodization is the crux here: the earlier period is considered to be the more significant one, and thus 'Being Just' then, in the formative period of the conflict, justifies the existence of Zionism and the whole of the Zionist project in Palestine. At the same time, one is allowed to cast doubt on the wisdom and morality of Palestinian actions in that period, to question their national narratives and, implicitly, to dispute their 'rights'. For the adherents to the 'Peace Now' scheme, Zionism may have 'misbehaved' in subsequent times, but its actions can never throw into doubt the very essence and justification of Israel's existence.

Peace and mutual recognition, however, entail bridging the *invisible* layers of the conflict—guilt and injustice. Guilt cannot be divided in the way of Peace Now, not if peace and reconciliation mean respect for and acceptance of the Other's narrative. The Palestinian narrative of 1948 is one of suffering, reconstructed on the basis of living memories, oral history, and of a continued exilic existence poignantly made tangible through property deeds people hold to lands that have been confiscated, photographs whose images are fading and latch keys to homes they are barred from returning to and that anyway in most cases no longer exist. The different Palestinian historical narratives are read backwards through the prism of contemporary misery and hardships—in the Occupied Territories, whose residents are subjected to routine house demolitions, sudden arrests, expulsions, and to the horrendous atrocities the Israeli army has increasingly been committing against them day in day out since the second Intifada broke out; and in exile, where they are subjected to the whims of their host countries and, in some instances, denied even their most basic civic and human rights. Through this prism, Zionism/Israel has for many come to represent absolute evil and the ultimate victimizer. How can this image be divided in the business-like approach to 'peace' the American and Israeli peacemakers have been advocating?

It never can, of course. When discussing peace in such a context, it may help to turn to communities of suffering around the world and see how they have tried to reconcile with their victimizers. Describing a collective evil in the past, narratives of suffering are an interpretative construct often resorted to by a given community in the present to help create a better future for itself. To avoid sounding reductionist, I wish to add that for all communities who continue to live the after-effects of the original wrong perpetrated against them, but especially in the case of the Palestinians, this narrative can have a redemptive value—for themselves. Another salient issue, of course, but one that I will not discuss here, is how—as the case of the Holocaust has shown—this narrative can be manipulated by a country's producers of culture and political actors for political ends.[18]

In most contexts, narratives of suffering are reproduced with the help of the educational and media systems, are sustained by a commemorative infrastructure of museums and ceremonies and are preserved through a variety of discourses.[19] At the same time, however much such a narrative of suffering can serve a community in conflict, it is more difficult to maintain as a means towards reconciliation.[20] In the

---

18 See, e.g., Moshe Zuckermann's article in this volume.
19 On ways in which Holocaust Memorials have been used to constitute collective memory as well as advance particular political ends, see James E. Young, *The Texture of Memory: Holocaust Memorials and Meaning* (New Haven and London: Yale University Press, 1993).
20 This concept was first developed by Elizabeth Fau in her *Community of Suffering and Struggle, Women, Men and the Labor Movement in Minneapolis, 1915-1945* (Chapel Hill: University of North Carolina Press, 1991).

case of the Palestinians, whether living under Israeli occupation or pushed into exile, commemoration takes on myriad forms, some of them traditional, others wholly unexpected. Lacking a basic societal infrastructure, and in the absence of a *terra firma* in which to ground these rituals, commemoration in the Occupied Territories is most explicit in the way the calendar is crammed with fateful or salient events and dates—for example, the 1917 Balfour Declaration, Israel's 'Declaration of Independence', the end of the Mandate, the 1947 UN Partition Resolution, the founding in 1964 of Fatah, the Palestine Liberation Organization, and so on. In exile, where, if not totally denied their political, economic and civic rights, people are often prevented from exercising them, re-telling the narrative takes on its own *couleur locale*. For example, in Lebanon—where the authorities view the Palestinian presence as a serious threat to the country's sectarian balance and its long-term political stability—the mass graveyard at the Sabra and Shatila refugee camps, where 2,000 Palestinian residents were massacred by rightwing members of a Lebanese militia following the Israeli invasion in 1982 and under the watchful eye and protective shield of the Israeli army, has been turned into one huge garbage dump for more than twenty years now. Each year anew, in September, this dump is removed and the site cleared, but it usually takes activists from outside the camps to generate some memorial event before the place disintegrates again into a dump. More recently, children in Sabra and Shatila have transformed the commemoration of the Nakbah through a re-telling of their own personal narratives and imaginative re-constitutions of a Palestine they of course never knew but long to return to. In another community in exile, Palestinian activists in Tunis between 1983 and 1993 would re-design their living rooms into actual museums of the catastrophe their people had suffered: a small corner would be set aside for the representation of their own narrative and discourse of national identity. For yet another example, Palestinians and others have been coming together in Cambridge, Massachusetts, on 13 December, the anniversary of the outbreak in 1987 of the first Intifada, to relay their own personal stories.

Thus, during times of conflict suffering and victimhood become a highly significant element in the constitution of the collective identity of the self and in the destruction of the collective memory of the Other. The negation of the Other, of his or her suffering and catastrophe, becomes a constitutive element in national identity formation.[21] In other words, violence and fear are two key factors in the construction of collective memories in the way they help reproduce and disseminate collective memories and ensure inclusion in or exclusion from a given historical reality and balance of power. This is especially the case when conflicts range over the definition of identity in a given territorial entity or over the definition of the territory itself.

In the case of Israel and Palestine, controlling the collective memory of *both* groups is part of the violent existential struggle for national survival. As the effort to shape collective memory is a dialectical process prompted by the fear of, and the wish to negate, the Other, it entails the usurpation of the other side's status of victim and the negation of their suffering. Conversely, recognizing the other side as the victim of your own actions becomes part of the healing process and is a major step towards reconciliation.

Fear thus plays a prompting role in the violence that is being per-petrated daily in the struggle over narrative, memory and victimhood. Victimizing the Other and negating their right to the position of victim are intertwined processes of this same violence. Jews who, in 1948, took part in the expulsion of almost a million Palestinians and in the massacring of thousands of others continue to deny the ethnic cleansing they perpetrated ever happened and refuse to acknowledge the destruction of the more than four hundred Palestinian villages and city neighbourhoods they were involved in.[22] Again, what undergirds

---

21 See, e.g., the articles in Bo Sarth (ed.), *Memory and Myth in the Construction of Community: Historical Patterns in Europe and Beyond* (Florence: European University Institute, 1999).

22 Ilan Pappé, 'Were They Expelled?: The History, Historiography and Relevance of the Refugee Problem', in Ghada Karmi and Eugene Cortran (eds.), *The Palestinian Exodus, 1948-1988* (London: Ithaca, 1999), pp. 37-62.

this constant self-declaration of victimhood by Israeli Jews is the fear they may lose their status as modern history's ultimate victims.

Fear, Justice and Retribution

What lies at the heart of this Israeli fear? And what would be able to undo it? The first and most difficult step for Israelis to take would be to recognize the cardinal role the Jewish state has played, and continues to play, in the dispossession of the Palestinian people and in transforming them into a community of suffering. The second step, no less difficult, would be for them to consider how to accept the consequences this recognition implies.

Out of no doubt many others, I will here briefly suggest three ways through which it might prove possible to extricate the element of violence that seemingly for ever has marked the relationship between the two communities. For guidance and advice I turn to the realm of civic and international law, sociological theories of retribution and restitution, and finally cultural studies, so as to probe and better articulate the dialectical relationship between collective memories and ways of manipulating them.

The very idea of considering 1948 in the realm of international law and justice is anathema to most Jews in Israel. As will be clear by now from the above, what most frightens Jewish society in Israel about having its past conduct scrutinized in the light of theories and procedures of law and justice is that this is likely to implicate some of their (prominent) members in war crimes and to have them convicted as war criminals. When Israeli philosopher of ethics Asa Kasher first heard about the 1948 massacre Jewish troops had perpetrated in the Palestinian village of Tantura, he publicly stated that the soldiers involved ought to be regarded as war criminals.[23] Tantura, however, was not the only—and arguably not the worst—massacre Zionist troops commit-

---

23 Asa Kasher was interviewed, together with MA author Teddy Katz and others, in *Ma'ariv*, 21 January 2000.

ted in Israel's first hour. Kasher was unique in his response—and soon 'repented'. Veterans of the Israeli unit who had taken part in the Tantura massacre sued the researcher whose MA thesis describes the massacre for libel. Similarly, any reference appearing in the Israeli press to expulsion, massacre or destruction is commonly denied as baseless or attributed to self-hatred on the part of the person who authored it; not seldom will it be portrayed as 'serving the enemy' in times of war.[24] Such reactions range across the board of Israeli society and include members of the academia, the media and the educational system as well most political circles.

At this point, let us try to imagine Israeli past conduct being debated or scrutinized along the lines of 'Inside the Law', a TV programme located on the premises of the Law School at New York University (NYU) and produced by PBS (the public TV channel in the United States). In a recent series on 'Justice, Restitution and Reconciliation in a Violent World', a first installment, called 'The Holocaust and Beyond', dealt with litigation arising from genocide and other crimes against humanity. It recognizes the *sui-generis* status of the Holocaust vis-à-vis other atrocities. However, when it breaks such crimes down into the discrete elements that destruction in these contexts consists of—social fabric, careers, culture, real estate, and so on—it puts them on the same level of guilt.

For our own purpose, a good example of how to approach this quantification of suffering we find in the reparations agreement Israel and West Germany signed on 10 September 1952. That agreement included pensions calculated according to inflation across the years, estimations of real estates and other such aspects of individual loss. A separate set of agreements was concluded about translating into money—in the form of grants to the state of Israel—the collective human loss the Jewish people had suffered. The Palestinian scholar Salman Abu Sitta has begun using a similar approach to assess the real value of assets the Palestinians lost in the Nakba.

---

24 Ilan Pappé, 'Breaking the Mirror: Oslo and After', in Haim Gordon (ed.), *Looking Back at the June 1967 War* (Westport: Praeger, 1999), pp. 95-112.

The second installment in the PBS series dealt with what kind of potential tribunals could handle such litigation and lawsuits. Centring on Pinochet and Slobodan Milosevic, it asks the question, 'Should war crimes and other atrocities be the subject of international or domestic jurisdiction?' The third installment, entitled 'Nation Building: Moving beyond Injustice', dealt with atrocities committed by regimes in transitory periods between occupation and liberation. The fourth pondered the legal right of the international community to intervene in local conflict in the wake of evidence of atrocities or war crimes. It looks critically at US military operations that by masquerading as international 'peace' actions effectively meant to achieve the exact opposite, i.e., exploit such situations for their own benefit.

Now, what would happen should legal experts on collective crimes appearing in PBS's 'Inside the Law' decide to incorporate the Nakba among their case studies of the former Yugoslavia, Rwanda and Chile and an installment were to be shown on Israeli TV discussing what procedures would be necessary to help rectify past evils and human atrocities? Few, if any, Jews in Israel today, I'm afraid, would be interested in watching such a programme or even bother to tune in: it would strike them as totally irrelevant to their own reality.

The reason for this is the persistent hold Zionist ideology has on the Jewish public in Israel. Being relentlessly disseminated from kindergarten to university, Zionist ideology has produced a self-image that is as pious about Zionist morality as it is insistent about Palestinian 'immorality'. Its level of sophistication may vary according to education, socioeconomic status and function, but its blunt overall message remains the same. Overt support for the Right of Return for Palestinians, for a Truth and Reconciliation Commission on the Nakba or for bringing Israelis to trial for war crimes committed in 1948 (and after) is out of bounds for most Jews in Israeli society, i.e., they refuse to accept these notions as legitimate, let alone as part of people's everyday knowledge. And as Foucault has argued in another context, people who advocate unpopular positions that challenge the majority's stronghold over what is allowed to enter the public realm are assessed as ideologically subversive and risk being sidelined as mentally ill.

But how difficult would it be to find a non-retributive paradigm of justice? The Rwandan author, Babu Aynido, in an article he published in January 1998 in the journal *Africanews*, 'Retribution or Restoration for Rwanda', elaborates upon one possible strategy. Dealing with the International Criminal Tribunal for Rwanda (ICTR), Aynido writes: 'Suffice it to say that the retributive understanding of crime and justice, upon which the ICTR is founded, is discordant with the worldview of many African communities. To emphasize retribution is the surest way to poison the seeds of reconciliation. If anything, retribution turns offenders into heroes, re-victimizes the victims and fertilizes the circle of violence.'

Ayindo here is inspired by Howard Zher's book *Changing Lenses* in which the author strongly comes out against the pro-punishment judicial system.[25] One of the questions Zher raises and that Ayindo picks up in his discussion of the Rwandan case is also relevant when we contemplate how Jews in Israel might be able to overcome their fear of facing the past: 'Should justice focus on establishing guilt or should it focus on identifying needs and obligations?' In other words, can it serve as a re-regulator of life where life was once disrupted or even destroyed? Ayindo states clearly that justice should not be allowed to inflict suffering on victimizers, let alone their descendants, but can be made to help the suffering stop. This claim, which Zher finds revolutionary, is easily understood, Ayindo explains, by many people in Africa as the only sensible way of dealing with victimhood. Even if one cannot compare between the genocide committed in Rwanda—an estimated 800,000 people murdered during 100 days in April–mid-July 1994—and the crime perpetrated in Palestine in 1948, whose repercussions remain with us until today, the mechanism of reconciliation itself proves highly relevant.

Ayindo distinguishes between two models in this context: the tribunal in Rwanda, which deals only with the past and does not enable a reconstruction of relationships there, and the Truth and Reconciliation

---

25 Howard Zehr, *Changing Lenses; A New Focus for Crime and Justice* (Ontario: Herald Press, 1990).

Commission headed by Bishop Desmond Tutu in South Africa, which he favours because of the way it looks towards the future. The power and authority underpinning the Truth commission, according to Ayindo, lie in its disinclination to inflict heavy penalties and in its insistence on discussing future relationships between the different communities—both victims and victimizers—in South Africa. In contrast, the Rwanda tribunal, he claims, is the fastest and surest way to turning the victims into victimizers themselves.

For a possible second way how this fear to face the past may be overcome I turn to the American psychologist Joan Fumia who focusses on the transformation of attitudes in conflictual situations.[26] Fumia bases her work on the relationships that develop between offenders and victims in the American legal system made possible by a recently introduced procedure that offers victim–offender mediation. This method involves a face-to-face meeting between offender and victim (obviously not applicable to murder cases and thus not appropriate in case of genocide, but certainly adaptable to the Israeli case). The most significant part of the procedure here is the readiness of the offender to accept responsibility for the crime he/she committed. In other words, not the deed itself but the consequences it worked in the lives of others are the focal point of the process. The search here is after restorative justice: what can the offender do to ease the loss and suffering of the victim. This is not a substitute for any criminal proceedings or, in the case of Palestine, it can never form an alternative for actual compensation or repatriation, but it certainly ought to be a supplement to any final solution. Fumia claims that her model was successfully implemented in South Africa.

Whenever Israeli responsibility for the Nakba will be discussed as part of the attempt to reach a permanent and equitable solution to the

26 Joan Fumia, 'Restitution versus Retribution: The Case for Victim-Offender Mediation, Conflict Resolution', *Conflict Resolution* (www.Suite101.com) and published for the first time in October 1988, in which she reports on the Victim-Offender Program (VORP) at work in the US legal system.

conflict—I admit, in 2006 a prospect more remote than ever—it is unlikely to reach the international court, as did the cases of Rwanda and the former Yugoslavia. Or, at least, this is what one assumes going by the distorted way the Nakba is seen by the US, Canada and most governments in Europe—political actors who largely accept the Israeli peace camp's perspective on the conflict, as set out above. However, in Africa and Asia governments have begun voicing different views, and the overall situation may change in the near future. Of course, as long as the balance of power remains as it is now, establishing a truth commission in Israel à la South Africa continues to be an unlikely possibility. At the same time, whether or not this may one day happen, the demands of the Palestinian victims of 1948 remain high on the peace agenda and the outcry over the crimes and injustices Israel perpetrated continues to follow the offenders. Still, in light of the above, if we want the solution of the conflict to move from the division of the visible to the restoration of the invisible, the fears of the victimizers will have to be taken into account as well.

The third route that might be possible I already hinted at earlier in this paper. It entails the need for a dialectical recognition by both communities of the other as a community of suffering: the demand that Israel recognize its role in the Nakba will find reflection among Palestinians in a growing awareness of and understanding for the salient place the Holocaust memory occupies among the Jewish community in Israel. This is a dialectics Edward Said was one of the first to highlight:

> What Israel does to the Palestinians it does against a background, not only of the long-standing Western tutelage over Palestine and Arabs [...] but also against a background of an equally long-standing and equally unfaltering anti-Semitism that in this century produced the Holocaust of the European Jews. We cannot fail to connect the horrific history of anti-Semitic massacres to the establishment of Israel; nor can we fail to understand the depth, the extent and the overpowering legacy of its suffering and despair that informed the postwar Zionist movement.[27]

27   Edward Said, *The Politics of Dispossession* (London: Chatto and Windus, 1994), p. 167.

Said immediately follows this by stating:

> But it is no less appropriate for Europeans and Americans today, who support Israel because of the wrong committed against the Jews, to realize that support for Israel has included, and still includes, support for the exile and dispossession of the Palestinian people.[28]

The universalization of the Holocaust memory, the deconstruction of the way Zionism and the state of Israel have been manipulating this memory, and an end on the Palestinian side to denying the Holocaust and underrating its significance are three elements that for Israeli Jews could open the road to the mutual empathy Said talks about.[29]

However, more may be needed to bring Israelis to recognize their role as victimizers. First of all, as I outlined above the self-image of the victim has been and continues to be deeply rooted in the collective conduct of Israel's political elite. It is the source the state tends to tap for moral international and world Jewry's support. In the face of such events as the 1967 war, Israel's 1982 invasion of Lebanon, Israel's brutal suppression of the first Intifada of 1989–1993 and its even more lethal approach to the al-Aqza Intifada that erupted in 2000, the self image of a 'righteous' Israel and of the modern David–vs.–Goliath myth has become quite ridiculous to maintain. Second, the fear of losing the position of the victim remains closely intertwined with the fear of having to face the ugly truth of the past and accept its consequences.

In the end, Israel's nuclear arsenal, its gigantic military complex and the octopus of its security services have all proved powerless in the face of the popular resistance of the Intifadas and the guerrilla warfare Israel encountered in Southern Lebanon. They will remain powerless when it comes to confronting the ever-growing disillusionment and radical-

28 Ibid.
29 Peter Novick, *The Holocaust in American Life* (Boston: Houghton Mifflin, 1999); Norman Finkelstein, *The Holocaust Industry, Reflections on the Exploitation of Jewish Suffering* (London: Verso Books, 2000).

ization of Israel's one million Palestinian citizens or the local initiatives of Palestinian refugees no longer able to contain their frustration at the opportunism and corruption of the Palestinian Authority or their dismay at a crumbling PLO. Neither Israel's huge sophisticated weapon arsenal nor the real or imaginary fears that are brought into play will enable Israel to silence its victims and escape the justice they demand. For Israel to put an end to its victimization of the Palestinians, recognize its role as victimizer and accept the Palestinian Other into the national discourse—these I see as constituting the only path that can bring us closer to reconciliation.

Reflections on Contemporary Palestinian History

Jamil Hilal

Palestinian historiography can largely be divided into two main strands, according to the way they build their narratives: one that adopts a vocabulary of surrender and defeat, and a second that highlights heroism and resistance. The 'defeat' narrative usually goes back to the failed rebellion of the people of Palestine against the rule of Ibrahim Pasha in 1834, i.e., it starts before the onset of Zionist colonialism in the 1880s. It will then incorporate all the revolts and uprisings that were intended—but failed—to put an end to the encroaching Zionist colonization of Palestine and to thwart the British policy that supported the creation of a 'Jewish national homeland' there. In the same vein, it will single out the 1936–1939 Revolt and the 1947–1949 war. Veiling the enormity of the defeat and the depth of the tragedy it brought upon the Palestinians, the latter is inscribed in the Palestinian collective memory—and in Arab political discourse—as 'al-Nakba', the Catastrophe. The 'defeat' narrative inevitably includes also the armed confrontations between the Palestinian resistance movement and the Arab states: the battles of September 1970 and 1971 in Jordan, the involvement of the PLO in the civil war in Lebanon and the de-

Author's note: This is an edited and updated version of an article that first appeared in Arabic in the special Nakba issue of the literary and theoretical quarterly *Al-Karmil* 55-56 (Spring-Summer 1998), pp.11-32.

struction of Palestinian refugee camps there. The invasion by Israel of
Lebanon in 1982 and the siege and bombardment of Beirut are re-
counted as yet another defeat for Palestinian resistance, deepened by
the Sabra and Shatila massacres and then also by the armed attacks the
Amal movement (a Lebanese Shiite political faction) carried out between 1985 and 1987 against the refugee camps in Beirut. It then
moves on to the failure of the first Intifada to achieve its objectives and
the Oslo Accords that only succeeded in setting back the Palestinian
national project further. Narrated as defeats, all the events I have listed
are viewed against the backdrop of national liberation movements
elsewhere that did achieve political independence.

The second strand narrates Palestinian history in terms of resistance,
heroism and sacrifice, and explains how the Palestinians were barred
from achieving their political objectives by the skewed historical circumstances and the imbalance of power that confronted them. The
Palestinians are portrayed here as the victims of various schemes—generally supported by international forces safeguarding their
own regional interests—that conspired to rob them of their homeland
and drive them into exile. The Palestinian people are seen as up against
colossal forces and tragic circumstances that, despite their own obdu-
rate and heroic resistance and the enormous sacrifices they made,
succeeded in depriving them of the national rights almost all other
peoples in the world enjoy. Hence, the emphasis on the uniqueness of
the Palestinian case. Hence also, the prominence of the term
'Nakba'—as it implies that the events of 1948 were the outcome of a
grievous destiny or the joint conspiracy of tyrannical forces.

Not surprisingly, the two narratives differ in the way they prioritize
events leading up to and following the Nakba. The first, for example,
will stress the lack of organization and the divisions and level of incompetence found among the leadership of the Palestinian national
movement as part of the explanation why the 1936 rebellion failed.
The second narrative highlights the acts of defiance, resistance and
heroism on the part of the destitute Palestinian peasants and workers
who, equipped with only primitive kinds of weapons but with tremendous courage, had confronted British Imperial army troops who
had crushed them with the brute force of the sophisticated artillery,

tanks and fighter planes they had at their disposal. The first narrative centres on the defeat of the rebellion and on its failure to achieve independence and an end to Zionist immigration into Palestine. It dwells on the weakening of the Palestinian national movement and the divisions and rivalries among its leadership, the destruction of the Palestinian economy that followed and the heavy human losses the Palestinian rebels incurred. For the second narrative, what counts most is the degree of courage the Palestinians revealed against overwhelming odds in resisting British occupation, Zionist colonization and the collusive attitude of Arab regimes. But where both narratives converge is in their unanimous agreement on the tragedy that was the outcome—the 1947–1948 war.

Narrating Palestinian history in terms of either recurring defeat and humiliation or sustained heroism and resistance entails, of course, a naive simplification. It reflects an attitude that views Palestinian history in essentialist terms—Palestinians appear as a people history has condemned to either constant defeat and/or permanent resistance. Both narratives relegate history to the realm of the mythical and politics to the domain of destiny. Neither allows for a pluralistic narration of history. What I want to argue here is that Palestinian history cannot be squeezed into one singular narrative, not even as a meta-narrative, because of the diversity and richness of the episodes in which it unfolded prior to, but even more so following, the Nakba. What is needed are attempts to narrate the history of Palestine in ways that will incorporate multiple events, will tease out different cross relationships and will do justice to plural contexts, and so from the past will extract new meanings for the present.

Two Irreconcilable Political Projects

A key approach to understanding the events that led up to and followed the Nakba is to view them as embodying a collision between two national projects. In this clash it was the Zionist project that came out on top, proclaiming success in the form of the Jewish state (Israel) the Zionists went on to establish on the land of Palestine. The success of the Zionists meant the defeat of the Palestinian national project. We can point to reasons for this defeat. For example, the Zionist project possessed a far superior organizational and material base, commanded the necessary logistical support and benefited from the configuration of favourable international and regional conditions. The Palestinian national project, on the other hand, even though it had the advantage that it owned the land and was rooted in the people that belonged to that land, enjoyed no such favourable conditions. In other words, the Palestinian national project was partly defeated in 1948 not because the Palestinians were unable to put up strong enough resistance to the Zionist project, but because that resistance lacked what it took to turn the odds in their favour: the agents of the Zionist project not only were far superior in the way they were organized, equipped and mobilized—they had international support on their side, and they were helped, indirectly, by the horrors of the Holocaust.[1]

How do we by-pass the dualism of defeat/resistance when narrating our history as Palestinians? We can narrate that history and do justice to all its forms of tragic defeat and heroic resistance, of dispossession and exile, of incompetence and shortcomings, and pay tribute to the normal ephemeral events of people's daily lives and so on, if we adopt the paradigms, concerns, issues and challenges of today. This, of course, is what good novelists do. One immediately thinks of the rich and colourful variety of the Palestinian characters and events we encounter in the stories by Ghassan Kanafani, Emil Habibi, Jabra Ibrahim Jabra, Antoine Shammas, Sahar Khalifeh, Rashad Abu Shawer and Elias Khoury, among others. It is perhaps even more true for Pales-

---

1   To give but one telling example, after having toured the Middle East, the United Nations Special Committee on Palestine (UNSCOP), established in May 1947 to help the Security Council decide on the future of Palestine after British withdrawal, visited the 'displaced persons camps [in Europe] where the Holocaust survivors had been gathered. [...] It does seem that those members who at the beginning of the inquiry had been quite neutral became pro-Zionist after their visit to the camps'; Ilan Pappé, *The Making of the Arab-Israeli Conflict, 1947-51* (London and New York: I.B. Taurus, 1992), pp. 27-28.

tinian post-Nakba poetry, which may choose to portray the Palestinian condition in either tragic or heroic terms, but which often resonates with the sentiments of ordinary Palestinian men and women and re-counts the numerous worries and personal dramas that make up their daily lives. The difference in impact of the 1948 defeat on the Palestinian cultural field and on the political field may well be due to the fact that the Palestinian cultural field has always been an integral part of the wider Arab cultural field—it transcends the constraints of the political fields. By saying this I do not, of course, aim to minimize the influence the political exerts on the themes and images of the cultural, but I do think that when we write the history of Palestine, we do well to adopt some of the insights our writers and poets offer us.[2]

The struggle the Palestinians waged against the Zionist project during the 1920s, 30s and 40s is a manifestation of their own project of building a state. Today, in the early years of the twenty-first century, state building remains as central as ever to Palestinians. It presents a challenge to our critical historians and social scientists for the salient questions it raises about how the state relates to society, and then also of course how society relates to the individual. These are not questions about economy and governance, but about freedom from external oppression and about emancipation from internal despotism.

The project of building a Palestinian national entity, in its early phases, evolved as a response to the incipient colonial settlement activities of

---

2   See, for example, Ibrahim Muhawi's Introduction to his translation of Mahmoud Darwish's *Memory for Forgetfulness*, where he writes: 'Darwish [...] offers us a multivocal text that resembles a broken mirror, reassembled to present the viewer with vying possibilities of clarity and fracture. [...] Each segment can stand on its own, yet each acquires a relational or dialectical meaning, a history, that is contingent upon the context provided for it by all other segments of the work. [...] Suspended between wholeness and fracture, the text, like Palestine, is a crossroads of competing meanings'; Mahmoud Darwish, *Memory for Forgetfulness. August, Beirut, 1982*, translated with an Introduction by Ibrahim Muhawi (Berkeley/Los Angeles/London: University of California Press, 1995), pp. xvi-xvii.

the Zionist movement in Palestine in the 1880s. It acquired momentum after the first world war with the collapse of the Ottoman Empire and the European colonialist invasion of Palestine and the rest of the Arab world in the form of so-called mandates. The project proceeded quickly, given the all too obvious objectives of the Zionist movement and the heightened pace and widening scope of its activities in Palestine following the Balfour Declaration. Like all other colonized peoples, the Palestinians drew for their national programme on the common model of the territorial nation-state. As this model became 'globalized', it was hailed as the only respectable form in which human beings can preserve or develop the actual and imagined solidarities or identities they view as particularly their own—national, linguistic, ethnic, religious, cultural. The nation-state came to symbolize independence, opening the way for the modern development of society and culture. It became a precondition for having one's collective rights recognized by the international community and being allowed to participate in the latter's activities—from membership in the United Nations to competing in the Olympic Games.

From the outset the Zionist movement was bent on establishing a 'Jewish' nation-state in Palestine. For the Zionists, the Jews of the world formed, not just a people sharing a religion, but one nation. Hence, although they were, in fact, themselves colonizing another people's land, the Zionists employed the discourse adopted by national liberation movements throughout the colonized world. In other words, Zionism articulated its project in terms of liberation and independence, but at the same time reconstructed a distant past to justify what was a blatantly colonialist project—the creation of a settler state in Palestine.

Territorial states or projects of nation states engender their own 'political fields' where political parties and social movements, with political programs, objectives, and stakes become active.[3] Political

3   Cf. Sami Zubaida, *Islam, The People and The State* (London-New York, 1993);
    describing the different patterns of formation the modern nation state took on
    after it was implanted in the Middle East, Zubaida explains: 'Alongside these state
    forms there developed a whole complex of political models, vocabularies, or-

parties and social movements compete for control over this field, in particular over the distribution of the resources of the territorial state, as such fields establish the rules of the game, define the dominant discourse and decide internal conflicts. Political fields generate their own language, symbols and sets of rules. They do not remain static, however, but are subject to constant change given the inherent conflicts they call up. That is, they are exposed to invasion and encroachment from forces representing social groups that have been excluded but that will keep trying to enter the field as players so as to change the dominant rules of the game. They are also affected by the ever-changing socio-economic and cultural reality they are part of and are liable to be impacted by regional and global processes. The project or the establishment of a political entity/state yields its 'imagined community', i.e., the membership of the social formation that has been defined by the state. Local media, novels, stories, poetry, songs, theatre and film play a crucial role in defining the features and boundaries of this 'imagined community', highlighting nation-ness as a cultural artifact. Population censuses, national maps, ID cards, passports, and various national symbols (the flag, the national anthem, the local currency, the postage stamp, etc.) further help define it.[4]

ganisations and techniques which have established and animated what I call a *political field* of organization, mobilization, agitation and struggle. The vocabularies of this field are those of the nation, nationality and nationalism, of popular sovereignty, democracy, liberty, legality and representation, of political parties and parliamentary institutions, as well as various ideological pursuits of nationalism, Islam and socialism' (pp. 145-146).

4   See, of course, Benedict Anderson, *Imagined Communities. Reflections on the Origin and Spread of Nationalism* (London & New York: Verso, 1991 [2nd ed.]); specifically Ch. 10, 'Census, Map, Museum' (pp. 163-185) which 'analyzes the way in which, quite unconsciously, the nineteenth-century colonial state (and policies that its mindset encouraged) dialectically engendered the grammar of the nationalisms that eventually rose to combat it' (p. xiv).

Problematics of the Pre-1948 Palestinian Political Field

The colonialist settlement activities of the Zionists in Palestine, the protection their patron, Britain, extended by supporting 'a Jewish national homeland' there and the simultaneous emergence of a number of territorial states in the Arab world—predicated on the independence the French and British Mandates were supposed to 'prepare' them for—set the stage for the appearance of a distinct Palestinian national political field. Naturally, this field, too, was constructed around the project of an independent Palestinian state.

However, the Palestinian political field differed from the other political fields in the region because, simultaneously and on the same land, the Zionist project was busy establishing a state of its own intended for an other community—'imagined' by the Zionist movement as the 'Jewish nation' it set out to create in Palestine. This 'imagined community' had its origin in the Jewish nationalist movement (Zionism) which had emerged in Eastern Europe following the wave of anti-Semitic pogroms that swept southern Russia and the Ukraine in the 1880s in which many Jews lost their lives. But the Zionist project only became possible when in the wake of the first world war the British realized the Zionists could help them implement their colonialist strategy in the region and East Asia and thus decided to give them their support. The Zionist project further gained a significant symbolic but also practical dimension during and following the second world war, in the aftermath of the Holocaust. But it soon came into sharp conflict with the Palestinian national project, that is, with Palestinians whose consciousness of their specific (Palestinian) and generalized (Arab) identity made them aware of the dangers looming ahead. As it based itself on a national religious model, Zionism had no problem in linking itself to the political colonialist structure the British Mandate imposed on Palestine. In other words, the Palestinian national project was directly confronted by both the imperialist policies of the British and the colonialist project of the Zionists.

Upon its creation in May 1948, the state of Israel lost no time in establishing itself as the natural successor of the Zionist movement by expelling as many of the indigenous population as possible from the nearly 80 per cent of Palestine it had taken over. Building colonial settlements and encouraging Jews to immigrate to Palestine remained an integral part of its policy. And since until today Zionism considers its 'national' project to be as yet incomplete, Israel has never agreed to define internationally accepted borders. Typical, too, is that it continues to hook its strategy onto that of the largest imperialist state in the world, the USA, which after the second world war took over from Britain as the dominant imperialist power in the region.

The 1947–48 War: The Palestinian National Project Defeated

The seeds of the Palestinian national project may be traced to the pan-Arab national identity we see developing within the framework of the Arab renaissance movement in the mid-nineteenth century and to the Arab resistance to the Ottoman 'Turkification' policy at the beginning of the twentieth. Some Palestinian historians highlight the significance for the development of Palestinian identity of the city of Jerusalem because of the special role it played in the lives of the people of Palestine. Other historians single out the revolt against the occupation of Palestine by Ibrahim Pasha, the son of Egypt's governor, Muhammad Ali, in the 1830s. But the history of the Palestinian national movement truly begins when we find organized endeavours emerging among the indigenous people of Palestine to create their own territorial state there. As we already saw, given its specific national political field this project came in conflict not only with the British Mandate, but also with the Zionist project. Again, unlike the Zionists, the Palestinians could anchor their political field in an existing society that had its own language, dialects, traditional dress and cuisine, one whose culture and history were deeply intertwined with the history of the entire region. The Zionist project differed in each and every one of these aspects. The Zionists wanted to create a society of immigrant settlers from a number of—often vastly different—societies, cultures and languages. Here then lies the crux: How did a project with such 'unpromising' features succeed in defeating an indigenous national project whose emancipatory features could nurture from a long-established society that for centuries had been an integral part of the wider Arab world?

I believe the answer to lie in the different nature and aims of the forces and alliances supporting the two projects and in the politico-historical terms in which the conflict unfolded. Both the British and the Zionist presence in Palestine were propelled by societies that had gone through industrial, technological and social revolutions which had helped consolidate them as modern nation-states. Palestinian society, on the other hand, confronted the presence of these two modern forces with the resources of a mostly traditional peasant society led by a class of city-dwelling large landowners, merchants and religious leaders. Palestinian society was as yet unfamiliar with modern forms of societal organization and lacked the political institutions, legal and administrative frameworks or the organizational apparatus of the modern state.

Still, between the two world wars Palestinian society saw rapid change partly in response to the European colonial presence and the quickening pace at which its economy became linked to the world market. Growing urbanization brought with it new educational institutions, a vibrant press, various forms of modern culture, and a sizeable working class that arose simultaneously with an underclass of destitute peasants. Moreover, as the struggle for independence intensified, local political parties and movements entered the political field and tried to seize control from the colonial state. These Palestinian political parties were not unified in their vision of pertinent national action: some saw in British colonialism the primary adversary while for others the Zionist settler movement was the main enemy. There was consensus over the need to halt Jewish immigration to Palestine, but this did not mean everyone agreed on how to deal with the British colonial state. Some called for an approach of reconciliation with the colonial state (the Istiqlal, i.e., Independence party), others instead wanted to direct the main front of the struggle against the British (the Izz ad-Din al-Qassam movement). Changing tactics among the political elite that activated the Palestinian political field coincided with the clannish alliances that invariably put up their heads. Admittedly, this was one of the main weaknesses of the Palestinian movement, eagerly capitalized on by both the British colonial authorities (who had extensive experience in implementing 'divide-and-rule' policies) and the

Zionist movement (that was quickly developing such experience). It was also a main contributory factor to the defeat of the Palestinian national movement in 1948.

The Palestinian elite during this period focussed primarily on trying to stop Jewish immigration, but failed to offer a vision of the future of Palestinian society. It denied that the Jews, as Jews, had any political or moral right to settle in Palestine so as to build a state there, but while it called for the establishment of an independent Palestinian state, it never offered a blue print of the kind of a state it envisioned. The elite did call upon Palestinians to place their national allegiance above all other allegiances (regional, family, and religious), but then showed itself incapable of mobilizing and restructuring society so as to optimally face the dangers that so clearly loomed ahead. For example, it did nothing to stop local and absentee landowners—people belonging to the same societal stratum!—from selling land to the Zionist movement. It was also completely nonplussed by the civil and military institutions the Zionists were erecting—crucial among them in the 1920s the Jewish National Fund—and, even more fatally, had no idea of how to deal with them. It failed to establish national institutions of its own to challenge those the Zionist movement was busy putting in place and never succeeded in generating political grassroots organizations to force the British to change or revert their policies. Most damaging perhaps was its inability to create a political vision that could somehow stymie the objectives of the Zionist movement and neutralize its British protector, for example by calling for a unified state in Palestine where Jews and Arabs would live side by side. When the Palestinian movement did endorse such a vision two decades following the Nakba, i.e., after the shock of the 1967 war, it was addressing a completely new situation and facing a totally different balance of power from the ones that existed in the 1930s and 40s.

Lack of a National Strategy

With only a few exceptions, the predominant form the activities of the Palestinian national movement took under British colonial administration was that of protest. But here, too, we find that this protest movement lacked a clearly defined overall strategy and, instead of taking the initiative, tended merely to react to policies, events, and situations as these evolved. This while it confronted a Zionist movement whose vision of how to expand its economic, social and military assets in the country and cultivate its international alliances was as focussed as it was unwavering.

Moreover, the leadership of the Palestinian movement somehow isolated itself from the changes that were taking place in Palestinian society. By the early 1930s Palestinians had become resentful of the divisions amongst the political elite and their inability to set out an appropriate course of action vis-à-vis the challenges Palestinian society was now facing. Impoverished workers who crowded the cities, particularly in Jaffa and Haifa, and peasant farmers crippled by the debts they had incurred to merchants and usurers began showing their frustration. Discontent was growing too among sectors of the intelligentsia—in the early 1930s fourteen different Arabic newspapers were being published in Palestine—who found themselves excluded from the decision-making centres and who were totally dismayed by what was taking place. The coastal cities, oriented as they were towards Europe, developed much faster than the country's other population centres, rural or urban. Between 1922 and 1944, in Jaffa and Haifa the Arab Palestinian population increased threefold compared with a twofold average population increase in Palestine as a whole. As Jaffa and Haifa were transformed into commercial, industrial, and cultural centres and the Jerusalemite families held the hegemonic leadership of the national movement, the internal mountain towns of Nablus and Hebron began to feel the impact of the rivalry and friction that followed. The working class grew rapidly in the 1930s and 1940s, as did the trade union movement—its membership comprised 20 per cent of the country's total wage labour by the end of the second world war—but they remained excluded from any form of adequate representation in the Palestinian movement.

We find these transformations clearly reflected in the political movements and uprisings that were typical of the 1930s and in the modern political discourse that began to emerge. The most prominent and popular of these movements was that of Shaykh Izz ad-Din al-Qassam, which supported and helped arm the peasants in their struggle against the colonialist policies of the British, who crushed his group with brutal force in 1935. Both the impact of Izz ad-Din al-Qassam and the popular rebellion that followed in 1936 took the leadership of the national movement—still tied to the traditional 'politics of notables'—by surprise and succeeded in deeply shaking it. But it remained incapable of creating vital national institutions or generating a tactical understanding of how to deal with—let alone, stay abreast of—the accelerating pace of events. Briefly put, it adopted the slogan of an 'independent secular state' in Mandatory Palestine, but did nothing to translate this into a comprehensive social and national project.

The 1948 Defeat

The deterioration of economic conditions of Palestinians in the 1930s, the continuing repressive policies of the British and the acceleration of Jewish immigration (in 1935 alone more than 60,000 Jewish immigrants arrived in Palestine) were behind the popular rebellion that erupted in 1936. It broke out largely spontaneously and would last until 1939 but few of those involved had drawn the necessary lessons from the way British troops only a few months earlier had quelled the Izz ad-Din al-Qassam movement and had murdered Shaykh al-Qassam himself. Though it was one of the most significant popular revolts to erupt in the Arab east between the two world wars, it was this lack of organizational preparation that ultimately spelled its failure. And it was this failure—the British killed or exiled most of the Palestinian leadership—that was critically to hamper the ability of Palestinians to tackle the catastrophic events of 1947–48.[5]

---

5   On the revolt, see, e.g., Mahmoud Yazbak, 'From Poverty to Revolt: Economic Factors in the Outbreak of the 1936 Rebellion in Palestine' (*Middle Eastern Studies* 36/3 [July 2000], pp. 93-119), where he describes how 'bitter resentment and long-simmering discontent among Palestine's fellahin [...] flared up into a full-blown revolt against British oppression and Zionist usurpation. Thus the eruption came from below—and it was the crowds who would dictate the moves of the rebellion, *the traditional leadership falling in behind* when they realized that because of its unmistakable nationalist overtones popular anger and frustration could also turn against them' (p. 109; emphasis added).

The pressure local national committees generated when they called the general strike in 1936 led to the formation of the Arab Higher Committee, mostly made up of notables and representatives of the rising professional middle class. But instead of acting as a government for Palestine and creating the necessary conditions (including economic measures) that could help the strike to succeed—for example, by setting up national representative institutions that could spearhead a civil disobedience campaign and support the armed revolt—and instead of developing some form of military capability, all the committee did was to present to the British authorities a list of demands calling for an end to Jewish immigration, a halt to the sale of land to Jews, and political independence for the Palestinian people. In other words, the Arab Higher Committee approached British colonialism in much the same way as the Arab national movements at the time approached their occupiers in the Arab East: in terms of the political independence the Mandate was supposed to lead to. The Arab Higher Committee did not see, or ignored, that the situation in Palestine was vastly different in nature: instead of their independence, the creation of a Jewish state there could only lead to the uprooting of the Palestinians from their land. Only thus can one explain why the committee was quick to respond to the request of the Arab kings and emirs (in Jordan, Iraq and Saudi Arabia, all three within Britain's 'sphere of influence') to bring an end to the general strike. In so doing, the committee acted in the narrow interests of most of the classes it represented (large landowners, big merchants and notables). Furthermore, the way it handled the Peel Commission report, whose solution to the worsening situation in Palestine was to divide the country into two states, was devoid of even a modicum of political shrewdness: again, while it rejected the plan out of hand, the Arab Higher Committee never put on the table the alternative of an independent Palestinian state.

Almost immediately upon the outbreak of the armed rebellion it was clear that Britain would react, not by engaging in dialogue, but by ruthlessly crushing its fighting force. For this purpose it marshalled the assistance of the Zionist forces. Even so, in the first phase of the uprising the Palestinians managed to achieve tangible successes and, during the summer and fall of 1938, succeeded in taking control of most of the urban and mountain centres in Palestine. At the same time, as the thrust of the revolt was located in the countryside, its 'peasant' character began to have its impact on the cohesiveness of Palestinian society as a whole (for example, the men's traditional headdress was enforced on urban residents, the hijab imposed on women, the use of electricity banned, debts and payment of rent cancelled, a kind of tax from the rich introduced, etc.). In other words, the rebellion never developed into a unified political movement nor did it proffer a vision that spoke to and could galvanize the various sectors of society. Britain summarily brought in land troops consisting of 20,000 soldiers—a large force for a Palestinian population that did not exceed one million—supported by warplanes and artillery and seconded by Zionist forces. It also manipulated the divisions within the Palestinian leadership and took advantage of the collaboration of some Palestinian groups (certain notables had formed anti-uprising forces which they called 'peace brigades') to quell the revolt. Nevertheless, Britain was sufficiently impressed by the force of the rebellion to issue a 'White Paper' in May 1939 that called for a limit to Jewish immigration, restrictions on the sale of land to Jews and the establishment of an independent Palestinian state within ten years, with a transitional period towards self-rule. However, without even stopping to consider how serious the British were or examining the potential advantages it contained, the Arab Higher Committee rejected the White Paper, thus further weakening the national movement and effectively aborting the aims of the rebellion. When four months later the British declared war on Germany, the revolt had been subdued.

Thus, the 1936 popular uprising, which had challenged the most powerful empire in the world at the time, had achieved none of its objectives when it was stifled in 1939. More than 5,000 Palestinians had been killed and more than 14,000 wounded. Crucially, it culminated in the dispersal and exile of the Palestinian leadership while no new leadership had as yet had a chance to emerge and replace it. Still, the 1936–39 *thawra*, as it is called in Palestinian discourse, is engraved in the Palestinian collective memory as a major act of defiance and resistance and elevated the Palestinian peasant to the status of heroic figure.

The first Intifada, which erupted in December 1987, similarly established the 'children of the stones' as symbols of defiance and resistance, much as in 1982 the 'RPJ kids' became symbols of Palestinian resistance against the Israeli invasion of Lebanon. Significantly, both the 1987–1993 Intifada and the al-Aqza Intifada of 2000 were quick to establish symbolic links with the 1936 rebellion, unifying Palestinian history as a history of struggle against Zionist colonialism and towards independence. The 1936 rebellion in particular served to establish Palestinian nationalism as a fact and both Intifadas borrowed part of its symbols (e.g., the *kufiyyeh*, and the name of Shaykh Izz ad-Din al-Qassam) and forms of resistance (especially the general strike). Israel, for its part, would adopt many of the brutally repressive measures the British had employed to quell the uprising of 1936, despite the non-lethal character displayed by the first Intifada (and the early months of the second Intifada), where throwing stones at heavily armed Israeli soldiers was the dominant method of resistance (in the 1936–1939 revolt stones had been secondary to firearms). Among the punitive measures the British used at the time against the Palestinians and the Israelis implement until today we find deportation, house demolition, administrative detention, shooting with 'live' ammunition at unarmed demonstrators, and banning political and popular activities.

The 1936–1939 revolt left Palestinian society exhausted and de-moralized—much as happened at the end of the first Intifada and, many argue, as is happening with the second. In 1939 Palestine's economy was devastated, its political society critically weakened (given the deportation and escape of many political leaders, most of whom never returned to Palestine) and its military capacity reduced to near zero. The sad irony is that in the end it was the Zionist movement that benefited from the general strike and the armed uprising as the Jewish settler community began implementing a policy of using exclusively 'Hebrew labour' and solidifying its separate 'Jewish' economy.[6] The

---

6   On how the Zionist ideological and institutional basis for separatism had already crystallized by the late 1920s, see Barbara J. Smith, *The Roots of Separatism in Palestine. British Economic Policy, 1920-1929* (Syracuse, NY, Syracuse University Press, 1993): 'That the Zionist settler movement, unable to make much headway under Ottoman rule, was nurtured by and eventually thrived within the British colonial context is undeniable. Within a few years of the inception of a British Administration, the Zionists had the beginnings of a national economic base underpinning their demonstrably nationalistic ideology' (pp. 3-4).

Zionists also succeeded in vastly improving their military capability since in return for the assistance they had given in oppressing the Palestinian uprising the British provided the Jews with the necessary military equipment.

Burdened by this legacy of cultural, economic and political disintegration the Palestinians faced the challenges and dangers of 1947 and 1948. For two decades they had often appeared as the most defiantly militant of the peoples British empirical rule had subjugated worldwide, now they seemed to have become docile and compliant. Before long, Palestinian society reverted to the pattern of divisive rule that pitted competing localized formations against one another (coastal town versus mountain town, village versus city), highlighted by the constant bickering between traditional notable families. Even the urban trade union movement, which in the early 1940s had been strong enough to worry the British, came under attack from traditional notables who tried to marginalize it. It is true that in 1947 and 1948 the Palestinians rallied together in their opposition to the Zionist project, but this unity commanded no effective organization, let alone a unified strategy or form of mobilization. By 1947 thousands of affluent families were leaving Palestine, at a time when tensions between Palestinians, Zionists and the British were mounting and Jewish immigration reached its highest peak—as most Western countries, notably the United States, had set quotas on Jewish immigration, it was Palestine that was taking in Jewish survivors of the Holocaust. There remained only a handful of notables and dignitaries who had been part of the leadership of the national movement during previous decades and a small number of new leaders who had emerged during the second world war. In other words, the Palestinians entered the 1947–48 war without a national leadership and a political strategy and with no fighting capability to speak of. These are major factors that help explain why the Palestinians responded the way they did as soon as the Zionist military forces began implementing their expulsion plans. There is no doubt that the Zionists' use of force and the premeditated massacres their military units committed played a decisive part in driving the majority of the Palestinians out and away from their homes, villages and towns. But it may well be that the ethnic cleansing of Palestine could have been resisted and its effects minimized, had the Palestinian leadership not been in such total disarray.

Their forced expulsion in 1948 is a cogent factor behind the way Palestinians, especially in the Diaspora, hold 'the land' sacred and behind the Diaspora's image of Palestine as a 'paradise lost', which is particularly strong in the refugee communities scattered in camps around Palestine. It may also have helped constitute the *fida'i* (freedom fighter) as a salient heroic symbol. In the Palestinian territories Israel occupied in 1967 the emphasis shifted to *sumud*, 'steadfastness'—staying put on the land—that during the Intifada became so strongly interwoven with the discourse of resistance.

The Roots of Defeat

Thus, I locate the factors for the 1948 defeat more in the weakness of the Palestinian national movement and its leadership than in the extraordinary political prowess of the Zionist movement. The Zionists also witnessed political confusion and internal splits—for example, the cooperation, even if short lived, of the Hagana with the British against the Irgun[7] after the escalating Zionist attacks on British forces in 1946. But the strength of the Zionist movement obviously rested on its successful institutionalization, its high level of mobilization and the vision and prodigious initiatives of its leadership, as well as on the way it succeeded in manipulating a whole range of international factors. Nowhere in the activities of the Palestinian national movement do we find anything approaching a process of building national, political, military, civil, and financial institutions at a time when the Zionist movement was busily involved in all of these. Neither did the Palestinian movement draw the necessary lessons from the failure of the

---

7   Irgun Zva Leumi (IZL), 'National Military Organization', a paramilitary Jewish underground unit established in 1936, that twelve years later, on 9 April 1948, would perpetrate the massacre at Deir Yassin.

1936 uprising, nor did it act upon the implications of the way Palestinian society was being transformed during and after the second world war by such momentous events as the collapse of the British Mandate in 1947 and the UN Partition Resolution of 29 November 1947.

Any comparison between the size of the Palestinian Arab population (about 1.4 million) and that of the Jewish population (about 620,000) in 1947/8 is misleading, if only because the demographic structures of the two populations were qualitatively different. Zionist immigration into Palestine produced a Jewish community with a majority in the arms-carrying age that was one and half times larger than the same age group among the Palestinians. On the other hand, the Palestinians were living in their homeland and constituted a majority there—until, that is, the Zionist forces in late March 1948 began carrying out their ethnic cleansing strategy.

When the Arab Higher Committee responded with a general strike two days after the United Nations had passed its partition resolution, it seemed as if it was copying the experience of the 1936 revolution. Even though it announced it would set up coordinating committees and form a national guard, it adopted a defensive strategy at the time when the Zionist forces were preparing for total war. When fighting erupted between Zionist and British troops and the British Mandatory administration collapsed, the Palestinian leadership reacted with little more than acts of protest. At no stage did it develop a plan of its own for the establishment of an independent Palestinian state, even when it had become absolutely clear to all sides that the Zionist leadership was gearing up towards creating a Jewish state in Palestine. Hence, the confrontation with the Zionist military forces took predominantly the form of clashes with unco-ordinated armed brigades that lacked a central strategy. When they began to realize that no national mobilization effort was underway, defenseless Palestinian civilians decided to move out of the line of attack—fighting raged particularly near Jewish settlements and coastal towns—and sought safety in the mountainous areas. Some of the wealthy families began leaving Palestine altogether. That these people were sure they were leaving their homes only temporarily again poignantly illustrates the absence of leadership and of any form of mobilization. With hindsight we can also point to the rising level of internal migration in the opposite direction that had become the trend in the previous two decades—i.e., from villages to coastal towns—as a first harbinger of the impending Palestinian defeat: these first waves of migration vacated areas of strategic importance to the Zionist project. However much the Palestinian leadership that had remained in Palestine tried to oppose or halt it, this internal migration seemed the only 'rational' response to the vicious war the Zionists unleashed against a Palestinian society that was totally unprepared for it. As such, internal migration seems to have paved the way for the ensuing waves of emigration to outside Palestine. The latter, however, were instigated by a deliberate Zionist policy of massacres, terror, co-ercion, and psychological warfare intended to create large areas void of Palestinians.

By the end of 1947 it was clear that the Zionist leadership was intent on waging a total war whose main aim was the ethnic cleansing of Palestine so as to make room for the Jewish state. The Deir Yassin massacre, which occurred on 9 April 1948 after the village (near Jer-usalem) had signed a peace treaty with the local Zionist troops, to-gether with similar massacres such as in the village of Tantura near Haifa, created a conception among Palestinians of the Jewish 'Other' as a treacherous killer of defenceless women, children and the elderly. Psychologically this played into the hands of the Zionists. Similarly useful, but among their own community, had been the Hebron mas-sacre of Jews in 1929, which served the Zionists to promote an image of Palestinians as hateful killers of innocent Jews.

As the war became more severe, Palestinian society began to im-plode. Though there were some noticeable military achievements by Palestinian fighters towards the end of 1947 and in the beginning of 1948, these victories were short lived. Despite his popularity, Haj Amin al-Husayni failed to unite the Palestinian forces under a single command and they—as much as he himself—remained without a clue as to the 'logistics' they would need if they were to stand a chance in the ongoing all-out war. The Zionist forces were thus able to exploit to the hilt the three main factors outlined above that worked in their favour: the internal flight of Palestinian civilian population, the lack of co-ordination amongst the Palestinian fighting units, and the absence of a unified national leadership. According to a variety of sources, the size of the Palestinian fighting units may never have been more than 15,000, including Abd al-Qader al-Husayni's Holy Jihad army and irregular armed groups in the villages. In no way did it reach the size of the Jewish Hagana forces of 35,000. By early 1948, after establishing a regular army in addition to Jewish militias, reserves and breakaway terrorist groups, the Zionist leadership had mobilized a military force that in number and combat power exceeded all Palestinian and Arab forces put together (the total number of Arab forces that came to the defence of Palestine upon the declaration of the establishment of the state of Israel never reached 15,000).

The prominent Arab states at the time of the 1947–48 war did not attach much importance to the creation of a Palestinian state. The Arab League opposed the idea of setting up an ad-hoc Palestinian government the moment the British would withdraw from Palestine and turned down a request for a loan to set up a Palestinian administration. It intentionally ignored the Arab Higher Committee, kept the Arab Salvation Army, led by Fawzi al-Qawqji, away from the command of the leadership of the Committee, and restricted the movements of al-Husayni's Holy Jihad army, thus preventing any coordination between Qawqji's Salvation Army and the Palestinian fighting units. Finally, it was no secret that because of his ambitions to annex parts of Palestine to Jordan, King Abdallah had been coordinating his policies with the Zionists and, crucially, kept his British-trained Arab Legion largely out of the fighting.[8]

Reconstructing Palestinian Identity

When the Palestinian national project was defeated in 1948, this was not just one more defeat in the ongoing confrontation between an indigenous liberation movement and a colonialist or settler force. It was

8   See, e.g., Avi Shlaim, *Collusion across the Jordan:King Abdullah, the Zionist Movement, and the Partition of Palestine* (Oxford: Clarendon Press, 1988).

the defeat of a whole society that then fragmented and disappeared as the territorial, cultural and political-economic entity it had been for centuries. The demographic and physical landscape of Palestine changed irrevocably, as the Zionists bulldozed hundreds of Palestinian villages and towns, in their place set up their own colonial settlements and split up or completely transformed Palestinian cities into Jewish ones. Expelled and dispossessed, the indigenous Palestinian people- —i.e., the barely more than 150,000 who remained in Palestine, now Israel, and the close to 800,000 who had fled to neighbouring Arab countries—found themselves governed by different political fields, each pursuing its own specific aims and agendas and involved in its own separate conflicts. Thus, a significant outcome of the 1948 defeat and fragmentation was a substantive social restructuring of the Palestinian people. Palestinian dispersal had its repercussions on the Arab political discourse and on the way the Arab world perceived itself and the Other—the Nakba not only laid bare the weaknesses of Palestinian society and its political elite, but also exposed the vulnerability of the Arab political regimes. The same would happen two decades later with the devastating defeat of the Arab regimes in the war of 1967, whose impact upon the Palestinians would be equally immediate and far ranging.

We can identify three watersheds in the history of the Palestinian people between 1948 and 1967. The first concerns the destruction of the national political field or space during most of this period. At the same time, we find Palestinian identity re-defining itself through mechanisms, discourse and symbols that vary with the conditions each of the main Palestinian communities now confronted. The second is the disappearance of Palestinian coastal cities and with it the control Palestinians had been able to exercise over urban space. After 1948, the remaining Palestinian towns—Hebron, Nablus and Gaza, among others—saw their role in Palestine's political, economic and cultural life almost totally eclipsed. This went hand in hand with the decline of agriculture, traditionally at the heart of Palestinian life and society. The third watershed was emigration, especially from the West Bank and the Gaza Strip, but also from other Palestinian communities—mostly for reasons of employment—that became a permanent feature of people's lives. One result was relatively large Palestinian work communities emerging in some of the Gulf States and permanent communities establishing themselves elsewhere, notably in Jordan.

The 1948 defeat, as I outlined above, dismantled the basic components that had gone into the making of the Palestinian national political field during the Mandate period. Following the defeat of the territorial Arab states in 1967, this national field would reappear, albeit in a completely new form. The Nakba resulted in the creation of Palestinian communities in territorial Arab states that enforced a wide range of restrictions on the expression of Palestinian nationalism and identity. But the liquidation of the Palestinian political field did not, as some historians have claimed, encapsulate the disappearance of Palestinian national identity. Palestinian identity did not disappear in the late 1940s and early 1950s to reappear in the late 1960s with the formation of the PLO. What reappeared in the form of the PLO was a new Palestinian political field linked to a state formation project. While national identity does not necessarily have to be tied to a territorial state, all state formation projects need their form of nationalism. What we find in the case of Palestine is that national identity emerged prior to and in a more radical manner than the state project. I want to suggest that this may well be the reason why Palestinian identity continued to regenerate itself after the Nakba even though the state entity project was delayed until two decades after that event. This explains also the ease with which Jordan in 1948 succeeded in annexing central Palestine—later called the West Bank—and the Gaza Strip found itself under Egyptian rule.

The actual processes of reconstructing Palestinian identity depended on the conditions that confronted each of the main Palestinian communities after 1948. But while this new national identity remained autonomous, i.e., was not connected to a territorial state project for two decades, it was engendered not within its own national political field, but in different political fields belonging to others. Therefore, in the 1950s and 60s the Palestinians had a main stake in the fortunes of pan-nationalism, which we see reflected in the widespread enthusiasm towards the pan-nationalist thesis the Nasserites, the Ba'athis and the Arab Nationalist Movement espoused during these years. Central to this thesis was the elevation of Arab unity and the implementation of socio-economic reform to the status of an emancipatory strategy that meant to undo the legacy of dependency, challenge the imperialist-Israeli Other and liberate Palestine. Most of the leaders of the Arab Nationalist Movement in its various territorial branches, for example, were Palestinian. The Islamic project, which had a limited following amongst Palestinians, shared the antagonism of the pan-nationalist project to the national territorial state. The fact that the pan-nationalist ideology transcended the notion of the territorial state (as did the religious ideology) made it very attractive to Palestinians, since it also promised to protect them from the repression of the existing Arab territorial states, and eventually from the Zionist state. The Palestinian communist faction reshaped itself according to the emerging territorial state formations—Palestinians would belong to an Israeli communist party, a Jordanian communist party, a communist party in the Gaza Strip, a Syrian communist party, etc. In fact, communism among them did not wear a Palestinian national garb until 1981.

One of the significant preludes to the emergence of a specifically Palestinian political field can be found in the support the pan-nationalist—Ba'athi and Nasserite—forces themselves gave to the formation of a Palestinian entity. The motive for this has to do with the strategies of the territorial state, whose structures and potential for re-producing itself perceptibly expanded in the 1950s and 60s (and actually continue to do so until today). The pan-nationalist support for the construction of a Palestinian 'entity' included the Arab Nationalist Movement, established in the early 1960s in the Palestinian region and in 1964 led to the establishment by the Arab League of the PLO. At the same time, the failure of Arab unity projects, most glaringly that between Egypt and Syria in 1961, worked in favour of the construction of a specific national political field. But the crucial element in the reconstruction of the Palestinian political field appeared with the defeat by Israel of the Arab territorial nationalist states in 1967 and the occupation that followed of the whole of Palestine, in addition to the Egyptian and Syrian territories Israel seized.

As outlined above, following the Nakba Palestinian communities became part of the spaces of various political national fields dominated by different territorial states. These fields fluctuated between suspicion of any expression of Palestinian identity or political formation to hostile rejection of these expressions. The 1948 defeat was followed by the annexation of the West Bank to the Kingdom of Jordan with the Gaza Strip coming under Egyptian control. The Palestinian Arab minority in Israel—a significant percentage of whom were subjected to forced internal migration—were given Israeli nationality. But at the same time Israel placed these Palestinians immediately under stifling military rule, until 1966, with severe restrictions placed on freedom of expression, of organization and of movement, as the authorities portrayed them as a 'fifth column', an internal threat to the state (and to its declared Jewish character). The Israeli political elite pursued a policy of suppressing any formation of national identity amongst the Arab minority, cultivating their economic dependency, isolating them from the Jewish community and state institutions and obstructing their urban growth.

Palestinians in the West Bank were granted Jordanian nationality but the regime curbed public expressions of Palestinian identity and nationalism as it saw these as potential threats to the Jordanian state. In the Gaza Strip, Palestinian identity was acknowledged, but Palestinians were restricted in their attempts to form national institutions. In all three cases, government officials promoted traditional clan leadership and local solidarities. In other words, territorial state policies viewed Palestinian identity with suspicion and felt more comfortable with primary identities. In Israel this took the form of dealing with Palestinians not only as clans but also as religious sects and ethnic groups (Circassian, Druze, Bedouin, etc.), with the government pursuing an active policy of separation.[9] In Jordan, the

---

9   See, for example, Kais M. Firro, *The Druzes in the Jewish State. A Brief History* (Leiden: E.J. Brill, 1999), which shows how ethnicity and ethnic issues were ready tools for the Zionists in the pursuit of their policy aims vis-à-vis the state's Arab population. Central among these was the co-optation of part of the Druze elite in an obvious effort to alienate Druzes from the other Arabs: creating 'good' Arabs and 'bad' Arabs served the Jewish state as a foil for its ongoing policy of dispossession and control (Introduction, esp. pp. 4 and 9).

regime first approached Palestinians as a 'tribal formation' that had to be incorporated into the Jordanian state, but held at a distance from the centres of political decision-making and kept outside influential positions in the military and security apparatuses. Later on this process of selective integration took the form of a division of labour, granting Palestinians relatively wide freedom in managing the private sector of the economy in the Kingdom, while keeping the political sphere firmly in the hands of the East Jordanian elite. This was further consolidated with the prohibition of political parties (with the exception of the Muslim Brotherhood) in 1957, which pushed the opposition (mostly Palestinian) underground.

In the Diaspora, Palestinians, particularly those in the refugee camps, were subjected to a series of procedures and controls that included confinement and discrimination (in Lebanon) and legal restrictions on labour immigration (in the Gulf countries) but also enabled integration (in Syria). UNRWA acquired a tangible presence in the life of the refugee camps as it was erected specifically to provide Palestinian refugees with some of their basic services, predominantly education and health. The UN institution used the curricula of the host states in the schools it ran in the refugee camps. Still, education became the basis for the articulation of a new identity that, in some cases, generated underground Palestinian organizations whose number by the late 1950s and early 60s had risen to more than forty, individually made up of between less than five to a few hundred members. All inscribed the right of return to Palestine in the heart of their political programmes.

This Palestinian dispersion over a number of political fields meant that the mechanisms and symbols people employed in the regeneration of their Palestinian identity varied according to the political space the different Palestinian communities were allowed. In the Diaspora, the construction of a new identity derived its dynamics from the conditions (physical, social, and legal) enforced on the refugee camps. These included not only the overall misery of living in a refugee camp and the marginalization that came with it, or the social and security-related siege they lived under in the suburbs of the Arab cities, but also the symbolism of the camp as a temporary place of residence. The refugee was a person awaiting return to what the politicized collective memory transformed into a 'paradise lost'. This dynamics was not limited to refugee camps in the Diaspora, but also arose in the camps located in the West Bank and the Gaza Strip. The entire Gaza Strip, with its large refugee majority, became one huge refugee camp—typified by extreme crowdedness, economic deprivation, social isolation, external restrictions—that remained cut off from the other Palestinian communities and from the wider Arab context until the 1967 June war. This may well be why in the 1950s guerrilla attacks against Israeli targets were launched primarily from here. Similarly, that the call for the Palestinization of the struggle against Israel first emerged from the Gaza Strip had much to do with the experiences and conditions that prevailed there. Albeit for different reasons, this call found a response in the Palestinian communities in the Gulf countries.

The experience of the Palestinians in the Gaza Strip and the Diaspora camps differed from that of those Palestinians who had not been expelled and found themselves, overnight, transferred into a dis-empowered minority in the newly established Jewish state. Here, political and literary activities combined to form the sources for the reconstruction of their Palestinian Arab identity—an identity that culturally came under attack from the 'civic religion', as some Israeli sociologists have called it, of the Israeli state (typified, e.g., by its 'Independence Day', by Saturday, i.e., the Jewish 'shabbat', being designated as the official rest day, the general observance of Jewish religious holidays, not to mention the instrumentalization of Jewish history in order to legitimize Jewish statism, etc.). Furthermore, as an Arab national minority, the Palestinians within Israel were assailed non-stop by systematic discrimination in political and economic terms. This proved the greatest challenge the Palestinian political parties encountered as they tried to operate within the narrow margins the Israeli political field had forcibly set aside for them. Among other things, this meant that we find them participating in parliamentary and local elections and setting up organizations and mechanisms as part of their efforts to claim and defend the rights of the Palestinian Arab minority.

That the Palestinian minority in Israel decided to take up this position in the Israeli political field inevitably evoked ambiguous attitudes towards them amongst other Palestinian communities. This ambiguity continued to be felt up to the occupation by Israel of the West Bank and the Gaza Strip in 1967, when social, economic and political interaction between these three Palestinian communities again to some extent became possible. Palestinians outside Palestine would remain ambiguous until the PLO decided to start interacting with the political parties that were dominant among the Palestinian minority in Israel and the latter gave its support to the PLO programme that in the mid-1970s came out in favour of the two-state solution. The true turning point came when the PLO adopted 'Land Day' as a Palestinian national day,[10] finally eliminating the suspicion with which Palestinians in Israel had been viewed. During these first three decades following the Nakba, the Palestinian political parties in Israel, especially the Israeli Communist Party, created material channels and opportunities for people to restructure and reshape their Palestinian identity as an Arab, i.e., not an Israeli, identity. That the Palestinian minority in Israel found itself up against a state that actively sought to erase its national identity and showed an open disregard for its collective rights gave the process of identity re-structuring a totally different direction from the ones other Palestinian communities were able to adopt. For example, whereas in the refugee camps a strong yearning for return was predominant, among the Palestinian minority in Israel we see a strong cultural and organizational dimension developing.

Significantly, the pre-1948 Palestinian political elite did not participate in the reconstruction of a new Palestinian identity. It was the offspring of poor or middle class families who had begun to find their way into the universities in the Arab world—particularly in Beirut, Damascus, and Cairo—who politicized and articulated the experience of camp existence. Traditional notable families played no role in this process.

---

10 Palestinian demonstrations protesting against the government's relentless confiscation of their lands culminated in the death of six Palestinian Israeli citizens on 30 March 1976 when the security forces opened fire on the crowd. The event is commemorated each year as 'Land Day'.

The defeat of the territorial Arab states in the June 1967 war, together with the collapse of Arab unification projects, formed the backdrop to the way the PLO succeeded, in 1969, in 'capturing' the official Arab custodianship of the Palestinian resistance movement. It was then that the PLO acquired the tools to reconfigure the Palestinian political field, almost immediately generating tensions with the territorial Arab states—armed conflicts erupted in Jordan (1970–71), Lebanon (1975–1982) and Syria (1983). In fact, this situation continued even after Oslo had given the Palestinian Authority its 'own' territory on parts of the West Bank and the Gaza Strip.

   Some historians see the period between 1948 and the late 1960s as a 'vacuum', whereby they mean that Palestinian identity formation lay largely dormant. But what disappeared during this period is a specific Palestinian national *political field*, not Palestinian national *identity*. That is, the reconstruction of Palestinian identity continued, but within the context of the experiences typical of the various Palestinian communities, i.e., a life of subsistence in refugee camps on the outskirts of Arab cities, marginalization and national oppression, particularly among the Palestinian minority in Israel, and discrimination and disempowerment in a large number of Palestinian communities in the Diaspora.

The Shattering of Palestinian Society

Following the dismemberment of their society and the defeat of their national political field in the Nakba, one of the most striking of the numerous transformations of their social structures the Palestinians faced was the total freeze of Palestinian urban growth, especially as the coastal cities, notably Jaffa and Haifa, had all collapsed. The only exception was Gaza City, but the town's isolation from other Palestinian communities generated problems of its own. Not only was urban life fractured and the development of its infrastructure arrested or even dismantled, no Palestinian metropolis was allowed to emerge after 1948. As we already saw, this suspension of Palestinian urban growth was further aggravated by a sharp decline in the role of agriculture in

Palestinian life. One of the ironies Palestinian national consciousness embodies has been the emergence of 'land' (*al-ard*) as a near sacrosanct symbol in the Palestinian collective imagination at the very time that the role and the importance of agriculture in their lives was rapidly fading away.

The establishment of the state of Israel on 78 per cent of Palestine robbed the Palestinians of their more important cities there. Jaffa and Haifa, Palestine's most cosmopolitan coastal cities as they had been open to the outside world, were taken over by the Zionists, and Jerusalem was torn in two. The occupation and annexation of the West Bank by Jordan at the same time marginalized the main Palestinian towns there while the Gaza Strip (under Egypt) became one huge refugee camp. Nablus and Hebron, as inland town always more traditional than those on the coast, remained dominant in the West Bank, but were soon overshadowed by Jordan's capital, Amman, which in the 1950s and 60s developed into a fast-growing metropolis. In the Galilee and the Triangle (incorporated into Israel following a territory exchange with Jordan in 1949 and including Kufr Qassem and Umm el-Fahm), Palestinian villages and towns became mere annexes to Tel Aviv and the expanding Israeli settlements. Most of the refugee camps in Lebanon, Syria and East Jordan were tucked onto the outskirts of the main cities there providing them with cheap labour. When Israel occupied the West Bank and the Gaza Strip in 1967, it brought also these territories within the orbit of Tel Aviv and other Israeli cities. Urban expansion in the West Bank and the Gaza Strip together with the incipient reversal of the Palestinian population movement—i.e., into and not away from Palestinian territory—only came after Oslo had established the Palestinian Authority. Even so, it remains threatened and constricted by the unabated expansion of Israeli settlement, not least in and around the Old City of Jerusalem.

The decline of the role of agriculture, as it continued in the decades following the Nakba, can be traced throughout the various Palestinian communities. While over half of the Palestinian labour force in 1945 worked in agriculture, this was no more than 5% in 1995. Amongst Palestinians in Israel, the ratio of the work force employed in agriculture went down to one-third in 1963, to one-fifth in 1973 to reach

8% in 1987 and a mere 4% in 1995. In the West Bank, those employed in agriculture constituted 40% of the total labour force in 1961, but already no more than 31% in 1972 and 26% in 1980, to reach 20% in 1987, which then dropped to less than 15% in 1997. In the Gaza Strip employment in agriculture as compared with the total labour force went down from 22% in 1965 to 18.5% in 1980 and to 9% in 1997. In Jordan, which contains a high ratio of Palestinian residents, the percentage of those employed in agriculture did not exceed 6.5% of the total labour force in 1993. Employment in agriculture varies but remains very small in Syria and Lebanon according to the geographical location of the Palestinian camps there, and is non-existent amongst Palestinians working or living in the oil countries or the USA and Europe. Therefore, one can say that fifty years on from the Nakba, less than 5% of the total Palestinian labour force are employed in agriculture, compared with no less than 50% on the eve of the Nakba.[11]

This transformation in the occupational structure of Palestinians went side by side with a high rate of emigration from the West Bank and the

---

11 Estimates on changes in the occupational structures of Palestinians since 1948 are based on various censuses, surveys, official statistical yearbooks, and studies. These include Palestine Government, *Census of Palestine* (Alexandria, 1933); Jamil Hilal, 'West Bank and Gaza Strip Social Formation Under Jordanian and Egyptian Rule (1948-1967)', *Review of Middle East Studies* 5 (1992); Jordan, Department of Statistics, *Jordanian Censuses*, data for 1952, and 1961; Jordan, Department of Statistics, *Statistical Yearbooks* for selected years afterwards for data on occupational structure of population in urban areas where the overwhelming majority of the Palestinians resided, as refugees or as migrants, in Jordan (East Bank); Israel Defence Forces, *Census of Population 1967* (Jerusalem, 1968); Israel Central Bureau of Statistics (ICBS), *Statistical Abstract of Israel* (Jerusalem, 2003); Palestinian Central Bureau of Statistics (PCBS), *Population, Housing and Establishment Census Preliminary Results 1997* (Ramallah, 1998); and PCBS, *Labour Force Survey*, Annual Report, since 1999; Palestine Economic Policy Research Institute (MAS), *Social Monitor* 6 (Ramallah, 2003); Jamil Hilal, 'Emigration, Conservatism, and Class Formation in West Bank and Gaza Strip Communities', in Lisa Taraki (ed.), *Living Palestine. Family, Survival, Resistance, and Mobility under Occupation* (Syracuse NY: Syracuse University Press, 2006); B. Kimmerling & J.S. Migdal, *The Palestinian People. A History* (Cambridge MA & London: Harvard University Press, 2003).

Gaza Strip, a phenomenon that would become ever more significant during the four decades following the Nakba—people were driven by a desire to escape from poverty and to seek improved living conditions elsewhere. Between 1950 and June 1967 some 400,000 Palestinians emigrated from the West Bank alone, either to the East Bank of Jordan or to oil-producing countries and elsewhere. The Israeli occupation in June 1967 of the Gaza Strip and the West Bank created a mass shift in the two or three months immediately following the war when Israel displaced about 200,000 Palestinians and immediately began forcibly colonizing both areas with Jewish settlers. After that, and well into the 1980s, an average of 20,000 Palestinians annually emigrated from the West Bank and Gaza Strip. This is a huge ratio considering the population size of about one million in these two areas in 1967. As a result, large Palestinian communities emerged in the Gulf States—some 400,000 Palestinians were living in Kuwait in 1991 and 150,000 in Saudi Arabia at about the same time. Most of the migrants were qualified professionals and highly skilled, while unskilled or semi-skilled labourers found employment in the Israel labour market, which by the mid 1970s employed one third of the Palestinian labour force of the West Bank and the Gaza Strip. This remained more or less the same until after the first Intifada and the 1991 Gulf War. That people had little or no choice but to seek employment in Israel and its colonial settlements led to the growing economic dependency of the West Bank and the Gaza Strip on Israel. Another factor was the transformation of both areas into a captive market for Israeli goods, second only in terms of size after the US market, a process that continued after the Oslo Accords of 1993.

Elusive Statehood

The political field that the PLO constructed in the late 1960s was based on a coalition of various Palestinian resistance groups, two among them extensions of the two Ba'ath regimes in Syria and Iraq. One of the PLO's first acts was to change the text of its Covenant, including the title, which from 'The Palestinian Pan-national Covenant' became 'The Palestinian National Covenant'. Some of its articles were amended consonant with the emerging

Palestinian political field's focus on liberation and the creation of an independent Palestinian state. For example, 'Palestinian identity is an original identity that cannot be eliminated, and is transferred from parent to child'; 'the armed struggle is the only means to liberate Palestine' and is 'a strategy and not a tactic'. Thus, the PLO gave Palestinian identity a heightened political and emancipatory dimension. In practice, the PLO adapted its tactics to the ever-changing conditions. Establishing an independent Palestinian state became the crux of its activities, its *raison d'être*. The Organization acquired a revolutionary legitimacy within a short period of time and was soon able to undergird the various Palestinian communities with a variety of political and organizational networks. It re-fashioned Palestinian history into a narrative of resistance and heroism in light of the dispersion, dispossession, annexation and occupation that the Palestinians experienced in 1948 and again in 1967. The goal of an independent state kept the PLO tightly focussed on the need for a national territory. The first attempts of the Palestinian resistance movement to secure a base on Palestinian land—the West Bank and the Gaza Strip—failed for various reasons. This forced it to seek bases in the neighbouring Arab states, a factor that we saw brought it into conflict with these states. At the same time, the political field remained wedded to the need to dislodge the Israeli colonial occupation from the West Bank and Gaza Strip.

Onto this overriding objective of establishing a sovereign national state the PLO focussed all its political, civic and paramilitary structures, brought to bear the symbols of its struggle, and directed the formation of its political discourse. Political forces that appeared on the fringe of the PLO's political field in the 1980s—e.g., the Islamist movement—found that, if they wanted to compete successfully, they had to adapt themselves largely to the norms and discourse of the PLO's political field. For example, when Hamas emerged out of the Muslim Brothers movement and participated in the 1987 Intifada, it at first sought to set itself apart by issuing statements and fielding activities that were intended to show its independence from the PLO-affiliated united leadership of the Intifada, but later—even though it continued to reject its secular motif and part of its political objectives—Hamas gradually began using the PLO's political idiom. This engagement with the PLO continued in 1994 when, prompted by the new political field that arose with the establishment after Oslo of the Palestinian Authority, the PLO itself began changing the terms There is no doubt that this way of having 'invaded' the national political field left its marks on Hamas. But it equally left its marks on the Palestinian political field itself: the PLO now had a political Islamic opposition to contend with and it had to work out new concepts defining the relationship between society and politics, on the one hand, and religion as interpreted by political Islam, on the other.

This transformation in the Palestinian political field was inspired by changes within the PLO during the 1970s and 80s. First of all, there was the bureaucratization that accompanied the shift from guerrilla type resistance—its high symbolism a clear component of the new Palestinian identity—to regular military formations whose discipline, rank, and local arrangements marked a separation of sorts between the military and the civil. Equally significant was the financial aid that gradually began to flow to the PLO and its factions from the Arab oil-producing countries during these years—it furnished the PLO with a 'rentier' dimension as the bureaucratic elite that administered the resources of the PLO was awarded certain privileges. In other words, the PLO by now had gained some of the attributes of a 'state' but lacked the essential element of national territory.

The PLO compensated for the fact that it existed outside its own national territory and that the armed struggle it tried to wage from neighbouring states remained highly ineffective by developing political and popular organizations. But the forcible ousting of the PLO from Lebanon in the summer of 1982, after Israel's invasion of that country and its siege of Beirut, had a deleterious impact on these. A further negative impact—this time from the inside—formed the 'quota' system that governed the way the leading organs of the PLO were set up as it confined the decision-making process to the small inner circle of the Palestinian leadership, i.e., the faction leaders. These and other factors weakened the PLO's ability to mobilize its resources but also marginalized other political organizations and parties. The inevitable result was a kind of political autocracy and the attendant 'client' relations.

At the political level, the most prominent transformation came in 1974 when the PLO adopted a programme that no longer spoke of establishing a democratic state on the whole of Palestine but only on part of

Palestine, i.e., the West Bank and the Gaza Strip. This created a split within PLO ranks resulting in a Palestinian 'rejection front' that was supported by Iraq and Libya. The second transformation was the gradual shift, in the 1980s, of the decision-making process from the PLO institutions (the National Council, the Central Council, and the Executive Committee) to what might be called the office of the chairman of the Executive Committee of the PLO. This period witnessed the formation of an opposition outside the PLO's political field by groups that split away from Fatah (the main PLO faction), supported this time by Syria and Libya. The third change was the shift of the Palestinian national struggle's centre of gravity to the West Bank and Gaza Strip, accelerated by the ousting of the PLO from Lebanon and by the ensuing fate Palestinian camps there suffered after 1982.

In November 1988, and under the impact of an ongoing Intifada, the Palestinian National Council openly adopted the two-state solution. However, the programme lacked a clearly defined strategy to help develop and sustain the Intifada so as to make the occupation politically, materially and morally so costly to Israel that the internal pressure this would generate would be strong enough for a new perception of Palestinian rights to emerge there. The Israeli authorities responded with brutal repression—deportations, house demolitions, curfews, sieges, detention of tens of thousands of Palestinians and outlawing the local popular self-help committees that had sprung up in their hundreds all over the West Bank and the Gaza Strip. PLO institutions failed to restructure themselves according to the dramatic changes taking place at that crucial juncture both inside the Palestinian territories and at the regional and international level. Particularly lacking again was a clear strategy, for example, to address the Israeli public in an effort to counter the racist and colonial discourse and policies of the Israeli ruling establishment. Nor did the Palestinian movement take effective notice of the international support the Intifada was generating for the two-state solution.

There is a striking resemblance between the way the 1936–39 Revolt evolved and the final stages of the 1987 Intifada, particularly after 1991. Both were met with ruthless and sustained repression, both had a leadership that resided outside the country or was in exile, and both were plunged into internal violence once they lost their grassroots character. Finally, both witnessed the emergence of groups that sought to define Palestinian society in terms of kinship, religion and a traditional outlook on the role of women in society.

The Palestinian Political Field after Oslo

It is no coincidence that challenges to the PLO's hegemony appeared from outside its political field, and shortly after the eruption of the 1987 Intifada, i.e., when the centre of the Palestinian struggle shifted to the 1967 Occupied Territories. It was especially the Islamist movement in the Occupied Territories that sought to change the 'rules of the game' in the national political field. This challenge was rooted in an organized popular base and a religious ideology that opposed the secular vision and the pluralistic structure of the PLO's political field. The signing, in September 1993, of the Oslo Accords between the PLO and Israel did much to erode that political field and to pave the way for a new one that centred on how to transform administrative self-rule in a few disjointed parts of the West Bank into a sovereign state on the whole of the West Bank and Gaza Strip, with East Jerusalem as its capital, and to do so without appearing to jeopardize the rights of the Palestinian refugees.

The establishment of Palestinian self-rule helped reinforce the shift in the centre of the national political field and altered the dynamics and rules of political activity. But the fact that the Palestinian Authority was created before any borders of the state, or even its own powers, had been defined meant leaving these for later negotiations—as issues that could at any time erupt into explosive conflict. The PLO leadership signed the Oslo Accords under the assumption—the illusion, rather—that they would lead to a solution of the Palestinian question on the basis of a 'historic compromise'. This explains why it committed itself to end the armed struggle and to amend its Covenant. But the PLO soon discovered that the main Jewish Israeli political parties were not attuned to such a compromise, but were out, rather, to entrench Israel further as a colonialist power. Hence, the Palestinian 'tunnel' uprising in 1996, which erupted when Israel decided to excavate a tunnel in the Old City of Jerusalem, and the outbreak of the second Intifada in September 2000.

Since it first emerged in the 1920s, the Palestinian national movement has lived through countless critical events whose impact differed according to when they occurred and in which of the communities Palestinian society had been fragmented into by the establishment of Israel. Similarly, the momentous conflicts and hostilities it has had to confront varied in intensity, location and type—above all the never-ending bloody confrontations with the Zionist movement before 1948 and then with the Jewish state. It has had to face military and political clashes with more than one Arab state. And it could not escape the impact of international and regional efforts for change that were often as unpredictable in occurrence as they proved violent in nature. The Palestinian collective memory carries the marks of tens of thousands of Palestinian martyrs and of the hundreds of thousands others who have been wounded, imprisoned or deported. Villages, towns and even refugee camps have been, and are being, destroyed and communities uprooted, others besieged, land confiscated and homes demolished. Powerless, they watch Zionist colonial settlements going up on their land in their stead.

Thus, Palestinian history demands to be told as a multi-layered narrative, each layer with its own characters, symbols, settings, and specific discourse. As a grand narrative, it needs to be continually enriched from the existing variety of its sources I have outlined here. Besides the long arduous fight against Zionist colonization and British colonial control stand the struggles of the Arab Palestinian minority in Israel for their national rights and for equal citizenship, before the 1976 Land Day, undiminished after that, and with shocking awareness since October 2000.[12] Then there is the struggle of Palestinians in the West Bank and Gaza Strip against the Israeli occupation before, during and

---

12 On 1 October 2000 Palestinians in Israel held a general strike in response to the massacring of Palestinians in al-Haram al-Sharif on 29 September, following Ariel Sharon's provocative entry onto the compound the day before. The Israeli police forces acted with violence and on 1, 2, 3, and 8 October, in what many saw as a pre-planned attack in which they used live ammunitions and rubber-coated steel bullets, killed thirteen unarmed Palestinian young men.

after the Intifada of 1987 and the al-Aqza Intifada. Our sources bear testimony to the steadfastness of the Palestinian refugee camps in Lebanon before 1982 and after. They include thousands of other small events and episodes that help form the consciousness of millions of Palestinians in their daily battle for survival in exposed surroundings and precarious situations.

The Oslo Accords have had an undeniable impact on the Palestinian struggle for self-determination and statehood. They resulted in the establishment of self-rule on patches of Palestine for the first time in Palestinian history. However, twelve years after Oslo, the Palestinian Authority retains no more than a semblance of self-government on dispersed bits of territory of the West Bank and Gaza Strip, its capital, East Jerusalem, still occupied, its territory strewn with colonial settlements, while it has no control over any of its natural resources and borders and millions of refugees are still awaiting recognition of their right of return. Oslo did nothing to resolve the one burning issue that goes back in the Palestinian struggle against the Zionist movement to before the establishment of the state of Israel—land. Nor did Oslo resolve that other most outstanding issue since the creation of Israel, i.e., the refugee question. Oslo epitomizes the issue of Palestinian national rights as no more than a territorial dispute over the land of the West Bank and Gaza Strip. In other words, the PLO leadership fell into the trap Israel's colonial designs had set for it. Exaggerated concern was given to symbols of sovereignty and fatally little attention to the fact of Israel's continuing and intensifying occupation of land. Moreover, the PLO's appetite for the symbols of sovereignty never went hand in hand with a felt need for genuine democratic institution building as a means for mobilizing all Palestinians against Israel's occupation. That the PLO agreed for issues of sovereignty and national rights to be dealt with at a later stage (during the so-called 'final status' negotiations) gave the colonial state not only the first but also the last word, as happened again with the US sponsored 'Road Map'. When that 'final status' stage came, in the summer of 2000 at Camp David, it was made clear to the Palestinian side that the state they envisaged would never be more than an Israeli protectorate—a state without political viability or popular legitimacy; a state without genuine sovereignty over East Jerusalem; a state whose territory was literally shot through with huge chunks of Israeli colonial settlements, a state delegitimized a priori by an Israeli refusal to accept any moral and historical responsibility for the Nakba. It is in this context that the outbreak of the second Intifada should be viewed and read, i.e., as the expression of the Palestinians' utter disillusionment with the Oslo process, which, they were told, would correct the historic injustice inflicted on them, but that actually has caged them further and further into an Apartheid system and continues to rob them of their land as Israel, relying on naked military aggression and overwhelming economic and diplomatic power, continues to deny the Palestinians their human and national rights.

The creation of an independent Palestinian state has been at the heart of the Palestinian national movement almost from the outset. Today, an independent and sovereign Palestine looks as remote as it did before Oslo. The outcome of the present confrontation remains unclear, but we are already seeing an Israeli imposed unilateral separation—as the wall Israel is constructing inside the West Bank makes cruelly obvious—i.e., with the Palestinians there confined within a kind of imposed Apartheid, or at best a client Palestinian state, a Bantustan, whose sovereignty is symbolic only. This could mean the re-emergence of a Palestinian resistance movement rekindling the struggle for decades to come.

But it could also give momentum to the emergence of a joint political vision for a pluralistic democratic territorial state over the whole of Palestine.

Palestinian Nationalism
The Difficulties of Narrating an Ambivalent Identity

Issam Nasser

'Nationalism' and 'nation' are pivotal notions for the way they have helped shape our modern world. In effect, one could say that since the early nineteenth century the nation has become the guardian and proclaimed itself the champion of all of history. For that reason alone, any historical study concerned with the present ought to give serious consideration to the impact the notions of nation and nationalism have had—and continue to have—on the way we understand certain historical events. National historical narratives were born when the 'nation' was born. For authoritative lineages and chronologies needed to be constructed to help present the nation as the ancient and primordial entity one imagined it to be, not as the historically recent phenomenon it actually was. And it became the task of the historian to provide the nation with the weight of the historical legitimacy it of course lacked at its all too recent birth.

Setting *past* apart from *present*, historical writing reconfigures the content of history and forces the silent body—the nation—to speak (de Certeau, 1988). Through this distinction between a *dead* past and a *living* present an historical chronology is invented that divides the past into different, ostensibly homogeneous periods, with the historian deciding where they begin and end. It is this separation between past and present that enables the nation to appear as history's messiah, not only because—as Walter Benjamin has written—the nation 'consummates all history', but even more so because the nation presents itself as the end of history (Benjamin, 1978:312). Thus, we should

217

see the study of how specific national identities were formed and developed, not as an historical search for the 'actual' roots of the nation,
but as an academic exercise almost in 'historical teleology'. In other
words, what we have here is a process that starts out from an already
known conclusion whereby historians select a particular series of events
and then narrate them backwards so as to arrive again at that same
already known conclusion they had set out from.[1]

   It is not surprising therefore that one often finds a number of different narratives for the evolution of each individual nation. And while
historians eventually will come to agree on the 'outcome', they rarely
agree about 'what came before'. Thus, the way a national historical
narrative unfolds depends on what historians decide will be its point of
origin and which its significant events. This, of course, is almost never a
conscious selection on the part of the historian: at play is a process in
which national interests intersect with ideology, the production of
knowledge and historical imagination, all of which influence the historian in the pursuit of his/her job of narrating the nation.

The history of Palestinian national identity is a salient example of the
multiplicity of historical narratives seen as the 'outcome' of a number
of historical imaginations. The implications are particularly important
here because the national existence of the Palestinians as a people has so
often been put into question. Most strikingly, of course, such questioning of Palestinian 'nation-ness'—the complete denial even that
there exists a Palestinian nation—is overwhelmingly connected with
Zionism and with the negation of Palestine and the Palestinian nation
that lies at the core of Zionism. But it also stems from contradictions
inherent within the Palestinian discourse itself. For, in the final anal-

1   Cf. Benedict Anderson (1991:205): 'Because there is no Originator, the nation's
     biography cannot be written evangelically, "down time", through a long procreative
     chain of begettings. The only alternative is to fashion it "up time"—towards Peking
     Man, Java Man, King Arthur, wherever the lamp of archaeology casts its fitful
     gleam. This fashioning, however, is marked by deaths, which, in a curious inversion
     of conventional genealogy, *start from an originary present.* World War II begets
     World War I; out of Sedan comes Austerlitz; the ancestor of the Warsaw Uprising is
     the state of Israel' (italics added).

ysis, the Palestinian discourse emerged out of historical processes that were often bent on preventing precisely that discourse from emerging.

What particularly stands out in the construction of a modern Palestinian identity is that the challenges and contradictions producing it have at the same time made that identity ambiguous. For example, the Palestinian discourse of the 1960s was essentially a pan-Arabist discourse that stemmed from a belief in a larger Arab nation embracing all Arabs. Simultaneously it argued that the Palestinians were very much a nationed people in order to counter a Zionist discourse that vehemently denied their very existence—Zionism insisted that Palestinians were simply Arabs who happened to live in Palestine and as such ought to be absorbed into the larger Arab nation envisioned by pan-Arabism. In other words, the Palestinian discourse rejected the Arab 'sameness' argument because Zionism used it against them, and at the same time hang on to it—for entirely different reasons. This 1960s' predicament no longer exists: today even the most fervent proponents of Arab nationalism accept the existence of different Arab identities, while Palestinians are recognized by the international community—even by Israel—as a nation. But, since the developments behind this change are essentially political in nature, they do not necessarily imply that there is agreement on how a collective Palestinian identity has come into existence, or what the nature and boundaries of such an identity are.

It is this that makes the study of the history of Palestinian identity through a reading of the past a matter of utmost importance to anyone who is Palestinian, not because this may somehow benefit any kind of negotiation process, but because it will enable us to see how Palestinians define themselves, envision their future and seek to determine the boundaries of their national political community. After all, ideas about—and imaginings of—history are neither mere illusions nor necessarily true depictions of reality. I suggest that we see them basically as epistemologies, critical tools that help us understand and deal with reality. When an identity is formulated and assimilated—be it individually or collectively—it becomes the spectacles through which the individual will see the world. As Ali Harb (1995:49) has saliently put it, it 'becomes a barricade behind which hides the believer [...] whether as a fundamentalist, as a universalist, or as a racist fascist.'

A closer look at some of the most important writings on Palestinian history reveals that most historians have never adequately delved into the question of Palestinian national identity or asked how it was formulated. The few studies dealing with the issue reveal, at best, disagreements among historians on the origins and evolution of the Palestinians as a people. Approaches range from total negation[2] to insistence on a long historical presence that goes back to the Canaanites.[3] Between these two extremes we find some historians—particularly Israeli—who see Palestinian identity as a reaction to the Zionist presence, with relatively recent origins dating back to the 1960s. In fact, some Israeli historians claim that 'the Zionist movement is one of the most successful national movements in history for it started with the aim of forming one national group, and it ended up with forming two.'[4] On the Palestinian side we find studies that view the formation of Palestinian identity as a historical process that goes back to the onset of Zionist immigration into Palestine in the 1880s and the events surrounding it, further determined by British Mandatory policies and the failure of the Arab nationalist movement in the aftermath of the first world war. On this view, Palestinian nationalism was 'ushered into its own independent existence mainly as a result of the chaos and disarray of the larger Arab nationalist movement' after the fall of Faysal's government between 1918 and 1920 (Muslih 1988:x).

The starting point for my own reflections on the history of Palestinian identity is the conceptual belief that nations are not infinite primordial

---

2   Both Arab-nationalist and Zionist historians hold this view. Among the latter, Ben Zion Netanyahu (the father of Israeli politician Benjamin Netanyahu) frequently stated: 'I do not believe that the Arabs who call themselves Palestinians have the right to demand a state. It is clear to me that there is no such thing as a Palestinian people' (*Al-Quds*, 18 September 1998).

3   The Palestinian historian Bayan Nweihed al-Hout adopted this position in a lecture she gave at the Beirut Theatre in April 1998. She argues something similar in her book *Filastin: al-Qadeya, al-Sha'b, al-Hadara*.

4   Attributed to the Israeli historian Meir Pa'el who is said to repeat it often (personal communication from the historian Ilan Pappé at a meeting in Ramallah, February 1998).

entities as some national thinkers claim; rather, a nation or people as a collectivity is basically an imagined political community produced at a specific time and place (Anderson 1991).[5] This is not only an economic and political process, but also, to a large extent, a cultural-rhetorical one. Therefore, writing the history of the nation as imagined community can never be limited to the political events that produce the nationed people, it must also include an analysis of the different discourses through which the nation has been produced and constructed—'imagined'—and the history put into service by this production process.[6]

Accordingly, as I see it, when we want to understand the emergence of the Palestinians as a nation, we must not only trace the development of their political institutions, but also study the Palestinian imagination, the type of discourse it produced, and the historical factors that influenced it. All of these contributed to the formation of a Palestinian consciousness whose loyalty is to the collectivity and which helped draw the boundaries of this collectivity. I realize that centring on consciousness and discourse may have dangerous implications, because many see in Palestinian self-consciousness a kind of 'false consciousness'. This surely is one of the political challenges one faces when studying the historical emergence and development of Palestinian identity, not to be ignored if we are seriously interested—in an academic sense—in the historical understanding of this identity. After all: consciousness influences reality and vice versa. Self-consciousness is not

5   Cf. also Hobsbawm, who speaks of 'that comparatively recent historical innovation, the "nation", with its associated phenomena: nationalism, the nation-state, national symbols, histories and the rest. All these rest on exercises in social engineering which are often deliberate and always innovative, if only because historical novelty implies innovation.' And he immediately explains: 'Israeli and Palestinian nationalism or nations must be novel, whatever the historic continuities of Jews or Middle Eastern Muslims, since the very concept of the territorial states in the currently standard type in their region was barely thought of before the end of World War I' (Hobsbawm and Ranger 1983:13).

6   There is a dominant tendency in the study of the evolution of Palestinian identity to focus on the history of the Palestinian political institution. A good example of this is the Palestinian historian Maher al-Sharif (1995).

only connected to the way one imagines the self, but also to the way others see, represent and interact with us and vice versa.

Rashid Khalidi rightly maintains that one of the main challenges facing us today is the fact that the emergence of a distinctive Palestinian identity on the political level intersects with—though it does not completely depend on—the exclusion of the Palestinians by and their becoming the Other for national groups who view themselves as notably different from the Palestinians and whose historical narrations underpin this difference. This is exactly the reason why the study of Palestinian identity, when we try to base it on its own textual sources, becomes a near impossible task. The historian of Palestine cannot solely depend on 'Palestinian sources', but must also turn to, and borrow from, historical narratives by other nations of the region, because they will often employ the same historical events on which the Palestinian narrative seeks to base itself. Instances of this are many. For example, could one claim that the period of Arab renaissance at the end of the nineteenth century, or the period of the political emergence of Arab national thought during the first world war, belongs only to Lebanese history, or to Palestinian history, or to any other single Arab history? Is Jewish history in Palestine a matter of relevance only to Israelis? Does it not also from part of the history of the Palestinians? Of course, we find these and many other historical issues echoed in numerous historical texts of different groups in our region.

It is this intersection of and frequent conflict between Palestinian history and the histories of others that poses yet another, closely connected, difficulty for students of Palestinian history and identity today. Because the development of Palestinian identity is frequently explained in terms of meanings produced by other texts that often ignore the Palestinians, it is our job as Palestinian historians to recover exactly those parts of Palestinian memory that have been colonized by these competing historical discourses. The historian of Palestine has the difficult task of defining modern Palestinian history and extracting it from its Israeli counterpart, from that of neighbouring countries and from the wider Arab history.

Palestinian history's lack of independence is one challenge confronting the historian, resisting the temptation to invent a totally independent

Palestinian narrative is another. After all, that the Palestinians' national identity is different from that of their neighbours does not mean that we can place it outside the context of those histories that are not, literally speaking, our own. The Palestinian Nakba of 1948, for instance, is wholly particular to the Palestinian narrative but is also irrevocably tied to its Israeli counterpart, whether Palestinians (or for that matter Israelis) like it or not. The main problem here is the inability of many historians to appreciate or even consider how difficult it is for Palestinians to be 'part of' the national identity of any of their neighbouring countries. Exactly this failure to recognize the connections between Palestinian history and competing histories has led to the view that Palestinian identity is a recent phenomenon, the product of political national activities that emerged only in the 1960s.

This perspective points to yet another problem facing historians, one that often leads them to the rather simplistic solution of viewing the evolution of Palestinian identity through the prism of the region's political history. This, I believe, totally ignores the complex roots of Palestinian identity. True, it is important to consider the impact on the formation of Palestinian identity of dominant Middle East ideologies, such as Arab nationalism and Islamism, of the divisions the West imposed on the region, and of Zionism. However, as important as they are, none of these factors explains why part of the urban intellectuals in Palestine, and in the Mashreq (the eastern part of the Arab world) generally, began to imagine Palestine as a distinct political unit—even though this imagining was not accompanied by a distinct Palestinian national consciousness—long before the West began imposing its colonial divisions on the region and Zionism, in its wake, began promoting intensive Jewish immigration.

For example, in 1908, the writer (and former Ottoman official in Jerusalem) Najib 'Azuri suggested to include northern Palestine into the *Sanjak* (district in the Ottoman Empire) of Jerusalem so as to encourage the economic development of the land of Palestine.[7] 'Azuri's

---

7   The Ottoman parliament (*Majlis al-Mab'outhan*) was restored in 1908; 'Azuri published his proposal in a newspaper article on September 23; cf. Rashid Khalidi, 1997:28-29.

vision of Palestine corresponds with both Palestine's borders as the British would drawn them a decade later, and those the first Arab Palestinian Congress would outline in Jerusalem on 3 February 1919. In the protest statement the Arab participants delivered to the Peace Conference in Versailles they announced that they represent 'all Muslim and Christian residents of Palestine, which is made up of the regions of Jerusalem, Nablus, Arab Acre'.[8] Moreover, when the Muslim-Christian committee in Jaffa sent a letter of protest to General Allenby in 1918, they signed it in the name of 'the Arab Palestinians'.[9]

The idea of the 'land of Palestine' that we see emerging here with defined borders similar to those the British Mandate were to draw later reveals that certain circles at the time definitely thought of Palestine as distinct from its neighbours. A number of historians accept this view and see the Palestinian imagining of the boundaries of their nation as a product of conditions that go back to the nineteenth century, even though they may differ on the main reason behind such an imagining. For example, Rashid Khalidi argues that the centrality of Jerusalem in the popular imagination of the Muslim, Christian and Jewish residents turned it into a symbol for all other places in Palestine and made visiting the city an important part of the religious identity of the residents of Palestine (Khalidi 1997:28–29). Other historians who share Khalidi's view usually highlight the importance of the administrative status of Jerusalem in the lives of the people of the region from the middle of the nineteenth century on, particularly after 1887 when it became the capital of the eponymous independent *sanjak* and started sending delegates to the *Majlis al-Mab'outhan* (the Ottoman parliament). For Kimmerling and Migdal, this special administrative status of Jerusalem was of signal importance for the eventual birth of an independent Palestinian identity in the aftermath of Ottoman rule

8   Documents of the Palestinian Arab Resistance to the British Occupation and to Zionism, 1918-1939 (Beirut: Mu'assasat al-Dirasat al-Filastiniyya):3.
9   Documents of the Palestinian National Movement, 1918-1939 (Beirut: Mu'assasat al-Dirasat al-Filastiniyya).

(Kimmerling and Migdal 1993:68–69). They quote an earlier article by Butrus Abu-Manneh arguing that the autonomous status of Jerusalem proved of 'tremendous importance for the emergence of Palestine' (Abu-Manneh 1978:25 [1999:46]).

Beshara Doumani, on the other hand, does not see the centrality of Jerusalem as crucial in Palestinian life, though, like the others, he too locates the emergence of Palestinian identity in developments during the final decades of Ottoman rule. Doumani argues that historians of Palestinian identity ought, first and foremost, to examine the 'economic, social, and cultural relations between the inhabitants of the various regions of Palestine during the Ottoman period [to understand] why Palestine became a nation in the minds of the people who call themselves Palestinians today' (Doumani 1995:245). As Doumani points out (1995:4), Palestine 'produced large agricultural surpluses and was integrated into the world capitalist economy as an exporter of wheat, barley, sesame, olive oil, soap and cotton during the 1856–1882 period.' Thus it was Nablus, and not Jerusalem, that in the nineteenth century formed the main commercial centre in a region that extended from Hebron in the south to the Galilee in the north. And it was its trade relations with the Greater Syrian hinterlands, particularly with Damascus, that in effect made Jabal Nablus the actual centre of Palestine.

Again other historians argue that the Western consciousness of the region in general, and of Palestine as the Holy Land in particular, that we encounter in writings of European and American travellers, missionaries and archaeologists in the nineteenth century, played an important role in shaping a local recognition of the distinctiveness of Palestine and its geographic unity, even though its borders were never clearly drawn.[10] For Alexander Schölch, for example,

> [i]t is possible to state with certainty that imagining Palestine as a unit (as the *Holy Land* or as the *Land of Israel*) was far more developed and precise in the minds of Europeans in the second half

10 I briefly refer to this possibility in my doctoral dissertation (Nassar 1997).

of the nineteenth century than it was for its own local population or for the Ottoman administration (Schölch 1988:27).[11]

Schölch goes on to show that the port of Jaffa—because of its connection with Jerusalem—was Palestine's window to the world. Using Ottoman and European statistics, Schölch (1988:163–174) argues that because from this port Palestine exported and imported numerous products to and from Europe, Jaffa played a central role in shaping and constructing a particular and independent 'meaning' of Palestine as an entity separate from its surroundings.

The different narrations of the emergence of Palestinian self-identification outlined above do not necessarily suggest that such identification was prevalent among the majority of Palestine's residents. Rather, these narrations point up the material conditions that laid the foundations for the eventual emergence of a Palestinian self-identification. There is near consensus that the loyalties and identifications of the residents of Palestine towards the end of the Ottoman period were not national, but rather combined local, regional and religious affiliations. Ottoman, Arab, tribal and religious identities coexisted simultaneously among the urban elite and the residents of villages, who often assumed primarily local identities (Khalidi 1997:63–88).

This multiplicity of identities did not necessarily produce any kind of conflict. That is, loyalty to the Ottomans did not negate being proud of one's Arab heritage, nor did it preclude defending Palestine against foreign greed. More significantly even, these coexisting loyalties were always part of Palestinian discourse and would become one of the features of Palestinian identity. Herein lies the main problem for Palestinian historians: the history of Palestinian self-consciousness cannot be characterized as chronological in the sense that it gained strength as time passed. On the contrary, Palestinian self-identification often appears to have oscillated between different historical belongings and

---

11 This translation is my own from Kamel al-Assali's Arabic 1988 edition of Schölch's original 1986 study.

loyalties. Sometimes, in one and the same event the historian will detect evidence of Palestinian particularity but will also find that a national identification broader than Palestine is at play. This multiplicity came especially to the fore during the Mandate period and from there can be traced well into the 1950s and 60s.

For instance, the conference in Jerusalem in 1919, mentioned above, was called 'the Arab Palestinian Congress' and the final statement it issued emphasized the importance of the independence of Palestine and of preserving its unity, but at the same time asserted that Palestine was part of Greater Arab Syria (*Bilad al-Sham*) (Nweihed al-Hout 1986:96). Examine the political programme of any the Palestinian political movements in the 1950s and 60s—say the Arab Nationalist Movement—and one will notice that concrete Palestinian concern with liberating Palestine from the Zionist movement was invariably couched in the language of Arab nationalism.[12]

Along with the colonial division of the Middle East by Britain and France (the Sykes-Picot agreement of May 1916), Jewish immigration to Palestine played a significant role in the evolution of a distinct Palestinian nation, as it prompted the people of Palestine to adopt new directions and develop new features. Because Jewish settlement initially was bent on setting up agricultural colonies, the clash with the Zionist project occurred first in the villages, not in the cities. This was to produce one of the most salient but also most problematic features of Palestinian identity: the peasant (*fallah*) character became an essential part of how Palestinians view and represent themselves. Later on, peasant ways of dress, the *kufiyye* headscarf, and the village dance, the *dabka*, would become symbols of Palestinian national identity. But as the city was not central in shaping local consciousness, consciousness was not generalized but always competed with a number of other

---

12 Established in the early 1950s by a number of Palestinian activists such as George Habash and Hani al-Hindi, the Arab National Movement declared that the liberation of Palestine was impossible without Arab unity; see the interview of George Habash with Mahmoud Soueid published in Soueid (1998:11).

national perspectives. What we see happening during the British Mandate period is how this peasant sense of distinctiveness then finds its *political* expression not in the rural areas but in the city, through articles in local newspapers, political discourse and emerging parties. Without exception, the various Palestinian newspapers—*Al-Karmel*, *Filastin* and *Al-Munadi*—conducted one campaign after another warning against the danger of the Zionist movement and its steadily unfolding project in Palestine, and demanded that Palestine continue to belong to its own people and be given political independence. In 1914, Najib Nassar, the most prominent of Palestine's journalists and owner of the Haifa based *Al-Karmel*, called upon the Arabs of *Bilad al-Sham* to show their support for the people of Palestine, 'the Palestinians'. In 1914, Nassar wrote: 'We, your Palestinian brothers, have been sharing with you all your difficulties. So why then don't you, at least, feel with us a little the disasters raining upon us [...] and on our country.'[13] Nassar's text is clear about the borders of 'our country', i.e., that of the Palestinian people. It also reveals that he was aware the Palestinians differed from the neighbouring people in the rest of Greater Syria. This awareness starts to take a political turn as it intensifies after the Balfour Declaration in 1917 and during the British Mandate period in general. In 1923, for instance, in its founding statement, the National Arab party stated that its goal is 'preserving Palestine for its people [...] and establishing a constitutional government in it' (Mahaftha 1989:225). Although the Arab identity of Palestine remained an important part of Palestinian discourse during the Mandate, this discourse focusses more and more on the separate identity of Palestine. In other words, despite the fact that Palestinian identity was rooted in historical conditions pre-dating the intensive Jewish settlement activity of the Zionists, it crystallized into a national consciousness only after the Palestinian encounter with Jewish settlements.

Thus, it is the combined rejection of Zionist settlement by Palestine's rural population and the political expression of this rejection

---

13   *Al-Karmel*, Haifa, 6 December 1914, quoted in Ali Mahaftha (1989:23-24).

through urban institutions that constitute the point at which Palestinians begin to view themselves as an independent people. And it is the emergence of Zionism in Palestine and the British support it succeeded in gaining through the Balfour Declaration that then prompted the development of a distinct political Palestinian identity to accelerate. This identity found expression through societies and organizations that saw themselves variously as Arab, Syrian, Islamic or Christian, but that all had only one aim—to save Palestine from the Zionist project. Imagining the Palestinian collectivity begins to take a practical turn when in reaction to Zionist threats several Palestinian conferences begin to come out with unambiguous demands for the right of self-determination for Palestine. This imagining takes on a more formal course in the post-1922 period, following the official establishment of the Mandate and the political borders it set out for Palestine. It later develops into a collective imagining that encompasses the majority of the population in Mandate Palestine—until 1948.

Palestinian national consciousness did not succeed in producing its own nation state, as was the case with the Arab neighbours of Palestine. Instead, a period of disruption and discontinuity followed in the wake of the Nakba. A tragic event on many different levels—familial, personal and national—the Nakba means, first of all, the destruction of the social structure for most of the population in Palestine, who became refugees; and, second, the disappearance of urban centres from the lives of those Palestinians who somehow had succeeded in remaining in Palestine but who from active city dwellers were now reduced to separate groups living on the margins of cities that were now Jewish. Both these consequences mark a turning point in the nature and continuity of Palestinian discourse. The first encouraged the emergence of the Palestinians as a distinct group of people united by their shared experience of dispossession and displacement. The second put an end to the development of the Palestinian collective imagining that, as I outlined above, had been formulated in Palestine's cities.

The two issues are closely related. The first is especially significant because it encouraged the emergence of a new kind of Palestinian identity. As Homi Bhabha has it, the 'nation fills the void left in the uprooting of communities and kin' (1994:139). That is, the forced expulsion of the Palestinians in 1948 and the appearance of refugee camps throughout the Middle East provided the context for the transformation of the old Palestinian local and communal belongings into a new national belonging. The construction of this new form of a living *locality* that is far more complex than the *old community* and far more symbolic than *society,* to a great extent altered 'the meaning of home and belonging' (Bhabha 1994:140).

Thus, their uprooting affirmed for the Palestinians their particularity and created the conditions for a new kind of national imagining to emerge. Within Palestinian national discourse the Nakba therefore represents more a rhetorical shift than the beginning or the end of an era. The identity that before 1948 had seemed so clear in the way the intellectuals of the city elite had expressed and finessed it was wiped out together with Palestine's cities. The destruction of more than 400 Palestinian population centres meant the loss of the old traditional local features, but also signified their replacement with a new kind of be-longing as distinctly Palestinian—the refugee experience. This experi-ence and the rhetorical shift that accompanied it did of course not affect all Palestinian Arabs in the same way at the time. It meant that the Palestinian remained the Other, but now in relation to new groups—the neighbouring Arab countries. That the refugees were ex-cluded from all other identities forming around them deepened this feeling of 'otherness'.

Residents of East Palestine (except, of course, the refugees among them) did not experience this exclusion in the same way. Significantly, Palestinian identity was 'at its weakest in Jordan and the West Bank, its emergence delayed until Israeli rule replaced Jordanian rule' (Budeiri 1995: 18). In the West Bank this new identity took longer to sink its roots mainly due to Jordan's active and repressive policy to Jordanize East Palestine and its people. Hence, the eager and complete adoption of the Palestinian identity we see happening in this part of Palestine following the war of 1967, prompted by both Palestinian political activity coming from abroad and the repressive policies of the Israeli occupation since 1967 that now socially and economically separated the West Bank from Jordan. In other words, Palestinian self-awareness in the West Bank appeared later in comparison with Palestinian self-awareness in the Diaspora and it was the product of discrete events and developments that did not affect the inhabitants of the refugee camps outside the West Bank. Mussa Budeiri (1998:39) best reflects this when he writes:

> Growing up in 'Jordanian' Jerusalem in the 1950s, what strikes me most today is the total absence of Palestine and Palestinian things in my worldview, both as a child and as an adolescent. True, on my daily trip to school I walked in the shadow of the wall built by the Jordanian army presumably to protect people from Israeli sniper fire [. . .] East Jerusalem and the West Bank, as the name implied, were no longer Palestine but Jordan; 'Palestine' was over there, beyond the flimsy wall that started at Damascus Gate and stretched all the way to Shaykh Jarrah.

Although it is hard to tell how representative Budeiri's own feelings may be of the entire population of East Jerusalem at the time, his description reflects sentiments that existed among at least segments of the West Bank residents. It is no secret that the residents of the 'West Bank' (both urbanites and villagers) were quite aware of the distinction between themselves, 'the residents', and those who arrived during and after the war in 1948, 'the refugees'. The notion of a Palestinian collective identity, which emerged among the refugees and dominated modern Palestinian national discourse, was essentially based on the refugee camp experience. The legal framework put in place by the 1993 Oslo Peace Accords—and hence centred on those who currently live in the West Bank and Gaza Strip—for determining who is legally a Palestinian and who is not will only make future studies of Palestinian identity more confusing because it excludes those Palestinians who do not reside in these areas. West Bank-Gaza centralism, in this sense, can only be described as a colonization of historical Palestinian discourse. The reductive transformation of the Palestinians into a single, local group deprives those who lived the Palestinian experience of their Palestinianism, once again casting them as 'refugees'. In a sense, those who lived through the Nakba are now facing a new catastrophe: the disappearance of their Palestinian identity, an identity forged through their personal diaspora experience in the years following the creation of the state of Israel.

This essay began by setting out the challenges that the articulation of the Palestinian identity has to confront. It then moved on to examine the difficulties historians face in their attempts to study the historical emergence of this particular identity. Here it is important to stress that this article is not about whether Palestinians possess a legitimate identity or not. The Palestinians constitute a national group with political and national rights that can never be ignored or denied, no matter how they—or anyone else—read their history. In other words, the issue of how legitimate a nation is may be relevant for international law, but from the perspective of history it is meaningless and futile.

The main point I have wanted to stress in this article is that nations 'lose their origins in the myths of time and only fully realize their horizons in the mind's eye' (Bhabha 1995:1). In other words, the question is not whether historians—of Palestinian identity in this case—can actually come to agree on the origins of their nation, but rather what kind of nation they envision. Thus, what matters most is the type of narration we choose for our nation's history. For not only will it present a certain vision of the past, in many ways it will form the foundations for how the nation will view its present and stake out its future. Realizing how elusive and ambivalent national identities are is essential for understanding that they are—and always will be—subject to change. What makes this so hard to accept in the Palestinian case is that the change is now affecting the different parts in which the Palestinian nation has been dispersed. In other words, creating an authoritative national history of the Palestinian nation will, in our case, almost certainly mean the marginalization of certain segments of our nation.

References

Abu-Manneh, B. 1978. 'The Rise of the Sanjak of Jerusalem in the Late 19th Century', in Gabriel Ben-Dor (ed.), *The Palestinians and the Middle East*

Conflict: Studies in Their History, Sociology and Politics (Ramat Gan: Turtledove); reprinted in Ilan Pappé (ed.), *The Israel/Palestine Question* (London and New York: Routledge 1999).

Anderson, B. 1991 (2nd ed.). *Imagined Communities: Reflections on the Origin and Spread of Nationalism* (London: Verso).

Benjamin, W. 1978. 'Theologico-Political Fragment', in P. Demetz (ed.), *Reflections* (New York: Schocken Books).

Bhabha, H. K. 1994. 'Dissemination', in idem (ed.), *The Location of Culture* (London: Routledge).

Bhabha, H.K. (ed.) 1995. *Nation and Narration* (London and New York: Routledge).

Budeiri, M. 1995. *Majjalat al-Dirasat al-Filastiniyya* 21 (Winter): 3–27.

Budeiri, M. 1998. 'Reflections on al-Nakba', *Journal of Palestine Studies* 109:31–35

de Certeau, M. 1988. *The Writing of History* (translated by T. Conley) (New York: Columbia University Press).

Doumani, B. 1995. *Rediscovering Palestine: Merchants and Peasants in Jabal Nablus, 1700–1900* (Berkeley: University of California Press).

Harb, A. 1995. 'Utrouhat fil-Fikr wal-Haweyya' (Reflections on Thought and Identity), *Abwab* 6:49.

Hobsbawm, E., and T. Ranger, 1983. *The Invention of Tradition* (Cambridge: Cambridge University Press).

al-Hout, N. 1986. *Filastin Al-Kiyadat al-Siyasiyya* (Political Leadership) (Beirut: Mu'assasat al-Dirasat al-Filastiniyya).

Al-Hout, N. 1991. *Al-Qadeya, al-Sha'b, al-Hadara* (Palestine: The Cause, the People, the Civilization) (Beirut: Dar al-Istiqlal lil-Dirasat wal-Nashr).

Khalidi, R. 1997. *Palestinian Identity: The Construction of Modern National Consciousness* (New York: Columbia University Press).

Kimmerling, B., and J.S. Migdal. 1993. *Palestinians: The Making of a People* (New York: The Free Press).

Mahaftha, A. 1989. *Al-Fikr al-Siyasi fi Filastin: Min Nihayet al-Hukm al-ʿUthmani wa hatta Nihayet al-Intidab al-Biritani 1918–1948* (Political Thought in Palestine: From the End of Ottoman Rule until the End of the British Mandate) (Amman: Markez al-Kutub al-'Urduni).

Muslih, M. 1988. *The Origins of Palestinian Nationalism* (New York: Columbia University Press).

Nassar, I. 1997. *Imagining Jerusalem in the Nineteenth Century: A Study in Religious and Colonial Imagination* (Doctoral Dissertation, Illinois State University).

Schölch, A. 1988. *Tahawulat Jathreyya fi-Filastin 1856–1882: Dirasat hawl al-Tatawwur al-Iktisadi wal-Ijtimaʿ wal-Siyasi* (Amman: al-Jamiʿa al-Urduniyya), Arabic translation of *Palästina im Umbruch 1856–1882* (Wiesbaden: Franz Steiner Verlag 1986); English translation by W. Young and M.C. Gerrity: *Palestine in Transformation, 1856–1882: Studies in Social, Economic, and Political Development* (Washington, DC: Institute for Palestine Studies 1993; repr. 2006).

al-Sharif, M. 1995. *Al-Bahth ʿan Kiyan: Dirasat fi al-Fikr al-Siyasi al-Filastini 1908–1993* (The Search for Being: Studies in Palestinian Political Thought) (Nicosia: Markez al-Abhath wal-Dirasat al-Ishtirakiyya fil-ʿAlam al-ʿArabi).

Soueid, M. 1998. ʿAl-Tajriba al-Nidaliyya al-Filastiniyya: Hiwar Shamil maʾ George Habashʾ, *Marjeʿiyyat Filastiniyya* 3 (Beirut: Muʾassasat al-Dirasat al-Filastiniyya).

Gender, Nakba and Nation
*Palestinian Women's Presence and Absence
in the Narration of 1948 Memories*

Rema Hammami

Between the spring of 1998 and summer 1999, a public project of memory narration and codification of the Nakba took place in the pages and over the airwaves of the semi-official Palestinian media. This 'official' project could build on a long history of Nakba narratives being produced across different genres and mobilized as part of the various collective identity making projects of Palestinian nationalism. The dramatic difference in 1998 was that, for the first time, Palestinians witnessed a collective and public commemoration that marked the Nakba off as a national ritual, as opposed to a series of texts and private memories. Practically, this was due to the fact that the 50-year commemoration took place in the context of Palestinian state formation and the existence of state apparati interested in generating a certain type of memory/ history and attempting to encode it as part of an official national narrative. The commemorations were produced as a public and collective exercise in which the carriers of this memory were the general public (of a certain generation) who undertook the role of story tellers as direct witnesses to this formative trauma in the Palestinian nation's history.[1]

---

1 I use the word 'nation' here as an analytic concept through which we can address issues of collective identity, belonging and representation of the Palestinian 'people'. Due to the specific history of nationalism in the region, 'nation' in Arabic is reserved for the larger Arab nation, while 'people' is considered the correct designation for national collectivities of existing (or emerging) nation states.

For weeks, on the 'Voice of Palestine' and in the pages of the Palestinian daily *Al-Ayyam*, a veritable deluge of personal testimonials poured forth—seemingly a whole generation of the public recalled the formative events in a collective process of witnessing.

Although the state formation politics of the 1948 commemorations is an important topic in itself, it is not the direct subject of this paper. Instead, dominant nationalist narratives of the Nakba are used as a window into issues of gender, nationalism and representation in the Palestinian context. While a large body of literature exists on Palestinian women as activists in the national movement, the more symbolic roles of women in the production and reproduction of Palestinian nationalism have rarely been touched upon. The ways in which women were positioned in the 1998 narratives (and those preceding them) of the Nakba provides insights into the larger positioning of women of different classes within the rhetorical and symbolic devices of Palestinian nationalism, history writing and ultimately identity making.

The direct problematic addressed here is why peasant women in particular have been excluded as narrators of the 1948 experience—especially in contrast to peasant men who are consistently mobilized as its paradigmatic voice. This absence of peasant women from the various memory-making projects also contrasts dramatically with the presence of urban middle class women—who have recently played (in film) a vocal but significantly different role in the production of a specific memory of 1948, as well as in representing a different aspect of the nation.

Only recently have feminists theorized the multiple and complex ways that women are implicated in nation-building projects; either in terms of concrete policies and actions or in the symbolic reproduction of various dimensions of nationhood.[2] In terms of the latter, Yuval-Davis

---

2   See Nira Yuval-Davis, *Gender and Nation* (London: Sage Publications, 1997); Cynthia Enloe, *Bananas, Beaches, Bases: Making Feminist Sense of International Politics* (London: Panorama, 1989); S. Walby. 'Woman and Nation,' in G. Balakrishan (ed.), *Mapping the Nation* (London: Verso, 1996).

says, 'gendered bodies and sexuality play pivotal roles as territories, markers and reproducers of the narratives of nations and other collectivities.'[3] Women as the biological reproducers of future members of the collectivity and social reproducers of the national culture are particularly apt symbols for representing a variety of myths, passions, and processes involved in nation making. For instance, as Benedict Anderson has pointed out, nations often depend on powerful con structions of shared origins, in some immemorial past which, however, seems 'to glide into a limitless future'.[4] In this process of implying a shared genealogical origin, nations often invoke the metaphor of family and, in particular the mother. 'Mother Russia', 'Mother Ireland' or 'Mother India' all imply the way in which nations are thought of as giving birth, life and a home to their members. And probably originating in peasant culture is women's association with land through notions of fertility, which is also found in nationalist mythology and metaphor. Through these associations, one can see how women become the national territory to be defended, the homeland, and the boundary markers with other collectivities.

Homi Bhabha and Partha Chatterjee[5] have both elaborated on Anderson's 'dual-time' of national imaginaries, that of the immemorial past and the limitless future. Both show that the immemorial past becomes conceived of in the present as an unchanging inner-core of national culture—a nation's spiritual essence. But Chatterjee goes on to identify women as charged with this particular burden of representation. As such, women's responsibility to reproduce the national culture simultaneously becomes the symbolic role of representing its fixity and time-less nature.

These insights have resonance for a reading of Palestinians women's location in narratives of nationhood. But national narratives are never seamless consensual undertakings. Different social groups—no matter

3   Yuval-Davis, *Gender and Nation.*
4   Benedict Anderson, *Imagined Communities: Reflections on the Origin and Spread of Nationalism* (London: Verso, 1983), p. 19.
5   Homi Bhabha, *Nation and Narration* (London: Routledge, 1990); Partha Chatterjee, *The Nation and its Fragments; Colonial and Postcolonial Histories* (Princeton: Princeton University Press, 1993).

their political cohesion within national liberation movements—have contending projects in terms of asserting particular images and symbols of nationhood. In the narratives of the Nakba produced across different genres in the 1990s contending projects of representing the Palestinian nation expressed themselves clearly through the representation of women.

The Nakba as National Corpus

Over the past fifty-seven years, the Nakba has been a recurrent theme in various forms of nationalist historiography and cultural production. The earliest treatment of it was the six-volume history by the chronicler 'Arif al-'Arif. This was followed in the 1960s by Mustafa al-Dabbagh's encyclopedic, *Our Country Palestine*, which included specific histories of each village and town and their fate during the war.[6] But perhaps the treatment of the Nakba, as history, has predominantly been undertaken through various works of oral history, emerging in the late 1970s with Birzeit University's Research Center's series on destroyed Palestinian villages being the main institutional innovator.[7] The genre of oral history remains the dominant textual strategy through which the Nakba is treated, as we see in the continuing production of village and town memorial books that reached its popular zenith in 1998 in the 50-year commemorations of the Nakba, when the local Palestinian press was awash with oral history testimonials of the events of 1948. In literature the Nakba has also been a constant source of inspiration. Its earliest treatment in the 1950s by poet Abdul Karim al-Karmi (Abu Salma) was followed in the 1960s by the short stories of Ghassan Kanafani, reaching

---

6   'Arif al-'Arif, *Al-Nakba, Nakbat Bayt al-Maqdis wal-Firdaws al-Mafqud 1947–1952* (The Catastrophe, The Catastrophe of the Holy Land and The Lost Paradise), (Sidon, Lebanon: Al-Maktaba al-Assriyya, 1956). Mustapha Murad al-Dabbagh, *Biladuna Filastin* (Our Country Palestine), (Beirut: Dar al-Tali'a, 1965).

7   This project, initiated in the mid-1980s by Sherif Kana'aneh and Rashad al-Madani and subsequently directed by Saleh Abd al-Jawad, has to date produced 22 histories of destroyed Palestinian villages.

perhaps it most famous novelistic treatment in Emile Habibi's *The Secret Life of Said the Pessoptimist*, first published in 1974. In the visual arts, representation of the Nakba also emerged early on. In the mid-1950s, Ismael Shammout produced the first series of what became known as *hijra* or emigration paintings depicting the expulsion and flight of Palestinians in 1948. Again, the *hijra* re-appeared in works by the Gazan artist Fathi Ghabin in both the early 1980s and early 1990s. The one anomaly is film; only in the period of the 50-year commemorations did there emerge a series of documentaries, predominantly undertaken by diasporic filmmakers, in which life in the pre-1948 coastal cities dominated thematically in their treatment of the Nakba.

The breadth and continuity of the treatment of the Palestinian experience in 1948 across a wide range of genres attests to its ongoing power as a foundational event in the creation and ongoing reproduction of the Palestinian national consciousness and identity. What is striking, however, is the relative fixity in its treatment since the 1950s until the present despite interceding history or the filter of different genres and writers.[8] Clearly, as a foundational moment whose very nature was one of trauma and loss that has yet to reach a redemptive *denouement*, the Nakba stands openly in the national imaginary as an unhealed wound. As such, the repetitive treatment of various aspects of it—the lost paradise of pre-1948 Palestine, the cruel and willful expulsion of the people from their homes and land—continues to provide a resonant allegory with the existential present. This is all the more so since Palestinian narratives of the Nakba, regardless of their currency within Palestinian society (and the wider Arab world), remain to this day subalternized counter-narratives to the hegemonic Zionist narrative of the creation of Israel in 1948 as a moment of national re-birth and political independence.[9]

8   Hasan Khader, 'One Event, Two Signs', *Al-Ahram Weekly* (Cairo), 31 December 1998.
9   This struggle against an overwhelming denial (with concrete political force) also explains why many of the narratives of the Nakba take the form of evidence and witnessing regardless of the fact that they are written for a local/national audience in the form of oral history, popular journalism, or even literature.

Homeland

But fundamentally, in whatever narrative form it takes, the Nakba is the story of the loss of the Palestinian homeland and thus represents the way in which Palestinians' relationship to 'homeland' has been profoundly defined by the experience of dispossession. It is from the location of political exile that the homeland has been dominantly imagined.[10] As such, very recently, even for Palestinians in the Occupied Territories, Palestine has been that place of the 'elsewhere' that was lost in 1948.

Collective identity based on an affinity with the lost space of Palestine clearly preceded other constructions of Palestinian nationhood. Given that Palestine had never existed as a sovereign entity, and prior to 1948 had a weak and divided national movement with an ill-defined nationalism, in the immediate aftermath of the Nakba Palestinian-ness was largely defined in this way by the majority of the Palestinians who were now refugees. Yezid Sayigh has described this as a form of 'regional patriotism' with a sense of collective identity being based primarily on a common territorial component rather than a common culture.[11] In this light, Nora Ratzel's[12] insight is apt: that political exiles (unlike natives who stay, as well as immigrant diasporas) express attachment to their homelands through the language of climate, smell and other physical characteristics rather than invoking people. Thus, in early—and continuing—Palestinian narratives of the homeland it is commonly evoked in personal memoirs, poetry and literature as a specific house, certain fields or even a particular tree.[13]

10 Slyomovics notes that, when looking at memorial books of destroyed Palestinian villages, 'we must learn from memorial books the ways in which the "here" of the place of exile is always opposed to the distant "there" of the Palestinian homeland'; see Susan Slyomovics, *The Object of Memory; Arab and Jew Narrate the Palestinian Village* (Philadelphia: University of Pennsylvania Press, 1998), p. 12.

11 Yezid Sayigh, *Armed Struggle and the Search for a State; The Palestinian National Movement 1949-1993* (Oxford: Clarendon Press, 1997), p. xiii.

12 In Yuval-Davis, *Gender and Nation*, p. 18.

13 Anton Shammas, 'Autocartography', *Three Penny Review* 63 (1995), in which an old exiled woman from Jaffa thinks of Palestine in terms of the lemon tree in her garden there.

Nation-ness based on a sense of collective experience and a shared political destiny emerged much later—with the latter dimension clearly linked to the rise of the PLO in the late 1960s.[14] The experience of the Nakba and affinity with the lost homeland remained pivotal components of these later constructions. The discourse of loss and longing remained, but with the 'maturation' of Palestinian nationalism, it was now the nation that would redeem the homeland through the dual resistance of memory and armed struggle. As will become apparent when we review the 1998 commemorations, these cornerstones of Palestinian identity begin to fissure post the PLO declaration of a two-state solution in 1988 and especially within the terms of the 1993 Oslo Accords. When the homeland and the nation-state no longer overlap and political negotiation is substituted for armed resistance, memory remains the only means of redemption.

Given the size, variability and long historical breadth of this corpus on the Nakba, it is impossible to treat the location of women within the entire range of narrative genres. Instead, I will focus on more recent texts where the contradictory positioning of women as signifiers of the nation appears most acute. Thus, the overwhelming absence of women from the historical narratives—including the range of oral history projects—is contrasted with visual art and media, where women become central referents used to express various forms of loss or survival. Specifically, this article will analyze representations of women in the oral history narratives of the Nakba (in the form of commemorative articles in Palestinian press and village memorial books), in nationalist art depicting the flight, and in the recent spate of films on pre-1948 urban life. The repetition and recurrence of particular representations of women in these narratives bespeaks the fact that these tropes are produced in a larger field of cultural and political practices. As such, individual authorship works within the existing cultural language and symbols—even when critiquing it.

---

14 Sayigh (*Armed Struggle*, pp. xiii-xiv) calls the former 'experiential nationalism' and the latter 'cognitive nationalism'.

The 1998 Narratives

An overview of the commemorative coverage the local Palestinian newspaper *Al-Ayyam* dedicated to the Nakba during 1998–1999 is exemplary of the gendered problematic outlined above.[15] *Al-Ayyam* is considered the most culturally sophisticated and socially 'liberal' among the local press and comes with a bi-weekly insert (*Kul al-Nis'a*, 'All Women') produced by the umbrella organization of the Palestinian women's movement. However, within the series of articles, columns and features commemorating the Nakba there was an almost total absence of women—tellingly, even *Kul al-Nis'a* never did a special commemorative feature. Given that the coverage spanned the period of more than a year and literally more than two hundred articles by a wide range of staff and guest writers, it is clear that this absence bespeaks a deeper problematic than the whim of an individual editor, or problems of column space.

Al -Ayyam's coverage of the Nakba took three basic narrative forms: political analysis by historians and political thinkers; local histories of the war based on interviews with witnesses; and first person testimonials reflecting personal experiences of the war and its immediate aftermath. In the first two types of articles women are completely invisible. In the third type—first-person testimonials—a small (and, I will argue, exceptional) handful of women appear among the 'popular voices', although they are absent among the testimonials of well-known public figures. In terms of column space, it is the first two types of writing that make up the bulk of the commemorations, comprised of political analysis and national and local histories of the war. Articles of political analysis overwhelmingly focus on why the population left,

---

15 The textual analysis here uses *Al-Ayyam's* Nakba coverage for a number of reasons. Although the newspaper *Al-Hayat al-Jadida* is the official mouthpiece of the PNA, *Al-Ayyam*, though also PNA supported, has a much wider readership and is much more publicly influential due to the quality and depth of its reporting. While not representing a unitary ideological line, it is the dominant journalistic forum for post-Oslo nationalist intellectual and political writing.

Zionist military strategy, and the failure of the Palestinian leadership.[16] Their role, among other things, is to lend the fragmented picture of national experiences in 1948 some overall coherence and spatial and temporal logic. In Bhabha's terms, they could be defined as pedagogical narratives.[17] They are texts that present the 'people' as pre-given and their history as a unitary national experience in an exercise of teaching a particular rendition of 'nationhood'. The authoritative voice inherent in this discourse is also belied by the title under which the series of political and historical analyses were published, '*L-kay la Nansa*' ('So As Not to Forget').

However, the dramatic elements of the story that they tell—of an in-nocent and mostly leaderless population facing a well-prepared, powerful military force supported by imperialist allies and the collusion of corrupt Arab leaderships, which results in dispersion and national destruc-tion—cannot override the picture of fragmented experiences that so powerfully imposes itself in the second type of articles, those representing local histories of the war.[18] In these, information provided by witnesses is deployed to create a narrative of specific events and moments in 1948, and while sources are identified by name, usually the narrator speaks on their behalf rather than directly quoting them.[19] What emerges from these

16 See, e.g., the five-part series by the Syrian writer, Haytham al Kilani: part 1 (22 March 1998), an overview of the phases of the war; part 2 (23 March 1998), the balance of power between Arab and Zionist forces; part 3 (24 March 1998), Zionist military strategy; part 4 (25 March 1998), civilian massacres and transfer of the population; part 5 (25 March 1998), the war's outcome. A number of analytical articles are devoted to understanding the fall of specific cities and the expulsion of their population; cf. Azmi Khawaja on the fall of Haifa (5 May 1998). All references are to *Al-Ayyam* newspaper.
17 Bhabha, *Nation and Narration*, p. 297.
18 Local histories of the war relying on witness information were published in two forms: throughout the years 1988-1999 they were produced on the cultural pages as a regular column by Nimr Sirhan called 'Shababik' (Windows); and during the spring and summer of 1998 they also appeared in feature form.
19 See, e.g., Safi Safi's three-part series on what caused the inhabitants of Beit Nabala near Lydda to flee in 1948. Safi uses the village as a case study in order to assess various hypotheses about why the population took flight. Through interviews with villagers he details the events and circumstances (as well as the psychological dimension) that was the backdrop to the dispersal of the villagers (*Al-Ayyam*, 11-13 July 1999)

narratives of particular battles, village and town resistance is a picture of extreme localism, atomization and non-coherence on any regional or national scale. The fragments of the national experience, however, constantly repeat themselves—regardless of whether they are about a city or village, or particular battle—and it is through this repetition that the partial and segmented local experiences begin to take on a unity as a national narrative. In that sense Homi Bhabha's concept of the performative nature of narratives of national representation can be seen in what appears to be the same story, but told from a myriad different voices and places within the space of the nation. While localized experiences of the war in 1948 clearly had their own specificity, both the telling of them and, more so, the writing of them are done within existent narrative strategies of nationhood.[20]

What are also apparent in these local histories (and subsequently in the first-person male narratives) are the dual dimensions of nationalist resistance: memory and armed struggle. The minute detail in the telling of the war in a myriad of small villages and battles is a conscious performance of a national memory that struggles against erasure. But these local accounts of the war always include the memory of village men buying or attempting to buy weapons to defend their communities.[21] The lost battle and subsequent dispossession from the home and land is thus rendered as a heroic but failed resistance—one that in 1998 can only continue on the battlefield of memory.[22]

20 Bhabha, *Nation and Narration*, p. 297.
21 For some examples, see Nimr Sirhan's interview with 'Abu Shawkat' (*Al-Ayyam*, 22-23 February 1999); article entitled 'He Doesn't Hide His Longing for Caesaria' (*Al-Ayyam*, 14-27 May 1998); article entitled 'We Found All of the Houses Destroyed' (*Al-Ayyam*, 17-30 May 1998).
22 This relationship is nicely summed up in the sub-heading of an article that brings together first person accounts of 1948; 'Subhi al Jalda: Manufactured Weapons: The Blood Flowed Like A River/ and Khalil Sirraj: Armed with His Property Deeds, Key and the Hope of Return' (*Al-Ayyam*, 18-19 May 1998).

Women's Absence

The absence of women in the analysis of 1948 and in the telling of local histories is clearly part of the larger problematic of women's absence from narratives of war. As Miriam Cooke cogently argues, war stories always attempt to order 'what is' along a line of binary opposites: war/peace, foe/friend, aggression/defense, front/home, combatant/civilian.[23] Women are always the absent presence in war narratives as they are located in the spaces of non-war—the home, and the peaceful spaces that need defending. In the narratives of local battles of 1948 women only appear in this guise—as the abstract women/children that heroic village men attempted to defend along with the land and the community.

However, it is in the third genre of writing in the commemorations in 1998, i.e., in first-person eyewitness accounts, that women's absence becomes most glaring.[24] In contrast to the local histories, here the individual comes to the forefront as witnesses who narrate their personal experience. While the local histories attempt to weave communities into the national narrative, the eyewitness accounts attempt to link individuals (of all backgrounds) as carriers of the national experience. Thus, there is an attempt to represent the full range of the 'citizenry' made up of the well-known and the unknown, wealthy and poor, former villagers and urban merchants, statesmen, artists and even a few women. Although all the voices are an attempt to assert the 'public' of the Nakba, women's voices are absent from the roster of well-known figures (political and cultural leaders) whose memoirs were rallied in a separate, regular feature called 'Shehada'. Between March and June 1998, sixteen of these testimonials were published in more

---

23 Miriam Cooke, *Women and the War Story* (Los Angeles: University of California Press, 1997), p. 15.

24 These also took two dominant forms: a regular feature during the spring and summer of 1998 called 'Shehada' (Witness, or Testimonial); and a range of features of remembrances by location, some under the heading 'Direct Witnesses to the Nakba'. Under the heading of 'Shehada' fall autobiographical accounts of the war, predominantly by intellectuals and political figures.

than twenty articles in the cultural pages of *Al-Ayyam*—without a single female voice, despite the fact that in more academic fora for the commemorations well-known women writers presented their own personal testimonials.[25]

The range of features that centrally mobilize popular voices, sometimes under the heading 'Direct Witnesses to the Nakba', were published predominantly in May 1998, during the height of the commemorations. Some of the voices are organized around the thematic of place: the cities of Jaffa, Haifa, and Akka; and the villages of Deir Yassin, Caesaria, al-Mansi, Walaja and al-Ammur.[26] While in other cases, individual refugees from a range of different villages are brought together as 'Direct Witnesses', in these testimonials 'regular people' narrate the personal experience of their families and communities in the war and in its immediate aftermath. Here, popular voices, the experiences of 'regular people', are uncovered and brought to centre stage in order to represent the collective experience. This function of popular voices was explicitly enunciated in the introduction the editor of the 'Testimonials', Ghassan Zaqtan (poet, and at the time editor of *Al-Ayyam*'s cultural section), wrote for the series:

> We chose the cultural section (of the newspaper) because of our conviction that popular memory is one of the most important sources of our cultural production. It is not for us to judge (these) texts on their literary merit, as much as to work to weave a collective vision, akin to a tremendous fresco that all participate in drawing, each with its own language, colours and analyses.

25 Hala Sakakini, the daughter of educator Khalil Sakakini, was the only woman to present her experiences at the Sakakini Cultural Center in Ramallah in 1998, and the literary critic, Salma Khadra al Jayyusi, was the only female public figure to present her experiences in the special issue on the Nakba of the *Journal of Palestine Studies* (109, Autumn 1998).

26 Articles in *Al-Ayyam* on the cities include the following: Akka, 14 April 1998; Jaffa, 14 May 1998; Haifa, 5 May 1998; on villages: Caesarea, 14 April 1998; Walaja and Ammur, 30 May 1998.

Women's Voices

Although a few women's voices finally emerge in the articles of popular witnessing, their presence is determined by the fact that only they can adequately signify certain dimensions of the national imaginary. They do not appear in order to represent the experience of the Nakba from a women's point of view, but because they are the over-determined symbols of two specific sites: the city of Jaffa and the massacre of Deir Yassin.

In the two part series, 'Direct Witnesses to the Nakba', seven individuals from different villages and towns of origin provide their testimony and among them are two women, one originally from Jaffa and another originally from the village of al-Na'ani near Ramle.[27] In terms of the testimonies by location, it is only Jaffa that once again allows for a woman to be among the three eyewitnesses, and of the villages covered it is only Deir Yassin where there is a woman's voice. Finally, in an article that is only incidentally about the Nakba, but actually about a woman reaching the age of 130, Hajja Salama Darwish, also originally from Jaffa, is the fifth female testimonial of the Nakba among a virtual ocean of male memory and voice.[28]

Clearly, given that three of the women are from Jaffa, it seems that they are somehow fundamentally associated with that city—it is the only place in which there is an inevitable female included in the commemorations.[29] Jaffa is also ostensibly the subject of the commemorative films produced in the period of the commemorations—films where female voices are central (see below).

The fourth woman is the central voice in the eyewitness article on the massacre of Deir Yassin, but she is identified in the following terms:

---

27 See *Al-Ayyam*, 9 and 10 May 1998.
28 'Al-Hajja Salama Darwish, 130 Years and 350 Descendants' (*Al-Ayyam*, 6 February 1999).
29 These are Subhiyya Sa'ad in the article dated 14 April 1998; Madiha Hinnawi in the article dated 10 May 1998; and Salama Darwish in the article dated 6 February 1999.

> Um Salah is considered one of the reliable witnesses who experienced the events of the massacre of Deir Yassin and she is an honoured guest in most of the conferences in remembrance of the massacre in which she provides historical evidence on Deir Yassin at every forum [...] over the past half century.

Unlike the myriad male testimonials of specific events (rather than simply personal experiences), Um Salah's capacity to represent such a central national event as the Deir Yassin massacre must be explicitly justified through an initial presentation of her credentials as 'expert witness'. But it is also clear that the massacre of Deir Yassin as the momentous event within the war of 1948 that led to the flight of so many communities, specifically because of the well-known murder of women and children there, has to have a female voice to represent it. Deir Yassin looms very large but singularly in the national imaginary. It is *the* referent for the brutality of the enemy in 1948, and it also *the* marker of national shame. Shame, because the story of it led to flight, but more fundamentally because it so centrally invokes the transgression of women's bodies by the enemy in war.

The only woman present in the commemorations without some form of extenuating circumstance is a peasant refugee woman, Miriam Marbu'a, from the village of al-Na'ani near Ramle, now living in al-Amari refugee camp near Ramallah. Her inclusion along with two 'ordinary' male witnesses is probably due to the article's authorship by a female journalist, Rana Annani, who just before it was published authored an article interviewing the head of a women's oral history project which sought to uncover women's contribution to national resistance.[30] Miriam's memory, however, interpellates itself as a hidden counter-narrative to the dominant ways in which women are supposed to represent the experience of 1948. As she describes how the villagers of Na'ani literally had to run for their lives because the Zionist forces

30 See Rana Annani's interview with Fayha Abd al-Hadi entitled 'Recovering the Role of the Palestinian Woman; Oral History Project Paints New Picture of Women's Struggle' (*Al-Ayyam*, 8 November 1998).

were immediately behind them shooting, she says, 'And from the amount of fear, some of the women left their children behind on the road without even realizing it.'[31] As will be addressed subsequently, such an admission stands in radical contrast to images of women in the pictorial representation of the Nakba by Palestinian artists.

A Continued Absence

This overwhelming absence of women as actors in and narrators of the foundational experience of Palestinian nationhood can partially be located in women's general absence from Palestinian historiography, such as their absence from the history of the 1936 revolt.[32] Again, that both histories of 1948 and 1936 fit into the larger genre of War Stories may well account for this. However, women are also absent from another genre of Palestinian history-writing, in which war plays only a partial and concluding chapter, i.e., oral histories of pre-1948 village life as exemplified in the oral history project on Destroyed Palestinian Villages set up by Birzeit University Research Center in the early 1980s. According to its founders, the project sought to:

31 *Al-Ayyam*, 9 May 1998, p. 18.
32 See Islah Jad, 'The Forgotten History: Who Remembers Women's Roles in Politics', in Huda Sadda et al. (eds.), *Women's History and Alternative Memory* (Cairo: Nur – Dar Alma'a al-Arabia li-Nashir [Nur – Arab Women's Publishing House], 1998) (in Arabic); Ted Swedenburg, *Memories of Revolt: The 1936-39 Rebellion and the Palestinian National Past* (Minneapolis: University of Minnesota Press, 1995). A singular and telling exception is the foundational work of anthropologist Rosemary Sayigh on the social history of Palestinian refugees. While Sayigh included a myriad of women's narratives in the formative work of Palestinian oral history, *Palestinians, From Peasants to Revolutionaries* (London: Zed Books, 1979), as well as in her subsequent work, *Too Many Enemies; The Palestinian Experience in Lebanon* (London: Zed Books, 1994), a generation of social and oral historians, highly indebted to her path-breaking work have tended to overlook its feminist emphasis. On the other hand, feminist scholars working on Palestine have been highly influenced by her insights but continue to focus overwhelmingly on gender in contemporary life.

describe the village in such a way that the reader is able to picture it
as living inhabited and cultivated as it was in 1948 before it was
destroyed [...] allowing Palestinians to feel tied and connected to the
villages society and real country as if they had lived in it rather than
being a name on a map.[33]

The twenty-two studies in the series covering different destroyed villages (and one town, Majdal) used oral history interviews with former
villagers, as well as maps, photographs and documents in an attempt to
re-create or 'preserve' a particular history of a now destroyed place.
Susan Slyomovics has typified the series as fitting into a larger genre of
'memorial books'—individual volumes that memorialize a village,
district or region that no longer exists.[34] Usually it is former inhabitants
of places lost to uprooting who compile memorial books, and their
authorship, readership and publication venues draw on this same
community of former inhabitants.[35] While Slyomovics' typification is
useful, in the Palestinian case village memorial books are not simply
about remembering a lost community—they are consciously nationalist narratives and their production is a conscious project of mapping
the lost homeland, destroyed village by destroyed village.

The Birzeit village memorial books have a set thematic structure and
a consistent narrative strategy.[36] The villages initially materialize
through dense geographic description; they are placed in a relational
map with other lost and living communities and natural landmarks.
They are then mapped internally and concretized through accounting
both the size and distribution of land and the relation of built with

33 Sherif Kana'aneh and Rashad al-Madani, 'The Destroyed Palestinian Villages,
    No. 7: Al- Faluja' (Birzeit, 1987).
34 See Chap. 1, 'Memory and Place', in Slyomovics, *The Object of Memory*, pp. 1-
    28.
35 Ibid., pp. 2-4.
36 While the first 17 were supervised by Sherif Kana'aneh, Saleh Abd al-Jawad, who
    supervised the subsequent five, moved them away from memorial books and
    more in the direction of local social history. However, the thematic components
    of the books remained relatively fixed.

agricultural space. The village is then located in epic history beginning in a mythic past and bringing them up to the period of the British Mandate that subsequently becomes the books' ethnographic present. The present and living village of the Mandate period unfolds in the sections on economic and social life. In each book, the concluding chapter is inevitably the local experience of the Nakba.

Women are consistently located in the books in only two specific areas: under the 'social' in the form of descriptions of local dress, and weddings.[37] In the former, they appear not as persons but as female costumes in relation to male ones. In the latter, they predominantly appear as objects in a set anthropological ritual. The only women's voices that consistently appear in the books are in the form of songs that women sang at weddings. There are a number of minor exceptions to this pattern and one exceptional case. The minor exceptions are when a particular economic activity is distinctive of the village itself and women's participation in the activity allows their mention. Thus, in the book on the town of Majdal, women are mentioned as involved in the local weaving industry and in the book on the village of al-Faluja, women are mentioned as being responsible for a prime agricultural activity (poultry raising). The one major exception in terms of gender is the study on the village of Abu Shushch,[38] the nineteenth book in the series, and the first produced under new editorship. The Abu Shusheh book is unique because researchers discovered that it was the site of a massacre by Zionist forces that included the killing of women, children and the elderly. Women become the central characters in the dramatic narrative of Abu Shusheh's fall because the majority of village men were absent fighting elsewhere when the attack took place. The women come to centre stage after the massacre because, during it, they were hiding with their children in caves within the village and only after Abu

---

37 For an example from the earlier series, see Kana'aneh and al-Madani, 'No 7: Al-Faluja'; for the later series, see Abdel Rahim al-Mudawar, No. 19: 'The Village of Tira'at Haifa' (Birzeit, 1995).

38 Written by Nasir Yaqub and Fahum al-Shalabi and edited by Walid Moustafa and Saleh Abd al-Jawad (Birzeit, 1995).

Shusheh was occupied for three days by the Zionist forces, was their presence discovered:

> The story doesn't end there, the defense of the village was a chapter, the massacre was another chapter, and the entry (into the village) was another chapter. And while it was men who were the heroes of these preceding events, here we are confronted with a new hero: the women.[39]

The narrative continues with the women of Abu Shusheh, negotiating and undertaking the burial of the dead scattered throughout the village; organizing access to food and water; and grouping together for physical protection. After a period of four terrifying days (in which two children were murdered in front of their mothers), the women began to flee in three waves until the majority were collectively 'transferred' by the Zionist Hagana forces on the final day.

Because women are central actors in the narrative of Abu Shusheh's resistance in the war, they are given a separate section in the Social Life chapter of the book under the heading of '*al-Mar'a*' (The Woman).[40] As in the other books, they make an appearance through topics of dress and weddings, but here for the first (and only) time in the village memorial book series is there an additional and separate treatment of their role in village life. But in comparison with the naturalizing voice that dominates throughout all the books in their treatment of village social and economic life, the narrative on women is full of uncertainty. The women's section begins with questioning: 'Did she live in darkness and enslavement or was she a partner of the man?'[41] But because the only available paradigm to write about peasant women in Palestinian village life is folklore, the text becomes a specific description of women's crafts and a superficial discussion of women's agricultural and domestic labour and roles within the family. There are no specific female characters; no age or social hierarchies as there are with village

39   Ibid., p. 208.
40   Ibid., p. 173
41   Ibid.

men. And the only specialization among the women that is mentioned is that of the mid-wife.

Peasant Men and Peasant Women

Thus, even in the exceptional case of the Abu Shusheh book women are predominantly encoded within village history and social and economic life through the genre of folklore. They appear as fragments of material and oral folk culture—either through costume, crafts, or folk songs sung at weddings. Similar to their positioning in narratives of the war, in the pre-war histories they also remain locked in the implicit space of private family life. In the former they are not on the battlefield and in the latter they are not in the public sphere of the village that the books so painstakingly attempt to 're-construct'.

In contrast, both in the village memorial books and in the later press commemorations of the Nakba in 1998, peasant men are central referents of the national experience. In the memorial books, they are the lived village and communities of lost Palestine, and in the commemorations they are the well-spring of insurgency against that of dispersal and dismemberment. Swedenburg's assessment of the representation of the peasant (*fallah*) in Palestinian historiography of the 1936 Revolt and beyond suggests the degree to which this iconic role of peasant men in Palestinian nationalism is longstanding:

> Owing to his crucial role in the 1936–39 revolt, the *fallah* epitomizes the anti-colonial struggle. The peasant additionally signifies a prolonged attachment to and intense love for the land of Palestine in the face of land expropriation and population transfers. The *sumud* (steadfastness) of the *fallah* is the model for confronting these dangers and maintaining a permanence of place.[42]

He goes on to show, however, that consistently in the political analysis of the revolt the insurgent peasant is ultimately assessed as incapable of

42 Swedenburg, *Memories of Revolt*, p. 22.

mounting an organized and strategic struggle; he is in need of an educated elite leadership that will overcome his localism, clannishness and
inherent deficiencies.[43] In the 1998 commemorations, this discourse is
reproduced but with a subtle shift whereby the onus of the defeat is
placed more squarely on the lack of a national leadership and Arab
solidarity: 'The burden rested on the villagers, and the initiative was left
to those with initiative, and in the absence of a comprehensive national
strategy and aware leadership and Arab support there was no hope.'[44]

However, peasant males were absent from earliest historical works on
the Nakba: in 'Arif al-'Arif's foundational work they play a secondary
role to the elites and the struggles in the towns. Their ascension to centre
stage in Palestinian nationalism can be dated to three moments and
geographical centres in the history of the national movement: first, with
the advent of Marxists streams within the PLO in the late 1960s, followed by the emergence of nationalist poets and novelists in the Galilee
in the mid-1970s, and completed in the rise of the 'heritage movement'
in the Occupied Territories in the late 1970s.[45] The historiographical
work reviewed by Swedenburg on the 1936 Revolt is exemplary of the
first wave of radical history writing that emerged around the PLO's
Palestine Research Center in Beirut, as are the short stories of Ghassan
Kanafani; the poets Tawfiq Zayyad and Mahmud Darwish and the
novelist Emile Habibi represent the second wave which emerged in the
Galilee; and the Birzeit village memorial books, as well as the Palestine
Folklore Society journal *al-Turath w-al-Mujtama* (Heritage and Society)
are exemplary of the third wave. While there are differences and nuances
in representations of the male peasant across these three waves,
Swedenburg's (above) assessment summarizes well the main components. But taking his analysis one step further, a central absence suddenly appears. Peasant men represent the timelessness of agricultural life

43   Ibid., pp. 19-21
44   Nimr Sirhan in his regular column 'Shababik' making the links between the 1936
     Revolt and resistance in 1948 (*Al-Ayyam*, 22-23 February 1999).
45   The basis for this conceptualization can be found in Salim Tamari, 'Soul of the
     Nation: The Fallah in the Eyes of the Urban Intelligentsia,' *Review of Middle East
     Studies* 5 (1988), p. 79.

prior to 1948, the cyclical relation of the seasons—a cycle and relationship that has existed for 'time immemorial'. He is not the land itself, but the signifier of dependence on it and an immutable attachment to it. 1948 suddenly thrusts him into non-cyclical time—he is forced into modern history. This rupture also moves him from a naturalized relationship with nature into an active political struggle with man. Through traversing these different ruptures (of time, space and the relationship to nature) he embodies the contradictory experiences and imperatives of the national past and its re-birth. He is, at once, the past and its subsequent loss. He represents the dual imperatives of continued attachment to that past, as well as the necessity of entering modernity in order to redeem it. He is loss and redemption, tradition and modernity, but he is neither the land, nor the homeland nor the nation.

While the peasant male's attachment to the land transforms him into a central symbol of its loss, it is the silenced peasant woman who remains outside of history and modernity. She is the marker of what has neither changed nor has been lost: variously the land, the homeland and the nation's inner sanctum. She represents the ontological link between past and present, land and nation, as exemplified in a concluding line in the 1988 Palestinian declaration of Independence where a tribute is paid 'to the brave Palestinian woman, guardian of sustenance and life, keeper of our people's perennial flame'. In their silence from history, peasant women have played central roles in representing the various fixities of nation-ness and the national experience. But their allegorical role has also shifted across the different phases of Palestinian nationalism. Her earlier incarnations were as land and homeland, ironically most exemplified in the allegories and metaphors that dominated the nationalist poets who emerged in the Galilee in the late 1960s. Palestine is always a woman, the beloved, or the mother addressed by the poet-lover.[46] Yearning and longing mark the

46 See Carole Bardenstein, 'Raped Brides and Steadfast Mothers: Appropriations of Palestinian Motherhood', in A. Jetter, A. Orleck and D.Taylor (eds.), *The Politics of Motherhood: Activist Voices from Left to Right* (Hanover–London: University Press of New England, 1997); Mary Layoun, *Wedded to the Land? Gender Boundaries and Nationalism in Crisis* (Durham–London: Duke University Press, 2001); and Cooke, *Women and the War Story.*

relationship with her. At other times she is the raped virgin, or the bride who the poet longs to re-unite with in the Palestinian Wedding. The quintessential expression of this can be found in the work of Mahmud Darwish from the late 1960s. For example, in his 1966 collection of poems entitled *A Lover from Palestine*, in the poem 'Diary of a Palestinian Wound' he insists, 'I am the lover and land is the beloved'.[47]

Darwish's early work exemplifies the period of Palestinian nationalism just prior to the emergence of the PLO as an independent liberation movement—and the positing of woman as homeland suggests that earlier affiliation of national identity based on lost territory. The relationship women/homeland is also apparent in the first period of Palestinian nationalist art, but is expressed through women's *absence* in depictions of refugee flight and the refugee experience. For instance, in the foundational depictions of 1948 produced by exiled artist Ismail Shammout in the mid-1950s the iconography of the Hijra (flight) is overwhelmingly expressed through peasant men and children. In his early painting of the Hijra, 'Where to?' (1953), still considered the iconic painted image of the Nakba, a peasant father carrying a sleeping son on his shoulder clasps the hand of another child, behind him is a third child and in the distance a silhouette of his abandoned village. In another picture representing the flight produced a year later and entitled 'We Will Return', again it is a peasant male in the forefront (this time a grandfather, possibly representing a mukhtar) holding a young boy and followed by more young boys that depicts the flight. Women did not flee in Shammout's depictions of the flight and in the paintings of others from the same period, they are not depicted in the paintings of refugee misery.[48] The particular representation of peasant males in

---

47 The depiction of women in nationalist poetry is beyond the scope of this paper, but according to poet Zakaria Muhammad, the metaphor of women as the land or homeland did not exist prior to the late 1960s, and found its fullest expression in the works of Mahmud Darwish. Prior to this period longing for the land, homeland, was expressed without the metaphor of woman.

48 For examples of the latter, 'Memories and Fire' (1956) depiction of an old man staring dejectedly into a fire, and 'Here Sat My Father' (1957), of a young boy with a refugee shack in the background staring at a stool.

these works suggests the degree to which his signification as the well-spring of national insurgency emerged later; for here he is scared, broken and passive. But peasant women's symbolism during this period is exemplified by their very absence in representations of the flight. Again, it is women's association with the land during this nascent period of Palestinian nationalism that suggests the inability to represent them as part of the community in flight or exile within art that is consciously nationalist.[49]

Peasant women as symbolic devices representing the land continued into the third wave of Palestinian nationalist production that centrally mobilized the image of the peasant, the 'Heritage Movement', which emerged in the Occupied Territories in the late 1970s. This nationalist culturalist movement[50] arose in the West Bank and Gaza at a time of rapid transformation of the agricultural base of the society brought on by the forced economic integration into Israel; the increasing land expropriations by Israel for the creation of Jewish settlements, and a period in which any expression of Palestinian nationalism was criminalized by the occupier. In this context, Palestine's heritage was that of the peasantry and the movements declared project was its preservation. Peasant dress, customs, sayings and folkways were collected, archived, exhibited and written up in book and journal form. The main intellectual forum of the movement was *al-Turath w-al-Mujtama* (Heritage and Society), founded in 1974. Salim Tamari has shown that between 1974 and 1988 only 3 per cent of the articles in the journal dealt with urban life, the vast majority focussing on peasant folklore.[51] A further analysis would show that the majority of peasant folklore

---

49 Shammout is considered the father of what later became known as the liberation art movement, which evolved in the context of the rise of the national liberation movement. His Hijra paintings, first exhibited in Gaza in the mid-1950s, exemplify a didacticism that continued to dominate nationalist art until the late 1960s.

50 The movement was made up of everything from visual artists, folklorists, and folk dance troupes. It was popularized by student-council organized 'Heritage Days' at the universities and in numerous folk museums that sprung up around the country.

51 Tamari, *Soul of the Nation*, p. 79.

addressed was that of peasant women or in which women were central.[52] While most of the folklorists are men, the vast majority of topics covered (popular sayings, folktales, traditional bread baking and craft activities, traditional child-raising practices) are female. Also produced during this period were an array of books on 'Palestinian costume' that overwhelmingly focus on the embroidered dress of peasant women and folklore books, such as the childhood and child-raising practices in Palestine. Peasant women are faceless and nameless icons of an authentic and unchanging national culture; they are not historical subjects but folk artifacts. They are the site of an array of 'norms and traditions' that are expressions of the unchanging and essential characteristics of Palestinian culture.

This positioning of peasant women as the sites for the reproduction of the nation's unchanging culture and heritage is also reflected in art from this period.[53] While some of the older metaphors continue, there is a subtle but significant shift. In one work of the artist Taleb Dweik, entitled 'The Land', three peasant women stand in a field and the pattern of their traditional costume mimics aspects of the landscape. In the work of Nabil Annani, peasant women figures mimic village homes, or in Vera Tamari's work, 'Courtyard in al-Bireh', where peasant female figures against silhouettes of traditional houses actively shape the clay from which they are made. She is also mother of the nation, dramatically so in Suleiman Mansur's 1988 painting 'The Village Awakens', which has a frontally seated monolithic peasant woman and emerging from between her legs a mass of characters, men, women, children, workers, peasants. In Nabil Ananni's work, she is also a monolith, but one whose body is formed from a home (represented by three windows) and three children. But peasant women throughout these works are not posed simply as direct allegories for

52 An overview of the first four issues shows that in more than half the articles peasant women are the central figures.
53 For further analysis of women in the art of this period, see Vera Tamari and Penny Johnson, 'Loss and Vision: Representations of Women in Palestinian Art under Occupation', in Annelies Moors et al. (eds.), *Discourse and Palestine; Power, Text and Context* (Amsterdam: Het Spinhuis, 1995).

land, village or mothers of the nation—they are mobilized to represent something more transcendent; an inner core of national culture. Overwhelmingly these works locate women within a context of built culture as opposed to nature. They are consistently presented in a field of cultural artifacts (clay pots, woven baskets, village homes) or ancient symbols from Canaanite or Islamic history (the sun, the hand of Fatima, etc.). In other cases these artifacts are encoded on their bodies. Her centrality to these works suggests the extent to which she is charged with the burden of representing the nation's unchanging cultural identity. While she is still a symbol of fertility, her role as mother in these works has shifted in the direction of guardian and reproducer of this identity.

The centrality of peasant women in nationalist art from this period is dramatically reflected in the change in Ismael Shammout's treatment of her in the 1980s when compared with the 1950s. In his 1986 painting 'Rummana' (Pomegranate), the context is a refugee camp, but the huge and central figure in the foreground is that of a young self-confident peasant woman selling grapes and pomegranates. Behind her to the left is the old peasant man who has fallen to the background; while immediately behind her (and integrated with her headscarf) is a peasant madonna figure holding a child. The old peasant male sits passively in the background surrounded by active and vibrant peasant women and children. The dramatic contrast can also be seen in depictions of the Hijra during this period. In contrast to Ismail Shammout's depiction of peasant men and children in flight in the 1950s, the Gazan artist Fathi Ghabin in a series of Hijra paintings produced in the mid-1980s centrally has a peasant woman in flight, who is always carrying a young child. It is now peasant men who are absent. Peasant women in this period have moved beyond representing the land or homeland. In this array of artistic and folkloric representation, they are the nation's spiritual essence—its inner sanctum. And as expressed by the ever-present child, she is not simply the life-giver of the nation but the protector and keeper of its future. In these depictions, the nation as an idea and collective spirit has superceded the nation as a specific place or location. She is the bearer of the nation's identity and thus represents its future redemption.

Peasant Women and Urban Women

Thus throughout the different phases and genres, peasant women are never narrators of the nation—rather, various narratives of it are inscribed on their body. In contrast, a handful of urban women, at least in the commemorations of the Nakba in 1998, are able to become active narrators of the nation's past. Specifically, as mentioned earlier, it is the city of Jaffa that is the recurrent site through which women are given a voice in which to narrate the experience of the Nakba, both in the newspaper commemorations of 1998 and in films produced during the same period.[54] Significantly, although other Palestinian cities (Haifa and Akka) were addressed in *Al-Ayyam*'s commemorations, neither of them involved the representation of women.

Narratives of Jaffa and its loss represent a profound counter-narrative to dominant nationalist representations of the Nakba. As suggested by the preceding analysis, since at least the late 1960s it is the peasantry that is configured as the main heroes and victims of 1948. To some extent, small towns (such as Majdal and Lydda) have been afforded a secondary place within the national narrative, but—as opposed to presenting a specifically urban experience—their representation tends to be conflated with the peasantry. In contrast to the heroic (but tragic) peasantry, urban elites are blamed for their inability to organize a national movement and lead national resistance in 1948. As such, the marginalization of the cities from (post-PLO) nationalist historiography of pre-1948 Palestine and the Nakba is partly an expression of their being discredited as a class. Additionally, while much of the pre-1948 urban elite were able to assimilate into the economic and political life of the Arab diaspora following the Nakba, it is the peasantry who populated the refugee camps that gave birth to the national movement. Thus, the centrality of the peasantry to Palestinian nationalism and the

---

54 As I mentioned above (n. 25), overall exceptions to the Jaffa case, outside of the context of materials already covered (*Al-Ayyam*'s commemorations and village memorial books), were the writer/translator Salma Khadra al-Jayyusi and Hala Sakakini, daughter of educator Khalil Sakakini.

marginalization of the urban elites from it is also a reflection of the social bases of the national liberation movement. However, what was lost in this process of the marginalization of urban narratives and narrators is a notion that modernity was also a dimension of Palestine's past. The past that was lost—and then re-born in the national culture represented by peasant women—was one of the peasants, not of the cosmopolitan urban elite with its motor cars and cinemas.

While there are other urban centres that could represent pre-1948 Palestine's modernity and cosmopolitan-ness (i.e., Haifa), Jaffa is singular for two reasons: it was a wholly Arab city (adjacent to Jewish Tel Aviv), as opposed to Haifa which was a 'mixed' city; and Jaffa almost completely lost its population in the ethnic cleansing of 1948 (as opposed to Haifa, where out of a total Arab population of around 72,000 barely 2,000 would survive the onslaught, but which then succeeded in absorbing back significant numbers of indigenous Palestinians the Zionists had expelled from surrounding villages and towns). As such, it is Jaffa that represents the double erasure of Palestinian modernity. Strikingly, it is Jaffan exiles in the Arab, European and North American diasporas that have been the main producers of narratives of the city— exiles who pose a counterpoint to the nationalist historiography projects that were either directly or indirectly implicated in the national identity making projects of the PLO. It is also clear that these narratives of the city have only been produced in the 1980s and 1990s.

In an example of memorial books on Jaffa produced by its exiles the narratives centrally locate Jaffa as pre-1948 Palestine's cosmopolitan and modern economic capital.[55] Its modernity is established through presentations not only of the spatial and built environment but also through a complex rendering of its public institutions, social clubs and the dynamic of a modern cultural life that includes sporting clubs, cinemas, and political organizations. In the memorial book referred to above (edited by Diab), out of the more than forty first-person narratives of former exiles that make up the bulk of the book, fully one quarter are by women.

---

55 Imtiaz Diab, *Yaffa: Misk al-Madina* (Jaffa: Fragrance of a City), (Beirut, 1991).

Additionally, women have appeared as central narrators of Jaffa's collective memory in a number of documentary films produced over the past decade. These films appeared in the context of the Nakba commemorations but were centrally configured around the experience of Jaffa and were produced by the children of Jaffan exiles, again predominantly based in the diaspora. Two examples are *Na'im and Wadi'a* by Najwa Najjar and *Far from Palestine* by Robert Manthoulis. In comparison to village histories, in these films, family history becomes the central narrative strategy through which the lost past of Jaffa is constructed. However, the female voices and images that centrally construct these films have a different story to tell than the dominant nationalist one produced by peasant male re-telling of village life. Here female voices and images are not mobilized to tell a 'missing' female history of the national narrative of loss and redemption, filling in missing gender spaces. There is also no explicit feminist message in either of the films. At the same time these upper- and middle-class women of the Jaffa films are incapable (by their language, dress and ways of speaking) of representing the continuity with the past that is the domain of the iconic peasant woman. Instead, they are bearers of a completely different nationalist imaginary—the lost nation as a lost modernity. The filmic images as well as those related by the narrators themselves, all work to produce an imaginary of the nation as a modern artifact through the accounting of a particular urban life and especially the material culture it contained. But most important is the fact that it is women (middle class, educated, modern) that are the bearers of this national narrative that fundamentally attests to the nations former attainment of the modern, most iconically symbolized through its 'liberated' women.

In contrast to the loss of an unchanging rural life or as exemplars of a nascent resistance (peasant men), what we have here is women representing an achieved and subsequently destroyed modernity of the nation. And in relation to (the fixity of) the peasant women, the Jaffan women of these films represent the thwarted dynamism and unfolding into the future of the nation.

In both films it is daughters seeking to reconstruct the histories of their parents that define their overall structure. However, in *Far from*

Palestine, the parents never appear and instead it is the daughters who tell of their parents past as a means to reconstruct the golden age of Jaffa. In *Na'im and Wadi'a* the film-maker is the granddaughter who seeks to re-create the history of the lost city through the stories of her aunts about her grandparents (who give the film its name). The narrative of *Na'im and Wadi'a* is exemplary of this genre, as the following excerpts show.

> Mother was a new graduate who came to her uncle's house in Jaffa to have fun.
> She saw how open life in Jaffa was compared to Nablus and wanted to stay.
> We had land in Jaffa near the sea—it was registered in the name of my grandfather and his four sons.
> She was 18 or 19 when she married. She taught one year at Birzeit, she studied French.
> Her family were also conservative Catholics, they taught her the Catholic faith. She had a habit of fasting during the holy month of Ramadan.
> She was known as a beauty queen at the Friends school.
> We had land. We weren't rich.
> Here's the house, it had a large family room, dining room and salon, three bedrooms. There's a picture of mother standing next to the buffet—she looked like Ava Gardner.
> At the time the fashion was iron (for furniture) but father had it made from wood.
> He was one of the first to own a car [...] he collected her for the wedding in his car.
> They went on their honeymoon to Cairo. [...] Cairo was like Europe then.
> We went to Cinema for free because father was one of the shareholders.
> He loved Esther Williams and even began a correspondence with her.
> He wrote many books on rules and etiquette [...] and he loved to dance—waltz, tango.

She wasn't a good dancer so she used to let him dance with the
Jewish women and then she'd dance the easier ones with him—she
didn't mind.
The people of Jaffa loved picnics.
Mother would swim in a slip, not a maillot—only the young ones
wore bathing suits.
Your uncle got married in 1948, they went on their honeymoon to
Beirut and never came back—he had (back in Jaffa) a furnished
house waiting, with a refrigerator
They only took photos.
When she knew she lost the house she knew she lost everything
He lost his library and I lost my toys.

The narratives told involve an accounting of the accoutrements of
modernity (dining room, buffet, car, cinema, refrigerator, photographs), icons of a culture of modernity (the beach, cinema, honeymoon, Esther Williams, beauty queen, picnics, dances, the tango etc.)
and finally elements of the institutions of modern life (women's schools
and colleges, shareholding). But these artifacts are presented as part of a
dynamic and unfolding rhythm of urban life, with the story of the
family standing in for the community, the city, and ultimately the
nation.

Images of a modern urban centre, cinemas, motor cars, women
dressed in glamorous 1940s Hollywood fashion and a music backdrop
of Jazz, interspersed with footage from Hollywood films and British
newsreels, all give the film its fast paced rhythm and—very centrally—give the overall sense of 'life on the move'. The sense of forward
movement and change is also suggested through the mention of 'firsts'
(father had the first car, he was the first to have a record player, etc.) or
by other internal contrasts (mother swam in her slip but young women
swam in bathing suits, Jaffa was freer than Nablus). This stands in stark
contrast to the peasant village narratives where accounting of the land,
the crops and by implication the seasonal cycle sets up a type of cyclical
and unchanging movement of time, a fixity that was shattered only
with war. The overall message in the Jaffa films is not one of a complete
modernity (as if it can ever be complete) but of an emerging one—a

modernity in the process of unfolding but then brought to a sudden and violent halt in 1948.

The positioning of urban women as the tellers and exemplars of the nation as an unfolding modernity is not uncommon in third world nationalism.[56] Women as exemplars of the backwardness of native society or traditional society in colonial discourse, or even as a justification for colonial rule, are by now well known in the literature on the Middle East and south-east Asia. Their obverse has also been established: 'modern' Middle Eastern or Indian women as symbols or exemplars of the progressive and modernizing nature of national liberation projects. However, as both Jayawardena's and Chatterjee's writings suggest, the contradictory positioning of women in Anderson's dual time of the national imaginary—as the inner sanctum and the unfolding future—breaks into the open as a tangible and critical dilemma in modernist nationalist projects that emerge in the context of colonialism. In nationalist discourse the dilemma is expressed as how to salvage modernity from its colonial genitors—to modernize our women (as part of the nation building project) without losing our identity or distinction from the colonizers, which is so profoundly marked by our women.

Chatterjee shows how this dualism was resolved in nineteenth-century Indian nationalist discourse through locating women within the realm of the home and the spiritual, which was to remain linked to, but autonomous from, the space of the public and the material. This inner/outer distinction he sees as a crucial in the formation of Indian nationalism:

> The subjugated must learn the modern sciences and arts of the material world from the West in order to match their strengths [...] but in the phase of the national struggle the crucial need was to

56 Partha Chatterjee, *The Nation and its Fragments; Colonial and Postcolonial Histories* (Princeton: Princeton University Press, 1993); K. Jayawardena, *Feminism and Nationalism in the Third World* (London: Zed Press, 1988).

protect, preserve and strengthen the inner core of national culture, its spiritual essence. No encroachments by the colonizer must be allowed in that inner sanctum. In the world imitation and adaptation to western norms was a necessity, but at home they were tantamount to annihilation of one's very identity.[57]

The home in this context is not the physical home but the private and personal inner realm of men, women and families

The Jaffa narratives are those of an exiled nationalist bourgeoisie. Even if the intended aim of the films reviewed here was to posit the loss of an uncontested and unproblematic modernity with women actively engaged in its production (or consumption), the narratives of the women themselves belie the fact that modern Jaffan women were also entangled in the dualism that Chatterjee problematizes. In the film *Na'im and Wadi'a* Wadi'a's religiosity is described (and amplified) by the fact that, although a Catholic, she fasted during Ramadan. She married at a respectable age of 18 and swam in a slip rather than a maillot. In line with local tradition, her father-in-law had left the family land only to his four sons. Additionally, all of Wadi'a's forays into the public (beyond school) take place in a familial context or at least in a conjugal one (the cinema, dancing, picnics)—she moves in the public not as an individual agent, but bounded by familial relations (uncle, husband, children, etc.). Wadi'a is not an autonomous individual—her experience of modernity is mediated by the familial. Through her beliefs and despite her dress, she continues to be the bearer of an authentic cultural identity that modernity does not undo.

Conclusions

This reading of Palestinian nationalism's foundational narrative shows to what extent it depends on symbolic, temporal and metaphorical devices common to other nationalisms, regardless of the specific con-

---

57 Chatterjee, *The Nation,* pp. 121-122.

tent of space, place and history. On the one hand, there is the selection of the peasantry, which, as the social group most capable of representing a relationship to the land, is elevated as the wellspring of national identity. This privileging of the peasantry in the context of Palestinian nationalism likely received added impetus due to the development of a national movement among a people in exile, the majority of whom were former peasants. On the other hand, there is the location of women within national narratives, exemplified here by division, but one that cannot ultimately overcome the spatial and temporal confines that national imaginaries depend on.

The dual time of nationalism, the contradictory need to bring an immemorial past into an unfolding future clearly imposes a range of conditions on the possible roles that men and women of different classes can play within narratives that carry the national imaginary. These conditions notwithstanding, there have been significant shifts in how and by whom these dimensions are represented within various historical periods of Palestinian nationalism. In the nationalist narratives prior to the advent of the liberation movement, the timelessness of the peasantry as a whole was counterposed to the dynamism and agency of urban upper-class males. A subtle but crucial difference can be discerned in artistic representation from this period, in which peasant women were configured as the land and peasant men as an ongoing attachment to it. In the following period, under the aegis of a full-fledged national liberation movement, the nation's urban past was marginalized along with the urban elites seen as culpable for the disaster of 1948. Instead, the peasantry came to the fore and the temporal dualism of nationalism was encompassed through juxtaposing and contrasting the fixity of peasant women with the relative dynamism of peasant men. Insurgency and agency of refugee men, sons of peasants, spoke to a redemptive future, while their unchanging origins and link to the past and the land was ensured through the folklorizing of peasant women. Simultaneously, as Palestinian nationalism became more elaborated and self-assured, peasant women were no longer simply allegories of the homeland, but also came to represent the essential nature of nationhood.

As such, the emerging modernity that prior to 1948 had been a central experience of the urban classes and peasantry alike was excised from dominant narrations of the national past. Modernity came to rest solely in the dynamism of the national liberation movement and its transformation of peasant males from refugees to revolutionaries. Peasant women's entry into the modern was inconceivable, and urban women's entry into modernity remained marginalized in national narratives until very recently.

The re-entry of urban-centred nationalist narratives in the late 1990s, predominantly from exile, marks a significant shift on multiple levels that bears further exploration beyond this paper. The timing is significant on a number of accounts. On the one hand, there is the passage of the 50th year since the loss of historic Palestine, and with it the loss of its original urban and cosmopolitan centres, the coastal cities. On the other, there is the coming home of the national movement in the guise of the PNA to build a Palestine on still occupied and highly contested fragments of the original homeland. The various projects to insert Jaffa as the missing voice of Palestine's modernist past are dominated by urban middle-class exiles, historically at odds with or marginal to the national movement. At the same time, Jaffa's inclusion in locally produced official narratives is suggestive of a national movement attempting to grapple with its own legacy of cosmopolitanism in exile as it confronts small-town parochialism on returning 'home'. Women as exemplars of the modern are crucial to the production of Jaffa's modernity. Simultaneously, nationalist imaginaries are fundamentally based on spatial as well as temporal binaries. As such, the modern woman, if a member and exemplar of the nation, carries with her into the public and the future the spiritual realm of the home and family.

'Ethnocracy'

The Politics of Judaizing Israel/Palestine

Oren Yiftachel

During Israel's fiftieth year of independence (1997–98), the country's High Court of Justice was grappling with an appeal known as Qa'adan vs. Katzir. It was lodged by a Palestinian Israeli citizen who was prevented from leasing state land in the suburban locality of Katzir—built entirely on state lands—on the grounds that he was not Jewish.[1] The court deferred decision on the case for as long as it could. Its President, Justice Aharon Barak, widely viewed in Israel as a champion of civil rights, noted that this case had been among the most strenuous in his legal career, and pressured the sides to settle out of court.

In March 2000 the court ruled in favour of Qa'adan, and noted that Israel's policies towards the country's Arab minority were discriminatory and illegal. Yet, the court did not issue an order to Katzir to let Qa'adan lease the land, and was very careful to limit the ruling to this specific case so as not to create a precedent. In addition, the local Jewish community continued to raise administrative and social ob-

Author's note: An earlier version of this paper appeared in 1998 in *Constellations: International Journal of Critical and Democratic Theory* 6/3, pp. 364-390. I am grateful for the encouragement and comments I received from Uri Ram, and for the useful remarks on earlier drafts from Adriana Kemp, Yossi Yona, Michael Shalev, As'ad Ghanem, Ian Lustick, Amnon Raz, and Nira Yuval-Davis.
1   IHC 6698/95, *Qa'adan vs. Israel Land Authority et al.*

stacles and frustrate Qaʻadan's plans to join the locality. By mid 2005 the family still had not moved to Katzir.

The fact that in Israel's fiftieth year, the state's highest legal authority still found it difficult to protect a basic civil right such as equal access of all citizens to state land provides me with a telling starting point for pursuing the goals of this paper. In the pages below I wish to offer a new conceptual prism through which the formation of Israel's regime and its ethnic relations can be explained. A theoretical and empirical examination of the Israeli regime leads me to argue that it should be classified as an 'ethnocracy'.

The paper begins with a theoretical account of ethnocratic regimes, which are neither authoritarian nor democratic. Such regimes are states that maintain a relatively open government, yet facilitate a non-democratic seizure of the country and polity by one ethnic group. A key conceptual distinction is elaborated in the paper between ethnocratic and democratic regimes. Ethnocracies, despite exhibiting several democratic features, lack a democratic structure. As such, they tend to breach key democratic tenets, such as equal citizenship, the existence of a territorial political community (*demos*), universal suffrage, and protection against the tyranny of the majority.

Following the theoretical discussion, the paper traces the making of the Israeli ethnocracy, focussing on the major Zionist project of *Judaizing* Israel/Palestine, i.e., 'making it Jewish'. The predominance of the Judaization project has spawned an institutional and political structure that undermines the common perception that Israel is both Jewish and democratic.[2] The Judaization process is also a major axis along which relations between various Jewish and Arab ethno-classes in Israel can be explained. The empirical sections of the paper elaborate

---

2   Here my work joins previous critiques of the Israeli regime; see, for example, U. Ben-Eliezer, *The Emergence of Israeli Militarism* (Tel Aviv: Kibbutz Meʻuhad, 1995) (Hebrew); B. Kimmerling, 'Religion, Nationalism and Democracy in Israel', *Zemanim* 56 (1995), pp. 116-131 (Hebrew); A. Ghanem, 'State and Minority in Israel: The Case of an Ethnic State and the Predicament of Its Minority', *Ethnic and Racial Studies* 21/3 (1998), pp. 428-447; J. Shapiro, *Democracy in Israel* (Ramat Gan: Messada, 1977).

on the consequences of the ethnocratic Judaization project on three major Israeli societal cleavages: Arab-Jewish, Ashkenazi-Mizrahi,[3] and secular-orthodox.

The analysis below places particular emphasis on Israel's political geography. This perspective draws attention to the material context of geographical change, holding that discourse and space constitute one another in a ceaseless process of social construction.[4] The critical political-geographical perspective problematizes issues often taken for granted among analysts of Israel, such as settlement, segregation, borders, and sovereignty. As such it aims to complement other critical analyses of Israeli society.

Theorizing Ethnocracy

The theorization of ethnocracy draws on the main political and historical forces that have shaped the politics and territory of this regime. It focusses on three major political-historical processes: (a) the formation of a (colonial) settler society; (b) the mobilizing power of ethno-nationalism; and (c) the 'ethnic logic' of capital. The fusion of the three key forces in Israel/Palestine has resulted in the establishment of the Israeli ethnocracy and determined its specific features. But the formation of ethnocracy is not unique to Israel. It is found in other settings where one ethno-nation attempts to extend or preserve its disproportional control over contested territories and rival nation(s). This political system also typically results in the creation of stratified ethno-classes within each nation. Other notable cases include Malaysia, Sri Lanka, Estonia, Latvia, Northern Ireland (pre-1972), and Serbia. Let us turn now in brief to the three structural forces identified above.

---

3   Ashkenazi Jews (Ashkenazim in plural) are of European origins, while Mizrahi Jews (Mizrahim in plural, also termed Sepharadim or Oriental Jews) hail from the Muslim world; see also above, p. 160, n. 10.

4   Following H. Lefebvre, *The Production of Space* (Oxford: Blackwell, 1991).

A Settler Society

Settler societies, such as the Jewish community in Israel/Palestine, pursue a deliberate strategy of ethnic migration and settlement that aims to alter a country's ethnic structure. Colonial settler societies have traditionally facilitated European migration into other continents, and legitimized the exploitation of indigenous land, labour, and natural resources. Other settler societies, mainly non-European, create internal migration and resettlement in order to change the demographic balance of specific regions. In all types of settler societies a 'frontier culture' develops, glorifying and augmenting the settlement and expanding the control of the dominant group into neighbouring regions.[5]

One common type of colonial-settler society has been described as the 'pure settlement colony', which has been shown to be most appropriate to the Israeli-Zionist case.[6] Further studies have shown that 'pure' settler societies are generally marked by a broad stratification into three main ethno-classes: (a) a founding charter group, such as Protestant-Anglos in North America and Australia; (b) a group of later migrants, such as southern Europeans in North America; and (c) dispossessed indigenous groups, such as the Aborigines in Australia, Maoris in New Zealand, Amerindians in North America, and Palestinians in Israel/Palestine.[7] The charter group establishes the state in its 'own vision', institutionalizes its dominance, and creates a system which segregates it from the other ethno-classes. But the pattern of control and segregation is not even, as immigrants are gradually assimilated into the charter group in a process described by Soysal as

5   See O. Yiftachel and T. Fenster, 'Introduction: Frontiers, Planning and Indigenous Peoples', *Progress in Planning* 47/4 (1997), pp. 251-260.
6   G. M. Fredrickson, 'Colonialism and Racism: United States and South Africa in Comparative Perspective', in idem (ed.), *The Arrogance of Racism* (Middletown: Wesleyan University Press, 1988); G. Shafir, *Land, Labour and the Origins of the Israeli-Palestinian Conflict 1882-1914* (Cambridge: Cambridge University Press, 1989).
7   D. Stasiulis and N. Yuval-Davis, 'Introduction: Beyond Dichotomies: Gender, Race, Ethnicity and Class in Settler Societies', in D. Stasiulis and N. Yuval-Davis (eds.), *Unsettling Settler Societies* (London: Sage, 1995). This broad classification fluctuates according to the specific circumstances of each settler society.

'uneven incorporation'.[8] Such a system generally reproduces the dominance of the charter group for generations to come.

The establishment of 'pure' settler societies highlights the political and economic importance of extra-territorial ethnic links that are crucial for the success of most colonial projects. The links typically connect the settler society to a co-ethnic metropolitan state or to supportive ethnic diasporas. As elaborated below, extra-territorial ethnic links are a defining characteristic of ethnocracies. These regimes rely heavily on support and immigration from external ethnic sources as a key mechanism in maintaining their dominance over minority groups.

Ethno-nationalism

Ethno-nationalism, as a set of ideas and practices, constitutes one of the most powerful forces to have shaped the world's political geography in general, and that of Israel/Palestine in particular. Ethno-nationalism is a political movement which struggles to achieve or preserve ethnic statehood. It fuses two principles of political order: the post-Westphalian division of the world into sovereign states, and the principle of ethnic self-determination.[9] The combined application of these two political principles created the nation-state as the main pillar of today's world political order. Although the nation-state concept is rarely matched by political reality (as nations and states rarely overlap), it has become a dominant global model due to a dual moral basis: popular sovereignty (after centuries of despotic and/or religious regimes) and ethnic self-determination.

The principle of self-determination is central for our purposes here. In its simplest form, as enshrined in the 1945 United Nations Charter, it states that 'every people has the right for self-determination'. This

---

8   Y.N. Soysal, *Limits of Citizenship: Migrants and Postnational Membership in Europe* (Chicago: University of Chicago Press, 1994).

9   A. Murphy, 'The Sovereign State System as a Political-Territorial Ideal: Historical and Contemporary Considerations', in T. Biersteker and S. Weber (eds.), *State Sovereignty as Social Construct* (Cambridge: Cambridge University Press, 1996).

principle has formed the political and moral foundation for the establishment of popular sovereignty and democratic government. Yet most international declarations, including the United Nations Charter, leave vague the definition of a 'people' and the meaning of 'self-determination', although in contemporary political culture it is commonly accepted as independence in the group's 'own' homeland state. Once such a state is created, the principle is reified, and issues such as territory and national survival become inseparable from ethno-national history and culture. This possesses powerful implications for other facets of social life, most notably male dominance, militarism and the strategic role of ethnic-religions, although a full discussion of these important topics is beyond the scope of this paper.

The dominance of the ethno-national concept generates forms of ethnic territoriality which view control over state territory and its defence as central to the survival of the group in question, often based on selective and highly strategic historical, cultural, or religious interpretations. As I argue below, the application of this principle has been a major bone of contention in the struggle between Jews and Palestinians and in the formation of the Israeli ethnocracy as it attempted to Judaize the land in the name of Jewish self-determination.

The global dominance of ethno-nationalism and the nation-state order has prompted Billig to consider national identities as 'banal'.[10] But despite its dominance, the political geography of nation-states is far from stable, as a pervasive nation-building discourse and material reality continuously remolds the collective identity of homeland ethnic minorities. Such minorities often develop a national consciousness of their own that destabilizes political structures with campaigns for autonomy, regionalism, or sovereignty.[11]

10 M. Billig, *Banal Nationalism* (London: Sage, 1995).
11 B. Anderson, 'Introduction', in G. Balakrishnan (ed.), *Mapping the Nation* (New York: Verso, 1996); W. Connor, *Ethnonationalism: The Quest for Understanding* (Princeton: Princeton University Press, 1994); A.D. Smith, *Nations and Nationalism in a Global Era* (Cambridge: Polity, 1995).

The Ethnic Logic of Capital

A third structural force to shape the political geography of Israel/Palestine and the nature of its regime has been associated with the onset of capitalism, and its ethnic and social consequences. Here the settings of a settler society and ethno-nationalism combine to create a specific logic of capital flow, development and class formation on two main levels. First, labour markets and development are ethnically segmented, thereby creating an ethno-class structure that tends to accord with the charter-immigrant-indigenous hierarchy noted above. Typically, the founding charter group occupies privileged niches within the labour market, while migrants are marginalized, at least initially, from the centres of economic power, and thus occupy the working and petit bourgeois classes. Indigenous people are typically excluded from access to capital or mobility within the labour market, and thus are virtually 'trapped' as an underclass.[12]

Second, the accelerating globalization of markets and capital has weakened the state's economic power. This went accompanied by the adoption of neo-liberal policies and the subsequent de-regulation of economic activities and privatization of many state functions. Generally, these forces have widened the socio-economic gaps between the charter, immigrant, and indigenous ethno-classes. Yet, in the setting of militant ethno-nationalism, as prevalent in Israel/Palestine, the globalization of capital, and the associated establishment of supra-national trade organizations, may also subdue ethno-nationalism and expansionism, previously fuelled by territorial ethnic rivalries. Particularly significant in this process is the globalization of the leading classes among the dominant ethno-nation, which increasingly search for opportunities and mobility within a more open and accessible regional and global economy. A conspicuous tension between the global and the local thus surfaces, with a potential to intensify intra-national tensions, but at the same time also to ease inter-national

12 Stasilius and Yuval-Davis. 'Beyond Dichotomies'.

conflicts, as has recently been illustrated in South Africa, Spain, and Northern Ireland.[13]

Ethnocracy

The fusion of the three forces—settler society, ethno-nationalism, and the ethnic logic of capital—creates a regime-type I have called 'ethnocracy'.[14] An ethnocracy is a non-democratic regime that attempts to extend or preserve disproportional ethnic control over a contested multi-ethnic territory. Ethnocracy develops chiefly when control over territory is challenged and when a dominant group is powerful enough to determine unilaterally the nature of the state. Ethnocracy is thus an unstable regime, with opposite forces of expansionism and resistance in constant conflict.[15] An ethnocratic regime is characterized by several key principles:

13 For the global process, see D. Held, 'The Decline of the Nation State', in S. Hall and M. Jacques (eds.), *New Times: The Changing Face of Politics in the 1990s* (London: Lawrence and Wishart, 1990); D. Harvey, *The Condition of Post-modernity* (Oxford: Blackwell, 1989). For its Israeli manifestations, see U. Ram, 'Citizens, Consumers and Believers: The Israeli Public Sphere between Capitalism and Fundamentalism', *Israel Studies* 3/1 (1998), pp. 24-44; G. Shafir and Y. Peled, 'Citizenship and Stratification in an Ethnic Democracy', *Ethnic and Racial Studies* 21/3 (1998), pp. 408-427.

14 The term 'ethnocracy' has appeared in previous literature; see J. Linz and A. Stepan, *Problems of Democratic Transition and Consolidation* (Baltimore: Johns Hopkins University Press, 1996), p. 69; J. Linz, 'Totalitarian Vs Authoritarian Regimes', in F. Greenstein and N. Polsby (eds.), *Handbook of Political Science* (Reading: Addison Wesley, 1975); A. Mazrui, *The Making of Military Ethnocracy* (London: Sage 1975); D. Little, *Sri Lanka: The Invention of Enmity* (Washington: US Institute of Peace, 1994), p. 72. However, as far as I am aware, it was generally used as a derogatory term, and not developed into a model or concept, as formulated here. For an earlier formulation, see my 'Israeli Society and Jewish-Palestinian Reconciliation: "Ethnocracy" and Its Territorial Contradictions', *Middle East Journal* 51/4 (1997), pp. 505-519.

15 As noted, ethnocracies have existed for long periods in countries such as Sri Lanka, Malaysia, and Northern Ireland (until 1972), and more recently in Estonia, Latvia, Slovakia, and Serbia.

(a) Despite several democratic features, ethnicity (and not territorial citizenship) determines the allocation of rights and privileges; a constant democratic-ethnocratic tension characterizes politics.

(b) State borders and political boundaries are fuzzy: there is no identifiable *demos*, mainly due to the role of ethnic diasporas inside the polity and the inferior position of ethnic minorities.

(c) A dominant 'charter' ethnic group appropriates the state apparatus, determines most public policies, and segregates itself from other groups.

(d) Political, residential, and economic segregation and stratification occur on two main levels: ethno-nations and ethno-classes.

(e) The constitutive logic of ethno-national segregation is diffused, enhancing a process of political ethnicization among sub-groups within each ethno-nation.

(f) Significant—though partial—civil and political rights are extended to members of the minority ethno-nation, distinguishing ethnocracies from *Herrenvolk* democracies or authoritarian regimes.

Ethnocratic regimes are usually supported by a cultural and ideological apparatus that legitimizes and reinforces the uneven reality. This is achieved by constructing a historical narrative that proclaims the dominant ethno-nation as the rightful owner of the territory in question. Such a narrative degrades all other contenders as historically not entitled, or culturally unworthy, to control the land or achieve political equality.

A further legitimizing apparatus is the maintenance of *selective openness*. Internally, the introduction of democratic institutions is common, especially in settling societies, as it adds legitimacy to the entire settling project, to the leadership of the charter ethno-class, and to the incorporation of groups of later immigrants. But these democratic institutions commonly exclude indigenous or rival minorities. This is achieved either formally, as was the case in Australia until 1967, or more subtly, by leaving such groups outside decision-making circles, as is the case in Sri Lanka.[16] Externally, selective openness is established

16 Here the advent of 'illiberal democracy' (F. Zakaria, 'The Rise of Illiberal Democracy', *Foreign Affairs* 76/6 [1997], pp. 22-43) is instrumental, by establishing

as a principle of foreign relations and membership in international organizations. This has become particularly important with the increasing opening of the world economy and the establishment of supranational organizations, such as the EU and NAFTA. Membership in such organizations often requires at least the appearance of open regimes, and most ethnocracies comply with this requirement.

Given these powerful legitimizing forces, ethnocratic projects usually enjoy a hegemonic status that originates among the charter group and is successfully diffused among the populace. The hegemonic moment, as convincingly formulated by Gramsci, is marked by a distorted but widely accepted fusion of a given set of principles and practices. It is an order in which a certain social structure is dominant, with its own concept of reality determining most tastes, morality, customs, and political principles. Given the economic, political, and cultural power of the elites, a hegemonic order is likely to be reproduced unless severe contradictions with 'stubborn realities' generate counter-hegemonic mobilizations.[17]

Ethnocracy in the Making:
The Judaization of Israel/Palestine

The analysis of the Israeli regime in this paper covers the entire territory and population under Israeli rule in Palestine. Prior to 1967, then, it is limited to the area within the Green Line (the 1949 armistice lines), but after that date it covers all of Palestine, or what Kimmerling has called the 'Israeli control system.'[18] While the Occupied Palestinian

---

a regime with formal democratic appearance but with centralizing, coercive, and authoritarian characteristics. See also Y. Yona, 'A State of all Citizens, a Nation-State or a Multicultural State? Israel and the Boundaries of Liberal Democracy', *Alpayim* 16 (1998), pp. 238-263 (Hebrew).

17 A. Gramsci, *Selections from the Prison Notebooks* (New York: International Publishers, 1971); see also Lustick's illuminating discussion of the notion of hegemony in his *Unsettled States, Disputed Lands* (Ithaca: Cornell University Press, 1993).

18 B. Kimmerling, 'Boundaries and Frontiers in the Israeli Control System: Analytical Conclusions,' in idem (ed.), *The Israeli State and Society: Boundaries and Frontiers* (Albany: SUNY Press, 1989).

Territories are often treated in studies of Israel as an external and temporary aberration, they are considered here as an integral part of the Israeli regime, simply because Israel governs these areas. This appears to be the situation even following the 1993 Oslo Accords, because the areas under limited Palestinian self-rule remain under overall Jewish control.[19] The appropriate political-geographical framework for the analysis of Israel/Palestine since 1967 is thus: *one ethnocracy, two ethno-nations,* and *several Jewish and Palestinian ethno-classes.*

Jews make up about 80 per cent of Israel's 5.9 million citizens and Palestinian Arabs about 17 per cent (the rest being neither Jewish nor Arab). An additional 2.7 million Palestinians reside in the Occupied Territories of the West Bank and Gaza Strip. Hence, the population within the entire contested 'Land of Israel', i.e., Palestine, is roughly 55 per cent Jewish and 43 per cent Palestinian Arab.[20]

Ethnic and religious division is also marked within each national community. About 41 per cent of Israeli Jews are Ashkenazi and about 43 per cent Mizrahi. The rest are mainly recent Russian-speaking immigrants, mostly of European origin, who form a distinct ethno-cultural group, at least in the short-term. Of the Palestinian Arabs in Israel, 77 per cent are Muslim (a fifth of whom are Bedouin), 13 per cent are Christian, and 10 per cent Druze. In the Occupied Territories, 95 per cent are Muslim and 4 per cent Christian. In both the Jewish and Muslim communities, a major cultural division has also developed between orthodox and secular groups. About 20 per cent of Jews are orthodox, as are about 30 per cent of Muslims on both sides of the Green Line.[21]

19 This is supported by repeated statements of Israeli leaders. For example, Netanyahu, prime minister in 1998, claimed that 'only one government has and will have sovereign power west of the Jordan' (*Ma'ariv*, 18 February 1998); similarly, then Minster of Justice Y. Hanegbi claimed on 14 September 1998 (Channel One, Israeli TV) that 'sovereignty in Eretz Yisrael will never be divided and will remain Israeli, and Israeli only.'

20 Israel's Central Bureau of Statistics (CBS), *Israel Yearbook* (Jerusalem: Government Printers, 1998); figures relate to 31 December 1997.

21 E. Rekhes, 'The Moslem Movement in Israel', in idem (ed.), *The Arab Minority in Israel: Dilemmas of Political Orientation and Social Change* (Tel Aviv: Dayan Centre, University of Tel Aviv, 1991).

Zionism has been a settler movement, and Israel a settler state, whose territory was previously inhabited by Palestinian Arabs. Despite notable differences with other colonial movements, the actual process of European settlement classifies Zionism (both before and after 1948) as a 'pure' colonial settler movement.[22] After Israel's independence in 1948 and following the mass entry into the country of Jewish refugees and migrants, conspicuous social stratification emerged. In broad terms, the Ashkenazim have constituted the charter group and have occupied the upper echelons of society in most spheres, including politics, the military, the labour market, and culture. The Mizrahim have been the main group of later immigrants, recently accompanied by a group of Russian-speakers and a small group of Ethiopian Jews. These groups are placed in a middle position, lagging behind the Ashkenazim, but above the indigenous Palestinian Arabs. Strikingly, and despite an official ideology of integration and equality towards the Mizrahim, a persistent socio-economic gap has remained between them and the Ashkenazi group.[23]

As is typical in settler societies, Israel's indigenous Arab minority has occupied from the outset the lowest strata in most spheres of Israeli life, and has been virtually excluded from the political, cultural and economic centres of society. Following Israel's conquest of the West Bank and Gaza Strip in 1967, their Palestinian residents became partially incorporated into Israeli economy, mainly as day-labourers, but were denied political and civil rights.[24]

22 The differences from 'typical' European settler movements include Zionism's nature as an ethno-national and not an economic project, the status of most Jews as refugees, the loose organization of diasporic Jewish communities as opposed to the well-organized metropolitan countries, and the notion of 'return' to Zion enshrined in Jewish traditions.

23 See, for example, Y. Cohen and Y. Haberfeld, 'Second Generation Jewish Immigrants in Israel: Have the Ethnic Gaps in Schooling and Earnings Declined?', *Ethnic and Racial Studies* 21/3 (1998), pp. 507-528; S.M. Lewi-Epstein and N. Semyonov, 'Ethnic Mobility in the Israeli Labor Market', *American Sociological Review* 51 (1986), pp. 342-351.

24 For the historical evolution of Israel's ethnic political economy and labour relations in Israel, see L. Grinberg, *Split Corporatism in Israel* (Albany: SUNY Press, 1991); M. Shalev, *Labour and the Political Economy in Israel* (Oxford: Oxford University Press, 1992).

A Jewish State

With its Declaration of Independence, in 1948, Israel announced itself as a 'Jewish state'. In some ways, the Declaration of Independence was quite liberal, promising non-Jews 'full and equal citizenship' and banning discrimination on grounds of religion, ethnic origin, gender or creed. The central political institutions of the new state were established as democratic, including a representative parliament (the Knesset), periodic elections, an independent judiciary, and relatively free media.

During the following years, however, a series of incremental laws enshrined the ethnic and partially religious Jewish character of the state (rather than its *Israeli* character, as accepted international standards of self-determination would have required). Chief among these have been the state's immigration statutes (Laws of Return and Citizenship), which made every Jew in the world a potential citizen, while denying this possibility to many Palestinians born in the country. Other laws further anchored the Jewish character of the state not only in the symbolic realm, but also as a concrete and *deepening* reality, covering areas such as citizenship, education, communication and land ownership. As the Israeli High Court declared in 1964—in what became known as the Yerdor case—'the Jewishness of Israel is a constitutional given.'[25] In 1985, revisions made to the Basic Law on the Knesset added that no party would be allowed to run if it rejected Israel's definition as the state of the Jewish people.[26] The combination of these laws created a structure nearly immune against democratic attempts to change its Zionist character.

During the early 1990s two Knesset basic laws defined the state as 'Jewish and democratic', thereby further enshrining the state's Jewish character, but also coupling it with a democratic commitment. As argued below, this coupling is problematic not as an abstract principle, but against the ongoing reality of Judaization, which has unilaterally

---

25 P. Lahav, *Judgment in Jerusalem: Chief Justice Simon Agranat and the Zionist Century* (Berkeley: University of California Press, 1997).
26 The 1985 Law also disqualifies parties using a racist platform.

restructured the nature of the state through immigration and land policies. This transformation was supported by the uni-ethnic arms of the state, including army, police, courts, economic institutions, development agencies, and most decision-making forums.

Hence, a main obstacle to Israeli democracy does not necessarily lie in the declaration of Israel as 'Jewish', which may be akin to the legal status of Finland as a 'Lutheran state' or England as 'Anglican'. The main problem lies in the mirror processes of *Judaization* and *de-Arabization* (that is, the dispossession of Palestinian Arabs) that are being facilitated and legitimized by the declaration of Israel as 'Jewish', and by the ethnocratic legal and political structures resulting from this declaration.[27] Let us now explore in some detail the dynamic political geography behind the establishment of the Israeli ethnocracy.

Judaizing the Homeland

Following independence, Israel entered a radical stage of territorial restructuring. Some policies and initiatives were an extension of earlier Jewish approaches, but the tactics, strategies, and ethnocentric cultural construction of the *Yishuv*—the pre-1948 Jewish community in Palestine—were significantly intensified. This was enabled with the aid of the newly acquired state apparatus, armed forces, and the international legitimacy attached to national sovereignty.

The territorial restructuring of the land has centred on a combined and expansionist *Judaization* and *de-Arabization* programme adopted by the nascent Israeli state. This began with the expulsion and flight of approximately 750,000 Palestinians during the 1948 war. Israel prevented the return of the refugees to their villages, which it rapidly demolished.[28] The authorities were quick to fill the 'gaps' created by

27 See D. Kretzmer, *The Legal Status of the Arabs in Israel* (Boulder, CO: Westview, 1990); Adalah, *Legal Violations of Arab Rights in Israel* (Shfa'amre: Adalah, 1998).
28 See B. Morris, *Israel's Border Wars, 1949-1956* (Oxford: Oxford University Press, 1993).

this forced exodus with settlements inhabited by Jewish migrants and refugees who entered the country *en masse* during the late 1940s and early 1950s.

The Judaization programme was premised on a hegemonic myth cultivated since the rise of Zionism, namely that 'the land' (*ha-aretz*) belongs to the Jewish people, and only to the Jewish people. An exclusive form of settling ethno-nationalism developed in order quickly to 'indigenize' im migrant Jews, and to conceal, trivialize, or marginalize the Palestinian past.

The 'frontier' became a central icon, and its settlement was considered one of the highest achievements of any Zionist. The frontier *kibbutzim* (collective rural settlements) provided a model, and the reviving Hebrew language was filled with 'positive' images such as *aliya lakarka* (literally 'ascent to the land', i.e., settlement), *ge'ulat karka* (land redemption), *hityashvut, hitnahalut* (biblical terms for 'settlement'), *kibbush hashmama* (conquest of the desert), and *hagshama* (literally 'fulfillment', but denoting the settling of the frontier). The glorification of the frontier thus assisted both in the construction of national-Jewish identity, and in capturing physical space on which this identity could be territorially constructed.

Such sentiments were translated into a pervasive programme of Jewish-Zionist territorial socialization, expressed in school curricula, literature, political speech, popular music, and other spheres of public discourse. Settlement thus continued to be a cornerstone of Zionist nation-building even after the establishment of a sovereign Jewish state. To be sure, the 'return' of Jews to their ancestors' mythical land and the perception of this land as a safe haven after generations of persecution had a powerful liberating meaning. Yet, the darker sides of this project were nearly totally absent from the construction of an unproblematic 'return' of Jews to their biblical promised land. Very few dissenting voices were heard against these Judaizing discourses, policies or practices. When such dissent did emerge, the national-Jewish elites found effective ways to marginalize, co-opt, or gag most challengers.[29]

---

29 According to Yoav Peled and Gershon Shafir ('The Roots of Pacemaking: The Dynamics of Citizenship in Israel, 1948-93', *International Journal of Middle East*

Therefore, 1948 should be regarded as a major political turning point, not only due to the establishment of a state pronouncing a democratic regime, but also as the beginning of a state-orchestrated, and essentially non-democratic Judaization project. Two parallel processes have thus developed on the same land: the visible establishment of democratic institutions and procedures, and a more concealed, yet systematic and coercive, seizure of the territory by the dominant ethnic group. The contradiction between the two processes casts doubt on the pervasive classification of Israel in the academic literature as a democracy, a point to which I return later.

The perception of the land as only Jewish was premised on a distorted national discourse of a 'forced exile' and subsequent 'return'.[30] A parallel discourse developed in reaction to the Arab-Jewish conflict (and Arab rejectionism), elevating the exigencies of national security onto a level of unquestioned gospel. These discourses have blinded most Jews to a range of discriminatory policies imposed against the state's Palestinian citizens, including the imposition of military rule, lack of economic or social development, political surveillance and under-representation, and—most important for this essay—large-scale confiscation of Palestinian land.[31]

Studies 28 [1996], pp. 391-413), the intensity of the Judaization project slowed down in the early 1990s, in part because of the global orientations of Israeli elites. But despite the decline, the logic of Judaization remains fundamental to Israeli-Jewish politics and should be treated as the historical 'genetic core' of the Israeli regime; it gained fresh impetus, of course, after Israel's 'disengagement' from the Gaza Strip in August 2005.

30 See U. Ram, 'Zionist Historiography and the Invention of Modern Jewish Nationhood: The Case of Ben Zion Dinur', *History and Memory* 7/1 (1995), pp. 91-124. Records show that Jews remained in the land of Israel for centuries after the destruction of the Second Temple, and in most cases emigrated voluntarily.

31 On policies affecting Palestinian Arabs in Israel, see also G. Falah, 'Israeli Judaisation Policy in Galilee and its Impact on Local Arab Urbanisation', *Political Geography Quarterly* 8 (1989), pp. 229-253; I. Lustick, *Arabs in the Jewish State: Israel's Control over a National Minority* (Austin: University of Texas Press, 1980); S. Smooha, 'Existing and Alternative Policy Towards the Arabs in Israel', *Ethnic and Racial Studies* 5 (1982), pp. 71-98; O. Yiftachel, *Planning a Mixed Region in Israel: The Political Geography of Arab-Jewish Relations in the Galilee* (Aldershot: Avebury, 1992); E.T. Zureik, *Palestinians in Israel: A Study of Internal Colonialism* (London: Routledge and Kegan Paul, 1979).

Prior to 1948, only about 7–8 per cent of the country was in Jewish hands, and about 10 per cent was vested with the representative of the British Mandate. The Israeli state, however, quickly expanded its land holdings and it currently owns or controls 93 per cent of the area within the Green Line. The lion's share of this land transfer consisted in expropriating Palestinian refugee property, but about two-thirds of the land belonging to Palestinians who remained and became Israeli citizens were also expropriated. At present, Palestinian Arabs, who constitute around 17 per cent of Israel's population, own only around three per cent of its land, while their combined local government areas cover 2.5 per cent of the country.

A central aspect of land transfer was its legal *uni-directionality.* Israel created an institutional and legal land system under which confiscated land could not be sold. Further, such land did not merely become state land, but a joint possession of the state and the entire Jewish people. This was achieved by granting extra-territorial organizations, such as the Jewish National Fund, the Jewish Agency, and the Zionist Federation, a share of the state's sovereign powers and significant authority in the areas of land, development and settlement. The transfer of land to the hands of unaccountable bodies representing the 'Jewish people' can be likened to a 'black hole', into which Arab land enters but can never be retrieved. This structure ensures the uni-directional character of all land transfers: from Palestinians to Jewish hands, and never vice versa. A stark expression of this legal and institutional setting is that Israel's Arab citizens are currently prevented from purchasing, leasing or using land in around 80 per cent of the country.[32] It can be reasonably assumed that the constitutions of most democratic countries would make such a blatant breach of equal civil rights illegal. But Israel's character as a Judaizing state has so far prevented the enactment of a constitution which would guarantee such rights.

---

32 I.e., the area of Israeli regional councils, where world Jewry organizations are part of most land leasing and ownership arrangements.

During the 1950s and 1960s, and following the transfer of land to the state, over 600 Jewish settlements were constructed in all parts of the land. This created the infrastructure for the housing of Jewish refugees and immigrants who continued to pour into the country. The upshot was the penetration of Jews into most Arab areas, the encirclement of most Arab villages by exclusively Jewish settlements—where non-Jews are not permitted to purchase housing—and the virtual *ghettoization* of the Arab minority.

Settlement and Intra-Jewish Segregation

Let us turn now to the issue of ethno-classes. Beyond its obvious consequences on the ethno-national level, the Jewish settlement project also caused processes of segregation and stratification between Jewish ethno-classes. This aspect is central for the understanding of relations between the various Jewish ethno-classes, and especially Ashkenazim and Mizrahim. Notably, it is not argued that relations between Jewish ethnic groups are non-democratic, but rather that the ethnocratic-settling nature of Jewish-Palestinian relations has adversely affected intra-Jewish relations. To illustrate the geography of these processes, let us outline in more detail the social and ethnic nature of the Jewish settlement project, which advanced in three main waves.

During the first wave, between 1949 and 1952, some 240 communal villages (kibbutzim and moshavim) were built, mainly along the Green Line. During the second wave, from the early 1950s to the mid-1960s, 27 'development towns' and a further 56 villages were built. These were mainly populated—usually through coercion—by Jewish immigrants and refugees from North Africa. During the same period large groups of Mizrahim were also housed in 'frontier' urban neighbourhoods, which were either previously Palestinian or adjacent to Palestinian areas. Given the low socio-economic resources of most Mizrahim, their mainly Arab culture—now affiliated with 'the enemy'—and lack of ties to Israeli elites, the development towns and 'the neighbourhoods' quickly became—and have remained to date—distinct concentrations of segregated, poor, and deprived Mizrahi populations.[33] This geography of dependence, achieved in the name of Judaizing the country, has underlain the evolution of Ashkenazi-Mizrahi relations to the present day.

The third wave, during the last two decades, saw the establishment of over 150 small non-urban settlements known as 'community' or 'private' settlements (*yeshuvim kehilatiyim*). These are small suburban-like neighbourhoods, located in the heart of areas on both sides of the Green Line. Their establishment was presented to the public as a renewed effort to Judaize Israel's hostile frontiers, using the typical rhetoric of national security, the Arab threat to state lands, or the possible emergence of Arab secessionism. In the Occupied Territories, additional rationales for Jewish settlement referred to the return of Jews to ancient biblical sites, and to the creation of 'strategic depth'. But, despite the continuation of a similar Zionist discourse, a major difference characterized these settlements—they ruptured, for the first time, Israel's internationally recognized borders, a point to which I return below.

From a social perspective, the people migrating into most of these high-quality residential localities were mainly middle-class Ashkenazi suburbanites, seeking to improve their housing and social status. In recent years, urban Jewish settlement in the West Bank accompanied the ongoing construction and expansion of small *kehilati* settlements. These towns have increasingly accommodated religious-national and ultra-orthodox Jews.[34]

Notably, the different waves of settlement were marked by social and institutional *segregation* sanctioned and augmented by state policies. A

---

33 See S. Hasson, 'Social and Spatial Conflicts: The Settlement Process in Israel during the 1950s', *L'Espace Geographique* 3 (1981), pp. 169-179; Y. Gradus, 'The Emergence of Regionalism in a Centralised System: The Case of Israel', *Environment and Planning D: Society and Space* 2 (1984), pp. 87-100; S. Swirski and B. Shoshani, *Development Towns: Toward a Different Tomorrow* (Tel Aviv: Brerot, 1985) (Hebrew).

34 See Falah, 'Israeli Judaisation Policy in Galilee'; Lustick, *Unsettled States, Disputed Lands*; D. Newman, 'The Territorial Politics of Exurbanisation: Reflections on 25 Years of Jewish Settlement in the West Bank', *Israel Affairs* 3/1 (1996), pp. 61-85; Yiftachel, 'Israeli Society and Jewish-Palestinian Reconciliation'.

whole range of mechanisms was devised and implemented not only to maintain nearly impregnable patterns of segregation between Arabs and Jews, but also to erect fairly rigid lines of separation between various Jewish ethno-classes. Segregation mechanisms included the demarcation of local government and education district boundaries, the provision of separate and unequal government services (especially education and housing), the development of largely separate economies, the organization of different types of localities in different state-wide 'settlement movements', and the uneven allocation of land on a sectoral basis.[35]

As a result, 'layered' and differentiated Jewish spaces were created, with low levels of contact between the various ethno-classes. This has worked to reproduce inequalities and competing collective identities. Movement across boundaries has been restricted as most new Jewish settlements (built on state land!) are allowed to screen their residents through tests of 'resident suitability'. This practice has predictably produced communities dominated by middle-class Ashkenazim. At least part of the ethno-class fragmentation and hostility currently evident in Israeli society can thus be traced to the Judaizing settlement system and its institutionalized segregation. In this process we can also note the working of the ethnic logic of capital I singled out earlier as a major force shaping social relations in ethnocracies. Development closely followed the ethno-class pattern prevalent in Israeli society. This created spatial circumstances for the *reproduction* of the 'ethnic gap' between Ashkenazim and Mizrahim, through location-based mechanisms such as education, land control, housing, social networks, local stigmas, and accessibility to facilities and opportunities.

Democracy or Ethnocracy?

As we have seen, the politico-geographic analysis of Jewish land and settlement policies highlights three key factors, often neglected in other interpretations of Israeli society: (a) The Israeli regime has facilitated a

35 See Yiftachel, 'Israeli Society and Jewish-Palestinian Reconciliation'.

constant process of expanding Jewish control over the territory of Israel/Palestine; (b) Israel is a state and polity without clear borders; and (c) the country's organization of social space is based on pervasive and uneven ethnic segregation. An elaboration of these assertions leads me to question the taken-for-granted notion that Israel is a democracy.[36] Instead, I would argue that the polity is governed by an ethnocratic regime, as defined earlier. It is a rule for and by an expanding ethnic group, within the state and beyond its boundaries, which is neither democratic nor authoritarian.[37]

Democracy, on the other hand, is a regime which follows several main principles, including equal and substantial civil rights, inclusive citizenship, periodic and free elections, universal suffrage, separation between arms of government, protection of individuals and minorities against the majority, and an appropriate level of government openness and public ethics.[38] A factor often taken for granted by regime analysts—but far from obvious in the Israeli case—is the existence of clear boundaries to state territory and its political community. The establishment of a state as a territorial-legal entity is premised on the existence of such boundaries, without which the law of the land and the activity of democratic institutions cannot be imposed universally, thus undermining the operation of inclusive and equal democratic procedures.

36 There exists a wide body of literature which debates the characteristics of Israeli democracy, all assuming *a priori* that Israel is governed by such a regime. See A. Arian, *The Second Republic: Politics in Israel* (Tel Aviv: Zmora–Bitan, 1997); B. Neuberger, *Democracy in Israel: Origins and Development* (Tel Aviv: Open University, 1998); S. Smooha, 'Ethnic Democracy: Israel as an Archetype', *Israel Studies* 2/2 (1997), pp. 198-241.

37 For elaboration of the historical evolution of the Israeli-Jewish 'ethnocracy', see my 'Israeli Society and Jewish-Palestinian Reconciliation'. A similar formulation of Israel as an 'ethnic state' can be found in N. Rouhana, *Palestinian Citizens in an Ethnic Jewish State: Identities and Conflict* (New Haven: Yale University Press, 1997); Ghanem, 'State and Minority in Israel.'

38 See D. Held, *Models of Democracy* (Stanford: Stanford University Press, 1988); Linz and Stepan, *Problems of Democratic Transition and Consolidation.* Needless to say, pure democracy is never implemented fully, although Linz and Stepan list 42 countries which fall over a democratic threshold. We use the democratic model here as an analytical tool with which the Israeli regime can be examined.

This brings us back to the question of Israeli boundaries and borders. As shown above, the Jewish system of land ownership and development as well as the geography of frontier settlement have undermined the territorial-legal nature of the state. Organizations based in the Jewish Diaspora possess statutory powers within Israel/ Palestine. World Jewry is also involved in Israeli politics in other significant ways, including major donations to Jewish parties and politicians, open and public influence over policy-making and agenda-setting, as well as lobbying on behalf of Israeli politicians in international fora, especially in the United States.[39] Hence, extra-territorial (non-citizen) Jewish groups have amassed political power in Israel to an extent unmatched by any democratic state. This is an undemocratic structural factor consistent with the properties of ethnocratic regimes.

As mentioned, Jewish settlement in the Occupied Territories has also ruptured the Green Line (Israel's pre-1967 internationally recognized frontiers) as a meaningful border. At the time of writing, some 340,000 Israeli Jews resided in the territories (including al-Quds, or East Jerusalem), and Israeli law has been unilaterally extended to each of these settlements.[40] The Green Line has been transformed into a geographical mechanism of separating (citizen from non-citizen) Palestinians, but not Jews.[41]

The combination of the two factors means that 'Israel', as a definable democratic-political entity, simply *does not exist.* The legal and political power of extraterritorial (Jewish) bodies and the breaching of state borders empty the notion of Israel from the broadly accepted meaning of a state as a territorial-legal institution. Hence, the unproblematic

---

39 A striking example of the involvement of world Jewry was the declaration by ultra-orthodox Australian millionaire, and major donor to religious parties, David Guttnick, that he would work to 'topple the Netanyahu government' in case it decides to withdraw from Occupied Territories (*Ha'aretz,* 14 August 1998).

40 Jewish settlements in the Occupied Territories were established under military rule; the settlements are closed to Palestinian Arabs.

41 For a thorough, ground-breaking analysis of the role of borders in Jewish politics, see A. Kemp, *Talking Boundaries: The Making of Political Territory in Israel 1949-1957,* PhD dissertation, Tel Aviv University, 1997 (Hebrew).

acceptance of 'Israel proper' in most social science writings (including some of my own previous work) and in the public media has been based on a misnomer.[42]

Given this reality, Israel simply does not comply with a basic requirement of democracy—the existence of a *demos*. As defined in ancient Greece, *demos* denotes an inclusive body of citizens within given borders. It is a competing organizing principle to the *ethnos*, which denotes common origin. The term 'democracy' therefore means the rule of the *demos*, and its modern application points to an overlap between permanent residency in the polity and equal political rights as a *necessary democratic condition*.

As we have seen, Israel's political structure and settlement activity have ruled out the relevance of such boundaries, and in effect undermined the existence of universal suffrage (as Jewish settlers in the Occupied Territories can vote to the parliament that governs them, but their Palestinian 'neighbours' cannot). The significance of this observation is clear from Israel's 1996 elections: counting only the results within 'Israel proper', Shimon Peres would have beaten Benjamin Netanyahu by a margin of over five per cent. Netanyahu's victory was thus based on the votes of Jews in the Occupied Territories (that is, outside 'Israel proper'), as were the previous successes of the Likud camp in 1981, 1984 and 1988. The involvement of the settlers in Israeli politics is of course far deeper than simply electoral. They are represented (1998) by 18 Knesset members (out of 120), four gov-

---

42 Most accounts of the Israeli regime, including critical analyses, have continued to treat Israel concurrently as (a) the land bounded by the Green Line *and* (b) the body of Israeli citizens (including Jewish settlers of the Occupied Territories). This contradiction was rarely problematized in the literature. For examples of critical accounts which take this approach, see Yoav Peled, 'Ethnic Democracy and the Legal Construction of Citizenship: Arab Citizens of the Jewish State', *The American Political Science Review* 86/2 (1992), pp. 432-443; U. Ram, 'Citizens, Consumers and Believers'; Rouhana, *Palestinian Citizens in an Ethnic Jewish State*; Smooha, 'Ethnic Democracy'. For earlier debates with this approach, see Kimmerling, 'Boundaries and Frontiers in the Israeli Control System'; J. Migdal, 'Society-Formation and the Case of Israel', in M. Barnett (ed.), *Israel in Comparative Perspective* (Albany: SUNY Press, 1996).

ernment ministers, and hold a host of key positions in politics, the armed forces, and academia.

Hence, a basic requirement for the democratization of the Israeli polity is not only to turn it into a state of all its citizens (as most non-Zionist groups demand), but into *a state of all its resident-citizens, and only of them.* This is the only way to ensure that extra-territorial and politically unaccountable bodies, such as the Jewish Agency, the Jewish National Fund, and Jewish settlers in Occupied Territories, do not unduly affect the state's sovereign territory. And it is only this principle that can lay the appropriate foundations for democratic rule, for and by the state's political *demos.*

Beyond the critical issue of borders, several other major impediments to the establishment of sound democratic regime have existed throughout Israel's political history. These have included a very high level of regime centrality, relative lack of political accountability, weakness of the judiciary, pervasive militarism, male dominance and associated discrimination against women in most walks of life, and the inseparability of religion and state. Lack of space prevents discussion on all but the last of these issues, to which we now turn.

Ethnocracy or Theocracy?

Some scholars claim that a growing influence of orthodox Jewish groups on Israeli politics is leading Israel towards theocratic—and not ethnocratic—rule.[43] Yet the orthodox agenda appears compatible with the Jewish ethnocratic project, as orthodox groups take the rule of the Jewish *ethnos* as their given point of departure, and chiefly aim to deepen its religiosity. As such, their campaign is geared to change the nature of the Israeli ethnocracy without challenging its very existence or the ethnic boundaries of its membership.

43 See Kimmerling, 'Religion, Nationalism and Democracy in Israel'; Y. Nevo, 'Israel: From Ethnocracy to Theocracy', paper delivered at a conference on 'The Conflictual Identities Construction in the Middle East,' Van Leer Institute, Jerusalem, November 1998.

Still, the orthodox agenda in Israeli politics is significant in another way, as it, too, challenges the prevalent perception of Israel as 'Jewish and democratic'. Despite important differences, all orthodox parties support the increasing imposition of religious rule in Israel (*Halacha*), as stated by the late leader of the National Religious Party, Z. Hammer, who was considered a moderate: 'I genuinely wish that Israel would be shaped according to the spirit of Tora and Halacha [...] the democratic system is not sacred for me [...].'[44] Likewise, one of the leaders of Shas, often considered a relatively moderate orthodox party, declared a few years ago: 'We work for creating a *Halacha* state [...] such as state would guarantee religious freedom, but the courts will enforce Jewish law [...] we have the sacred Tora which has a moral set of laws, why should anyone be worried?'[45] Although the initiatives these bodies have taken in recent times attempt to mainly influence the character of public (and not private) spheres, there exists a fundamental contradiction between the orthodox agenda and several basic features of democracy, such as the rule of law, individual liberty and autonomy, civil equality, and popular sovereignty.[46]

This challenge is somewhat obscured by the duality in the interpretation of Judaism as ethnic and/or religious. The secular interpretation treats Judaism as mainly ethnic or cultural, while orthodox and ultra-orthodox groups interpret it as an inseparable whole (that is, *both* ethnicity and religion). This unresolved duality is at the heart of the tension between the secular and orthodox Jewish camps: if the meaning of 'Jewish' is unresolved, how can the nature of the 'Jewish state' be determined?

The challenge to democracy from the orthodox agenda has become more acute because the orthodox political camp has grown stronger in Israeli politics over the last decade. In the 1996–99 period it held 28 of

44 Quoted in Neuberger, *Democracy in Israel,* p. 41.
45 Interview of Rabbi Azran, *Globs,* 28 September 1998.
46 Kimmerling, 'Religion, Nationalism and Democracy in Israel'; C. Liebman, 'Attitudes towards Democracy among Israeli Religious Leaders', in E. Kofman, A. Shukri and R. Rothstein (eds.), *Democracy, Peace and the Israeli-Palestinian Conflict* (Boulder, CO: Lynne Reiner Publishers, 1993).

the Knesset's 120 seats (with orthodox parties holding 23 and the rest being orthodox members of other parties). The orthodox camp has held the parliamentary balance of power for most of Israel's history.

Notably for this paper, the rising power of orthodox sectors in Israel is closely linked to the state's political-geography, and to the Zionist project of Judaizing the country. There are four main grounds for this. First, all religious movements in Israel, and most conspicuously Gush Emunim ('Loyalty Bloc', the main Jewish religious organization to settle the West Bank), fully support the settling of Jews in Occupied Palestinian Territories and the violent military occupation of these areas. This is often asserted as part of a divine imperative, based on the eternal Jewish right and duty to settle all parts of the 'promised land'. Such settlement is to be achieved while ignoring the aspirations of Palestinians in these territories for self-determination or equal civil rights. Needless to say, this agenda undermines even the possibility of democratic rule in Israel, and has already caused several waves of intra-Jewish religious-secular violence, including the assassination of Prime Minister Rabin in 1995.

Second, repeated surveys show that the religious public in Israel is the most intransigent in its opposition to granting civil equality to Israel's Arab citizens. This does not mean that the entire orthodox public opposes democratic rule, or that it is homogenous in its political views. But nearly all opinion studies, as well as the platforms of main religious political organizations, rank democratic values lower than the Jewish-ness of the state or Jewish control over the entire territory that is Palestine.[47]

Third, there is a discernible link between the rising power of orthodox bodies and the rupturing of Israel's borders. Political analyses and surveys show that as the Judaization of the Occupied Territories deepened, so have the Jewish elements in the collective identity of

---

47 See Y. Peres and E. Yuchtman-Yaar, *Between Consent and Dissent: Democracy and Peace in the Israeli Mind* (Jerusalem: Israel Democracy Institute, 1998); S. Smooha, *Arabs and Jews in Israel: Change and Continuity in Mutual Intolerance* (Boulder, San Francisco, Oxford: Westview, 1992).

Israeli-Jews at the expense of Israeli components.[48] This trend stems from the confusion in the meaning of 'Israeli', when both state borders and boundaries of the Israeli polity are blurred. In other words, the breaching of Israeli borders with settlement activity and the involvement of world Jewry in internal politics have eroded the territorial and civil meaning of the term 'Israeli', and simultaneously strengthened the (non-territorial and ethno-religious) Jewish collective identity. This process has grave implications for the future of democracy in Israel, principally because it bypasses the institution of territorial citizenship, on which a democratic state must be founded. In the Israeli context it legitimizes the stratification between Jews (with full rights) and Arabs (second-class citizens), thus denying Arabs much of the status attached to their 'Israeli' affiliation. Only the demarcation of clear Israeli borders, and the subsequent creation of a territorial political community, can halt the undemocratic ascendancy of Judaism over Israeli-ness.

Finally, the Judaization project is perceived by many in the orthodox camp not only as ethnic-territorial, but also as deepening the religiosity of Israeli Jews. This is based on interpretation of a central percept: 'all Jews are guarantors for one another'. Here 'guarantee' entails 'returning' all 'straying' non-believers to God's way. This mission legitimizes the repeated—if often unsuccessful—attempts to strengthen the religious character of laws and public spaces. The state's religious character is already anchored in a variety of areas: the Jewish Sabbath is the official Israeli day of rest; public institutions only serve *kosher* food; no import of pork is allowed; all personal laws are governed with the national rabbinate (which prohibits civil marriage); and most archaeological digs need approval from religious authorities.

Orthodox parties justify the imposition of these regulations on the secular public by asserting that they ensure the state's ethnic-cultural character for future generations. As such, this would prevent the incorporation of non-Jews and create a state which 'deserves to be called

48 See Migdal, 'Society-Formation and the Case of Israel'; Peres and Yuchtman-Yaar, *Between Consent and Dissent*.

Israeli [...] and Jewish'.[49] Accordingly, the theocracy sought by religious parties already presupposes a Jewish ethnic state (ethnocracy). Their agenda is simply to transform it into a *religious ethnocracy*.[50] In this light, we should note not only the conflict between orthodox and secular Jews, but also their long-standing *co-operation* in the project of establishing a Jewish ethnocracy.

Hence, the religious challenge to the democratization of Israel and the relations between orthodox and secular elements in Israeli society cannot be separated from the political geography of a *Jewish* and *Judaizing* state. The leading Israeli discourse in politics, academia, and the general public tends to treat separately Arab-Jewish and religious-secular issues. But, as shown above, the conflicts and agreements between secular and orthodox Jews cannot be isolated from the concerns, struggles and rights of Palestinian Arabs. This is mainly because at the very heart of the tension between orthodox and secular Jews lies the drive of Israel's Palestinian citizens to see the state transformed from ethnocracy to democracy, and to halt and even reverse the ethnocratic Judaization project.

A Segregative Settling Ethnocracy

As we have seen, the project of Judaizing the state, spearheaded by Jewish immigration and settlement, and buttressed by a set of constitutional laws and a broad consensus among the Jewish public, has

---

49 See Stukhammer, 'Israel's Jubilee and Haredi-Secular Relations from a Haredi Perspective', *Alpayim* 16 (1998), p. 219 (Hebrew); the leader of the Religious National Party in 1998, Rabbi Y. Levi, claimed that the main goal of his party was to ensure the Jewishness of the state for future generations (*Ha'aretz*, 12 August 1998).

50 As observed by E. Don-Yehiya (*The Politics of Accommodation: Settling Conflicts of State and Religion in Israel*, Jerusalem: Floresheimer Institute for Policy Studies, 1997), the most striking feature of orthodox-secular relations is their co-operation, and not conflict, as the two groups differ sharply on most values, goals and aspirations. I suggest here that the central project of Judaizing the country has formed the foundation for this co-operation.

been a major (indeed constitutive) feature of the Israeli regime. Israel thus fits well the model of an ethnocratic regime presented earlier in the paper. More specifically, and given the importance of settlement, it should be called a *settling ethnocracy.*

But beyond regime definitions, and beyond the fundamental chasm between Palestinians and Jews, the fusion of ethnocentric principles and the dynamics of immigration, settlement, and class formation created uneven and segregated patterns among Jews. This was exacerbated by the geographic nature of the Jewish settlement project, which was based on the principal unit of the locality (*Yishuv*). The Jewish settlement project advanced by building localities which were usually ethnically homogeneous, and thus created from the outset a segregated pattern of development. As noted, this geography still stands behind much of the remaining tension between Mizrahim and Ashkenazim in Israel.[51] The political, legal, and cultural mechanisms introduced for the purpose of segregating Jews from Arabs were thus also used to segregate Jewish elites from other ethno-classes, thereby reinforcing the process of 'ethnicization' typical of ethnocratic regimes.

To be sure, these mechanisms were used differently, and more subtly, among Jews, but the persistent gap between Ashkenazim and Mizrahim cannot be understood without accounting for the geography of intra-Jewish relations. In the main, Mizrahim were spatially marginalized by the Israeli settlement project, whether in the isolated periphery or in poor and stigmatized neighbourhoods of Israel's major cities. This has limited their potential economic, social, and cultural participation.

There is a clear nexus connecting the de-Arabization of the country with the marginalization of the Mizrahim, who—culturally and geographically—have been positioned between Arab and Jew, between Israel and its hostile neighbours, between a 'backward' Eastern past and a 'progressive' Western future. But, we should remember, the depth

---

51 See E. Shohat, 'The Narrative of the Nation and the Discourse of Modernisation: The Case of the Mizrahim', *Critique* (Spring 1997), pp. 3-18; S. Swirski, *Israel: The Oriental Majority* (London: Zed Books, 1989).

and extent of discrimination against Palestinians and Mizrahim has been quite different, with the latter included in Jewish-Israeli nation-building project as active participants in the oppression of the former.

A similar segregationist logic was also used to legitimize the creation of segregated neighbourhoods and localities for ultra-orthodox and orthodox Jews, the more recent Russian immigrants, and Palestinian Arabs. In other words, the uneven segregationist logic of the ethno-cratic regime has been infused into spatial and cultural practices that have worked to further ethnicize Israeli society.

Of course, not all ethnic separation is negative, and voluntary separation between groups can at times function to reduce ethnic conflict. But in a society which has declared the 'gathering and integration of the exiles' (*mizug galuyot*) a major national goal, levels of segregation and stratification between Jewish ethno-classes have remained remarkably high. Referring back to our theoretical framework, we can note the fusion of settler-society mechanisms (conquest, immigration, and settlement) with the power of ethno-nationalism (segregating Jews from Arabs) and the logic of ethnic capital (distancing upper and lower ethno-classes) in the creation of Israel's conflict-riddled contemporary human geography.

This process, however, is not uni-dimensional, and must be weighed against counter-trends, such as growing levels of assimilation between Mizrahim and Ashkenazim, and increasing formal equality in social rights among all groups. In addition, solidarity among Jews in the face of a common enemy has often eased internal tensions and segregation, especially between Mizrahim and Ashkenazim, as both have merged into a broadening Israel middle class. Here we can also note that the original Ashkenazi charter group has broadened to incorporate the Mizrahim, especially among the assimilated middle and upper classes.[52] Yet, the ethnicization trend has also been powerful, as illustrated by the growing tendency of political entrepreneurs to exploit 'ethnic capital'

---

52 T. Bensky, 'Testing Melting Pot Theories in the Jewish Israeli Context', *Socio-logical Papers* (Sociological Institute for Community Studies, Bar Ilan University) 2/2 (1993), pp. 34-62.

and draw on ethno-class-religious affiliations as a source of political support. In the 1996 elections such sectoral parties increased their power by 40 per cent, and for the first time in Israel's history over-shadowed the largest two parties, Labour and Likud, which have tra-ditionally been the most ethnically heterogeneous.

Moreover, the situation has not been static. The strategy of Judaization and population dispersal has recently slowed, responding to the new neo-liberal agendas of many Israeli elites.[53] It has also encountered growing Palestinian Arab resistance and Mizrahi grievances, which in turn have reshaped some of the strategies, mechanisms, and manifestations of Israel's territorial, planning, and development policies. Both Arabs and Mizrahim have seen a rise in their absolute (if not relative) socio-economic standards, partially due to Israel's development policies. Likewise, Palestinian resist-ance to Israeli occupation and oppression, culminating in the first Intifada that broke out in the Occupied Territories in December 1987, worked to slow Jewish expansion in several regions, brought about the 1993 Oslo Accords, and achieved a measure of limited Palestinian self-rule.[54] But these changes, important as they were, still occurred within the firm boundaries of the dominant, ethnocratic Zionist discourse, where Jewish settlement and control and the territorial containment of the Arab pop-ulation are undisputed Jewish national goals both within the Green Line and in large parts of the Occupied Territories, as the outbreak of the second Intifada in September 2000 has made so abundantly clear.[55]

---

53 Peled and Shafir, 'The Roots of Peacemaking'.
54 On protest and resistance in the Israeli peripheries, see my 'Israeli Society and Jewish-Palestinian Reconciliation.'
55 For the events that led to the second Intifada and its short-term consequences, see O. Yiftachel, 'Contradictions and Dialectics: Reshaping Political Space in Israel/ Palestine', *Antipode* 36 (2004), pp. 607-613; and idem, 'From "Peace" to Creeping Apartheid: The Emerging Political Geography of Israel/Palestine', *Arena* 16/3 (2001), pp. 13-24. It can also be argued that Oslo accelerated the process of Judaizing large parts of the Occupied Territories, by legitimizing the construction of further Jewish housing and pervasive land confiscation for 'by-pass roads'. In this vein, the long closures of the territories, and the subsequent importation of hundreds of thousands of foreign workers to replace Palestinian labour, are also part of the post-Oslo process of Judaization.

Conclusion:
The Enigma of Distorted Structures

In the foregoing I have attempted to probe the nature of the Israeli regime from a political-geographic perspective. I have showed that three main forces have shaped the Israeli polity—the establishment of a settler society, the mobilizing force of ethno-nationalism, and the ethnic logic of capital. The fusion of these forces has created a regime I have termed ethnocracy, which privileges *ethnos* over *demos* in a contested territory seized by a dominant group. Ethnic relations in Israel are thus comparable to other ethnocracies, such as Malaysia, Sri Lanka, Serbia, or Estonia, but not to western liberal democracies, as commonly suggested in scholarly literature or popular discourse.[56]

More specifically to Israel, I have shown that the Israeli regime has been significantly shaped by the ethnocratic project of *Judaizing* the Land of Israel/Palestine. This has been legitimized by the need to 'indigenize' 'deterritorialized' Jews in order to fulfill a claim for territorial self-determination. The momentum of the Judaization project has subsequently led to the rupture of the state's borders, the continuing incorporation of extra-territorial Jewish organizations into the Israeli government system, the persistent and violent military rule over the Occupied Palestinian Territories, and the subsequent undermining of equal citizenship. As shown above, the Judaization project provides a 'genetic core' for understanding the Israeli polity because it did not only shape the Jewish-Palestinian conflict, but also the relations between Ashkenazim and Mizrahim as well as between secular and orthodox Jews.[57]

---

56 For recent attempts to compare Israel to western democracies, see A. Dowty, *The Jewish State: One Hundred Years Later* (Berkeley: University of California Press, 1998); G. Shefer, 'Has Israel Really Been a Garrison Democracy? Sources of Change in Israel's Democracy', *Israel Affairs* 3/1 (1996), pp. 13-38.

57 I do not claim, of course, that the Judaization process can explain every facet of ethnic relations in Israel/Palestine; rather, it is a factor which helped shape these relations while remaining largley overlooked in scholarly literature. But the Judaization process has also greatly affected power relations between groups not covered in this paper, including military-civil society, gender relations and local-central tensions; see K. Ferguson, *Kibbutz Journal: Reflections on Gender, Race and Nation in Israel* (Pasadena, CA, Trilogy Book, 1993).

A key factor in understanding the Israeli regime thus lies in uncovering the sophisticated institutional setting that presents itself as democratic, but at the same time facilitates the continuing immigration of Jews—and only Jews—to Israel, and the uni-directional transfer of land from Arab to Jewish hands. Here we can observe that the legal and political foundations of the Jewish state have created a distorted structure that ensured a continuing uni-ethnic seizure of a bi-ethnic state. Once in place, this structure has become self-referential, reifying and reinforcing its own logic.

But the dominant view unequivocally treats Israel as a democracy.[58] This view is augmented by the durable operation of many important democratic *features*—as distinct from *structures*—especially competitive politics, generous civil rights, an autonomous judiciary, and free media. In particular, Israel's democratic image has also been promoted in the Israeli academy by nearly all scholars in the social sciences and humanities.

Israeli scholars use a range of definitions for the Israeli regime, including liberal democracy,[59] constitutional democracy,[60] con-sociational democracy,[61] and ethnic democracy.[62] The enactment of two new basic laws during the 1990s has prompted a wave of writing hailing the 'constitutional revolution' as a major move towards legal liberalism.[63] Even critical writers such as Azmi Bishara, Shlomo Swirsky, Uri Ram, Yoav Peled, Yonathan Shapiro and Uri Ben-Eliezer

---

58   This includes some of my own previous writings, such as *Planning a Mixed Region in Israel* (1992), where I classified Israel as a bi-ethnic democracy.

59   Neuberger, *Democracy in Israel*; Shefer, 'Has Israel Really Been a Garrison Democracy?'

60   S.N. Eisenstadt, *The Transformation of Israeli Society* (London: Weidenfield and Nicolson, 1985).

61   Don-Yihiya, *The Politics of Accommodation*; Liebman, 'Attitudes towards Democracy among Israeli Religious Leaders'; D. Horowitz and M. Lissak, *Trouble in Utopia: The Overburdened Polity of Israel* (Albany: SUNY Press, 1990).

62   Smooha, 'Ethnic Democracy: Israel as an Archetype'; Shafir and Peled, 'The Roots of Peacemaking.'

63   See Arian, *The Second Republic*; A. Barak, 'Fifty Years of Israeli Law', *Alpayim* 16 (1998), pp. 36-45 (Hebrew).

still treat 'Israel Proper' (the imaginary unit within the Green Line) as a democratic—albeit seriously flawed—regime.[64] Most Palestinian writers have refrained from analyzing the specific nature of the Israeli regime, although here a number of significant challenges to the common democratic definition of Israel began to appear, most notably by Elia Zureik,[65] Asad Ghanem and Nadim Rouhana, with the latter two defining Israel as a non-democratic 'ethnic state'.[66]

Yet, none of these works has incorporated seriously the two principal political-geographical processes shaping the Israeli polity: the ongoing Judaization of the country, and the vagueness of its political borders. Even critical writers tend to ignore the incongruity between the definition of Israel within the Green Line and the residence of people considered as full Israelis in occupied territories beyond the state's boundaries. This is not a minor aberration, but rather a structural condition that undermines the claim for a democratic regime. 'Israel Proper' is a political and territorial entity which has long ceased to exist, and hence cannot provide an appropriate spatial unit for analyzing the nature of the polity.

In many ways, the situation resembles the hegemonic moment observed by Gramsci, when a dominant truth is diffused by powerful elites to all corners of society, preventing the raising of alternative voices and reproducing prevailing social and power relations. From the above it appears that this hegemony has reached even the most enlightened and putatively democratic realms of Israeli-Jewish society.

How can this enigma be explained? How can enlightened circles that declare themselves to be democratic square the 'Jewish and democratic'

---

64 See A. Bishara, 'On the Question of the Palestinian Minority in Israel', *Teorya Uvikkoret* (Theory and Critique) 3 (1993), pp. 7-20 (Hebrew); U. Ben-Eliezer, 'Is Military Coup Possible in Israel?', *Theory and Society* 27 (1998), pp. 314-349; Peled, 'Ethnic Democracy and the Legal Construction of Citizenship'; Shapiro, *Democracy in Israel*; Swirsky, *Israel: The Oriental Majority*; Ram, 'Citizens, Consumers and Believers'.

65 E. Zureik, 'Prospects of Palestinians in Israel (I)', *Journal of Palestine Studies* 12/2 (1993), pp. 90-109.

66 See Ghanem, 'State and Minority in Israel'; Rouhana, *Palestinian Citizens in an Ethnic Jewish State*.

account with the continuing process of Judaization? I suggest here a metaphor in which Israeli-Jewish discourse is analogous to a tilted tower, such as the Tower of Pisa. Once one enters the tower, it appears straight, since its internal structural grid is perfectly perpendicular and parallel. Similarly, the introverted discourse about the Jewish and democratic state: once inside this discourse, most Jews accept the Jewish character of the state as an unproblematic point of departure, much like the floor of the tilted tower. From that perspective, Judaization appears natural and justified—or perhaps does not appear at all.[67]

On the basis of this tilted foundation, Israel has added laws and policies over the years that can be likened to the tower's walls. Given the tilted foundation, these walls could only be built on an angle, yet they appear straight to those observing from the inside. One needs to step outside and away from the tilted building and measure its coordinates against truly vertical buildings in order to discern the distortion. In the Israeli case, then, scholars are urged to step outside the internal Jewish-Israeli discourse and analyze the Israeli regime systematically against the 'straight' principles of a democratic state.[68]

In this vein, let us explore briefly the principle of self-determination, which forms the basis of popular sovereignty and thus of democracy itself. Because the modern state is a legal-territorial entity, and because the fullest expression of self-determination is the governance of a state, it must be exercised on a territorial basis. But Israel maintains a placeless entity (the Jewish people) as the source of its self-determination, and thus defines the state as 'the state of the Jewish people'. This non-territorial definition presents two serious problems for democratic rule: (a) it prevents the full political inclusion of non-Jews

---

67 Here we can note that the political disagreement between the Jewish left and right in Israel, which is often portrayed as a bitter rivalry, is not on the broadly accepted 'need' to Judaize Israel, but only on the desired extent of this project.

68 Some steps in this direction have already been taken; cf. Ghanem, 'State and Minority in Israel'; Rouhana, *Palestinian Citizens in an Ethnic Jewish State*; Yiftachel, 'Questioning "Ethnic Democracy"', *Israeli Studies* 3/2 (1998), pp. 253-67.

by degrading the status of (territorial) state citizenship,[69] and (b) it reinforces Judaization through the role of world Jewry in immigration and land transfer.

Returning to the case of Finland may help illustrate the problem: while that state is declared to be Lutheran, it is also defined as a (territorial) *Finnish* political community. As such, it allows non-Lutheran minorities to fully identify as Finnish. But because the state of Israel is defined (non-territorially) as Jewish, and Arabs can never become Jewish, their right to equal citizenship is structurally denied. Hence, a democratic state requires a *territorial* form of self-determination that enables the equal inclusion of minorities into the state's civil society.[70] This recognition casts doubt over the validity of one of the most significant statements made by the Israeli High Court, which declared in 1988, that 'Israel's definition as the state of the Jewish people does not negate its democratic character, in the same way that the French-ness of France does not negate its democratic character'.[71] This statement harbours a conceptual distortion: if France is French, Israel should be *Israeli* (and not Jewish). Hence, stepping outside the internal Israeli-Jewish discourse reveals that the maintenance of a non-territorial (Jewish) form of self-determination structurally breaches central tenets of democracy. It constitutes, instead, the foundation of the Israeli-Jewish ethnocracy.

69 This affects adversely the political rights of Israeli-Jews too, as it undermines the extent of their own sovereignty.

70 Political theorists discuss in recent debates the possibility of cultural or linguistic forms of self-determination, which may be non-territorial; cf. W. Kymlicka, *Multicultural Citizenship: A Liberal Theory of Minority Rights* (Oxford: Clarendon Press, 1995). However, these forms also allow the possibility of civil entrance into the collectivity. This is different in Judaism, which is neither territorial, cultural or linguistic, and thus prevents the possibility of civil inclusion.

71 *Neiman v. Central Elections Committee*, Judgement of the then High Court President, Justice M. Shamgar.

Epilogue: Ethnocracy and Negev Lands

To conclude, let us return once again to the 'coal face' of land control issues in Israel. Since September 1997, the Israeli government has announced on several occasions the introduction of new strategies to block the 'Arab invasion' into state lands within the Green Line, and to curtail 'illegal' Bedouin dwellings, construction and grazing. In most cases, 'illegal dwellings' and 'Arab invasion' are code terms for Bedouin residence on traditional tribal land and resistance to involuntary concentration in a small number of towns designated by the state in the Negev and Galilee.[72] The recently announced strategy would combine the development of small Jewish settlements (mainly in the Negev's north-eastern hills), the establishment of single-family Jewish farms, the sale of Negev land to the Jewish Agency and diaspora Jews, and the application of greater pressure on Bedouin to migrate to the state-planned towns. The initiator of the policy was the (then) director of the Prime Minister's office, Avigdor Lieberman, an immigrant from the former Soviet Union and a resident of a Jewish settlement in the Occupied Territories.

A closer look at this latest land control strategy raises several hard questions about its basic assumptions: if the Bedouin-Arabs were Israeli citizens—which they are—why would their use of state land be considered an 'invasion'? How do other sectors of Israeli society, such as *moshavim* and *kibbutzim*, which regularly build without planning permission, escape treatment as 'invaders'? Given that the initiator of the policy is a West Bank settler (illegal according to international law), who is actually the invader here? How can a recent immigrant to the country campaign to evacuate residents who have been on the land for several generations, since well before the state was established? How can the state lease large tracts of land to non-citizen (Jewish) organ-

---

72 On this issue, see the detailed analysis by T. Fenster, 'Settlement Planning and Participation under Principles of Pluralism', *Progress in Planning* 39/3 (1993), pp. 169-242.

izations and continue to block its own (Arab) citizens from using it for residential purposes?

At the end of its first Jubilee, then, Israel's *ethnocratic* features keep surfacing: the ongoing Judaization project, the stratification of ethnic rights, the fuzziness of geographical and political boundaries, and the legal and material involvement of extra-territorial Jewish organizations. Against this reality, scholars, students, and activists are called upon to help dislodge the hegemonic Jewish discourse of a 'Jewish and democratic state', and participate in the task of transforming Israel from ethnocracy to democracy.

Democracy...
and the Experience of National Liberation
The Palestinian Case

Musa Budeiri

> 'When *I* use a word,' Humpty Dumpty said in a rather scornful tone, 'it means just what I choose it to mean—neither more nor less.'
>
> 'The question is,' said Alice, 'whether you *can* make words mean so many different things.'
>
> 'The question is,' said Humpty Dumpty, 'which is to be master—that's all.'
>
> Lewis Carroll, *Through The Looking Glass*

Historically the struggle for democracy has been synonymous with the struggle for fundamental liberties. Universal suffrage in itself is only the first step on the road to the creation of a fully democratic society. If in the narrow sense the essence of democracy is taken to be the process of choosing between elites competing to govern, this itself requires a degree of freedom. The contending parties must be allowed to publish programmes and to make competing claims. The electors must be able to question them and to voice their doubts and their support. Choice in itself implies debate, and this necessitates a degree of freedom. Yet, the fact remains that it is possible to have pluralism without democracy, and to have participation without democracy. But pluralism and participation can be important stations towards a measure of democratization. Democracy viewed as popular power should and can be seen

Author's note: An earlier version of this article appeared in Arabic in G. Giacaman, A. Bishara, S. Zaidanai, B. Ghalioun and M. Budeiri, *The Democratic Choice: Critical Readings*, Beirut 1994: Centre for Arab Unity Studies.

as a 'continuous process of interaction between government and society, with the maximum involvement of the people in public decision making at every level' (Arblaster 1993). As such there are today no existing states that can serve as models to be reproduced carbon-copy fashion throughout the world.

The struggle for democracy has essentially been a quest for equality and social justice. Not merely formal equality, but the construction of a new and as yet non-existent world, a Utopia, which early on took a socialist form. The entrenched powers of wealth, property and privilege saw democracy as a threat. They skirmished and waged numerous battles in order to preserve their power and privilege. The reform of the political process, which was the outcome of the steadfast struggle waged by such movements as the Chartists in England, was agreed to reluctantly. The ruling classes consented to the surrender of part of their privileges in order to maintain their wealth and hegemony. Eventually a new state structure was built in Europe that paid homage to the principles of freedom, consent and participation. Tensions continued, however, to abound and eternal vigilance was necessary to ensure that there would be no defaulting. Inevitably there were regressions, as with the rise of Nazism and Fascism between the two world wars, and the betrayal of the promise of the Bolshevik Revolution. Yet, on the whole, the ruling classes succeeded in establishing their hegemony politically, while economically their long and profitable dominance of the colonial world enabled them to establish an economic order that gave the people a previously undreamed-off standard of living. It can be and has been argued that they 'manufactured consent' for this new power sharing arrangement. Whether this is true or not, it is undeniable that democracy currently means the Western Liberal model—'neither more no less'. We will now turn to the rest of the world where democracy does not obtain and try to observe whether the historical experience of those countries, inextricably interwoven as it has been with that of the imperialist capitalist countries of Western Europe, can have any meaningful impact on their current political make-up and practice.

The Colonial Experience

The struggle of the colonial peoples of Africa, Asia and Latin America for independence and the control of their native resources has been an intrinsic part of the worldwide struggle for freedom, justice, equality and democracy, despite the differences and variations that exist between country and country and continent and continent. It is worth bearing in mind at this juncture that the freedoms and liberties wrung by the powerless and the underprivileged in the emerging capitalist order in Europe had no parallel in the colonial world. Irrespective of the degree of political liberalization exercised at home, no colonial authority would sanction even the bare minimum of political or any other sort of rights when it came to the indigenous peoples of the colonies. Whereas the European working class was able to establish its right to its own political organization in order to press what it perceived to be its just demands—political, social, and economic—no parallel situation obtained in the colonies. The indigenous peoples were not allowed to establish their own parties and independence movements in order to press the case for self-determination and statehood in an open and public fashion. Brutal repression was the traditional and inevitable response to any attempts at self-organization for whatever purpose. Indeed, the colonial masters were unable to comprehend the motives behind the natives' constant violent outbursts. The problem presented itself as one of law and order. Given the premise of 'the white man's burden' and the 'basic inferiority' of the coloured races, the situation could not be otherwise.

In specific colonial situations—North America, Australia, parts of South America—the aboriginal races were wiped out. Colonial possessions were seized by force and maintained by force. Neither consent nor participation was part of the process of government. Indeed, even when changes were reluctantly being introduced back home and a measure of power and autonomy was surrendered to the public at large, the inhabitants of Europe's colonial possessions remained outside the pale. This should not be surprising. Athenian democracy excluded its slave population and of course Athenian women, while in most European states it is only well into the first half of the twentieth century that women are being given the vote. The need, therefore, does not arise to try and explain why the indigenous peoples of the colonies resorted to violence to achieve their liberation. There was no other avenue open to them. Thus, throughout the long history of colonialism indigenous movements of rebellion and revolt against foreign rule continued unabatedly irrespective of the guise they happened to assume at any given historical moment.

The first world war heralded a watershed, both in Europe itself and as far as the colonial peoples were concerned. The League of Nations was established, and a new world order was declared, based on the principles of national self-determination and the freedom of all nations as embodied in President Woodrow Wilson's fourteen points. But, despite the rhetoric and the new discourse, for the colonial peoples the aftermath of the war merely signified a re-division of the spoils of war. As far as the Arab provinces of the Ottoman Empire were concerned, the dismemberment of the Empire was to result in a re-division between Britain and France, giving Britain the lion's share of the booty. The new boundaries drawn on the map simply aimed at concluding a compromise between the rival claims of the victorious colonial powers. Under the umbrella of the League of Nations, mandated territories and protectorates were established furthering the fiction that the aim of foreign rule was the well being of the indigenous peoples. Neither the peoples of Asia or Africa reaped any benefits from this new world order. The only bright star on the horizon was the successful Bolshevik Revolution in Czarist Russia. This was to be the new ally—decidedly out of self interest—of the yet to be established national liberation movements in the colonies. Lenin, the architect of this new alliance, looked to the colonial peoples to play a supporting role. Capitalism's chains had to be broken where they had been forged. Only the worldwide overthrow and transformation of capitalism would ensure the freedom and independence of the colonial peoples. The struggle for freedom could not be separated from the struggle for democracy, equality and social justice. The struggle of the working peoples of the capitalist countries and that of the colonial peoples complimented each other. They were natural allies. The First Congress of the peoples of the East was held in Baku in 1921 with the aim of forging this grand alliance (Tarabulsi 1972:14). Later the Communist International was entrusted with the task of coordinating revolutionary activity world wide. The story of the twists and turns of Comintern policy do not concern us here. What is of import is the perception shared by revolutionary communists, by nationalists, and by the colonial authorities themselves, that this indeed was a single and unified struggle.

A real new world order or, perhaps, a different world order was ushered in as the second world war came to an end. This indeed was to be the signal for the demise of colonialism and the beginning of the decolonization process. National independence and national liberation movements sprung up everywhere. Self-selected groups of young people who had studied, fought or worked in the colonial heartlands, returned home and took up arms against the continuing presence of foreign rule. Violent means were employed to make the presence of the new movements felt and to mobilize the indigenous masses. In the writings of the theorists of the anti-colonial struggle, Franz Fanon foremost among them, violence assumed a central place. It was necessary and it was cleansing. For all their protestations of civilization and morality, the colonial masters did not hesitate to resort to violence in order to defend their interests. It was only when the downtrodden, the exploited and the oppressed took up arms to defend themselves and to assume control of what was rightfully theirs, that the civilized world shook in horror at the unspeakable violence being committed, and which cast doubts on the validity and sanctity of their claims.

The borders of many of these colonial possessions had been drawn without taking into consideration anything other than the greed of the colonial settlers, thus they cut across tribes, races, nations, and ethnic groups. In some places more than one nationalist party vied for the affections of the masses, and sought to be recognized as the standard bearer of the national liberation struggle. Consequently, this resulted in inter-ethnic or inter-tribal conflict that was to have dire consequences in the post-liberation period. In numerous colonized territories, the reigning colonial power nurtured an indigenous class of traders and officials who were accorded economic privileges and some of the trappings of authority to be wielded on behalf of the colonial authorities. Inevitably, this led to internal divisions as certain groups from among the local rich and privileged sided with the colonial authorities in an attempt to protect their privileged status. Different colonial powers pursued different paths in their efforts to extend and maintain their control. Thus, Britain and France behaved in different ways. The French pursued a civilizing mission. In theory at least, they wanted to convert the indigenous people everywhere into loyal French citizens. This did not, however, imply extending the rights and privileges which French citizens in the metropolis enjoyed to the inhabitants of France's far-flung empire. Liberal rhetoric and racist practice co-existed side by side. The British, on the other hand, preferred to rely on an indigenous class of collaborators to carry out their policies and to exercise their dominance through them. For the rest they left well alone. They did their best to tamper as little as possible with the existing social and economic order in so far as their interests were not involved.

The first world war, in addition to leading to a redrawing of the map of the world and the dismemberment of the Ottoman Empire, also created a new colonial discourse. The establishment of the League of Nations went hand in hand with the propagation of a new myth to the effect that old-style colonialism had come to an end. The member states of the League, or at least the leading members, took upon themselves the task of watching over and leading the peoples of the colonial world to nationhood and self-determination. Until such a time as the indigenous peoples achieved maturity their affairs would continue to be managed by the European powers according to the agreements they had reached among themselves.

Palestine was singled out as a unique case. In the first place, it had to be concocted by dismembering natural Syria into a number of parts. Thus Syria, Palestine, Lebanon, Trans-Jordan, and Iraq were established as separate entities. But, whereas the neighbouring territories were administered under the rubric of the new colonial discourse, Palestine was elected for greater things. Its indigenous population was eventually to make way for an ongoing wave of immigration and settlement led and instigated by East European Jews, mostly under European protection, and with the support of the then existing world order. Thus, the terms of the Balfour Declaration were included within the terms of the Mandate that was bestowed on Britain by the League of Nations. Paradoxically, the major part of this enterprise took place at the same time as the overwhelming part of European Jewry was being wiped out in the gas chambers of Hitler's Germany, with little being done by the family of nations to thwart this early example of ethnic cleansing (at least as far as the twentieth century was concerned).

The post-second-world-war era witnessed the attainment of independence by the overwhelming majority of colonized peoples in Asia and Africa. Algeria, in 1962, was the last Arab country to break the chains of foreign rule. Save for a few isolated instances—Rhodesia, Portugal's African colonies, Namibia, etc.—the age of colonialism was over. There were notable exceptions, however. The Apartheid regime in South Africa continued to enslave the country's black population; the Kurdish people, ignored and marginalized at the close of Great War, remained divided in three different nation states; and the Palestinians remained uprooted and dispersed, Palestine itself dismembered, and those Palestinians who somehow had remained on their land pauperized and denied their national identity.

Invariably, the national liberation and national independence movements were born in violent opposition to the European colonial powers, Whether the Mau Mau in Kenya, the FLN in Algeria, or the Vietminh in Vietnam, none of these movements possessed or could ever have hoped to achieve the legitimacy accorded to political movements in the metropolitan country, even those totally opposed to the established order and advocating its overthrow by force. These movements were born underground, or soon driven there after their creation, and persisted in their struggle until they achieved victory. Whether tribal coalitions, or national fronts grouped around a leading party or movement, their internal structures were shaped by the actual conditions of the struggle and of developments in the respective countries. They were not, and could not be, mirror images of conservative, liberal, or revolutionary political groupings in the countries of the metropolis. Survival in the harsh atmosphere of violent repression unleashed by the colonial power in its desperate attempt to hold on to its colonial possession necessitated secrecy and conspiratorial methods. These, in turn, gave birth to the required organizational forms, hierarchies and structures that enabled the struggle to continue. By necessity, consensus politics obtained at the early stages; people joined voluntarily. There could be no compulsion at the start of such an adventure. With the passage of time, the increase in size and tasks and the widening of the struggle to embrace large masses of people and multi-faceted forms, a centralized form of organization was established. This was borrowed from the Stalinist parties of the Communist bloc. In the aftermath of victory and the realization of independence, this was to make its presence felt, invariably with negative consequences. In the case of the Palestinian national movement, the picture is similar, yet at the same time different, due to the peculiarities of Palestinian history and to the unique features of the Palestinian problem, which became intertwined both with the still unresolved Jewish problem, and the struggle for Arab unity. Both were to have an effect that dictated the form and path the Palestine National Movement was to adopt for a large part of its existence, and perhaps account for its many failures and rare successes.

The Pre-History of the Palestine National Movement

It is commonly pointed out that powerful barriers inhibit the growth of democracy among Palestinians. Various arguments are called upon to validate this self-evident assertion. The most important, of course, has been the inability of the Palestinians to realize statehood or—to put it more plainly—the success of the Zionist settlement project in transforming Palestine into Israel. For the Palestinians, the age of colonialism has not come to a close. A colonial settler regime—showing many similarities with the White settler regime in South Africa while departing from it in some fundamental aspects—has prevented the Palestinians from achieving statehood and continues to do so up to this date. Not only was Palestine itself transformed into an alien entity, Israel, but a large part of Palestinians fell under Israeli occupation, while those who found refuge in the neighbouring Arab states were manipulated and kept under strict control by the regimes there. Is it any wonder, then, that the Palestinians have been unable to develop a democratic process?! In a blatant attempt to forward a specific political agenda, belatedly revisionist efforts are being made to point out the existence of a democratic process, albeit 'starting in a superficial elitist form under the British Mandate' (Maoz 1993:214) and highlighting the unique experiences of the Palestinians which render them 'likely candidates to spearhead democratization reforms in the Middle East' (Kaufman 1993:46). Nothing in the historical record gives substance to such claims.

In most of the countries of Africa and Asia which were under colonial tutelage of Western liberal democratic states, it is the colonial experience itself that has militated against the development of democratic practices and structures. Moreover, as has been noted by all students of the de-colonization experience, the requirements of the struggle for independence more often than not favoured the emergence of a dominant single party or mass movement. This was the expression of a people totally united in a single and overriding will to throw off the yoke of foreign domination. Inevitably, this was then usually carried into the post-independent state structure as a one-party system. Even where multi-party politics were tried in the immediate aftermath of the establishment of independence, these have been found wanting—they soon degenerated into tribal politics and served as a disguise for the promotion of inter-ethnic tensions. The coming of independence forced the fledgling states to face the political implications of population mobility, displacement, statelessness, the absence of a bureaucratic cadre, and unresolved border disputes. It soon became apparent to all that a political independence that lacked economic substance was a mere charade.

In order to come to grips with and comprehend the current workings of the contemporary Palestinian national movement, it is necessary to cast a look at its historical antecedents. For this we have to travel further back than the 1967 Israeli occupation of the West Bank and the Gaza Strip, or the 1948 war when Palestine was dismembered and the Palestinians were expelled. Actually, in order to witness the birth of Arab nationalism we have to go back even further than the period of the British Mandate and survey the final days of the Ottoman Empire.

Such an enquiry would confirm one important fact: Palestinian national sentiment, or Palestinian nationalism, is a phenomenon of fairly recent origin (Budeiri 1997:195–198).

It was the attempts of the Ottoman Empire to reform itself in order to withstand and repulse the ongoing encroachments of the European powers that gave birth to a specific Turkish nationalism which served in the end to dissolve the ties that linked the peoples of the Empire together. Once national or ethnic origin replaced the religious bond, the non-Turkic peoples of the Empire began going their separate ways. This held also for the Empire's Arab subjects. In this sense, Arab nationalism was the twin brother of Turkish nationalism, and raised the call for national political rights and freedoms for the Arab nation. This was a collective nationalist demand, not a democratic demand in the strict sense of the term. Shedding the non-Turkic parts of the Empire, Mustapha Kemal succeeded in establishing a Turkish nation state. The Arabs were not so fortunate. The demise of the Czarist regime in Russia had earned the Turks a respite, while the British and the French were busily trying to digest those parts of the Empire which had already fallen under their control. The forcible termination of Faysal's rule in Damascus signalled Arab inability to withstand the combined onslaught of Anglo-French power. Syria was partitioned between the victorious allies with scant attention given to the demands of the nascent Arab movement. The new conditions forced themselves on the constituent parts of the Arab national movement. Already the foundations of a narrow local nationalism were being laid (Khalidi 1997:167). By necessity each component of the national movement began to struggle for its own emancipation and against its 'own' colonial regime.

In Palestine the issue was compounded as a result of the Balfour Declaration and the Mandatory power's declared intention of honouring the provisions it contained. The Palestinian National Movement, a junior part in any case of the larger Arab national movement, was torn between its enmity to British colonialism and the perceived need to address itself to the Mandatory authorities to put a stop to Jewish immigration and the transfer of land. The mainstay of its policy was the demand for the termination of the Mandate and the establishment of an independent Arab state in Palestine. Any attempt to cooperate with the Mandatory authorities would in fact imply acceptance of the provisions of the Mandate, and the granting of legitimacy to the Zionist movement and its settlement activities in the country. Of necessity, it could not raise democratic demands and address itself to the British to grant these, while at the same time calling for a struggle against continued British control and domination. The numerous political organizations that mushroomed in the 1920s and 30s were not democratic, whether in form or in content. They were indistinguishable, and did not require or solicit popular democratic recognition for their claims to address the Mandatory power on behalf of the Arab inhabitants of the country. Without exception, these organizations were controlled by members of the traditional elite, an oligarchy of notables and wealthy families, whose authority was based on traditional elements of prestige, possession of land and senior religious and government positions. In other circumstances they would have been the natural mediating agents of colonial rule, and this in fact accounts for a lot of the tension that did exist within the Palestine national movement and the dissension that was rife within its ranks.

In retrospect, the death, in October 1935, of Shaykh Izz ad-Din al-Qassam and his followers at the hands of the British marks a watershed. A national leadership centred round the Mufti of Jerusalem, the appointed head of the Supreme Muslim Council, was intermittently engaged in a dialogue with the Mandatory authorities in an attempt to curtail Jewish immigration and prevent the continuing transfer of land to Jewish settlers. The British colonial presence itself did not figure prominently on the nationalist agenda. Indeed, looking at the experience of neighbouring states, a modus vivendi of sorts would have been worked out between colonized and colonizer based on the implicit undertaking that foreign control and domination would necessarily come to an end some time. Britain's commitment to the terms of the Balfour Declaration militated against such a possibility. Changing conditions within Palestine and the transformations wrought by the influx of hundreds of thousands of European Jewish immigrants forced a different set of policies on a national leadership than the ones they would have been naturally inclined to pursue. Targeting the British colonial presence itself as the main enemy was not a choice the Mufti and the social and economic elite of the country made consciously. The beginnings of the armed struggle, symbolized by Qassam and his small band of rural 'desperados', was a spontaneous act of self-defence at the grass roots level, which affected first and foremost the countryside and the peasantry (Swedenburg 1995:2, 30).

The years 1936–1939 saw the eruption and unfolding of the Great Arab Revolt that assumed and continues to assume a central place in Palestinian nationalist history and mythology. The military and political defeat the Palestinians suffered at the hands of British imperialism brought the period of independent Palestinian political activity to an end. This defeat was the outcome of an unfavourable balance of forces and British determination not to part with Palestine. Although internal dissension made itself felt in the Palestinian camp, especially during the latter part of the Revolt, this was not a factor of magnitude as far as the defeat itself was concerned. It is naive to deny that the Palestinians committed themselves to the revolt in a total fashion. The way they organized themselves, the fighting methods they adopted, etc. could have been improved upon. This was, however, a relatively backward society fighting a perceived threat to its existence with the materials available to it and under the command of its traditional leadership. The neighbouring states did not fare better in their attempts to challenge the colonizing power on the field of battle. Changed circumstances ten years later, with Britain just having emerged weakened and impoverished from a war with Hitler's Germany, would cause British policy makers to react differently in the face of a Jewish rebellion with very much the same aims—bringing the British presence in the country to an end and securing the country's independence. From then on, the neighbouring Arab states, particularly those with close ties to Britain, were to assume a paramount role in speaking on behalf of Palestine and its Arab inhabitants. Palestinians would no longer be able to play a sovereign and independent role in determining their own and their country's future. This was to make itself felt on the termination of the Mandate in 1948 and the withdrawal of British forces from Palestine. The newly established state of

Israel fought a halfhearted war (Zionist and Arab myths notwith-standing) with the neighbouring Arab states, primarily in an effort to settle their common borders and effectuate the partitioning of the country. This was a fate that had already been decided on by the recently established United Nations Organization, the successor body to the League of Nations, and the embodiment of international legitimacy and the international will.

Part-time actors in their own tragedy, the Palestinians found themselves in 1948/49 displaced refugees. Even those who had not budged but remained in their towns and villages had to undertake a novel form of exile: the denial of their identity. Just under a million Palestinians became homeless as a result of their eviction from the newly established Israeli state. They made their way to the surrounding Arab states, Lebanon, Syria and Trans-Jordan, while large numbers converged on a strip round Gaza occupied by Egyptian troops, and similar numbers made their temporary abode in those areas of Palestine that fell under Trans-Jordanian occupation, the West Bank. Palestine was thus divided into three parts, with only an insignificant minority—about 150,000—allowed to remain in its native habitat within Israel, while the largest concentration of Palestinians which now was in areas annexed to Trans-Jordan was forced to undergo an identity change——instantaneously transformed into Jordanian citizens by royal decree, they were no longer Palestinians (Wilson 1987:194).

For the next nineteen years, the Arab states of the Mashreq played the role of guardians, calling for the return of the dispossessed Palestinians to their homes and the implementation of the United Nations Partition Resolution 181 of 29 November 1947. Yet, no move was made to take the first step by allowing the Palestinians to establish their own independent state on those parts of Palestine that had not fallen under Jewish control, nor were the Palestinians allowed any autonomous form of activity. To be sure, there were differences in the situation of the Palestinians in the various host countries (Brand 1988:229–233). While in Jordan every attempt was made to absorb them and facilitate the assumption of their new identity to the extent of issuing them with Jordanian passports and enabling them to travel freely, in Lebanon, on the other hand, they lived in camps which were controlled by the Lebanese security authorities, and where they were denied permission to work and even to travel and deliberately kept outside the fabric of Lebanese political and social life. This situation began to change in 1964 as a result of the intensification of inter-Arab rivalries. When the Palestine Liberation Organization was founded in the same year under the auspices of the Arab League, the prime mover was Egypt (Shemesh 1988: 40). Given Egypt's conflict with Syria and Jordan, the PLO was to serve the interests of Egyptian foreign policy, both by garnering Palestinian support for Nasser's Pan-Arab policies, and by portraying Egypt as steadfastly working to realize the cherished aim of every Arab from the Ocean to the Gulf, the liberation of Palestine.

To head the organization the Egyptians chose a professional diplomat, Ahmad Shuqairy, the scion of a well-known family originally from city of Acre (Akka), whose father had been one of the leaders of the Palestinian national movement during the Mandate. He had previously served both the Syrian and Saudi governments in diplomatic postings abroad. Shuqairy established the PLO from the top down so to speak. It was he who appointed its leading body, the executive committee. The same went for what was to become the Palestinians parliament in exile, the Palestine National Council (PNC), which was similarly chosen, though with the ostensible aim of reflecting the wide geographic dispersion of the Palestinians after their exile in 1948. So long as Shuqairy enjoyed the confidence of the Egyptians, he was able to steer the organization in the way he thought best; this ensured that it would not contradict the basic tenets of Egyptian foreign policy. This was basically a one-man show, albeit with an attending chorus. Shuqairy, as it turned out, did not enjoy a free hand. The executive committee boasted a number of well-known personalities (among whom was Haydar Abd al-Shafi from the Gaza Strip), and the PNC was not altogether supportive of Shuqairy, as the pro-Jordanian faction was well represented in its ranks. The tasks the PLO was expected to fulfill were of the diplomatic and ceremonial type. Being the legitimate offspring of the Arab League Council, it was unable to operate in any fashion without securing a consensus, which was seldom forthcoming.

It is difficult to speak with any justification of the PLO as an autonomous Palestinian organization in this formative period. There is no denying that its establishment stuck a responsive chord both among the Palestinians and the wider Arab public, but its history in the pre-1967 period can best be understood as a function of Arab feuds, and the need to manoeuvre carefully in order to ensure survival. There is no doubt that Shuqairy performed successfully in carrying out this task.

The confrontation of June 1967 resulted in a total Arab defeat. Paradoxically, this freed the Palestinians from the tutelage and guardianship of their Arab hosts, but it also meant that the total area of geographic Palestine was now under Israeli military and political control. Well over a million Palestinians were now resident in 'Palestine', transformed into 'Israel', and found themselves under the direct military rule of their enemy. That is, for the first time since the expulsion and dispersal of 1948 there was a sizeable portion of the Palestinian people living on their own land, though as a minority under foreign rule and bereft of all civil and political rights. This was to prove of tremendous importance in the future, and would enable the Palestinians twenty odd years after the event to re-formulate their national demands in more realizable forms, and ones more acceptable to the international community.

The earthquake which shook the Arab world in 1967 could not but bring about change within the PLO itself. The Arab regimes, discredited as a result of their performance on the battlefield, had lost all credibility and were now more than ever pre-occupied with the immediate task of self-preservation. As a result, the PLO was transformed from an instrument of inter-Arab feuds into a relatively independent and autonomous Palestinian organization, mirroring to some extent the reality of the Palestinian's own condition and their efforts to create their own distinctive space as autonomous actors. Arab politics and inter-state feuds would continue to influence the deliberations and policies of the PLO, but only as part of the necessary environment in which the organization had to operate and as a reflection of the predicament of the hundreds of thousands of Palestinians who were unwelcome guests-cum-hostages in the neighbouring states. The PLO stopped being an organization of individuals appointed by one person to carry out his bidding. It was now transformed into a Front bringing together Palestinian armed groups, pan-Arab political parties, leftist organizations, refugees, and the representatives of the remnants of the old social classes who had been dispossessed in 1948.

The Transformation of the PLO

For having committed the sins of being unable to defeat the British, preventing the Zionist movement from realizing its objectives, and failing to achieve independence and statehood, the Palestinians have been regarded by their Arab brethren as not fully qualified to lead their own emancipatory struggle. The stigma of illegitimacy has repeatedly lent itself to any attempt on their part to assert themselves as fully independent actors. By strictly adhering to their own narrow patriotic interests as Palestinians, they were deemed to be betraying the broader Pan-Arab cause. Curiously, it was only the Palestinians who were held to this lofty standard. It was an accepted failing when Syrians, Jordanians, Lebanese, Iraqis, Egyptians, etc. acted in accordance with their own narrow interests. The Pan-Arab ideal, which to many appeared as a source of strength, proved instead a curse in disguise.

The creation of the PLO in 1964 was not an autonomous Palestinian act. In fact, the various Palestinian political groups which ostensibly were engaged in preparing for liberation and return did not welcome its establishment. They regarded the act, with justification, as one more in a long chain of events stretching back as far as 1937 when the Arab kings and leaders prevailed on the Palestinians to call a halt to their revolt. When the First Palestine National Council did meet in Jerusalem in May/June 1964 it was regarded by politically active Palestinians as an inter-Arab affair. The delegates themselves had been chosen by Ahmad Shuqairy himself and were not seen as legitimate representatives of the Palestinian diaspora. For example, of the twenty-nine delegates from Lebanon, which played the reluctant host to nearly a quarter of a million Palestinian refugees the overwhelming majority of whom lived in squalid camps, not one came from a refugee camp. The delegates did represent the geographical spread of the Palestinians, but were not representative of political parties, professional associations, groups, and trade unions. They were chosen as individuals. Thus, they were accountable to nobody but the person who had chosen them. In practice, over half the delegates came from Jordan. These were prominent members of society and pillars of the Jordanian establishment—ministers, members of parliament, mayors, leading business figures, etc. (Hourani 1986:100). One of the first prominent Palestinian figures to oppose this gathering was the Mufti of Jerusalem and former head of the defunct Arab Higher Committee (AHC). He called the legality of the whole exercise into question as the Palestinian people had not been given the opportunity to vote for their representatives, and dispatched a telegram to King Husayn of Jordan calling on him to ban the meeting. Within the Arab League itself, Saudi Arabia called on Arab states to boycott the gathering declaring it to be illegal, and went so far as to prevent the Palestinian delegates living in Saudi Arabia from travelling to Jerusalem. At the grass-roots level the conference was opposed by six radical organizations that came out with a statement a few days before its scheduled opening calling for the unity of all organizations wishing to carry out a revolutionary struggle for the liberation of Palestine. They condemned the conference for being held under official state auspices.

Despite this opposition and confident of Egyptian support, Shuqairy continued with his efforts. He was faced with two main obstacles. First there was the opposition coming from the small radical Palestinian organizations at the head of which stood Fatah, a little heard-of group which was preparing to engage in armed struggle. With this and similar organizations he tried to engage in a dialogue so as to win them over to his side. He wanted to do this without making any material concessions, as he was not in a position to meet any of their demands. Already at its inaugural meeting in Jerusalem, the PNC had decreed that all members of that body should be chosen by a process of direct election. This was not deemed to be practical in 1964, and indeed it was not. But Shuqairy was not averse to co-opting individuals if he was certain of winning them over to his side. His real problem, however, was in his dealings with Jordan. These were very much a function of the relationship between Egypt and Jordan and of the friction between the two so-called revolutionary and reactionary blocs led by Egypt and Saudi Arabia respectively. The collapse of the third Arab Summit in September 1965 signalled renewed confrontation between these two blocs. This led to clashes between the Jordanian regime and the PLO. Jordan had been uneasy all along with the creation of the PLO and had gone along only so as to accommodate Nasser. In 1966 open hostility erupted. PLO officials were arrested in Jerusalem and the organization's main offices in the city were closed. Soon after, the Jordanian government in a memorandum to the Arab League declared that it had withdrawn its recognition of the organization. It was only a few days before the outbreak of war in June 1967 and as a result of reconciliation between Nasser and Husayn that Shuqairy was readmitted to Jordan and the organization was allowed to resume its activities within the kingdom.

Just as the defeat of June 1967 discredited the Arab regimes, so did it help bring the opposition to Shuqairy to a head. As his name was associated with the policies that led to the defeat of 1967, the transformation of the PLO came from within when seven members of the executive committee submitted a memo to Shuqairy asking for his resignation and accusing him of pursuing harmful policies and leadership practices. Finding himself isolated and his patrons in no position to offer him support, Shuqairy was forced to resign. To many it seemed that he was being used as a scapegoat. He was after all only doing the bidding of others. An interim period ensued in which members of the executive committee of the PLO tried to revive the PLO in cooperation with the armed resistance groups by seeking to entice them into joining the organization on a power-sharing basis. This, however, was not to be. Fatah, along with the numerous groups that had sprouted following the breakdown of authority and the loss of legitimacy the various ruling regimes had suffered as a result of their defeat in June 1967, met in Cairo in January 1968 and called for unity on the basis of armed struggle (Cobban 1987:43). There was to be no place for the old-style politicians and power brokers and all the leftovers from 1948 Palestine. In a bid to wrest the organization from the control of the old guard, Fatah proposed the establishment of a preparatory committee made up of delegates of the armed resistance groups, representatives of unions and independents to choose a new PNC. The PLO was to be the framework for unity and for the escalation of the armed struggle. The aim was to reorganize it as a broad-based representative organization, a front of all groups actively engaged in the struggle for liberation. A new executive committee was to be elected by the council which itself would elect its chairperson, and the decisions of the council should be binding on the executive committee.

Already differences were emerging between Fatah and the Popular Front for the Liberation of Palestine (PFLP) with the latter preferring to remain outside the framework of Fatah sponsored/controlled activities. This was to prove to be the hallmark of PFLP activity in the future. From that early period the PFLP has chosen to play the role of opposition. Significantly, Oslo and the collapse of the USSR contributed greatly to its marginalization and its position has now been overtaken by the Islamic movement and even factions within Fatah itself. By occupying this ambiguous space, neither in nor out, the PFLP proved unsuccessful in exerting a great deal of influence, but has contributed strongly to giving the Palestinian scene the semblance of diversity and pluralism.

The battle of Karameh in March 1968 merely accelerated a process that, albeit at a much slower pace, was already underway. It gave added legitimacy to the armed struggle and especially to Fatah as the organization which was now undoubtedly the pace setter in the field. The perceived outcome of the battle engendered great enthusiasm for the armed struggle and for those participating in it, in that it was deemed to have shown that an alternative existed to the regular armies of the Arab regimes who had been unable to bear the brunt of the Israeli attack of June 1967. Indeed, this was the first victory, for so perceived, since the shattering defeat of 1967.

The stage was now set for a transformation of the PLO and this took place in the fourth PNC meeting in Cairo in July 1968. Of a total membership of one hundred, sixty-eight were official delegates of the armed resistance groups. Disagreements already surfaced in the allocation of seats to the various armed resistance organizations. In the absence of elections—and nobody seriously contemplated holding these—a quota system was devised to allocate seats to each organization according to its actual strength and popular support. The PFLP boycotted the fifth PNC meeting in Cairo, in February 1969, on the grounds that the quota system agreed to by all the other organizations would give control of the PNC to Fatah, which according to its own way of thinking would be harmful to the cause of national unity and lead to splits and dissensions. Despite this discordant note, the meeting went ahead as agreed to by the two main organizations Fatah and the Syrian sponsored Al-Saika, and Yasser Arafat was elected head of the Executive Committee.

Factionalism, an ominous feature of Palestinian politics, made itself felt even at the very moment of its historic conception. In 1968 and 1969 the PFLP had undergone a number of splits, giving birth to the PFLP-GC, the Democratic Front, and the Arab Palestine Organization. At the same time, Issam Sartawi and a small group of supporters split from Fatah in 1969, while another group, the Popular Struggle Front, had departed a year earlier. In April 1969, the Iraqi Ba'athist regime established its own Palestinian organization, the Arab Liberation Front, while in 1970 various Arab communist parties established their own armed resistance organization, Al-Ansar. Eventually, all these organizations would be accorded representative status within the PNC, while the most important ones would also be represented within the Executive Committee itself.

This mosaic-like structure could not hold together except on the basis of a continuing consensus, if not unanimous, at least among the recognized major groups. It also rested on the quota system by which each group was accorded representatives and received financial allocations, but which simultaneously was the cause of numerous disagreements and conflicts. Fatah was determined for the PLO to remain the framework which embodied Palestinian national unity, as it represented the official Arab commitment to the Palestinian people and to the Palestinian cause. Any weakening in its all-encompassing character as the united national front of the Palestinian people as a whole and as the spinal cord of the Palestinian armed struggle would allow the Arab regimes to withdraw their support and renege on their commitments.

Two features are important to note even at this early phase of the development of the PLO. The first has to do with its internal structure, while the second highlights the narrow limitations imposed on its operational ability by its surrounding environment. As far as structure is concerned, nothing major was accomplished until the eleventh PNC, held in Cairo in January 1973. There it was decided to establish the Central Council as a connecting link between the PNC and the Executive Committee, whose members would be chosen according to the time-tested quota system—each organization would receive a fixed number of seats, in addition to a number of 'independents' who would also be nominated by the various organizations (Hameed 1975:38). Significant here is that the number of PNC delegates continued to be increased at regular intervals (in 1968 there were 100 members, while in 1973 the number had risen to 180). This is accounted for by the desire to draw in ever-larger circles of the various Palestinian strata and involve them in the PLO's activities. Thus, the quota for the 'independents' and the various professional and union associations continued to be expanded (in 1968, three seats were allocated to the various associations, and twenty-nine to the independents, while in 1971 twenty-six seats were allocated to the associations etc., and forty nine to the independents). At the twelfth PNC meeting, in June 1974, three members were added to the Executive Committee as representatives of the Palestine National Front within the Occupied Territories. Although these three were from among a group of political activists who had been expelled by the Israelis, this was both an attempt to accord representation to a hitherto unrepresented section of the Palestinian people, and an indication of the increasing importance which the PLO was according, for the first time perhaps, to the territories Israel held under occupation since June 1967. It is no coincidence that this same meeting adopted the transitional political programme that called for the establishment of a Palestinian national authority in the Occupied Territories.

The second feature, relating to the geopolitical environment in which the PLO operated, was to prove of paramount importance in narrowing the choices available to the Palestinians. Gradually recovering from the deep state of shock and the threat of disintegration in which the defeat in June 1967 had thrown them, the Arab regimes began trying to assert their authority. Already in 1968 there were clashes between Jordanian troops and Palestinian armed groups, with 1969 seeing more numerous clashes both in Jordan and in Lebanon. This was to culminate in the September 1970 war the Jordanian regime initiated in order to re-assert its authority in the country and curtail the Palestinian armed presence. It eventually dawned on the Palestinian armed organizations that they would have to fight on two fronts—against Israel, which after all was the ostensible reason for their existence, and against the neighbouring Arab states, which wanted Palestinian armed activity as a lever to create pressure on Israel to come to the negotiating table, but could not tolerate an autonomous Palestinian role as it might jeopardize their very survival. When the first opportunity to reach an accommodation with Israel appeared to present itself, in the shape of the Rogers proposals in 1970, the verbal and material support a wide variety of Arab official sources extended to the PLO's various constituent groups came to an abrupt halt.

Until their final expulsion from Jordan in the middle of 1971, the armed organizations that had become synonymous with the PLO were pre-occupied in a defensive battle which they were unable to win. Without a secure and safe base in Jordan, they could not pursue an armed struggle against Israel. At the same time, without organizing the Palestinians in that base and being able to present a credible choice to the Jordanian component of the population, they could not begin to consolidate that safe base. Circumstances did not allow the PLO the luxury of choice: there was neither the time nor the opportunity to make a serious attempt at establishing the prerequisite political presence. A new phase was to start with the move to Lebanon where the PLO would continue to be tested as it now became engulfed in what was soon to become a multifaceted conflict that would further detract from the primary task of liberation.

The Lebanese Period

For the next twelve years the PLO set up camp in Lebanon. Events, however, did not allow the Palestinians to catch their breath. From the very beginning, clashes would erupt between one or the other armed resistance group and the Lebanese army. The Lebanese feared that the Palestinian presence would threaten the delicate internal political balance on the one hand, while inviting Israeli punitive retaliation on the other. Later the PLO became embroiled in the civil war which broke out in 1975 and which continued well after the Israeli siege of Beirut in the summer of 1982 that forced its expulsion also from this country. All this notwithstanding, it was in Lebanon that the PLO established itself as a quasi-state and acted out its role regionally and internationally.

The initial task of the PLO had been to embark on an armed struggle against Israel with the aim primarily of mobilizing the Palestinian people. By losing its major operational and social base in Jordan in 1970–71, it could no longer operate freely against Israel from Jordan or draw on the resources and power of the large Palestinian population there. The latter not only constituted the largest concentration of Palestinians anywhere, but also made up a majority of Jordan's inhabitants. Unable to exercise its authority over this larger part of the Palestinian people, it was forcibly prevented from doing so in the occupied West Bank and Gaza Strip by the ubiquitous repressive Israeli security apparatus. Likewise, the Syrian authorities, for all their verbal support for the armed struggle, would not sanction an autonomous situation for the inhabitants of the refugee camps in their country. The PLO had to make do with the Palestinian population of Lebanon, who now assumed the role of surrogates.

It was clear from the very beginning that the PLO and its constituent groups conducted themselves on the basis that the Occupied Territories were not the main arena of the national struggle. Increasingly, voices from left leaning organizations would argue that they had a role to play there, perhaps an important role, but even the proponents of increased involvement in the affairs of the Occupied Territories regarded this as merely a supportive role. The inhabitants of the Occupied Territories constituted only a part of the Palestinian people, and so long as the PLO was entrenched in Lebanon, it was the Palestinians in the diaspora who mattered most. Some observers would belatedly claim that the shift of the centre of gravity of the Palestinian national struggle from the diaspora to the Occupied Territories began in a sense with the massive defeat in Jordan in 1970–71. This by itself would help explain the abandonment of the slogan of liberation in favour of that of statehood as the goal of the movement. The 10–point 'Transitional' programme adopted at the twelfth PNC in 1974 is likewise regarded as an early manifestation of this trend. Yet, the course of development and transformation the PLO underwent during the 1970s indicates that this was not the case. It was only the loss of autonomy as a result of the forced departure from Beirut in 1982 that placed the organization in a quandary and forced it to re-orient itself and set out a new course.

The PLO had been created to play a unifying role, to reconstitute a shattered Palestinian society, and to maintain and develop Palestinian national identity. The PLO was the organizational expression of this national identity. Its role went beyond that of a traditional national liberation or resistance movement. The mission for which it struggled was not only to realize the national rights of the Palestinian people and to end foreign colonial rule, it simultaneously had to rehabilitate a fragmented and dispossessed Palestinian society and to embark on nation building. Thus, its task was twofold. Ostensibly, its raison d'être was the armed struggle against Israel. The more fundamental task was the building of a civilian institutional infrastructure that catered to the needs of the Palestinian nation in exile. The situation existing in the Palestinian diaspora affected both the evolution of the PLO and the organizational shape it took. Objective differences existed between the conditions of Palestinians and of Palestinian society in the Occupied Territories and their counterparts abroad. But the framework the PLO established in Lebanon was meant to create the institutions necessary for the conditions that existed in the diaspora—when the time for a shift of focus came after the departure from Beirut, this was to prove difficult. The existence of an 'inside' and an 'outside' would present itself as a reality that had to be taken into consideration and overcome and not merely as a political construct that could be discarded at will.

In order to carry out its 'nation building' role, the PLO in Lebanon was forced to provide state-like functions. These ranged from health care, education, employment and judicial aspects to police and military protection (Sayigh 1994:100–109). It had to meet the needs of a people spread among various countries and this tended to increase a predisposition towards bureaucratization within its ranks. The semi-autonomous status it came to enjoy in Lebanon reinforced this trend; furthermore, its involvement in the Lebanese civil war led to enlarging and regimenting the military formations of the PLO and its constituent groups. It cannot be denied that in the prevailing conditions, it was the PLO itself and its constituent groups that initiated 'civil-society' type institutions in the wider Palestinian community. These ranged from youth and women's associations to clinics and artisan shops. This meant that the growth of community features for the Palestinians of the diaspora during the 1970s and early 1980s was generally confined to areas where the PLO had control or was allowed to function. Once the situation changed, as it did after 1982, these community-like structures the PLO had erected, financed and administered collapsed, withered away, or were banned. With the loss of its territorial base in Lebanon—first as a result of the forced departure, later because of the split within Fatah's own ranks and soon after when, with the backing of the Syrian government, Amal unleashed its war on the refugee camps—the PLO was severed from direct interaction with the largest Palestinian community that had so far given it support. The cohesiveness and effectiveness of many of the institutions built during this period did not weather this loss. The reason is simple. Most of the mass organizations and popular unions had been established primarily as political vehicles rather than with regard to the community's social, economic or educational needs. These bodies were thinly disguised political fronts not primarily concerned with protecting and promoting the interests and rights of their members. Throughout that period, the large sums of money the oil rich Arab states contributed made possible the employment of large numbers of individuals in the organization's offices, departments and mass organizations. True to form, in adopting a state form the PLO also became a significant employer. Large numbers of Palestinians were dependent on it for a livelihood, while numerous organizations owed their existence to the direct subsidies they received. This bureaucratization was not restricted to the PLO's top leadership as all its various constituent groups duplicated the state functions developed by it (Hilal 1993:52–53). Each acted as a mini state and reproduced as far as its resources allowed the functions of the parent organization, maintaining their own military units, security apparatus, clinics, prisons, publications, nurseries, workshops, etc.

The modus operandi of the PLO during its sojourn in Lebanon faithfully reflected the objective situation of the Palestinians: dispersion, social divisions, fragmentation, the existence of numerous small groups and the absence of a single authority. The Fatah organization itself was indeed the largest, the wealthiest and the most influential. Yet it was neither able nor willing to set policies without coordinating with the other small groups for fear of further fragmentation and loss of the representative image of the PLO. Thus, right from the very beginning a plurality of groups arose each claiming to speak for Palestine and the Palestinians, and each pretending an equal measure of legitimacy.

Whether by choice or as a matter of necessity, tolerance of division and diversity was typical of the PLO right from the very beginning. This is not to deny that armed clashes did take place at an early stage, with Fatah dealing severely with those contending to embody Palestinian will and authority. By and large however, the existing plurality was preserved and national unity always given pride of place. Perhaps this can be partly accounted for by the Arab environment in which the PLO was forced to operate. Both Iraq and Syria at various times intervened forcibly in Palestinian affairs through their surrogate organizations. Other Arab states intervened in more covert forms. This patronage itself provided protection and forced the PLO to accommodate these smaller groups and permit them political leverage far beyond their size and capabilities. Some Palestinian groups were extensions of Pan Arab parties, while others were still ideologically based. Another factor that helped preserve this plurality of organizational frameworks was that Israel did not distinguish between one Palestinian group and another. The constant threat and persistent military harassment by Israel made national unity all the more important. Although the basic constitution of the PLO requires a simple majority for most decisions, the PLO leadership more often than not used to strive for consensus decision-making. Thus the aim was to arrive at a balance among the diverse political factions, and the tools employed were those of persuasion and bargaining. Undoubtedly, as the largest and strongest faction Fatah could impose its will without serious opposition, but usually chose not to do so. When an opposition did constitute itself outside the framework of the usual organizational structures on a major issue—as the Rejection Front led by the PFLP did in the 1970s—this was tolerated.

It has been argued, correctly, that the non-centralization of PLO authority in a finite territorial state has helped to thwart the development of an authoritarianism that would aim at the crushing of any and all opposition (Hassasian 1993:268). It could, of course, be argued that Fatah did not really have much choice in exercising such tolerance. On the one hand, there were always various Arab states in the wings ready to intervene on the behalf of their own surrogates, while on the other, dispersal and the absence of a territorially based national authority constituted objective constraints that forced Fatah and its leadership to seek the politics of consensus with its rivals, and to try and accommodate factionalism (Muslih 1990:26). Thus the 'Republic of Fakhani', as the Palestinian presence in Lebanon was called, with its semi-state institutions and several security apparatuses and prisons, was a situation that allowed for a large measure of tolerance and co-existence between the various constituent groups of the PLO.

In theory at least, the Palestinian National Council is the Palestinians highest political authority. Only with the election, in 1996, of a legislative council to represent the inhabitants of the West Bank and Gaza Strip did the PNC find itself relegated to a secondary position. But since from the beginning a quota system was in operation, the locus of real power was situated elsewhere. Historically, it is not difficult to understand how such a situation arose. It was established in order to guarantee the hegemony of the armed resistance organizations within the old style PLO in 1969. This assured the resistance organizations a majority of seats in the PNC and the Central Council, and assured that each group would be represented on the executive committee regardless of its size. Thus, in effect, the power of decision-making on national issues is in the hands of the political factions and not the representatives of the various Palestinian communities. The Palestinian establishment ensured that the PNC remained an empty shell through which various charades could be carried out, and it never became a platform for different social groups to put forward their demands and views in opposition to the executive authority (Khatib 1993:14).

Furthermore, the actual role of the PNC has always been to provide a formal legitimacy, without playing any role in mapping out Palestinian policy, or carrying out the task of control and overseeing the actual practice of the executive committee. The actual members of the PNC perform the role of rubber stamps for policies decided by others. Their acquiescence in this role is a function of the 'quota' system. One third of the seats are allocated to the organizations, one-third to the mass or-ganizations, and one third to independents. The first and second are of course the same, while the third group is chosen by the organizations themselves. The 'quota' system exists within the mass organizations as well. Each of the factions has a given number of seats in the PLO leadership bodies and a set representation in the mass organizations irrespective of its size, ideology or influence or popularity among Pal-estinians. As positions in leading public institutions are not filled by elections, it is not possible to determine objectively the degree of support enjoyed by the various political organizations. On top of this, some Arab state-sponsored factions are disproportionately represented in the leading bodies of PLO institutions and in the mass organizations for reasons of expediency and in order to curry favour with the sponsoring states.

That there have always been major political disagreements among the political groups, leading to vigorous arguments and debates, does not alter the fact that PNC sessions have always been rather formalistic and ceremonial in nature. Thus, we find the PNC, as the ultimate source of legitimacy, holding a session in Gaza in 1998 to ratify the new political reality post Oslo by revoking those articles in the charter that talked about armed struggle and the 'liberation of Palestine'. The democracy practiced by the Palestinians in Lebanon, it is correct to surmise, was the democracy of the leaders of the various factions. Decision-making has always been outside the national legislative and executive institutions of the PLO. By denying these institutions any authority, a vacuum was created at the top of the power structure, which was then filled by one man. The leader, historically, took the place of the institution. The left factions within the PLO have repeatedly called for collective leadership and for the introduction of a measure of democracy in the working of PLO institutions. The Fatah leadership has always been accused of running PLO institutions in an autocratic manner, and of dominating the PLO's institutions, departments, etc. through the appointment of its own followers and the appropriation of the bulk of its funds. These calls the left made always assumed a party factional aspect. They never gained active popular support because they were seen as little more than bids to improve the left's share in the 'quota' system (Hillal 1993:54–55). That is, the left was demanding a larger piece of the pie. This was reform behind the scenes and in the corridors of power. Its tools were pressure, manoeuvre, threats of withdrawal, etc. The aim was to increase the representation of one faction, to gain one more seat in one more council. There was no perception that there was a sincere striving for real representative democracy based on the verdict of the ballot box (Khatib 1993: 12). If on the other hand, collective leadership was going to be anything more than a confederal alliance between general secretaries of the various factions, then elections would have to take place from the popular base at every level in every faction before it is introduced in the institutions of the PLO. Candidates to PLO bodies would no longer be appointed by the factions. Fatah legitimately countered by accusing those claiming to be democrats of opportunism.

The argument over democracy in the PLO's bodies was itself a manifestation of a larger malaise. Israel's siege of Beirut, and the forced expulsion which ensued, put an end to the debate, as the very survival of the PLO was now at stake. The period extending up to 1988 was one of continuing declining fortunes what with dispersal, splits, further interference by Arab states, the loss of prominent leaders by assassinations, and a general weakness that reflected itself in an increased marginalization of the PLO's role both regionally and internationally.

Inside the Occupied Territories

The loss of its territorial base in Lebanon not only created difficulties for the PLO in maintaining the cohesiveness and effectiveness of its institutions, it also meant the end of the armed struggle and the legitimizing role this played as a source of authority for its historic leadership. A new source of legitimacy was required, and this was to be provided by the Palestinians living under Israeli occupation in the West Bank and the Gaza Strip. As the Occupied Territories were now the only field open to the PLO, they acquired increasing significance. The first Intifada, which erupted in December 1987 when Arab support was at its lowest, was crucial in renewing the PLO's waning legitimacy. Historically, there was, however, a certain tension in the relationship between the two wings of the Palestinian national movement. This is usually explained in terms of the sharp difference in conditions and experiences between the widely dispersed Palestinian community outside and the Palestinians within the Occupied Territories. The outcome has been dissimilar paths of development. This became clearly evident after the return of the Tunis-based PLO leadership and cadres to the Occupied Territories in the aftermath of the Oslo Accord. The 'external' leadership continued to have the upper hand and a number of local functionaries and activists were co-opted to the official bodies of the Palestinian Authority. Undeniable as this description of objective reality is, it ignores the actual policies, or lack of them, pursued over the years by the Palestinian leadership towards the Occupied Territories and their inhabitants.

Until the loss of the Lebanon as an autonomous base of operations, the PLO and its constituent groups accorded the Occupied Territories the status of a sideshow. The expectation was that its inhabitants would perform a secondary role; at best, all that was required of them was to be supportive spectators. Jealous of its standing as the sole and legitimate representative of the Palestinian people, and having continuously to safeguard this status against the encroachments of one Arab state or the other, the PLO was wary of any independent political activity emanating from the Occupied Territories. It regarded any divergent political attitudes exhibited there as manifesting a challenge to its legitimacy and representative status.

In the immediate aftermath of the occupation by Israel of the West Bank and the Gaza Strip in June 1967 attempts were made to establish an opposition focus that would gather round it political groups and individuals engaged in active resistance to the new reality of military rule. The National Guidance Committee (NGC; *Lajnat al-Tawjih al-Watani*), a semi-clandestine group, was established in Jerusalem bringing together representatives of the Jordanian Communist party, the Arab Nationalist Movement, the head of the Islamic Council, and Jordanian notables and officials. A co-ordinating committee, *Lajnat al-Tawjih al-Watani fi al-Daffa al-Gharbiyya*, brought together the NGCs established in the main urban centres, in addition to the Islamic Council. The membership of the committees was markedly conservative, and their main plank was the return of the West Bank to Jordan and the implementation of Security Council Resolution 242. In the Gaza Strip, both the nature of the Egyptian regime in control prior to the occupation and the existence of units of the Palestine Liberation Army in the strip before 1967 generated a different political atmosphere. Right from the very beginning resistance activities in Gaza assumed a violent form. In the West Bank, the NGCs did not, however, have a long life. The Israeli authorities carried out a policy of harassment, imprisonment and deportation against their members. When Israel deported Sheikh Abd al-Hamid Sayeh, the chairman of both the NGCs and the Islamic Council, the committees became defunct.

The growth of the Palestinian resistance organizations and their increasing clashes with Jordanian army units led to a growing rift within the Occupied Territories themselves. While trying to assert itself on the East Bank, the Jordanian regime was also trying to re-establish its authority vis-à-vis the inhabitants of the West Bank, even though they were under Israeli occupation. The Islamic Council itself was rapidly transformed into a bureaucratic department of the Jordanian Ministry of Awqaf. The Jordanian Communist Party attempted to set up an underground political resistance movement and established for this purpose the Popular Resistance Front (*Jabhat al-Muqawama al-Shaabiyya*). In the prevailing atmosphere, when the Palestinian resistance organizations in Jordan were calling for rejection of Security Council

Resolution 242, armed struggle and the liberation of Palestine, the Communists were swimming against the tide. After nineteen years of Jordanian rule, a Palestinian identity was being forged on the basis of Palestinian independence and separateness. A call for the return of the West Bank to Jordanian rule was not going to find a receptive ear. Moreover, in the prevailing atmosphere of guerrilla operations and armed struggle, talk of 'political' resistance to the occupation was even more incongruous. The current was flowing in a different direction altogether. To those who wanted to act out their resistance to the occupation, mere verbal opposition did not suffice. Thousands of mostly young people with roots predominantly in the Palestinian countryside enrolled in the resistance organizations eager to engage in the armed struggle, not merely against the occupation, but with the aim of liberating Palestine and establishing an independent Arab state in place of Israel.

The war the Jordanian regime unleashed in 1970 against the Palestinian armed resistance organizations, which was to culminate in their expulsion from Jordan, dealt a heavy blow to resistance activities within the Occupied Territories. With the move of the PLO to Lebanon the 'armed struggle' itself assumed a new form: infiltration across the Lebanese border. Meanwhile, the transformations wrought by the Israeli military occupation were bringing about changes in the social and class structure of the Palestinians living under its control (Budeiri 1982:63). These would further contribute to endowing them with a distinct and separate identity, as a social formation with its own particular characteristics. And with the passage of time we find these features becoming markedly different from those possessed by other Palestinian communities, whether in Jordan, Kuwait, Syria, Lebanon, or other places of exile.

Already in 1967, the Palestinians of the Occupied Territories, unlike those in the diaspora, possessed a socially differentiated society, rooted in the land, with its own economy, agriculture, crafts and service sector, and with its own civil institutions, etc. Thus side by side with secret and clandestine organizations engaged in carrying out armed-struggle type activities against Israel, a whole range of grass roots organizations began to take shape trying to effect changes in the existing social and economic order. The norms of military occupation itself prompted and facilitated the development of mass organizations and open organizational frameworks allowing for public participation in those civil society types of structures. The result was the establishment of numerous welfare, voluntary, professional and mass associations and trade unions, research centres, universities, colleges, clinics, newspapers, magazines and information centres. Later on there would also be a flowering of political organizations operating in conditions of semi-legality.

The Palestine Patriotic Front (PPF) was formally established towards the end of 1973 in the aftermath of the October 1973 war, although first incentives dated back at least a year (Dakkak 1983:75). Again, the core group was the Jordanian Communist Party, but this time it managed to bring in representatives of Fatah, and those of the Democratic Front for the Liberation of Palestine (DFLP), in addition to a number of active independents, like the mayors of West Bank towns. Although contacts were maintained with the PFLP, this organization preferred to remain outside the ranks of the Front. For the first time since the Israeli occupation of the West Bank and the Gaza Strip, the Palestinians fielded a political leadership that not only was made up of the representatives of political groups, but also included within its ranks delegates from labour unions, professional associations, student councils, women organizations, etc., and was seen to represent the prevailing mood within the Occupied Territories.

Initially, relations between the PPF and the PLO were cordial. Prior co-ordination and consultation had been carried out with delegates from the Occupied Territories travelling to Damascus and Beirut to ensure the endorsement of the PLO's leading bodies. The PPF for its part expressed its commitment to the leading role of the PLO, while leading PLO members declared that the PPF represented the organization in the Occupied Territories. The request of the PPF that a number of deportees be included in the National Council was acceded to, but no answer was forthcoming to the demand that the Palestinian communists be represented in the PLO's Executive Committee (Dakkak 1983:76).

Soon, however, relations between the PLO and the PPF took a turn for the worse. The PPF was portrayed from within the PLO as communist controlled, while the PLO was accused from within the PPF of trying to control its own activities. The PPF was now regarded as a rival, and what ensued was an attempt on the part of the 'outside' to exercise its control over the 'inside' and relegate it to a subordinate position. While already in the summer of 1974 the Israelis had initiated an assault on the PPF with a wave of mass arrests and deportations, they were soon to be aided by the PLO's attempts to dismantle the Front from within. The outcome of this double assault to all intents and purposes was the paralysis of the Front, and by the end of 1976—some would say even earlier—it had ceased to exist as a functioning organization.

During its short life span the PPF succeeded in accomplishing two tasks, both of which would prove to be of lasting importance. First, it created a public debate within the Occupied Territories, and consequently within the PLO, over the desirability of establishing an independent Palestinian state in the areas Israel had occupied in 1967, and over the implementation of UN resolutions concerning the refugees. Implicitly this was an endorsement of the two-state solution long favoured by the Palestinian communists. This was eventually to become the official policy of the PLO, but only fourteen years later with the declaration of statehood in 1988. These were early days though, and the PPF's stand was a far cry from the PNC-endorsed transitional programme of 1974 which called for the establishment of a 'national authority' without spelling out the practical implications of such a step. Second, it created a tradition of open political activity, utilizing the margin tolerated by the Israeli occupation authorities, especially as regards political activity in Jerusalem itself, which according to Israeli law did not fall under the jurisdiction of the occupation authorities. This was to be expanded in the following years to such an extent that the various constituent groups of the PLO, or at least the major ones which had created a political presence for themselves in the Occupied Territories, existed quite openly and acted as if they were in possession of legal immunity.

If the Fatah leadership thought that by getting rid of the PPF they would ensure a more pliable political movement in the Occupied Territories, they were soon to discover that they were very much mistaken. Already during the elections for the municipal councils in 1976 they were unable to guarantee the success of their candidates in opposition to the wishes of other political actors in the Occupied

Territories. In the event, a large number of leftist councillors were elected, and it soon became apparent that the mayors of Nablus and Ramallah were in alliance with the leftist forces (Maoz 1984:167). Moreover, when Sadat decided to visit Jerusalem in 1977, this provided the impetus for a new radicalization of the national movement.

Opposition to the Camp David agreement and the autonomy scheme of Israel's then prime minister, Menachem Begin, which was first made public in December 1977, helped spur the nationalist forces to launch a new organizational framework with the aim of subverting the scheme. The 'Jerusalem Conference' was held in October 1978 and attended by a majority of mayors and council members of West Bank municipalities and local councils in addition to representatives of national institutions (Gresh 1985:218). Despite calls for restraint by the leadership of the PLO, which let it be known that it was still studying the Israeli Egyptian agreement, the conferees issued a statement condemning the Camp David Accords and the autonomy plan. A follow-up committee was set up and in November another meeting was held at which a National Guidance Committee (NGC-2) was set up, and an executive committee was elected. It was also decided that this new committee, unlike the PPF, was to function in the open. This was made up of mayors, representatives of trade unions, students, professional groups, women's movements, charitable associations, the Gaza strip, and individuals in their personal capacities. It is also claimed that representatives of the Islamic trend were later co-opted to its ranks. Despite pressures by the outside to include pro-Jordanian figures and mayors who had expressed support for Sadat within the ranks of the NGC, its leadership was successful in repelling these attempts. Although scepticism was initially exhibited by various political groups concerning the credibility of this new structure, it operated successfully until it was banned in 1981 by the then Israeli Minister of Defence, Ariel Sharon, when he summarily dismissed the nationalist mayors and councils.

It is noteworthy that in the two instances when the Occupied Territories themselves established a political and organizational framework to give expression to their resistance to the Israeli occupation, they found themselves in opposition to the established PLO leadership. In

both instances the division took the form of an ideological clash between right and left. Of course the quota system also operated in the
Occupied Territories, though this was not the case at the beginning,
and even then differences made themselves felt. Unlike in Lebanon,
initially, only groups with some local following could be represented in
the various representative bodies. As a result of factionalism, necessarily
imported from the outside, each of the main political groups established its own trade unions, professional associations, women's groups,
and mass associations. Leftwing groups possessed an advantage, in that
they had started their activities at a much earlier date and found it
easier to make an appeal to young workers, students, and women who
presented themselves as their target audience. Despite its financial clout
and bureaucratic weight, Fatah was not initially able to make itself felt.
It was, in fact, a latecomer to the field. This was soon to change after
the exile to Tunis, when the Occupied Territories became the main,
perhaps even the sole arena of competition and struggle and when even
Arab-sponsored organizations reared their heads.

Most observers who have written about this period have un-
reservedly noted the grassroots nature of the organizational structures
established within the Occupied Territories, and view both the PPF
and the NGC as representative bodies. They are regarded as legitimate
not because they are elected bodies, which evidently they are not, but
because they are perceived to be the outcome of a broad-based political
participation, and to embody a measure of democratization in Palestinian society. It is indeed true that repeated calls for 'democratization'
have come from within the Occupied Territories. But what these calls
have in common is a rejection of the political strategy adopted by the
PLO leadership at any given time. Thus often the main motive behind
this 'democratic' position is an opposition to the policies pursued by
Arafat and the groups around him.[1] This was the case for example

---

1   It is indicative that current (2005) calls for democratization do not come from the
    mainstream political opposition to the PA, i.e. the Islamic movement, but from
    factions within the ruling party itself, Fatah, and the self-appointed representa-
    tives of the inhabitants of the West Bank and Gaza strip, namely the local NGOs,
    a large part of which are staffed by ex-political activists from the left.

when Arafat tried to effect a rapprochement with Egypt and with Jordan, with the aim of arriving at an agreement with the United States. In both instances he was termed 'authoritarian and anti-democratic', which he most evidently was, but his accusers lacked the credibility that comes with consistency and the determination to stick to principled positions. So long as decision-making remained an individual and not an institutional affair, calls for democracy proved meaningless (Arafat's replacement with Abu Mazen after his death in 2004 opened up various possibilities for internal change, if only because the latter does not possess the former's legitimacy and lacks an internal power base). Furthermore, so long as institution building was and continues to be a factional affair, these institutions, however much they multiply, will continue to lack any democratic content.

Bourguiba's Revenge: The New Palestinian Discourse[2]

Summarizing the period since the Palestinians were forced to transfer their headquarters from Beirut to Tunis in 1982, the assertion can be safely made that at both the regional and international levels, the balance of power tilted more heavily than ever in favour of Israel and against the Palestinian struggle for national self-determination and independence. In retrospect, the first Intifada itself did not in any way contribute to transforming this unfavourable situation, but provided the PLO with the means and the impetus to accommodate itself to this new reality.

In 1982, Israel embarked on a multi-frontal attack on the Palestinian national movement. The Israeli army invaded and occupied the larger part of Lebanon and laid siege to the PLO in Beirut. In the same period the Israeli occupation administration issued an order banning the

---

2   In 1965 Tunisia's president, Al-Habib Bourguiba, suggested that the Arabs should accept the UN 1947 partition decision, endorsing a two-state solution and implicitly recognizing Israel. There was unanimous official and unofficial Arab rejection of his proposal. For the official Palestinian position, see Sayigh 1965.

National Guidance Committees and dissolving a number of the most active elected municipal councils in the Occupied Territories. In an effort to re-establish its waning authority, Israel unleashed the Village Leagues, and installed the Civil Administration to carry out the day-to-day affairs of the occupation. To a large degree this was made possible by, and complemented, Israel's success in concluding the Camp David Agreement with Egypt.

The PLO's forced departure to Tunis signalled a downward spiral in its own and the Palestinians fortunes. The organization had of course already reached a dead end prior to that, but this remained camouflaged by the need to carry on its state-like functions in Lebanon and as a result of its involvement in the ongoing armed conflict in the country. The semi-state apparatus (military, diplomatic, administrative) which had been built up over the years became, in the new conditions, a political and financial burden. Political disagreements had already erupted over the choice of Tunis as a final destination, Arafat's decision to re-open contacts with the Egyptians while still under siege in Beirut, and his choice of President Mubarak as his first port of call after embarking from Beirut.

Within Fatah itself a split took place in 1983 that paralyzed the PLO, though in retrospect it appeared to have given Arafat greater freedom of movement to pursue his own policies. The loss of Lebanon as a territorial base led to increasing difficulties in maintaining the effectiveness and cohesiveness of the PLO's institutions, which consequently contributed to increasing the role and power of individual leaders in possession of the requisite resources. This was to become evident on the outbreak in December 1987 of the first Intifada in the Occupied Territories, when control of financial resources became a matter of paramount importance in the 'institution building industry'.

Until the first Intifada accorded a much needed legitimacy to a largely impotent and inoperative PLO, it appeared as if the Camp David Accords and Israel's war on the Palestinians in 1982 had served to marginalize the PLO and render it ineffective. The separate peace between Israel and Egypt had undoubtedly shifted the regional balance of power. The holding of the seventeenth PNC in Amman in 1984 was an early sign that a core group of the Palestinian leadership was edging towards recognition and acceptance of the new geo-political realities created by Egypt's withdrawal from the struggle with Israel. There had always been two strands within the Palestinian movement. One called for armed struggle and social transformation as the path to liberation. The other, more pragmatic and in tune with the existing Arab state system, preferred to work within the international system, as embodied by the United Nations, international public opinion and what was termed 'international legitimacy'. So long as Israel pursued the Jordanian option and refused to recognize the Palestinians as independent players this path was blocked. The demise in 1977 of Israel's Labour Party as the country's main ruling party transformed the situation. The Likud, in its desire to retain the whole of the Occupied Territories, recognized in the Camp David Accords the Palestinian issue as a question to be dealt with in partnership with the Palestinians themselves, albeit narrowly defined to exclude all Palestinians who were not resident in the Occupied Territories.

The first Intifada provided the opening that allowed this pragmatic group to pursue its aims. Already by holding the seventeenth PNC in Amman in flagrant disregard of the opposition, not only from within Fatah, but also that coming from other political groupings within the PLO, it was becoming clear that the era of consensus politics within the PLO was over and that a shift to a majority politics was taking place (Sahliyeh 1986:198). By the time the unification conference of the PLO took place in Algiers in 1987 (the eighteenth PNC) the battle over 'numerical democracy' had been won. Henceforth—and this was to prove of crucial importance once the decision had to be made whether or not to enter the US-brokered negotiations—a numerical majority was all that was needed to arrive at binding decisions in the leading bodies of the PLO. To all intents and purposes formal democracy was being observed.

Indeed, dialogue and heated debates have been a hallmark of Palestinian politics since the inception of the PLO. When consensus was the basis of Palestinian decision-making, dialogue and debate had their role in fostering negotiations and compromise. Even then, some opposition groups had found it difficult to abide by consensual decisions and more often than not, some groups, notably the Popular Front, preferred to remain outside the organizational framework of Palestinian politics rather than abide by decisions they could not agree to. Even so, they were careful not to stray too far. Once majority voting replaced consensual decision-making as accepted 'democratic' procedure, this called into question the whole issue of the PLO's representative bodies and the method of their selection. The 'quota' system, in operation both in the selection of representatives for the PNC and the Central Council, has also been used in the ongoing task of building a civilian infrastructure and institution building within the Occupied Territories. What the PLO did was simply to export its bureaucratic structures to the inside. The various groups within the organization wanted to be represented in every institution, with the aim of safeguarding their factional interests and those of their members. While paying lip service to democracy, the election process was shunned under a variety of excuses, not all of which were illegitimate. The end result was the institutionalization of the quota system, which continues to be inseparable from political alliances among like-minded groups.

Easy though it is to criticize this set up, it is necessary perhaps to pose the question whether in the prevailing circumstances there could have been a more suitable form of democratic procedure, and, if yes, what the aim of introducing such a procedure would have been. There are those of course who argue that the quest for democracy has become a 'global phenomenon', and that it is now 'a universal political norm'. There is thus no need to put forward such questions.

In many ways this is undoubtedly true. For example, on New Year's Day, January 1994, peasants in the southern province of Chiapas in Mexico staged an uprising against the continued rule of the Institutional Revolutionary Party, which had been democratically in power in Mexico since 1929, the world's oldest one-party state. The Zapatista Army of National Liberation, in a statement issued on that very same day, called on the Mexican people to support the struggle for 'work, land, housing, food, health, education, independence, freedom, democracy, justice and peace.' Emiliano Zapata, murdered in 1919, was the foremost leader of the Mexican Revolution of 1910–1919, whose rallying cry had been the slogan 'Land and Liberty'. That according to a World Bank estimate 32 million of Mexico's 85 million people today live in poverty does not detract from Mexico's democratic credentials. It is not clear whether the rebels' choice of 1 January to embark on their revolution was in any way connected to the fact that it was the date set for the implementation of the North American Free Trade Agreement (NAFTA) between the United States, Canada, and Mexico. The Mexican government's immediate response was to send in the army and to carry out aerial bombardments of suspected rebel positions.

It could, of course, be argued that in some regions of the world the groundwork necessary to accommodate liberal democracy has not yet been accomplished. There is Charles Issawi's well-known and often repeated argument that democracy does not exist in the Arab world because the economic and social basis which it requires is still non-existent. Others, characterizing the state in the Middle East as a rentier state, argue that because revenue is not raised by the state through taxation—which is necessarily associated with demands for popular reform and legitimization—but through the sale of oil, no social differentiation has taken place in society, and the state is immune to any popular pressure or influence. Furthermore, having experienced a brief interlude of liberal democracy between the ending of colonial rule and the onset of the military regimes that have become so well entrenched in the Arab world, democratization is regarded by many as essentially elitist and inequitable. The ruling elites, using the rhetoric of socialism, have maintained themselves in power and enjoyed the benefits of material privileges denied to the overwhelming majority of the populations of the Arab world. Currently, under the banner of economic liberalism, an aspiring elite is employing the rhetoric of multi-party democracy, markets, trickle down, etc., to challenge the ruling elite. Democracy, no less than socialism, is consequently regarded as merely a smoke screen hiding what is essentially a struggle for wealth and power between rival factions of the same social and economic elite.

It is hardly necessary to observe that the Palestinian national movement does not exist in a vacuum. It is affected and influenced by what goes on in its surrounding environment. The PLO itself differed from the existing Arab ruling establishments only in so far as it lacked a territorial base, and in that, due to its peculiar circumstances, it was unable to confront head on its own civil society. In 1993, the PLO, reduced after Oslo to the Palestinian Authority, was called upon to perform a predominantly security role, but unlike the neighboring Arab regimes it did not even possess the semblance of sovereignty. In Algeria, Iraq, Egypt, Syria, Saudi Arabia, Kuwait, we see how state and society interact. The current popularity of the concept of civil society conceals the unique characteristics of specific civil societies, and imbues them with the very much-desired qualities of the 'ideal type'. It is for this reason that it is important to cast a more inquiring eye at civil society in the Occupied Territories, and to examine its antecedents.

Observers have enthusiastically recorded the multifaceted activities of the grassroots movement that over the lengthy period of over twenty years of Israeli occupation has created a civil society representing the 'inside'. This seems to carry the promise of a regenerated Palestinian national movement, as juxtaposed to a bankrupt and bureaucratic 'outside', which is portrayed by the media, Arab states, the United States, Israel, and indeed the whole wide world, as constituting a barrier to the establishment of peace in the region and settling once and for all the Arab-Israeli conflict.

In this respect, the thesis has been put forward that the Israeli occupation itself has been the 'incubator' of this particular civil society and so has fostered the development of a democratic pluralist Palestinian politics (Maoz 1993:231) and that Israel's military control in the Occupied Territories has itself 'promoted the stirrings of democracy among people who are ruled undemocratically' (Kaufman 1993:47). Furthermore, the occupation has been credited with familiarizing the Palestinians with the election process, thanks to its having allowed elections to be held for municipal councils (notwithstanding that the last such election before Oslo took place in 1976) and professional associations. Even the repressive policies directed against Palestinians have been termed beneficial, in that they have accelerated the dispersion of decision making power to the grassroots level and to the younger generations. Thanks to the continuation of the occupation, so the argument continues, the Palestinians embarked on the Intifadas, which established new patterns of collective behaviour and prompted people to take new initiatives. Even the forced dispersal of the Palestinians round the world has contributed further to decentralize decision making, as diversity is the outcome of exile, and only democracy can encompass this diversity. More importantly, the constant defeats suffered by the Palestinians and the transformation of the regional environment as a result of the 1991 Gulf War, and the international environment as a result of the demise of the Communist world and the end of the Cold War, have made the Palestinians realize that they cannot afford to alienate Western countries by creating a non-democratic state. Strengthening this trend towards democracy is the fact that the professional and political elite currently occupying centre stage is almost exclusively Western educated and Western oriented. Thus the issue of freedom is fundamental to its outlook and it will not accept anything less than a future democratic state. But, of course, though in perhaps slightly less vulgar or perverse fashions, these and similar arguements have been employed by the apologists of every colonial power.

In reality, Palestinian civil society has been stunted and deformed by the workings of the Israeli military occupation. The forty-two years of military occupation of the West Bank and the Gaza Strip have been instrumental in accelerating the proletarianization process of the Palestinian peasantry and in prompting an ongoing emigration from the country. This has markedly affected those with more marketable skills. Those who remained, despite continued resistance to the occupation by a militant minority of the population, and despite the outbreak of the first Intifada, which at the outset possessed a popular mass character, have acquired a unique political outlook. This differentiates them both from the Palestinians who somehow stayed put in 1948 and consequently became 'Israeli' citizens, though of course without ever relinquishing their Palestinian identity. It also separates them from Palestinians who were dispersed further afield and continued to hold on to the myth of Palestine and the dream of liberation and return. The realism and pragmatism that observers tend to spot among the more eloquent spokespersons of the Occupied Territories, and indeed even the proverbial man in the street, is perhaps more the outcome of resignation and impotence, rather than political maturity or a newly found faith in peaceful processes. If the aim of procedural democracy is to ensure that popular sentiments become the arbiter of political decisions, the enthusiasm exhibited by civil society is indicative of the desire to seize on any alternative to the existing state of affairs, and legitimizing it by consecrating the inhabitants of the Occupied Territories as the spokespersons for the whole Palestinian people.

This new Palestinian discourse has been greeted as a sign on the one hand of a 'philosophical commitment to the development of democratic institutions', while at the same time demonstrating the beginnings of a new and welcome pragmatism—'Palestinians realize that they cannot afford to alienate Western countries by creating a non-democratic state.' Democratization is deemed to be positive because it serves to enhance the political process. But what is actually required from it? And what is it exactly that it is supposed to achieve? Is the aim to allow those with vested interests to make their voices heard? Or is the aim perhaps to give weight to the voice of the silent majority? Is it necessary in order to enhance the legitimacy of both national goals and national leaders? Is it a more useful way of combating the Israeli occupation and enhancing national solidarity? Will it allow for the redressing of a balance of power which is so markedly tilted in favour of Israel?

These and similar questions are meaningful only if they are posed in a concrete way. What was at stake, until 1993, was the division of power and authority between the PLO bureaucracy marooned 'outside', and the new intelligentsia which had grown up 'inside' and had been shaped by its experiences under Israeli occupation. The constant battering the PLO has been subjected to and its failures, the two Intifadas and the so-called 'peace process' in between, the changed regional and international environment, the increased differentiation created by the workings of the occupation and the false re-introduction of the democratic discourse to the area following 9/11, all these and many more factors have served to provide an opening for articulate social groups to appear who insist on taking part in the political process and having a share in determining their own future.

So long as the PLO operated at a distance from its very own 'civil society', it was possible to carry on with the process of 'manufacturing consent'. All that was required was arriving at a compromise acceptable to half a dozen general secretaries. With the Oslo Accords of 1993, however, the Palestinians were at the threshold—or so it appeared—of some form of self-rule and new rules had to be formulated to establish the relationship between the incipient Palestinian Authority (an Oslo-created pre-state formation) and Palestinian society in the areas under Israeli occupation. The returning PLO leadership touted Oslo as an 'historic compromise'—which, together with part of the Palestinian people, it entered into hesitantly. On the other side stood a reluctant Israel—as yet unclear in its own mind how best to take advantage of this transitional phase to ensure that any final resolution of the conflict would mirror the balance of forces as it 'actually existed' on the ground.

For the Palestinians, the new institutional structure called for by the reality Oslo had created had to reflect the material interests that had prompted them to accept its conditions in the first place. It also had to be able to endow the Palestinian leadership with sufficient strength to satisfy its domestic constituency and at the same time to allow it to wrest from the negotiation process a resolution of the conflict that would not lead to a loss of national legitimacy.

The true nature of Israel's reluctance became more manifest after the assassination, on 4 November 1995 (two years into Oslo), of Yitzhak Rabin, while the advent of Ehud Barak as Israel's prime minister proved to be the closing chapter of the Oslo 'peace' process. At Camp David, in the summer of 2000, success was not the main preoccupation of the Israeli negotiating team—even they themselves didn't take seriously the diktat they offered the Palestinians. Barak seemed to be saying that the Israeli leadership had had second thoughts about the process initiated at Oslo and it now wanted out. Rabin himself had already gone on record saying that there were no sacred timetables: Israel would determine the pace of developments according to its own strategic interests. Sharon's visit to Jersualem's Haram al-Sharif that followed in September was the spark that ignited the second Intifada. If they wanted to achieve a 'minimalist' state in the territories Israel has held under occupation since June 1967, the Palestinians seemed fated to wage a true 'blood-and-tears' war of national liberation. Israel would accept no less. Moreover, the 'secret potion' the United States had prepared in the form of plans for the 'export of democracy' to the Arab world aimed to secure, in the case of the Arab-Israeli conflict, a more pliant Palestinian leadership.

The first elections in 1997 were necessary to endow Yassir Arafat and his leadership with international legitimacy and to grant the seal of approval to the Oslo process and the establishment it had engineered of Palestinian self-rule in the territories that Israel continued to occupy. But Arafat baulked at agreeing to a final resolution of the conflict that would bring peace to Israel but withhold justice from the Palestinians. He paid for this with incarceration by Israel in a *Muqataa'* Israeli troops had first almost totally demolished and with the threat of death daily hanging over his head. But Arafat remained, and continued to remain 'relevant'. His death, when it came on 11 November 2004, was received with loud relief by both Israel and the United States, and no doubt by some Arab capitals as well. Similarly, when, in January 2006, new elections for the Palestine Legislative Assembly brought the unambiguous victory of Hamas in this 'test for democracy', the event was greeted with howls of alarm and despair not only in Israel and the United States this time, but also in Europe and in parts of the Arab world. Arafat had passed on the torch to Hamas: they were his genuine successors, at least of Arafat in his post-Camp-David incarnation.

But the 'democratic wave' the second Bush administration has unleashed with its occupation of Afghanistan and Iraq does not leave much leeway for the actual wants and needs of people, the Palestinians included. This is not what democracy is supposed to mean. Which brings us back to Humpty Dumpty: 'When *I* use a word, it means just what I choose it to mean—neither more nor less.'

References

Arblaster, A. 1993. *Democracy* (New York: Oxford University Press).

Brand, L.A. 1988. 1988. *Palestinians in the Arab World* (New York: Columbia University Press).

Budeiri, M. 1982. 'Changes in the Economic Structure of the West Bank and Gaza Strip Under Israeli Occupation', *Labour, Capital and Society* 15/1.

Budeiri, M. 1997. 'The Palestinians: Tensions between Nationalist and Religious Identities', in Israel Gershoni and James Jankowski (eds.), *Rethinking Nationalism in the Arab Middle East* (New York: Columbia University Press).

Chomsky, N. and E. Herman. 1988. *Manufacturing Consent: The Political Economy of the Mass Media* (New York: Pantheon Books).

Cobban, H. 1984. *The Palestine Liberation Organization: People, Power & Politics* (Cambridge: Cambridge University Press).

Dakkak, I. 1983. 'Back to Square One: A Study in the Emergence of the Palestinian Identity in the West Bank 1967–1980', in A.Schölch (ed.), *Palestinians over the Green Line: Studies on the Relations between Palestinians on both Sides of the 1949 Armistice Lines since 1967* (London: Ithaca Press).

Deegan, H. 1993. *The Middle East and Problems of Democracy* (London: Open University Press).

Gresh, A. 1985. *The PLO, The Struggle Within: Towards an Independent Palestinian State* (London: Z Books).

Hameed, R. 1975. *Mukarrarat al-Majlis al-Watani al-Filastini 1964–1974* (Beirut: PLO Research Centre).

Hassasian, M. 1993. 'The Democratic Process in The PLO: Ideology, Structure and Strategy', in E. Kaufman, S. Abed and R.L. Rothstein (eds), *Democracy, Peace and the Israeli Palestinian Conflict* (Boulder, CO: Lynne Rienner Publishers).

Hillal, J. 1993. 'PLO Institutions: The Challenge Ahead', *Journal of Palestine Studies* 23/1.

Hourani, F. 'Munathamt Al-Tahreer wa al-Nitham al-Urduni 1946–1974', *Majallat al-Urdun al-Jaddid* 7.

Kaufman, E., and S. Abed. 1993. 'The Relevance of Democracy to Israeli Palestinian Peace', in E. Kaufman, S. Abed and R.L. Rothstein (eds), *Democracy, Peace and the Israeli Palestinian Conflict* (Boulder, CO: Lynne Rienner Publishers).

Khalidi, R. 1997. *Palestinian Identity: The Construction of Modern National Consciousness* (New York: Columbia University Press).

Khatib, N. 1993. *Munakasha Hawl al-Dimokratiyya al-Filastiniyya* (Paris: Al-Mujtama al-Madani).

Macpherson, C.B. 1991. *The Real World of Democracy* (Oxford: Clarendon Press).

Maoz, M. 1984. *Palestinian Leadership on the West Bank: The Changing Role of the Mayors under Jordan and Israel* (London: Frank Cass).

Maoz, M. 1993. 'Democratisation among West-Bank Palestinians and Palestinian Israeli Relations', in E. Kaufman, S. Abed and R.L. Rothstein (eds.), *Democracy, Peace and the Israeli Palestinian Conflict* (Boulder, CO: Lynne Rienner Publishers).

Muslih, M. 1990. 'Towards Co-existence: An Analysis of the Resolutions of the Palestine National Council', *Journal of Palestine Studies* 20/4.

Sahliyeh, E.F. 1986. *The PLO after the Lebanon War* (Boulder, CO: Westview Press).

Sayigh, F. 1965. *Hifna min Dabbab: Bahth fi-Mafahim al-Bourguibiyya wa-Shiarateha* (Beirut: PLO Palestine Research Centre).

Sayigh, R. 1994. *Too Many Enemies: The Palestinian Experience in Lebanon* (London: Z Books).

Semyonov. M., and N. Lewin-Epstein. 1987. *Hewers of Wood and Drawers of Water: Non-Citizen Arabs in the Israeli Labor Market* (Cornell, CO: ILR Press, Cornell University).

Shemesh, M. 1988. *The Palestine Entity 1959–1974: Arab Politics and the PLO* (London: Frank Cass).

Swedenburg, T. 1995. *Memoirs of Revolt: The 1936 Rebellion and the Palestinian National Past* (Minnesota: University of Minnesota Press).

Tarabulsi, F (tr.). 1972. *Al-Ummamiya al-Shouiya wa-Taharrour al-Sharq: al-Muatamar al-Awal li-Shououb al-Shark*, Baku, 1–8 September 1920. Beirut.

Telos 95 (Spring 1993).

Wilson, M.C. 1987. *King Abdullah, Britain and the Making of Jordan* (Cambridge: Cambridge University Press).

The Derailment of Peace
Rabin's Assassination, Democracy and Post-Conflict Agendas

Lev Grinberg

When Yitzhak Rabin was murdered at a peace rally in Tel Aviv, on 4 November 1995, large numbers of Israelis—Jews and Arabs, secular and religious, from both the right and the left of Israel's political spectrum—vowed to 'continue along his path'. In the days that followed, there was an overriding feeling not only that the assassination would fail to achieve its intended aim, but that it would boomerang: it would strengthen the ranks of the country's peace-camp and weaken its opponents. When, at the end of 1995, IDF forces withdrawing from Palestinian cities in the Occupied Territories encountered no opposition from Israeli settlers there, this was seen as part of this 'continuing along the path Rabin had set out'. Similarly, severe criticism was levelled at opposition leader Benjamin Netanyahu for his role in the violent incitement typical of the demonstrations he had led against Rabin and his public support dropped sharply. Also, a number of Israeli rabbis called for soul-searching and a rethinking of the worldview national-religious education was imparting to Israeli youth, while castigating those rabbis who had seemingly encouraged the person (or persons?) behind Rabin's assassination.

This sentiment of 'continuing along his path' soon proved to be an illusion. It evaporated almost as quickly as it had arisen, to be replaced by a feeling of regression marked by a return to the days of violent conflict with the Palestinians. The assassination, on 5 January 1996, by the Israeli Security Services of Hamas member, Yahya 'Ayyash ('al-Muhandis', the Engineer), and the Hamas suicide attacks this provoked,[1] Israel's military operation in Lebanon ('Grapes of Wrath') and the Israeli government's refusal to honour the agreement of troop withdrawal from the town of Hebron (al-Khalil) were all factors in this regression. The process culminated in the electoral victory in 1996 of Benjamin Netanyahu, who thus came to power within a year of Rabin's death. Ehud Barak's 1999 victory and his first year in office as prime minister did not herald a return to the 'peace-making' that had characterized the government of Rabin. Barak excluded from his coalition those political parties that had the support of the country's Arab citizens, Jewish settlements in the Occupied Territories regained their pre-Oslo 'pioneering' aura, and the government sought out the Jewish National Religious Party (NRP) so as to be able to create a broad national consensus. Typically, while thus ignoring Israel's Palestinian citizens en bloc, Barak referred to his government as a 'government of all'.

Rabin's assassination plunged Israel into one of the most severe political crises it had known until then. The Oslo Accords, signed on 13 September 1993, had initiated a process of far-reaching change within Israeli society and politics. A little over two years later the murder of the country's foremost political leader, who had staked his career on them, already seriously undermined the legitimacy of the process. But it also stymied new political forces from emerging that could have supported the continuation of Oslo. In other words, at the height of an ostensibly irreversible process the legitimate political forces that could have brought this change to its rightful conclusion were dealt a fatal blow. The old political system had come apart with no new system as yet in place. In critical situations such as these leadership and the ability to provide political legitimacy for change prove of decisive importance. However, legitimacy is not conferred personally by this or that leader. Rather, it derives from the nature of the relationship between political leaders, on the one hand, and the groups that they claim to lead and represent, on the other.

---

1   Ayyash had come to the fore as one of Hamas' chief explosives expert after the murder, on 25 February 1994, of 29 Palestinian civilians during Friday prayers in the al-Ibrahimi Mosque in al-Khalil (Hebron) by Baruch Goldstein, a physician in the IDF.

When trying to understand the nature of the relationship between Israeli politics and society that comes to the fore here, the first question to capture my attention was: What is the nature of Israel's democracy that it allows for a long-term historical process to be derailed by a lone assassin? For an answer I will first highlight the features that appear to make Israeli politics and democracy unique and focus on how political leaders mobilize, lead and represent their electorate. I will then ask whether the Oslo Accords made a difference to this system, and then also what difficulties prevented movements and leaders from emerging that identified with and could have spearheaded the powerful historical transformation that Yitzhak Rabin initiated.

As I hope to show, the crisis is closely interlinked with the features of Israel's party system and the peculiar nature of the democratization process the Oslo Accords set in motion within Israel. My argument differs from other political studies because I choose to analyze the link between the 'peace process' and Israel's internal process of democratization through a novel theoretical framework. More specifically, I argue that these two processes—the 'external' one of peace-making and the 'internal' one of democratization through change of the party system—are intertwined in such a complex manner as to endanger the survival of both. The unique way in which both processes come together makes up what I want to call the Oslo 'process'. That this process could be derailed by the assassination of Rabin was, first and foremost, because within Israeli politics people had difficulties in pinpointing the anti-democratic content of the assassination and then linking this with what the killing of Rabin aimed to achieve—namely, ruling out Israeli reconciliation and compromise with the Palestinians and preventing Israel's occupation apparatuses from being dismantled. As we shall see, two of the most vulnerable aspects of Israeli democracy are exactly the nature of this distinction I outlined above between 'external' and 'internal' within Israeli society and the question of who has the authority to determine where the boundaries of the 'internal' and 'external' will be drawn.[2]

2   Cf. also L. Grinberg, 'Imagined Democracy in Israel—Theoretical Background and Historical Perspectives', *Israeli Sociology* 1/2 (1999), pp. 209-240 (Hebrew).

Democracy and the Process of Democratization

Democracy is often portrayed in the literature as a 'substance' that can be defined without much difficulty. Some scholars see it as a legal framework where what counts are the 'rules of the game', others choose to emphasize the values and principles inherent in democratic systems. Still others, however, stress the dynamics of social conflict and group interests that lead to the institutionalization of democracy and guarantee its stability. In the same way, I propose here to conceptualize democracy not as a substance, but rather as a process shaped by struggles between different social, political and economic interests and capable of containing these struggles within a shared framework of agreed-upon rules. This shared framework, in turn, is the outcome of a balance of power that aims to prevent one monolithic political force from usurping power and unilaterally enforcing its rule.

In the 1980s the literature began to distinguish between two stages of dynamic transition to democracy: installation and consolidation, the former putting in place the institutional conditions necessary for the latter to take root. Here, I propose my own definition of these concepts.

Installation—This stage occurs after social and political forces supporting openness and flexibility within the political system have become empowered vis-à-vis the ruling groups and elites that neglect and repress their demands. Groups that benefit from non-democratic rules and procedures—whether directly, through their participation in government, or more indirectly, through the benefits and privileges they reap from them—are likely to oppose those forces that seek democracy. No social group can be called democratic or anti-democratic by nature or in essence. Rather, the positions of different groups depend on the balance of power and the historical context that prevails when the political struggles take place. Groups, organizations and classes that benefit from oppressive, non-democratic and authoritarian regimes tend to support the status quo. People who know they are being oppressed will seek to subvert the prevailing power relations and by struggling for democracy open up new political spaces that will facilitate the mobilization of their own forces and help them achieve their demands.

Consolidation—This stage includes decision-making processes within institutional frameworks and recognized regular procedures that are acceptable to all organizations participating in the political system. The institutions and the rules of the game that will be agreed upon evolve out of historical processes according to the specific conjunctures of transition, the balance of power between state apparatuses and social groups demanding democratization and the power relations among these groups themselves, however different they may be from country to country.

Democratic processes can take place only after the achievements of democratization have been consolidated and the democratic in-stitutions put in place grant universal citizenship, equal rights, freedom of expression and freedom of organization to all. Democratic processes mediate between state institutions and groups represented by parties that are in competition with one another for the support of citizens. A democratic process is possible when institutions and rules—including the legal procedures required in order to change the rules—have been agreed upon and cannot be undermined. Political parties are the key agents of democracy, and the free competition between them at regular intervals for the support of citizens is one of the most distinctive signs of democratic processes.[3]

Political processes are democratic when equal rights are attributed to all citizens, who are free to participate in public debates and struggles. The elected political party leadership is responsible for the well-func-tioning of these processes. Its members must be exposed to public criticism while transparency demands they will be held accountable for their actions and decisions, and a periodical electoral vote can change the power relations between the parties. In a democracy, no body is

3   Cf. A. Przeworski, *Democracy and the Market* (Cambridge: Cambridge University Press, 1991).

above public sovereignty, and every public body is subordinated to the law and the elected institutions of the state.[4]

Decisive here is the role played by the elected leadership of political parties: without parties and without the ability of leaders to have dialogues and to compromise—with their electorate and with other parties—democratic decisions and processes cannot take place. Again, a party's ability to design strategies, goals and positions that aim both to mobilize support and represent its electorates and to address and satisfy their demands, depends on the historical context within which the party is acting. This context includes the formal framework of the state and the balance of power between different social groups and between social groups and the state.

For democratic processes in which parties mediate between civil society and the state to be successful a number of institutional pre-conditions needs to be met. However, the obfuscation in Israel of the boundaries between 'internal' and 'external' has resulted in a defective democratic process. Israel lacks four of the institutional components that make up these fundamental pre-conditions for the existence of democratic processes: borders, universal citizenship, separation of religion and state, and separation between politics and the military.[5]

Borders

A democratic system of government exists within the framework of a state that is defined as the sovereign authority within borders that have been recognized by the international community. The existence of clear borders is indispensable for the definition of a citizenry that is eligible to demand civil equality. When borders are undefined, it is impossible to talk about a democratic process as it remains unclear which citizenry

---

4   See Philippe C. Schmitter and Terry L. Karl, 'What democracy is ... and is not,' *Journal of Democracy* 2/2 (1991), pp. 75-88.
5   Only the first pre-condition—fixed borders—is not linked with democratization, which, as I show below, makes it a unique feature of the peace process.

the political system in question is supposed to represent.[6] That is, the 'people' cannot decide in a democratic way who the 'people' are.[7] The determination of state borders is not based on internal democratic struggles within the state, but rather on external power relations between states, for example as the outcome of wars, of colonial expansion or of decisions by international bodies.[8] A combination of factors— that Israel, in 1948, was established as a Jewish state, that between 1948 and 1966 this state imposed military rule on its Palestinian citizens and that, in 1967, Israel expanded its territory through military conquest—turned the determination of borders between the state of Israel and the Palestinians into a fundamental component of Israel's democratization process.[9] Unlike colonial regimes that established state apparatuses overseas, the rule Israeli occupation imposes on the Palestinians possesses territorial, administrative and economic contiguity with the 'colonial' state, i.e., Israel, itself, and this intentionally obfuscates the boundaries between the 'areas' of democracy and the 'territories' administered by military rule.

One of the greatest challenges posed by anti-democratic forces in Israel supporting continued military rule over the Palestinians is the question of who has the authority to determine the future borders of the state. Israel's rejection of the right of Palestinian citizens of Israel to participate in this decision is glaringly anti-democratic and as such is a basic component of the de-legitimization of the peace process. This rejection is linked to Israel defining itself as the state of the Jewish people, that is, to the religious founding principle, as interpreted by

6   Oren Yiftachel discusses this point within the Israeli context in his 'Israeli Society and the Jewish-Palestinian Question: "Ethnocracy" and its Territorial Contradictions' (Negev Center for Regional Development, Working Paper No. 12, Ben-Gurion University, 1991)(Hebrew); see also his article in this volume.

7   See C. Offe, '"Homogeneity" and Constitutional Democracy: Coping with Identity Conflicts through Group Rights', *The Journal of Political Philosophy* 6 (1998), pp. 113-141.

8   See especially J. Linz and A. Stepan, *Problems of Democratic Transition and Consolidation* (Baltimore: Johns Hopkins University Press, 1996).

9   Cf. Grinberg, 'Imagined Democracy in Israel'.

Zionism in the late nineteenth century, that God had promised the 'Land of Israel' (*Eretz Yisrael*) to the people of Israel. This means that there is no democratic consensus either within the country's 1948 border that Israel's Palestinian citizens should have equal rights. Still, the question of 'fuzzy' borders comes mainly to the fore—and saliently so—where it concerns the Occupied Territories, i.e., where the fate and future of the Palestinians living in the West Bank and the Gaza Strip are concerned.

The vast majority of Israelis unconditionally accept that the Palestinians of the West Bank and the Gaza Strip should be refused their democratic political right to take part in any 'national' referendum that is to have a direct impact on their own fate. But then, the clearly anti-democratic groups in Israel—who benefit from the privileges accruing to them because of the occupation—also reject the right of the country's Jewish majority to determine the borders of the state. The major obstacle, as I argued above, is that border demarcation is not an issue of democracy, but rather one of the foreign relations a country maintains with other countries and the way these evolve. The legitimacy of a country's borders depends on international recognition or, at the very least, on recognition by neighbouring countries.

Universal Citizenship

Historically and in the majority of cases, citizens' struggle for recognition of equal civil and political rights regardless of class, race, gender, religion or area of residence, evolves only after a state's borders have been demarcated. Well-known struggles for democratization are those waged by the working class, women and slaves, all demanding to be recognized as equal citizens. It is possible that after 'external' territorial borders have been defined, the issue of the 'internal' borders—the unequal citizenship of people Israel defines as 'non-Jewish', i.e., its Arab citizens, its foreign workers and many of its new immigrants from former Soviet Union countries—will remain open and unresolved. A battle may well ensue between democratic forces wanting equality for all and anti-democratic forces attempting to preserve the privileges Jews are granted by virtue of the state's definition as Jewish. Making citizenship universal, therefore, means nullifying ethnic distinctions on the part of the state.[10]

Separation of Religion and State

The granting of sovereignty to the people together with the rejection of monarchical regimes brought in its wake the end of special rights and extra privileges certain groups, organization and individuals routinely enjoyed because of their special relationship with the ruling power. In this way, democratization for example annuls the special status of official religious institutions that had once provided the monarch with legitimacy. Religion, formerly a state institution, becomes part of the free civil society and subject to the personal decision of free individuals.

The unique historical process that led to the state of Israel forged an inseparable link between the state and Jewish religious institutions, one that actually encumbers the democratization process. At issue is not just Jewish religious parties positioning themselves at the forefront of the struggle against peace and democratization, but the anti-democratic structural position of all Jewish parties. Since the special privileges Jews in Israel enjoy derive their 'legitimacy' exactly from the fundamental fact that the state of Israel is defined as Jewish, the majority of secular Jewish parties are in no particular hurry to demand the separation of religion and state. What is more, since there is no non-religious definition of Judaism, ensuring Israel will be preserved as a Jewish state will always require a religious stamp of approval.

This was the core of the limited democracy we had in Israel even before the expansion of the country's borders through occupation after

10 Cf. O. Yiftachel, 'Debate: The Concept of "Ethnic Democracy" and its Application to the Case of Israel', *Ethnic and Racial Studies* 15/1 (1993), pp. 36-125; S. Smooha, 'Class, Ethnic and National Cleavages and Democracy in Israel', in E. Sprinzak and L. Diamond (eds.), *Israeli Democracy under Stress* (Boulder, CO: Lynne Rienner, 1993), pp. 309-342.

June 1967. This is also where it will remain if and when the issue of 'external' border demarcation with the Palestinians of the West Bank and Gaza Strip is ever resolved. The immigration of non-Jews to Israel during the 1990s—whether as *olim hadashim* ('new immigrants') from the former Soviet Union or as 'foreign workers'—accentuates this problem and places it outside the already complex context of the 'national conflict'.

Separation between Politics and the Military

Democratization requires the military to be subordinated to civilian rule. The phenomenon of military officials advancing within a hier-archical structure that is able to force its will on civilians restricts the power of political parties to plan the direction they want the state to take and to freely represent its citizens. For the clear demarcation between the military and the civil spheres, the definition of borders and the achievement of peace are fundamental preconditions.[11]

Though clearly visible in the Israeli context—with its numerous instances of the military interfering in state affairs—few people perceive the issue as problematic for the democratic process. When military officials rise to power,[12] they do so as free civilians, while when they are in uniform they express their opinions as experienced professionals in the realm of defense and security. This erasure of boundaries between politics and national security within Israel's political system runs par-allel to the obfuscation of the 'external' borders of the state itself, and both are tightly linked to Israel's military occupation of the Pales-tinians. Although a classic instance of an undemocratic situation,

---

11 C. Tilly, *Coercion, Capital and European States, AD 990-1992* (Cambridge: Blackwell, 1992).

12 This applies primarily to army chiefs of staff and generals who move into decisive political positions within the highest echelons of civilian rule (examples that come readily to mind include Moshe Dayan, Yitzhak Rabin, Ezer Weitzman, Ariel Sharon and Ehud Barak).

public discussion for the most part overlooks this feature and regards the active involvement of military officials in politics largely as self-evident or, at best, as a sad necessity. According to all international criteria, the involvement of people in uniform in political decisions, especially that of former army generals in politics as a whole, only works to set limits to the overall freedom of the civilian sector.[13]

In Israel, the routine involvement of military officials in the country's politics has transformed them into the highest authority on major political, i.e., 'security' issues—the definition of state borders and relations with neighbouring countries. In order to clarify my argument and present a balanced picture of the implications this fuzzy boundary between the military and political has, I should immediately add that, had it not been for the support of the Israeli army's general command, there would have been no Oslo process. But then, as a bureaucratic body that controls both the land and the population, the military will always be interested in borders that facilitate the efficient waging of war.[14]

Oslo as a Process of Democratization and Peace

The historical process Yitzhak Rabin set in motion was one of democratization and not just of peace. By that I mean that it awakened political struggles in Israel for the creation of the four institutional conditions I defined above as necessary preconditions for the existence of a democratic process. The path Rabin charted would have led him—consciously and directly or even unintentionally and indirectly—to achieve these institutional preconditions. The definition of Israel's external borders became an explicit goal of the state's negotiations with the Palestinians. But such a decision would also have paved the way—once peace had been concluded—for the exclusion of mili-

---

13 Cf. Linz and Stepan, *Problems of Democratic Transition and Consolidation.*
14 See Dov Tamari, 'Borders are a Condition for Security', *Ha'aretz,* 19 October 2000.

tary officials from politics, the separation of religion from state, and a discussion of the rights of Israel's Palestinian citizens.

While questions about the last two issues had emerged already without connection to the Oslo process, they were in fact an essential part of it, as Oslo made the future of these two issues uncertain. On the whole, putting an end to the Jewish people's exclusive right to *Eretz Yisrael* by recognizing the political rights of the Palestinian Other directly challenges both Israel's negative discrimination of the Palestinians and its positive discrimination in favour of the Jewish religion. And it is exactly that understanding of the link between the peace process and the weakening of the status of the Jewish religion within Israel that lies at the heart of the politicization of Orthodox circles and their opposition to the Oslo process.[15] The warming relationship between Orthodox and national-religious circles, including their unified support of Benjamin Netanyahu, is indicative of the connection between peace and the democratization aspects inherent within the Oslo process. Similarly, the 'secular' awakening against the influence of the Orthodox and their refusal to perform military service, for example, should be seen as a reaction to the politicization of the Orthodox parties since the beginning of the process. In other words, by combining democratization and peace Oslo resulted in, among other things, the politicization of the struggle over the place of the Jewish religion within the state of Israel.

While the path laid down by Rabin in Oslo did in fact initiate a process of democratization in Israel, it was problematic—like other processes of democratization—in that it was embarked upon while consolidated

15 Rabbi Ovadia Yosef's support for the return of Occupied Territory as '*piku'akh nefesh*' ('saving life' as an overriding injunction in Jewish religion) is a unique exception in this context, as it contradicts the position of the majority of his followers. While an explanation of his attitude lies outside our scope here, it should be pointed out that the Oslo process was made possible to a large degree by Ovadia Yosef's exceptional stance, beginning with the 'dirty trick' affair of 1990 (see below) and ending with the establishment of Rabin's government in 1992.

democratic preconditions and agreed-upon rules of the game were as yet absent. This meant that leadership became an extremely critical factor. It is the authority of political leaders to give legitimacy to the arrangements and compromises they conclude that enables the results of the process to be consolidated. Democratization processes take place during periods in which old political arrangements and procedures are in crisis and new legitimate ones have yet to be put in place. In other words, for democratization to develop satisfactorily, it is crucial that leaders succeed in legitimizing new arrangements and procedures by force of their personal status.[16]

The forces that opposed Yitzhak Rabin and succeeded in stopping him (even if only temporarily, i.e., until suitable conditions re-emerge and the political power necessary to turn the tables again has been regained) targeted him personally because the legitimacy for the changes in question stemmed from his personal authority. This legitimacy did not actually result from the acceptance of rules of the game that were now democratic, as Rabin's opponents rejected the mandate he had received from the people. In addition to his clear victory in the 1992 elections, Rabin's authority was rooted in a personality that struck people as honest and reliable, in his military record, in the strong image he projected as 'Mr. Security', and in his personal history. What provided Rabin with the legitimacy to bring about a change in public opinion was, of course, his transformation from IDF Chief of Staff in 1967 and the 'bone-breaking' Minister of Defence during the first Intifada, into the leader of peace and reconciliation he became with Oslo. The wider public that supported his policy of profound change in Israel's official attitude towards the Palestinians

---

16 In the literature these processes are referred to as a 'transition to democracy' whereby the ability of the elites to lead and administer during such processes is seen as decisive; cf. G. O'Donnell and P.C. Schmitter, *Transitions from Authoritarian Rule: Tentative Conclusions about Uncertain Democracies* (Baltimore: Johns Hopkins University Press 1986). Max Weber speaks of 'charismatic' authority, when, in the absence of consolidated, understood procedures of governing, it is faith in the authority of leadership that legitimizes new values and institutions.

readily identified with Rabin's frequently awkward body language and
his often terse statements. Examples of this included the clearly visible
aversion he showed on the lawn of the White House when it came to
actually shaking hands with Arafat because for Rabin Arafat remained
au fond 'the terrorist leader', and his disparaging attitude towards the
Jewish settlers who rallied against him. Because Rabin's leadership
within the Oslo process was so central, it became necessary to strike at
him personally, initially by attacking his public image through slander
and defamation (for example, through posters that showed him dressed
in Nazi uniform), and, when that proved not effective enough, by
assassinating him.

The groups that opposed Rabin and the Oslo process acted against
not only peace and compromise, but the process of democratization as
well. They represented the anti-democratic forces in Israeli society that
refused to give up the special rights and privileges they were provided
by the Jewish state, by Israel's military rule over the Palestinians, and
by the continuous official confiscation of Palestinian lands. These
groups did not hesitate to resort to anti-democratic methods, such as
the violation of laws and the exercise of violence against the government's peace policy, of which Rabin's assassination then became the
most extremist expression. For the majority of his opponents, at the
heart of their rejection of Rabin was the claim that his rule and authority to make peace with the Palestinian people was illegitimate, as he
had been given 'no mandate' to make concessions and it was un-
acceptable to them that in order to achieve his goal he relied on the
support of Palestinian citizens of Israel and their parties.[17]

Why do these groups oppose peace and democracy? The sub-
ordination of the Palestinian 'non-citizens' in the Occupied Territories
and of the Palestinian citizens discriminated by the Jewish state pro-

17 The rejection of Rabin's authority to make decisions was at the heart of the
    struggle of the opponents of the process. The barrage of propaganda directed at
    him at one point became so extensive that even the then President of Israel, Ezer
    Weizmann, a few days before the assassination called for halting the process on
    the grounds of this alleged lack of authority.

vides the opponents of democracy with special rights and privileges that are most likely to be jeopardized by conditions of peace, defined borders and a democratic state ruled by law. This, of course, also means that democracy does not constitute a fundamental value in the eyes of these people, who argue that there is a higher authority than the state. In addition, they seek to force their position on the majority of Israelis, confident that ultimate truth is on their side and not dependent on the public 'mood'. If the extreme political right wing in Israel succeeds in forcing its position on the public, it will be regarded as 'peace among us', while if the public decides to continue along Rabin's path, it will, most likely mean 'civil war'.[18] In the peculiar reality of Israel, peace and brotherhood among Jews disappears when the majority does not go along with the positions of the anti-democratic minority. This was the case before Rabin's rise to power, and has been the case again since his assassination.

Mythological Politics

Institutional openness and flexibility to allow change are key features in all democratic political systems. In the previous section I highlighted the limitations on Israel's democracy that have been there from the outset. The question I now want to look at is how a political system could have evolved in Israel that actually sets limits to its democracy—in effect stymieing the political changes that should have enabled the country to adapt itself to the changes happening around it—and how this system was then consolidated. In this section I will address how Israeli party politics were being constructed during the 1980s, before the onset of the Oslo process.

After its removal from office in 1977, the Labour party found it difficult to play the democratic game from the benches of the oppo-

---

18 Since these lines were written, the slogan 'Brothers do not abandon [one another]' has come into use, providing legitimacy for 'civil war', as 'abandonment' implies endangering someone's life.

sition, that is, to offer an alternative policy significantly different from that of the party in government and one that could help it win the next elections. This was a result of the new political discourse that arose after 1967 exactly because of the limitations on Israel's democracy that I outlined above and here will call 'mythological'. The consolidation of this mythological discourse created a balance of power that was in favour of the so-called 'right' wing in Israel. There were now two collective cultural identities in Israel, the 'right' and the 'left', with the 'right' enjoying a permanent electoral advantage based on demography. That is, the cultural groups belonging to the 'right' enjoyed numerical superiority. I will call this superiority 'the structural advantage of the right'.

The mythological discourse fixes the occupation as permanent and denies the Palestinians in Israel political space by creating two polarized collective identities—'them' (Palestinian Arabs) and 'us' (Jewish Israelis). In this debate, the Jewish parties defined and delimited the boundaries between 'right' and 'left' within the Jewish collective, now referred to as '*ha-'Am*' ('the [Jewish] people'). '*Eretz Yisrael*' became the myth of the 'right', 'peace and security' (*shalom ve-bitahon*) that of the 'left'. The 'right' presented itself as the guardian of national pride and appealed to 'traditional' voters, the Orthodox and the Mizrahi (Oriental) Jews, and pledged to continue Israel's rule over the Palestinians by rejecting their legitimate rights as equal citizens. The 'left' presented itself as moderate and willing to compromise, but rejected negotiation with the PLO and the establishment of a Palestinian state, justifying continuing the occupation by creating the slogan 'there is no partner to negotiate with'.

This debate dominated the election campaigns of 1981, 1984 and 1988, which all showed that in electoral strength the Likud and Labour parties were more or less equal, but that the 'right' enjoyed the 'demographic' advantage it had over the 'left'. This raises such questions as what is 'right' and what is 'left' in Israeli politics, where does the 'right' derive its structural advantage from, and how is that advantage connected to demography.

The terms 'right' and 'left' in Israel have been transformed over the years into code words, symbols of entities that define cultural communities and social groups making up two hostile camps. Each camp has its own language, symbols, myths, narratives and heroes, and promotes its own way of understanding the past, present and future of the state of Israel. The separate, collective social identity of each camp is primarily defined by its hostility to the other and has no real connection with the practical political positions of their leaders. In other words, these are not political positions at all, i.e., they are not part of a democratic process ensuring a dynamic, changing interaction between parties and citizens capable of making changes.

It is this centrality of the cultural element in the mythological definition of 'right' and 'left' in Israel that gives demography its decisive importance in the country's politics. Studies on Israeli voting behaviour indicate that support of 'right' and 'left' is often closely linked with categories such as ethnicity, religion, level of education, class and area of residence. An Israeli who is Ashkenazi, secular, well educated, lives in a prestigious neighbourhood and enjoys a high socio-economic status is most likely to be a supporter of the 'left'. Israelis who vote for the 'right', on the other hand, are often Mizrahi, religious, living in the periphery, without higher education and of lower socio-economic status. This is the source of the 'group pride' for each camp: the 'left' regards itself as rational, modern and moderate, and the 'right' regards itself as nationalist, loyal and proud. The 'left' refers pejoratively to the right as 'irrational', and the right refers self-righteously to the left as 'traitors to the nation'.

A fundamental component of the paralysis of mythological politics has been what I called above the structural advantage of the 'right'—the fact that, since 1977, the 'right' wins elections due to the demographic aspect. In other words, in any election based, not on political positions, but on mythological collective identities, the groups that support the 'right'—religious, Mizrahi, members of the lower class and people living in the periphery—have a permanent numerical advantage over the social groups that constitute the 'left'. This was especially true when the 'right' and the 'left' agreed that parties predominantly supported by Israel's Palestinian citizens could not be part of the legitimate political process of coalition building.

The way these two mythological identities function is based primarily on the sense of belonging of their members, of having something 'in common' with other members of the collective, and but then also on a feeling of hostility towards the Other, most notably the leadership of the opposing group. Neither camp assesses or criticizes the actual political positions taken up by the parties and their leaders, nor do these serve as rallying points. In retrospect, it was the Labour Alignment that institutionalized military rule over the Palestinians and began obfuscating the borders of the state of Israel with building settlements in the Occupied Territories after 1967. By doing so, Labour indirectly strengthened the messianic belief in 'Greater Israel' (*Eretz Yisrael ha-Shlema*), the founding myth of the 'right'. And it was the policies of the 'left' after 1967 that encouraged the formation of the core group of religious settlers, Gush Emunim ('The Bloc of the Faithful'), and thus, ironically, contributed to the empowerment of the Likud between 1967 and 1977.

In contrast, it was the Likud, just after coming to power, that dropped its ideological claims to sovereignty throughout 'Greater Israel' by signing the 1978 Camp David Accords. The agreement defined Israeli rule in the West Bank and the Gaza Strip as temporary and as subject to negotiation, within the framework of a proposed Palestinian 'autonomy'. These are actually the major components that made up the 'peace and security' myth of the 'left': the temporary nature of the occupation of the Palestinians and its reversibility through the signing of peace agreements. Following Sadat's visit to Israel in 1979 Peace Now was established, a political group that resembles the 'left' and which mobilized the popular support for Begin's negotiations and agreements with Egypt.

The national unity governments in power between 1984 and 1990 are perfect examples of how the political hatred between 'right' and 'left', on the one hand, and their common daily political cooperation, on the other, fail to connect. The 1978 Camp David Accords laid the political foundation for co-operation between 'right' and 'left' for the sake of the 'peace process',[19] and at the same time consolidated their symbolic

---

19 It was his keen political sense that led Rabin in the 1990s to introduce the term 'peace making', to distinguish his approach from the 'peace process' which since 1978 had actually served the Likud as a cover for holding on to the status quo and as a pretext to prevent results from being achieved in that direction.

polarization. In practice, while adopting the slogan of peace, the government never stopped expanding settlements, while on the symbolic level the 'right' continued to be labelled as irrational and the 'left' as traitors who lacked all national pride. The national unity governments illustrated how disconnected Israel's political parties and their positions were from the interests of the public in terms of political, cultural, social, and other issues.

The mythological debate between the 'right' and the 'left', the mutual hostility they showed each other but also the ways they found to co-operate with one another, were all in the clear interest of Likud as well as Labour. Both large parties stood for policies they were unable to realize on their own, but having lost ideological orientation, each still sought to remain the dominant political power in Israel. The Labour party could not realize its vision for a democratic Jewish state separate from the Palestinians, and the Likud was not interested in annexing all of 'Greater Israel' because it meant transforming more than one million Palestinians into equal citizens of this 'Greater Israel'.

In order to hide the inconsistent reality they had created, both the Likud and the Alignment now began mobilizing public support through a discourse whose symbols and myths were geared to polarize its members against the other party, whereas in fact they were co-operating with each other on the basis of shared policies that maintained the occupation. This mythological discourse and the mutual hatred it engendered perpetuated the existence of Israel's undemocratic political system because it closed off all political space: every new political organization would immediately be placed within the framework of the mythological right-left discourse and forced to identify with one of the sides and to accept the centrality in Israeli politics of the Likud and the Alignment. More significantly, this political construction supplied a formula for successfully negotiating the contradictions on the symbolic and practical level. That is, their mythological discourse enabled the national unity governments to co-ordinate between the undemocratic discourse, disconnected and conservative in terms of internal Israeli politics, and the undemocratic reality of forced military rule over the Palestinians. Crucially, the mythological discourse marginalized all relevant discussions of, and practical solutions to, the major problems facing Israel, most notably its relations with the Palestinians, by keeping them off the public agenda.

The upshot of the hostile debate between the mythological 'right' and 'left' during the 1980s was the creation of a kind of 'cartel'. This was very different from the 'monopoly' situation created by MAPAI between 1948 and 1977 because now the pie was divided between the two large camps—'right' and 'left', while each small party had to join either one of them. Clearly, there was no room for centre parties like the short-lived Dash,[20] as the polarization was mythological and not based on practical political positions. The bargaining power of the smaller parties only came to the fore when Labour and Likud began trying to form governments on their own, independent of one another. This happened during the 1990s when confrontations with major changes occurring outside the Israeli party system—in particular the first Intifada and the massive wave of immigration from the former Soviet Union—rendered the stagnation the national unity governments had engendered aimless and even dangerous. The turning point came in March 1990.

Rabin's Path

The trap inherent in the mythological politics of 'right' and 'left' is, of course, that the collective identity and 'group pride' of one camp depends on the resentment towards and hatred fostered for the other camp. Neither side was able to succeed by relying only on their own official political platform, as these were both purely mythological. In such an event, change could only be achieved following the simultaneous weakening of both collective identities. The nurturing of mutual hatred became the primary mechanism to help mobilize voters, as well as paralyzing the political system. The latter, in turn, functioned to

---

20 Dash was established as a centre party and performed impressively in the 1977 elections when it obtained 15 Knesset seats; however, almost immediately the party split between 'left' and 'right' and disappeared from the scene.

preserve the strength of both large parties, regardless of the interests, needs and positions of their electorate, by disregarding the crisis emerging in the country.

Yonathan Shapiro has called this phenomenon 'populist politics': leaders address the public directly, mobilizing them by means of myths that have no connection with open and direct debates on practical issues that citizens care about.[21] In other words, the first enemy of any change in the political system defined by the 'right-left' discourse is the tribal loyalty to mythological identities that are disconnected from the interests of the citizens and their actual political positions on different issues. Shapiro argues that democracy in such circumstances cannot function because democracy is meant to mediate between the practical interests of groups of citizens and the necessity of the state to define a general, accepted policy. The populist debate and the crisis in Israeli democracy reflected the weakening of the two large parties. Myths and tribal mobilization brought out voters on elections day, not party members and activists who believed in their party's platform. Both Likud and Labour became devoid of all meaningful content and lost their ability to recruit activists for year-round political work.

The non-functioning of the two large parties was the primary obstacle preventing a practical, non-mythological policy from emerging that could have addressed, with any measure of success, the problems Israeli society was increasingly facing. This paralysis of Israeli politics was reinforced because there were no alternative policies on offer and all democratic commitment to implement policies promised during election campaigns was lacking. The democratic mechanism that was supposed to generate alternative policies against inefficient governments was not functioning, and the national unity governments of the 1980s embodied the lack of alternatives. Thus, the party system was in need of far-reaching change for the political conservative discourse and practices to be transformed. The problem was how to infuse a politics

---

21 Y. Shapiro, *Herut: On the Road to Power* (Tel Aviv: Am Oved, 1989) (Hebrew); idem, *A Society Imprisoned by Politicians* (Tel Aviv: Sifriat Hapoalim, 1996) (Hebrew).

that had become mythological and irrelevant with real positions on the political and social issues that called out for action.

As I already outlined, a number of 'external' changes between 1987 and 1992 forced the Israeli political system to start functioning—the outbreak of the first Intifada, the fall of the Soviet bloc, and the subsequent massive wave of immigration to Israel from the former Soviet Union. The Labour party was the first to understand the new conjuncture[22] and began introducing internal changes in its organization. As early as March 1990, the Labour party tried to establish a 'peace government' based on the Knesset that had been elected in 1988. It was at this point, however, when both large parties sought to form narrow governments without the other, that their dependency on smaller parties became obvious.

In March 1990 Shimon Peres, behind Rabin's back, tried to bring an end to the unity government with Yitzhak Shamir by attempting to form a coalition between Labour and the two leading Orthodox parties, Shas and Agudat Israel. After new elections, Peres expected to become prime minister. Peres's 'dirty trick', as Rabin lost no time in calling it, set a whole series of changes rolling in Israeli politics, among them the legislation of fundamental laws (*chukei yesod*) and the amendment of the Prime Minister Law. They also helped propel Shas into a position of influence on the national level. And, finally, they were crucial for the internal reform of the Labour party that paved the way for Labour's 1992 electoral victory and Rabin's commitment to seek a political agreement with the Palestinians within four years.

Though Peres could not have foreseen all these ramifications when he embarked on this piece of 'dirty tricks' policy (which initially backfired—Yitzhak Shamir formed the government in 1990), the resulting situation had extremely positive effects on the democratization

---

22 Actually, the first changes were visible already during the election campaign of 1988, when the Alignment (Ma'arakh) was dismantled at the initiative of its smaller partner, Mapam, which ran independently and then, in the run-up to the 1992 elections, together with Ratz and Shinui established Meretz. Ma'arakh again became Labour.

process of Israel. As it was now moved into opposition, the Labour party was forced to come up with alternatives to the policies of the Likud government, if only to attract new voters and gain their trust.

The Labour party changed its internal election system within the party by adopting a system of primaries for both Knesset and prime ministerial candidates. It was especially the shifts Labour succeeded in introducing between 1990 and 1992 that led to a democratic transformation in Israel. That is, Labour adopted a system that facilitated the influence of citizens on the party and their representatives; set out new policies and formulated relevant issues on the public agenda; and promised to bring an end to Israel's occupation of the West Bank and Gaza and to abolish military rule over the Palestinians.

That this was a policy that worked was shown by the 1992 elections when Labour increased its Knesset mandates from 39 to 44, while the Likud's dropped from 40 to 32. The 1992 elections represented a watershed not only in terms of their outcome, but also in the way they were carried out: the mythological 'us' and 'them' of 'right' and 'left' were replaced by a relevant debate on the practical present and future issues facing Israel. Labour's main campaign slogan had been a call for a change in priorities—among them a promise of negotiations and political settlement with the Palestinians—but also a full Israeli domestic (post-conflict) agenda, something that had been ignored for years. Equally important for Labour's success in the polls were the votes of new immigrants from the former Soviet Union, as it reversed the structural or demographic advantage of the 'right', further encouraged by Labour's insistence that the government's economic policy had failed.

Under the banner of a 'change in priorities' the general nature of the election campaign now moved towards relevant political debates that addressed a broad variety of issues on the new public agenda—unemployment, health care, roads and education. All parties that ran on a pragmatic, non-mythological platform in 1992 emerged victorious. The decline of those parties that continued to raise the banner of '*Eretz Yisrael*'—Likud, Tehiya and the National Religious Party—was unmistakable, as was the relative electoral successes of right-wing parties that had adopted a more 'matter-of-fact', 'pragmatic' but also more militaristic language.[23]

An additional element was the strategic position of the Knesset factions that had the support of Israel's Palestinian citizens. The five Palestinian Knesset members who were voted in were indispensable in creating a 'bloc' of 61 Knesset members able to prevent the formation of a government of the 'right'. This made them by necessity an 'internal' part of the political game, thus further encouraging democratization. In other words, the electoral defeat of the Likud prevented it from being able to form a government without the Labour party, as it had done between 1990 and 1992. But this time round a national unity government was no longer in the cards precisely because the change in political discourse would not allow a return to the stagnation and paralysis that had characterized the national unity governments of the 1980s.

After the elections of 1992, Labour's candidate for prime minister, Yitzhak Rabin, showed his electorate he was fully committed to achieve a number of targets, first and foremost regarding Israel's relations with the Palestinians, but also regarding a new agenda in education, health and employment. This, then, was the final and perhaps most fundamental element in the process of democratization the Labour party had initiated, as it compelled all parties to begin addressing new agendas that concerned Israel's civil society and to build a mutual relationship between civil society and politics.

This promising situation, however, suffered from one potentially fatal set-back. Despite the construction of a pragmatic, democratic and de-mythologized political discourse, the political system itself remained virtually unchanged and thus, as Likud opposition exerted pressure against a government identified with the 'left', there was the looming danger of sliding back again into the polarization of 'right' and 'left'. A

---

23 Labour and Meretz together obtained 56 Knesset seats, while the two militaristic right-wing parties got 11 seats, i.e., Tzomet 8 and Moledet 3. The 'mythological' Tehia party disappeared.

possible regression into the mythological discourse would imperil the process of democratization as well as the peace process, while threatening to make the elections of 1992 a one-time event. It was this very real and serious threat that reinforced Rabin in his determination to strike out on a new path, aware that the full burden of Israel's political transformation lay on his shoulders.

The question was how to continue dismantling the mythological politics of 'left' and 'right'. Rabin's step was historical—though, again, to what extent he himself was aware of this is not clear—in that he sought the complete transformation of Israeli politics, one that included political, economic, educational and symbolic elements. Part of the broader overall system of changes was legal-procedural, the election of prime minister. After Rabin's death, these policy changes were again abolished except for this law—it was to tear the old party system to shreds.

In order to ensure the system would not slide back again into mythological polarization and political paralysis, Rabin worked to eradicate the basis upon which mythological politics rested. First, he set out to change the nature of Israeli rule over the Palestinians, a step that was intended to destroy the 'right' wing's myth of *Eretz Yisrael ha-Shlema*, but also designed to jolt the Labour party out of the stagnated conservative policy it had stuck to since 1967.[24] He did this not only through dialogue with (as he defined them) moderate, pragmatic Palestinians, but also through the discourse he employed in the public media. Whenever he spoke in public or was interviewed in the media, Rabin sought to de-legitimize the national-religious extremists and the

24 It is crucial to recognize the transformation that occurred in Rabin's approach between 1988 and 1992, apparently due to global changes but in particular to the first Intifada. Rabin led the Labour party into a national unity government in 1988, much against the wish of then party leader Shimon Peres (as we saw, the attempt by Peres, Beilin and Ramon to form a peace government in 1990 Rabin called a 'dirty-trick'). It was only after two years in opposition (1990-1992) that Rabin formulated positions that were in opposition to those of the Likud.

myth of *Eretz Yisrael,* claiming that the settlements in the Occupied Territories did not serve a security function but only a clearly political one.[25] Rabin also 'revived' the borders of 4 June 1967 as he moved checkpoints to re-establish the Green Line as the line of separation between Israel and Palestine. These steps brought about a new political, non-mythological definition of collective identity: no longer a question of 'right' or 'left' but of peace-supporters (including voters from the 'right', but also Palestinians) and their opponents.

Because he wanted to ensure legitimacy not only for the peace process but also for the political participation of Palestinian citizens, Rabin openly supported their democratic right to be full political partners. He did so in the face of the demand of the 'right'—which he rejected—that he 'rely on a Jewish majority only'. By thus opening up political space for the Palestinians both in the Occupied Territories and within Israel, Rabin forged a linkage between peace and democracy. After all, those who reject a Palestinian state also reject equal political rights for the Palestinian citizens of the state of Israel. In his now increasingly frequent confrontations with Jewish extremists, Rabin denounced the opponents of peace as covert partners of the Islamic movement, Hamas, as both were out to derail the Oslo process.

The new collective identity and the new political map Rabin's leadership created were to underpin the legitimacy of his steps towards peace. The new 'we' meant Israelis and Palestinians striving for peace, and the new 'they' were the religious and extremist Jews and Muslims who wanted war to continue. Obviously, these identities functioned as substitutes for the former mythological identities and had not yet been fully consolidated, but when Rabin was assassinated they were crystallizing rapidly. In my opinion, it was Rabin's success in building new

25 This was problematic because the settlements the Labour party had built had always been classified as 'security' settlements. When he came to power in 1999, Ehud Barak, though calling himself '*mamshikho shel Rabin*' (Rabin's successor), took the complete opposite course by highlighting his ties with *Eretz Yisrael,* the settlements, and the NRP.

political collective identities—as reflected in the demonstration on Kings Square ('Kikar ha-Melachim', today's Rabin Square) in Tel Aviv on 4 November 1995 and the wide-spread mourning following his murder that day—that propelled the Yigal Amir gang towards their decision to kill him. This was a strategic political decision that was borne out by an accurate analysis of the process by people who deliberately wanted to derail it: as Rabin had constructed new identities whose legitimacy was based on his personal authority, he himself had to go.

Rabin was the enemy of the mythological 'right'—the 'right' that wanted the occupation to go on—because he had succeeded in dismantling the mythological 'left' that had been structurally inferior to the 'right'. The demonstrators who flooded into Tel Aviv's Kings Square that fateful night were not members of the 'left' as such, but rather supporters of peace, and included Israeli Palestinians and Likud supporters. This was Rabin's achievement, and it blocked the way back to the traditional mythological polarization of 'right' and 'left'. In order to destroy Rabin's path, the 'right' had to target Rabin the man because Rabin and his path were one. For example, in posters they carried at rallies against him Rabin was portrayed as an Arab (with a *kafiyya*), while Yigal Amir, his assassin, would later claim that the square had been 'full of Arabs'. It was of course true that Rabin's policy had succeeded in getting thousands of Jews and Arabs demonstrating together and singing along with the 'Song for Peace' that rang out over the square in protest against violence (of the settlers and Hamas) and in favour of peace (of Rabin and Arafat). Peace had become the interest of the 'left', while the assassin was the representative of the 'right'. The three bullets that killed Rabin reversed the situation instantly—with Rabin dead, the two polarized mythological camps sprang back into life.

Imagining Peace:
Assassination and Post-Conflict Agendas

Even before being implemented, the policies Rabin set out enabled people to start *imagining* peace and to envisage the new agenda Israel would pursue once the national conflict had been brought to an end.

This new 'post-conflict' agenda, as I suggest calling it,[26] was meant to address the issues that mythological politics had always pushed aside—social causes, the economy, questions of identity and citizenship, culture and religion. The political party system set out to prepare itself for the post-conflict agenda immediately after the signing of the Oslo Accords. I single out the following signposts that helped shatter the traditional identities of 'right' and 'left':

1. City council elections in 1993 witnessed the formation of new coalitions that ruptured the right-left dichotomy, the most striking of which was Meretz's support of Roni Milo, the Likud candidate for mayor in Tel Aviv. There were many other examples of such non-mythological coalitions as well.
2. Within the Histadrut—a major symbol of the mythological politics and the identity of the 'left' that historically had always remained alien to Mizrahi workers[27]— Meretz and Shas formed a coalition against Labour led by Haim Ramon and Amir Peretz, who left the Labour party before the elections (May 1994). The joint Meretz-Shas list received 46% of the vote, Labour 32% and the Likud shrunk significantly. That is, for the first time in 74 years the Labour party lost control of the Histadrut.
3. David Levy, a political leader who more than anyone else symbolized the connection between the peripheral Mizrahi Jews and the 'right' and Likud, split from the Likud and, in June 1995, established Gesher ('Bridge'), a party whose platform mainly addressed social issues.
4. In coordination with Yitzhak Rabin, Haim Ramon began working with the Likud's Roni Milo on establishing a new centre party. Such a party had a chance only when 'right' and 'left' had stopped being dichotomous and mythological in nature.

26 This term differs from 'post-Zionist', which, as I see it, is often employed by people with conservative views to de-legitimize critical ideas and research.
27 See L. Grinberg, *Split Corporatism in Israel* (Albany: SUNY Press, 1991), idem, *The Histadrut Above All Else* (Jerusalem: Nevo Publishing, 1993) (Hebrew).

The idea to create a centre party was based on the assumption that it would enable to split the vote in the direct elections for prime minister, which would favour Rabin. In other words, the new system of direct prime ministerial elections and the law that instigated them were deliberately designed to reduce the power of mythological messages to attract votes while it was also expected to result in both the loss of votes for Labour and Likud and gain support for the evolution of a new party system. The law was enacted in an effort to facilitate the democratic transformation and to create rapport between the party system and all citizens who identified with the post-conflict agenda. The law's sophistication lay in the fact that democratization was likely to preserve—even if only temporarily—the centrality of the Labour party. Labour, it was expected, would be able to field candidates with realistic chances of winning prime ministerial elections. Not coincidentally, Benjamin Netanyahu was the only Likud MK to support the law, as he was the only Likud politician convinced he could win a direct election. In this regard, the law's major problem was not its role in bringing about the disintegration of the large parties—this had already started—but that it was based on the assumption that there was only one indisputable prime ministerial candidate during the transit period: Yitzhak Rabin.

As with all transitions to democracy, the greatest challenge for the democratization process that took place in Israel between 1990 and 1995 was that for it to be successful it depended on the political acumen of its leaders to create the alliances and make the compromises necessary to help consolidate the process and underpin its legitimacy.

For decades the Labour party had trumpeted its opposition to the establishment of a Palestinian state, to negotiations with the PLO and to the return to 1967 borders: why trust it now? Trust was given to Rabin, whose positions had changed due to the new conjuncture. But the new discourse and the new post-conflict party system mediating between civil society and the state had not yet been sufficiently consolidated. As Claus Offe accurately observed, the contradiction inherent in democratic processes is that they invariably take place in non-democratic conditions; democracy does not as yet exist, but a struggle goes on to have new democratic and agreed rules and procedures established.[28]

This was also Rabin's problem. He led a process in which peace with the Palestinians was supposed to redefine the boundaries of Israeli politics, while having at his disposal neither legitimate rules and procedures (to change Israel's borders and to implement post-conflict politics) nor a new party system with alliances that could successfully meet the challenges of the new agenda. On the contrary, in the old 'right-left' discourse the Palestinians were outsiders to the political system. And as to political and national rights, Palestinians possessed none—in the Occupied Territories—or only some—within the Green Line. This was perceived as 'democratic' and 'legitimate'. Israel, after all, prides itself on being 'the only democracy' in the Middle East.

On the eve of his assassination Rabin spoke out against this anti-democratic approach that had abrogated the voting rights of Palestinian citizens: he regarded it as racist. It was a typical case of the legitimacy for change deriving directly from the leader's image and authority. In times of crisis, when there is no other source of authority, the public readily accepts the authority of a leader or a group of leaders who appear to herald a new orientation. Max Weber defined this as the source of his 'charismatic authority'—not a quality of an individual leader, but rather a characteristic feature of a period of crisis in which the personality and ideas of leaders come to represent the change their supporters expect and thus instilling respect for their leadership.[29]

In his 1992 victory speech, Rabin announced that he himself would be the exclusive leader of the process: there would be no one else. He apparently meant to say how deeply aware he was of the weight of the burden history had placed on his shoulders and of the danger of Israeli politics regressing back into the old mythological mobilization of 'right'

---

28 See Offe, '"Homogeneity" and Constitutional Democracy'.
29 See Max Weber, *Economy and Society*, ed. R. Guenther and W. Claus (Berkeley: University of Berkeley Press, 1968).

and 'left'.[30] At the same time, he intended to dampen the enthusiasm voters of the 'left' felt because of his victory. As I see it, Rabin's speech and policies were intended to leave the 'left' de-mobilized in order to forestall the re-mobilization of the mythological 'right' as a counter-reaction. In Rabin's eyes, the polarization of 'right' and 'left' played clearly into the hands of the 'right' and would be a blow to the process of liberation from the mythological right-left construction.

In order to expand his base of support and minimize that of his opponents, Rabin promoted the identity formation of supporters of 'peace', to be distinguished from supporters of the 'left'. A fact is that many Likud followers expressing support for the process stayed away from the extremist and often violent demonstrations organized by Likud leader Benjamin Netanyahu, especially after he had aligned himself with the Jewish settlers in the Occupied Territories. By consolidating his image as national leader ('Mr. Security') Rabin sought to undermine the traditional sources of support for the 'right'. He achieved a major success when he managed to isolate Netanyahu, who now became prisoner of the extremist religious groups and the mythological discourse of *Eretz Yisrael.*

In de-mobilizing the 'left' so as to prevent Netanyahu from galvanizing the entire collective 'right' against him, Rabin was more successful than expected. Only when he was sure that the violent image the opponents of peace projected was there for all to see, and when among those who identified themselves with his path and the peace camp he recognized a significant number of people from the 'right', did he agree for a mass demonstration in his support to go ahead. Moreover, most of the Likud-voting public did not take part in demonstrations against Oslo, preferring to follow the process on their TV sets, just as voters of the 'left', the vast majority of whom accepted Oslo as irreversible.

30 This was Rabin's response to a number of political leaders identified with the 'left' (Meretz's Yossi Sarid prominent among them) who, either publicly or privately, had let it be known they would 'lead' Rabin according to their interests.

But the masses of people that had turned up at Tel Aviv's Kings' Square and the thousands who promised to 'continue along his path' after Rabin's assassination, soon woke up to the fact that the path to peace and democracy was as yet largely uncharted. Rabin had paved only part of it on his own, through his work and actions. He had served as prime minister in 1974–1977 and as defense minister in 1984–1990, but he had not then been seen as the charismatic leader capable of instigating significant changes he became in the early 1990s. The transformation he underwent was engendered by the unique circumstances the first Intifada had created and the dissolution of the national unity government that followed. With Rabin's assassination, there was no one of equal leadership stature to take his place, certainly not Shimon Peres, the ultimate symbol of the mythological 'left-right' politics of the 1980s, and Israeli politics began to slide back into the old 'safe' and familiar mythological party solidarity, with its hatred for the other and its 'right-left' polarization.

Immediately following Rabin's assassination, the 'left' put all the blame on the 'right' which, although now in gradual decline, still stood for a collective that also included Rabin supporters. The 'right', in turn, indirectly held Rabin responsible for his own assassination, explaining it as a result of the 'polarization of the people' (i.e., Jewish Israelis). This polarization, they claimed, was caused by Rabin's efforts to legitimize peace while de-legitimizing Jewish settlers and the concept of Greater Israel, and by the violent reaction he elicited on the part of extreme right-wing demonstrators. In the wake of Rabin's death, the 'left', under the leadership again of Shimon Peres, revived the old mythological discourse of 'right' and 'left' as it adopted the idea of the 'right' that the crisis had been caused by the polarization of the people, and not by the aggressive, extremists and anti-democratic features of the opponents of peace.

Peres's line of policy derived from the immediate need to appease the Jewish settlers and to nurture the 'unity of the people', which explains why Peres refrained from holding elections immediately after Rabin's assassination. Instead, he attempted to bring the National Religious Party (NRP) into the coalition by promising them he would leave most of the Jewish settlements under Israeli jurisdiction. Adopted by the leaders of the 'left', this policy indirectly reflected an understanding of the assassin's motives: since they proved a reaction to the assassination, Peres's policies indirectly justified it. For, only someone who considered Rabin himself responsible for the polarization in Israel's political system could decide to invite his most aggressive opponents to join the government immediately after his assassination and promise not to evacuate settlements. As with the unity governments of the 1980s, national unity and the mythological right-left polarization were two sides of the same coin, which served to close the political space of the Palestinians by means of creating an 'internal' Jewish discourse.

When the sides in the political arena are 'right' and 'left', the occupation can go on. Discourse formation will then exclude anything referring to dialogue with the invisible other side—the Palestinians—except when, in order to preserve their power, internal competition between Likud and Labour over Jewish public opinion is at stake. The factors that prevented the establishment of a national unity government were the elements that remained from Rabin's policies: (1) the Oslo Accords, which were based on continuing dialogue with the Palestinians; (2) the Direct Election Law, which determined on election day who would be prime minister; (3) the post-conflict agenda and its expanding parties, which prevented polarization based solely on 'right' and 'left'.[31]

Post-Assassination Leadership and Politics

That Peres could initiate this sharp reversal away from Rabin's policies was due to the immense vacuum of leadership Rabin's death had created. Although ministers expressed shock at Peres's new policies, no

---

31 This article was originally published in September 2000. What made the formation of a national unity government possible in 1999 was the significant weakening by then of the legitimacy of Oslo Accords and of the chances for the post-conflict agendas outlined above, and the cancellation of the direct election law for prime minister.

one dared oppose him. Relevant discussions and pragmatism were replaced by blindly following the party leader and an overall inability to either formulate policy or develop leadership that could walk the path Rabin had set out. This kind of paralysis of will was typical of Labour, but a similar trend took hold of the Likud party when it elected Benjamin Netanyahu as leader. In other words, one primary result of Rabin's assassination was the internal paralysis of both Israel's main parties that now regressed back into dependency on their leaders and the mythological discourse that helped perpetuate this situation. Neither 'Bibi' the 'magician', nor Barak, who displayed similar elements, invented this kind of leadership: from the first days his government was in place after Rabin's assassination, senior ministers of the party lost all ability to influence Peres in the policies he set out. Like Netanyahu and Barak after him, Peres can be said to have made all his wrong decisions on his own, i.e., without party consultation or a process of checks and balances.

This all occurred in the direct aftermath of Rabin's assassination. As Rabin's path was reversed, the renewed conservative mythological mobilization of 'right' and 'left' prevented people from thinking freely and stymied all open discussion. No one came forward with alternative policies during the elections of 1996, as Peres retracted from implementing the Oslo Accords. He never began 'final status' negotiations in May 1996 as the Oslo Declaration of Principles required (thinking this would harm his chances for re-election), he did not approve the agreement Israel's Yossi Beilin and the Palestinian Authority's Abu Mazen had reached just before Rabin's assassination, and he postponed withdrawing the Israel army from Hebron (al-Khalil). Two prime ministerial candidates debated with each other which of them had the experience necessary to achieve maximum peace and maximum security, but they never put on the table a concrete programme for any final status. The symbols they used were similar, and the colourful phrases they bandied about were near identical, with both sides engaged predominantly in obfuscating their positions. The vote for prime minister reflected the mythological mobilization of 'right' and 'left', a competition 'between our chief and their chief', and saw the return of the demographic structural advantage to the 'right'.

With Rabin dead, the leaders and groups that had started to gear themselves up for the post-conflict agenda and the new party system returned to their home base (Haim Ramon and Amir Peretz to the Labour party, David Levy and Roni Milo to the Likud). The split vote, however, still gave the public a chance to voice its dissatisfaction with both large parties, effectively ensuring that, with the procedural change in the electoral system, the old mythological politics continued to crumble. But the crucial problem was the total lack of a new politics, new parties and new alliances capable of articulating a discourse that would give legitimacy to the process of compromise with the Palestinians and the post-conflict agenda.

This is the root of the crisis that Rabin's assassination provoked: the lack of continuity in leadership, policy design and political articulation. The type of leadership evolving within the parties as represented by personalities like Netanyahu and Barak was a symptom of the crisis and not its cause. Post-Rabin politics encouraged the rise of leaders symbolizing old myths intended to mobilize the support of 'right' and 'left'. For example, Peres can be said to symbolize all the failures of the Labour party since 1977, but because of his experience and seniority he was immediately elected as Labour's leader; Netanyahu is a revisionist 'prince' who is loyal to the myth of *Eretz Yisrael* of the 'right'; Barak is the ultimate symbol of militarism and the myth of security on the 'left'. All of them embody the efforts to preserve the power of the two large parties and to prevent their decline in public opinion.

In order to succeed, these leaders began addressing the public opinion over the head of their parties so as to bolster their personal position of leadership, only accelerating the deterioration of the parties that constituted their power-base. This type of leader easily produces the illusion that he represents a new agenda as election day draws near, but then finds it much harder to keep his promises due to the weakening of his party vis-à-vis parties with post-conflict agendas. The post-conflict situation became the dominant agenda during the 1999 election campaign, when we find the majority of the public voting for parties that presented positions on the major issues that are likely to face the country when—one day—peace will have been achieved: collective identity, culture, ethnicity, religion, economics, etc.

The mutual decline of both parties throughout the 1990s is the most salient phenomenon during the period (from a combined total of 76 Knesset mandates in 1992 to 45 in 1999).[32] The fate of the two mythological parties (still referred to as the two 'large parties') completely depends on their ability to present an attractive candidate for prime minister. Beyond that, the fundamental problem of the two mythological parties is their complete dependence on their leaders (forcefully illustrated by Peres holding on to power—in February 2001 he became foreign minister in the government of Ariel Sharon). This phenomenon results in a problematic, centralized decision making process that no longer represents the electorate. The neutralization of both large parties and the simultaneous aggregation of power in the hands of their prime ministerial candidates (including their direct addressing of the 'people') were the clearest expressions of the crisis in the democratic system caused by the assassination of Rabin and the halting of the democratization process.

Conclusion

In this article I have wanted to outline a theoretical distinction between the democratic processes that take place within the framework of already accepted, agreed-upon rules and procedures and democratization processes that first seek to establish such a framework. Accordingly, I see Rabin as a major figure who led forces, groups and organizations in Israel in a process of democratization before new rules and procedures of the democratic process had come into existence. As I have highlighted, peace is one of the necessary preconditions for the stabilization of democratic institutions, rules and procedures in Israel.

---

32 Mythological mobilization of support reached its height in 1981, when Labour and Likud received a combined total of 95 mandates. It would be misleading, however, to regard these results as measure for comparison. In the elections of 1977, with the first appearance of a centre party, the two large parties received a combined total of only 76 mandates, as in 1992. In the other two elections of the 1980s, they received combined totals of 81 and 85 respectively.

Rabin's assassination brought a halt to both the peace process and democratization because they are inseparable. It was only a coincidence that the assassination attempt succeeded precisely at the symbolic juncture (in time and place) of the peace process and democratization. The linkage between the two processes was forged by the mass demonstration in Tel Aviv in support of peace and against the violent rallies of Jewish settlers and Islamic organizations who opposed peace. At the same demonstration, support for peace and the struggle for democracy were unified for a moment under the banner flown there of 'Yes to Peace, No to Violence'. One anti-democratic activist fired three bullets at both processes. He fired those shots in order to halt the Oslo process, and he succeeded. This article sought to explain how the assassination succeeded in derailing both processes despite the public's great support for them especially in the immediate aftermath of the assassination.

Given the absence of democratic conditions, in particular after Israel imposed military rule upon the Palestinian territories it occupied in 1967, the mythological discourse that evolved in Israel enabled the country's two large parties to mobilize public support by means of symbols that were totally irrelevant to pragmatic issues and their actual policies, in both the political and the socio-economic realms.

Rabin's project led to the liberation of Israeli politics from the paralysis of mythological discourse, whether intentionally or as a pragmatic reaction to changing circumstances. While it is true that the mythological discourse evolved as a result of the anti-democratic realities of the Occupation, it also became a factor that perpetuated the Occupation and prevented it from being dismantled. Rabin's assassination returned Israel to the mythological debate, but with one very serious addition—the growing power of post-conflict parties and agendas detached from and unable to legitimate the process of reconciliation with the Palestinians.

This lies at the bottom of the political crisis that has characterized Israel ever since Rabin's assassination: just when it was possible to imagine peace and the process seemed irreversible, Rabin's assassin targeted the democratization process and succeeded in derailing it. Israeli civil society was ready for a post-conflict agenda, but its political leadership and party system still is not.

The major political challenge after Rabin remains changing the party system in order to co-ordinate it with social developments, positions and struggles within the civil society. This co-ordination is expected in democratic regimes, but Israel, as I argue, is a highly deficient democracy. Yigal Amir's success, no matter how temporary, is made especially clear by the periodically recurring violent threats coming from anti-democratic circles each time Israel's political leadership dares to move towards compromise with the Palestinians. That is, the anti-democratic reality engendered by Israel's treatment of the Palestinians has changed little. Thus, the primary challenge that confronts Israel's political leadership is the gap between the process of democratization and the politics of conflict that divides the 'people' into 'right' and 'left'. The challenge is all the greater since the path that Rabin had laid out in order to bridge this gap was destroyed when he himself was murdered.

Naming the Colonizer in Geographical Palestine

Conceptual and Political Double Binds and their Possible Solution

Uri Davis

Introduction

A narrative—any narrative, including academic narrative—is at one and the same time part of the overarching context of constituted human reality and, correlatively, a representation of the power relationships and intentions of individuals, organizations and political parties acting within this context. In other words, as a representation, narrative reflects an existing power system—including the activity necessary to maintain that system—as well as the intended political efforts to change and reform it.

Economic, social and political action is thought and imagined, inter alia, in conceptual narrative, and the importance of the narrative is in that it simultaneously and correlatively conceptualizes both the existing social and political reality—as well as the power relations obtaining therein—and the intentions and the value orientations of the narrators.

The emphasis on clarity and accurate (politically correct) conceptual definitions is thereby not motivated by the phenomenological or semantic interests of the authors alone, but also and typically by their political and pragmatic commitments.

The purpose of this paper is to make a contribution towards the constitution of an academic and political narrative on the subject of the 1948 Palestine refugees that does not implode into a conceptual and moral self-contradiction. Needless to say, developing such a narrative is of particular significance for individuals, organizations and political parties in the Middle East and elsewhere who are committed to act for a reform of the existing power relations in the region and work to see them replaced with democratic regimes predicated on the principles of separation of religion from the state, equality of rights and reciprocity.

As noted above, economic, social and political action is thought and imagined, inter alia, in conceptual narrative. In order to project an alternative political future predicated on democratic power relations it is necessary to formulate an academic and political narrative that is able to represent such a reform as a worthwhile objective in consistent terms.

Thus, it is incumbent upon individuals, organizations and political parties who are committed to help such a reform come true to construct such a narrative as reflects their intentions as clearly as possible. Words, as we all well know, can illuminate as well as veil. As an academic and a documentalist, it may be in order for me to underline the observation that it is only in the relationship between text and context that we can hope to find enlightenment.

Assuming the characterization of the Israeli-Palestinian conflict as an inter-communal conflict—i.e., not an inter-state conflict, but a colonial conflict between the colonized native or indigenous people and the colonial people originating from the Zionist immigration to Palestine—there are no serious conceptual difficulties in identifying the colonized people, the people dispossessed in the course of the conflict, the Palestinian-Arab people. On the other hand, there remains a persistent conceptual difficulty, which haunts most projects critical of political Zionism, namely, the inability of critics of political Zionism to correctly name the said colonial people. Who are the colonial people? Are they the 'Jewish people'? The 'Israeli people'? The 'Israeli-Jewish people'?

And there is the added difficulty of laying out a conceptual framework in terms of which a solution can be developed to the Israeli-Palestinian conflict based on the principles of separation of religion from the state, equality of rights and reciprocity. Reciprocity between which parties? Between Jews on the one part, Christians on the second part and Muslims on the third part? Between Jews on the one part and Arabs on the second part? Between Israelis and Palestinians?

In this paper I wish to suggest that a possible resolution of these difficulties could be developed by reviving the term 'Hebrew' as an appropriate politically correct—that is, not a Zionist—name for the designation of the people originating from the Zionist immigration to Palestine. I present this paper as part of an ongoing effort to conceptualize a terminological frame of reference to discuss a solution to the conflict that is not a political Zionist solution, but one that conforms to the values of the Universal Declaration of Human Rights.

The analysis presented below is inspired by the success of the European Economic Community to move via the Maastricht Treaty of 1992 towards greater European Union, and the transformation of the Apartheid Republic of South Africa into a democratic South Africa. This paper is not intended as a descriptive reading. It is normative par excellence and directed at those among the intellectual and political elites in the region and beyond who are interested in helping create a new political narrative that will be compatible with democratic values, and who are committed to contribute in thought and action to the transition of the Middle East as a whole, and of individual states separately and together, from confessionalism—the supremacy of the religious community over the state—to democracy—the supremacy of the values of the Universal Declaration of Human Rights over the state.

It is in order, therefore, that at this point I make explicit the normative orientation that underpins my work, including this paper. I am indebted to Stanley Diamond for his teaching and Yeshayahu Leibowitz for his writings.

I understand secularism to be the principle of separation between religion (Mosque, Church, Synagogue) and the state. Secularism so understood says nothing about the existence (or otherwise) of God or the origins of human values. But it does say something important about the state: the state, being a human construct, has no value in and of itself. Its only significance is as a tool, an instrument to implement given values, and as such it may or may not deserve various degrees of respect. The proper subject of human loyalty is values. Loyalty to the state, the worship of a human construct, is the secular equivalent of idolatry. State worship, or loyalty to the state, is represented, inter alia, in the violation of the rights of the individual and the abrogation of the principle of equality before the law in the name of the alleged supremacy of reasons of state and the interests of a putative nation. In contemporary political terminology this is called fascism.

I take my normative point of departure from the United Nations Universal Declaration of Human Rights (UHDR) of 1948 and I declare that my personal and professional loyalties are to the values represented in this Declaration. I regard the state to be an instrument whose proper use is the enhancement of human welfare in terms of the said values and whenever there arises a conflict between loyalty to the values of the UHDR and respect for the law of the state, the values of the UHDR ought to take precedence. It may be in order to obey the state: it is never in order to be loyal to the state.

In the best tradition of critical anthropology I propose to begin with the deconstruction of the identity label the writer of this paper carries himself, namely, 'Palestinian Hebrew anti-Zionist Jew of Dual Israeli and British Citizenship'. I will give an explication of each term included in the title above in reverse order, starting with 'citizenship'.

Citizenship versus Identity

I suggest that citizenship be conceptualized as a certificate, a datum. Conceptualizing citizenship in this way underlines the distinction between citizenship on the one hand and identity on the other, notably secularized tribal identity.

As will be discussed specifically below, tribal identity is an emotion, a feeling, a fact of consciousness, whereas citizenship, I suggest, is a datum, a certificate. One can touch and observe one's citizenship: being a certificate it can be held in one's hand. Unlike orthodox religious identity, one cannot touch or observe one's secularized tribal identity.

For instance, secular Jews primarily 'feel' their identity to be Jewish, whereas orthodox Jews primarily act out theirs. 'Jewish identity' for secular Jews is primarily a fact of consciousness, while for orthodox Jews it is primarily a matter of observance. Conducting their life in conformity with the precepts of religious law, for orthodox Jews 'Jewish identity' is primarily observable behaviour—not a 'feeling'. They do not have an identity crisis such as the one haunting secular Judaism. For them the question 'Who is a Jew' does not arise, let alone represent a problem.

The certificate of citizenship regulates the relationship between the individual and the state. In western liberal democratic states, citizenship represents a legal recognition of a basic claim of the individual vis-à-vis the state of which he or she is a citizen, namely, a legal recognition by the state of the right of the individual to equal access to the resources of the state: equal access to the civil resources of the state (e.g., standing before courts of law, civil service appointments), the power-political resources (e.g., vote and elections), the social services resources (e.g., welfare, education) and the material resources (e.g., land, water).

Citizenship in western liberal democratic states is not a certificate of loyalty to the state or to the regime. It is a certificate of rights. Conceived in this way, dual, or multiple, citizenship does not entail dual loyalties or multiple loyalties. All dual or multiple citizenship entails is the recognized status of the individual concerned to the right of abode in two or more states and the right of equal access to the resources of the two or more states where he or she is a citizen. A citizen of a single state has the right of abode in one state. A dual or multiple citizen has the right of abode in two or more states. There is little doubt that dual or multiple citizenship improves the choice of the individual and should be viewed as a good thing, not otherwise. In this context it is remarkable that, rhetorics of Arab unity notwithstanding, the provisions of the League of Arab States—notably, the Agreement of 5 April 1954 on Provisions Regarding Citizenship Among Member States of the League of Arab States—prohibit dual or multiple Arab state–Arab state citizenship.

In the final analysis, whereas citizenship determines the rights of the individual in the state where he or she is citizen, secular tribal identity determines the ethnic affiliation of the individual. The coupling in law of tribal identity with citizenship results in ethnocracy, not democracy—in Apartheid, not nationalism.

Israeli/British

In the identity construct above the term 'British' does not designate an identity. It designates a legal relationship to the state of the United Kingdom. Likewise the term 'Israeli' does not designate an identity. It also designates a legal relationship, namely, a legal relationship to the State of Israel. The United Kingdom is an old state, founded with the 1066 Norman conquest of the Isles of Albion. The State of Israel is a new state, founded in 1948 with the Zionist conquest of the land of Palestine.

'British' does not mean 'English'. Under the sovereignty of the United Kingdom there is one, British, citizenship but there are at least four nationalities (English, Scottish, Welsh and Irish). In terms of this analysis, any individual who is a citizen of the United Kingdom is British. The United Kingdom is a democratic state in a way that Israel is not because it has one citizenship for all British citizens, regardless of national origin (English, Scottish, Welsh, Irish or other). All British citizens are equal before UK law.

'Israeli' does not mean 'Jewish'. Some 20 per cent of the citizens of the State of Israel are non-Jews, most of them being Palestinian–Arabs. In terms of this analysis, any individual who is a citizen of the State of Israel is an Israeli. Israel is a bi-national state, but under Israeli sovereignty there is not one Israeli citizenship for the two nationalities, rather, there are two unequal citizenships: one for the so-called 'Jewish nation', representing full access to the resources of the state (including land and water), and one for the so-called 'non-Jewish (Gentile) nation(s)', representing access to only some resources of the state (excluding land and water). In fact, under Israeli sovereignty there are at least three classes of citizenship, one for 'Jewish' citizens, one for 'non-Jewish' citizens and one—nullified—citizenship for 'absentees', namely the Palestine refugees of 1948 (not to mention the abomination of the truncated citizenship of the internally displaced persons, 'present-absentee' Palestinian Arab citizens of Israel) who today together with their descendants total over five million people outside and inside the State of Israel. Under the terms of the 1947 UN partition plan for Palestine—i.e., into two states with Jerusalem as *corpus separatum* under an international regime administered by the UN, all three components bound together by economic union—they are all entitled to the citizenship of the 'Jewish state'. Israel abrogated this right. Before legislating the Law of Return in July 1950, the Knesset (Israeli Parliament) in March passed the Absentees' Property Law stripping away the right of the 1948 Palestinian refugees to Israeli citizenship and to their massive rural and urban properties (not to speak of bank accounts) inside Israel with the view to making these properties vacant for new Jewish settlement.[1] It is estimated that at least 70 per cent of the total land area of pre-1967 Israel is Palestinian refugee property, classified in Israeli law as 'absentees property'.

Jew

Viewed from an orthodox Jewish point of departure, the answer to the question 'Who is a Jew' is simple and straightforward: a Jew is any person who submits to the 613 orthodox Jewish precepts, the codex of Jewish orthodox religious law (Halakha) as formulated in the standard text of *Shulhan Arukh*, who is born to a Jewish mother or who has converted to Judaism according to orthodox religious law.

As noted above, an orthodox Jew has no Jewish identity problem. His or her identity is not primarily a fact of consciousness, but a fact of behaviour; not a feeling, but an action. The Halakha determines his or her life from birth to death—from daybreak to sunset; from week to week; month to month; season to season; year by year. It determines how he or she dresses, eats, makes love, celebrates, mourns.

The problems for Jewish identity, as for any other tribal identity, begin with secularization. The only viable answer to the question 'Who is a (secular) Jew' is: 'anyone who says that he or she is a Jew' or 'anyone who "feels" that he or she is Jewish.' The attempt, notably by the legislator of the State of Israel, the Knesset, to formulate a different answer collapsed into echoing the Nazi definition of 'Who is a Jew'.

1   On the Absentees' Property Law, see above p. 126, n. 58.

For the Nazi state and the Nazi occupation authorities a 'Jew' was defined as any person with 'Jewish blood' in their family three generations back. For the Israeli Knesset, a 'Jew' for the purpose of the Israeli Law of Return, 1950, is defined as follows: '4B For the purpose of this Law, "Jew" means a person who was born of a Jewish mother or who [...] has become converted to Judaism and who is not a member of another religion.'

And, again echoing the Nazi definition, the privileges and rights accorded in law to persons recognized by the said Law of Return as 'Jews'—notably, the virtually unhindered right of immigration, citizenship and settlement in Israel—are also vested in the children and the grandchildren of Jews, the spouse of a Jew, the spouse of a child of a Jew and the spouse of a grandchild of a Jew, with the exception of a person who was born a Jew and willingly changed his religion.

In other words, unlike the orthodox definition of 'Who is a Jew', the foundation of the secular legal definition of a 'Jew' in the State of Israel for the purpose of the Law of Return, 1950 (the mainstay of Israel's Citizenship Law, 1952) rests not on observance of religious Law, nor on Jewish sentiment, but rather on biology ('born to a Jewish mother'). The Jewish state in the political Zionist sense of the term is founded on the idea of a state that aims to guarantee in law and in practice an ethnic majority of citizens who are recognized, in the first instance, as being biologically Jewish. The racialist logic of the Nazi definition of 'Who is a Jew' has thus been incorporated into Israeli legislation. Thus, the Jewish State in the political Zionist sense of the term is not and has never been a democracy in the Western liberal sense of the term.

Anti-Zionist

Zionism is a political programme embodied in the institutions of the Zionist organization, founded at the First Zionist Congress in Basel in 1897. The aims of political Zionism were first formulated in this First Zionist Congress ('establish for the Jewish people a home in Palestine, secured under public law') and since then have been reformulated by successive such congresses a number of times, the last formulation to date being in the 'Jerusalem Programme'. The executive arms of the Zionist Congress include the World Zionist Organization (WZO), the Jewish Agency (JA) and the Jewish National Fund (JNF). An individual or a political party should be defined as Zionist if they support the aims of Zionism and/or are affiliated to the WZO, the JA, the JNF or any other part of the Zionist organization.

Zionism is not Judaism. Zionism is a (negative) political and practical programme which until 1948 worked to establish a Jewish state in the land of Palestine and since 1948 works to consolidate the continued existence of this state, the State of Israel, as a Jewish state in the political Zionist sense of the term, namely, as a state that aims to guarantee in law and in practice an ethnic majority of such people who are identified by the state as 'Jews' (see above). Thus, again, the State of Israel is not a democracy in the Western liberal sense of the term. It is an ethnocracy, an Apartheid state. The political Zionist idea of a 'Jewish state' is not and has never been compatible with the liberal idea of a democratic state.

Judaism is alleged to be a divine religion, not a man-made political programme. There is an important part of orthodox Judaism (Neturei Karta) that regards Zionism to be the worst expression of Jewish religious apostasy. They are anti-Zionist Jews. Secular humanists ought to regard political Zionism to be a form of Apartheid colonialism. To be anti-Zionist means to be opposed to the political programme of the Zionist organization. To be anti-Jewish means to be a racist. Anti-Zionism is not anti-Semitism, just as in South Africa anti-Apartheid has not been anti-White. Thus one might add that, notwithstanding its subsequent nullification in December 1991, the UN General Assembly, recalling the UN Declaration on the Elimination of All Forms of Racism and Racial Discrimination, was correct to determine that Zionism is a form of racism and racial discrimination (Resolution 3379 of November 1975).

Hebrew

For the purpose of this paper, the term 'Hebrew' designates a language. Hebrew is also the national language of those citizens of the State of Israel whose origin is the Zionist colonial settlement in Palestine. If, for the purpose of this paper, we define the term 'Arab' as any person whose national language is Arabic and 'Hebrew' as any person whose national language is Hebrew, it is possible—as will be shown below—to construct identity equations that are not Zionist and meet the requirement of separation of religion from the state, equality of rights and reciprocity in terms which allow us to identify both today's colonized people and today's colonizer people as tomorrow's citizens on equal footing of a future democratic state.

Palestine/Palestinian

I take as point of departure the modern political definition of the term 'Palestine' as the territory whose political boundaries were defined by the League of Nations in the 1922 Mandate for Palestine the Principal Allied Powers had granted Britain. There is no similar consensus regarding the definition of 'Who is a Palestinian'.

For the purpose of this paper the term 'Palestinian' is defined as: (1) any person who has a predecessor born in British Mandate Palestine as defined above, regardless of that person's place of birth; (2) any person born in geographical Palestine as defined above; (3) any person married to a Palestinian (man or woman); (4) all the citizens of the State of Israel, including all those identified today by the State as Arab citizens as well as all those identified as Jewish citizens.

It is in order to note in this connection that UN Resolution 181 of 29 November 1947 recommending the partition of geographical Palestine into two states, one 'Jewish' and one 'Arab', with Jerusalem as *corpus separatum* under an international regime administered by the UN, all three components bound together by economic union, was *not* pronounced and was *not* intended as a license for the war crime of mass expulsion of the indigenous Palestinian Arab people from the territories of which Israel took control in the course and in the aftermath of the 1948 war, nor as endorsement of political Zionist ethnic cleansing. The UN Resolution 181 *did not* envision a 'Jewish state' ethnically cleansed of all Arabs, nor an 'Arab state' ethnically cleansed of all Jews. Quite the contrary, Resolution 181 envisaged two essentially democratic bi-national states, with Jerusalem as *corpus separatum,* bound together by economic union, one with 'Arab' trappings (such as, I would have thought, the first line on road signs being in Arabic, the second in Hebrew and the third in English) and the second with 'Hebrew' trappings (such as, I would have thought, the first line on road signs being in Hebrew, the second in Arabic and the third in English). Under the terms of Resolution 181 *all* Arabs ordinarily resident in the territories designated for the 'Jewish state' would have been entitled to 'Jewish state' citizenship and *all* Jews ordinarily resident in the territories designated for the 'Arab state' would have been entitled to 'Arab state' citizenship. Both states were to have democratic constitutions and Resolution 181 includes a Declaration to the appropriate effect.

Conclusion:
1948 Palestine Refugees, Return and Compensation

It is now possible not only to reject the political Zionist designation of the people originating from the Zionist immigration to Palestine, but also to give a politically correct name—that is, not a Zionist name—to the said people and lay out a conceptual framework for a solution to the conflict that is based on the principles of separation of religion from the state, equality of rights and reciprocity—a democratic solution, an anti-Zionist solution.

In parenthesis, it is in order to note that collective punishments are illegal under international law and incompatible with the values of the UDHR. A child born in a Jewish settlement to Jewish settler parents carries no guilt for such crimes as may have been committed by his or her parents. The right of a Jewish child born in the illegal settlement of Alon Moreh in the West Bank to live in the country of his or her birth is equal to the right of an Arab child born in Nablus to live there. The Jewish child has an equal right to live there—not to be a settler there. To live there as citizen on equal footing to the Arab citizen—not to occupy and dispossess. The child of a settler family may choose to leave the country when the regime is liberated from political Zionism and is reformed into democracy and Alon Moreh is transformed from a settlement designated

'For Jews Only' into a locality open to all, but every effort should be made that he or she should not do so. The African National Congress (ANC) won the battle for democracy in South Africa because it saw it to be a matter of principle that the ANC regard itself not as the representative of Black South Africans but the democratic political home for all South Africans, whites and non-whites on equal footing. The PLO lost the struggle for democracy in Palestine because to date it regards itself to be the sole legitimate representative of the Arab Palestinian people—not of all Palestinians, Arabs and non-Arabs on equal footing.

So what is the politically correct alternative name, that is, not a Zionist name, for the colonial people originating from the Zionist immigration to Palestine that is consistent with the principles of separation of religion from the state, equality of rights and reciprocity?

The political Zionist designation of a 'Jewish people' must be rejected on the grounds that Judaism is a term of reference properly designating a religious community—not the collective of citizens of any given state. The term 'Israeli people' must be rejected on the grounds that Israel does not have one single citizenship for all, but, as we saw, at least three unequal citizenships, one for 'Jewish' citizens, one for 'non-Jewish' citizens and one—nullified—citizenship for 'absentees', i.e., the Palestine refugees of 1948, not to mention the truncated citizenship of the internally displaced persons, the 'present-absentee' Palestinian Arab citizens of Israel. And 'Israeli-Jewish people' must be rejected on grounds that it represents a blatant violation of the principle of separation of religion from the state in that it weds a political term 'Israeli'—namely, 'pertaining to the State of Israel'—with a confessional term, 'Jew'.

On the other hand, the name proposed here for the people originating in the Zionist immigration to Palestine, namely, the 'Palestinian Hebrew people', has, I submit, considerable merit. It must be pointed out at the outset that it is not suggested here that the proposed name and the classifications detailed below are acceptable today to the mainstream of those citizens of the State of Israel who the State classifies as 'Jews'. It is, however, suggested that they might be accepted by a future political coalition that—applying where appropriate the lessons learned from the South African experience—will generate and oversee the dismantling of the Zionist legal structures in Israel and have them replaced with democratic structures.

The political correctness of the term comes into sharp focus when one attempts to imagine and spell out democratic alternatives predicated on the principles of separation of religion from the state, equality of rights and reciprocity, that could be better than the Zionist future envisaged for the country of Palestine and for the region of the Middle East as a whole.

Thus, for instance, under the sovereignty of a future democratic State of Palestine, or a future democratic State of Israel (assuming that the Zionist State of Israel is transformed into a democratic state like Apartheid South Africa was transformed under the leadership of Nelson Mandela into democratic South Africa), there will reside on equal footing at least two peoples, the Palestinian-Arab people—consisting of all Palestinian Arabs, citizens of the State of Israel and those declared 'absentees' under the Absentees' Property Law, 1950, and their descendants—as well as the Palestinian-Hebrew people—consisting of all persons who are citizens or permanent residents of the State of Israel and were classified as 'Jew' under that state's Law of Return, 1950—not as colonizer people versus colonized people, but on the basis of equality before the law and reciprocity of rights. The Absentees Property Law and the Law of Return, both of 1950, will be abolished. There will be one citizenship: Palestinian or Israeli or, should the solution of the conflict result in a federated state, dual Palestinian and Israeli citizenship. All 1948 Palestine refugees will have their right to return to all and any part of geographical Palestine, to the title of their properties inside and outside the State of Israel, and to compensations secured and underpinned by their rights as citizens, either Palestinian or Israeli or dual Palestinian-Israeli citizens.

In such a framework, the Identity Card of an Arab resident of the State of Palestine would read:

Citizenship (*al-Jinsiyya/Ezrahut*):	Palestinian
Peoplehood (*al-Shaab/'Am*):	Palestinian-Arab
Nationality (*al-Qawmiyya/Le'um*):	Arab
Religion (*al-Din/Dat*):	None/Muslim/Christian/ Jewish/Other

The Identity Card of a Hebrew resident of the State of Palestine would read:

Citizenship (*Ezrahut/al-Jinsiyya*):   Palestinian
Peoplehood ('*Am/al-Shaab*):   Palestinian-Hebrew
Nationality (*Le'um/al-Qawmiyya*):   Hebrew
Religion (*Dat/al-Din*):   None/Muslim/Christian/
                                        Jewish/Other

The Identity Card of an Arab resident of the State of Israel would read:

Citizenship (*al-Jinsiyya/Ezrahut*):   Israeli
Peoplehood (*al-Shaab/'Am*):   Palestinian-Arab
Nationality (*al-Qawmiyya/Le'um*):   Arab
Religion (*al-Din/Dat*):   None/Muslim/Christian/
                                        Jewish/Other

The Identity Card of a Hebrew resident of the State of Israel would read:

Citizenship (*Ezrahut/al-Jinsiyya*):   Israeli
Peoplehood ('*Am/al-Shaab*):   Palestinian-Hebrew
Nationality (*Le'um/al-Qawmiyya*):   Hebrew
Religion (*Dat/al-Din*):   None/Muslim/Christian/
                                        Jewish/Other

It is now possible for us to answer the questions posited in the 'Introduction', namely 'Who are the colonial people? The Jewish people? The Israeli people? The Israeli-Jewish people?' It is now possible for us not only to reject the terms 'Jewish people', 'Israeli people', 'Israeli-Jewish people' as inappropriate, but also point to a positive and constructive alternative and say that the future democratic State of Palestine or the future democratic State of Israel or the future democratic federal state of Palestine and Israel, after abolishing the 1950 Absentees' Property Law and Israeli Law of Return, will recognize the Palestinian-Hebrew people, namely, all current citizens of the State of Israel who are classified as 'Jews' and their descendants, not as colonizers, not as settlers, not as occupiers, but as equal citizens under the law on equal footing to the Palestinian-Arab people, including all current Arab citizens of Israel and all Arabs currently classified by Israel as 'absentees'.

References

African National Congress, *Freedom Charter,*
    http://www.anc.org.za/ancdocs/history/charter.html
Asad, Talal, *Anthropology and the Colonial Encounter* (London: Ithaca Press, and Atlantic Highlands, NJ: Humanities Press, 1973; repr. 1975).
Brenner, Lenny, *Zionism in the Age of Dictators* (London: Croom Helm, 1983).
Davis, Uri, *Citizenship and the State: A Comparative Study of Citizenship Legislation in Israel, Jordan, Palestine, Syria and Lebanon* (Reading: Ithaca Press, 1997).
Diamond, Stanley, *In Search of the Primitive: A Critique of Civilization* (New Brunswick, NJ: Transaction Books, 1974).
Leibowitz, Yeshayahu, *Judaism. Human Values and the Jewish State* (Cambridge, Mass: Harvard University Press, 1992).
Orr, Akiva, *Israel: Politics, Myths and Identity Crisis* (London: Pluto Press, 1994).

One-State Palestine

Past, Present and Future

Ilan Pappé

A clear sense of 'Palestine' as a coherent geo-political unit dates back—both Palestinian and Zionist narratives will grant us this—to at least 3000 BC. Roughly stretching from across the Jordan River to the Mediterranean and running from the mountains of the Lebanon to the Sinai desert, it was then, and for another 1,500 years, the land of the Canaanites. In around 1500 BCE Canaan fell under Egyptian rule, not for the last time in its history, and then came successively under Philistine (1200–975), Israelite (1000–923), Phoenician (923–700), Assyrian (700–612), Babylonian (586–539), Persian (539–332), Macedonian (332–63), Roman (63 BCE–636 CE), Arab (636–1200), Crusader (1099–1291), Ayyubi (1187–1253), Mamluk (1253–1516) and Ottoman rule (1517–1917).

Administratively, each of these ruling powers may have divided the land in ways that suited its own political culture and time, but in ethnic, cultural and religious terms the country's population itself (apart from some shifts during the early Roman and early Arab periods) remained much the same as its society moved through the different historical eras. And, as even a cursory journey into Palestine's more recent past reveals, the deeper layers of ancient existence on which it rests help explain the emergence and consolidation of the unique features that today we recognize as typically Palestinian: the dialects people have in common, the traditions and customs they share, the culture and poetry they cherish, and of course the local patriotism (*wataniyya*) that binds them together.

In modern times, colonialist and, later, nationalist narratives singled out and then manipulated one of the above historical periods to justify their taking control of the country. Not unlike the Crusaders before them, the historical chronology was co-opted in this way both by European colonialism and, arriving on its coat tails, the Zionist movement. But the Zionists were different. Originating in Europe and first emerging on the shores of Palestine in the early 1880s, these immigrant Jewish nationalists put the historical reference at the very heart of their colonization of Palestine in order to conquer the country and claim it for themselves. This is why they talked about the 'return' to and the 'redemption' of a land that once upon a time had been ruled by 'Israelites'. As the above historical checklist makes clear, this means they singled out a mere eight decades from a total of four millennia of morphological layers while mythologizing the country as the 'land of the Bible'.[1]

---

1   We are here, of course, in the realm of 'nationalism', so powerfully re-conceptualized in the 1980s and 90s by scholars such as Ernest Gellner, Eric Hobsbawm, Benedict Anderson, and many others; for a brief outline, see my 'Fear, Victimhood, Self and Other' and the references there, and the articles of Ehud Adiv and Issam Nassar in this volume. What comes strongly to the fore in their works is 'the element of artifact, innovation and social engineering which enters into the making of nations' and the insight that 'nationalism comes before nations. Nations do not make states and nationalisms but the other way round'; see Eric Hobsbawm, *Nations and Nationalism since 1780. Programme, Myth, Reality* (Cambridge: Cambridge University Press, 1990), p. 10. Somewhat further on (pp. 47-48), Hobsbawm works this out as follows:
'Again, while the Jews, scattered throughout the world for some millennia, never ceased to identify themselves, wherever they were, as members of a special people quite distinct from the various brands of non-believers among whom they lived, at no stage, at least since the return from the Babylonian captivity, does this seem to have implied a serious desire for a Jewish political state, let alone a territorial state, until a Jewish nationalism was invented at the very end of the nineteenth century by analogy with the newfangled western nationalism. It is entirely illegitimate to identify the Jewish links with the ancestral land of Israel, the merit deriving from pilgrimages there, or the hope of return there when the Messiah came—as he so obviously had *not* come in the view of the Jews—with the desire to gather all Jews into a modern territorial state situated on the ancient Holy Land. One might as well argue that good Muslims, whose highest ambition is to make the pilgrimage to Mecca, in doing so really intend to declare themselves citizens of what has now become Saudi Arabia.'

Since those who ruled the country before the onset of nationalism were quite often the vassals or local representatives of empires with faraway capitals in Baghdad, Rome, Cairo and Istanbul, any form of local sovereignty was out of the question. But sovereignty, of course, did become the issue with the break-up of empires in the early and mid-twentieth century and the emergence amidst their collapsing structures of individual nation states; that is, when either through peaceful means or wars of liberation the indigenous peoples achieved independence. Where the vestiges of imperialism or colonialism refused to let go—as for example in the case of white settlers' communities in the Maghrib or South Africa—national wars of liberation lingered on. In places where the indigenous populations had been annihilated by invading settler societies—as happened in the Americas and Australasia—the latter became that country's 'nation'.

As many of those writing on nationalism see it, the take-over by the new nation states was generally wedded to a longer process of achieving social and cultural cohesiveness. Looking at the Middle East, we find that the nation states that emerged upon the disintegration of the Ottoman Empire were partly the result of a political sleight-of-hand: Britain and France drew their borders but then withheld independence through the Mandates they were able to impose following the first world war. As a result, these Arab lands-turned-nation-states differed in political structure and demographic composition. Some, like Iraq and Lebanon, contained heterogeneous ethnic, religious and cultural communities, which naturally encumbered the nation building process. Others were more fortunate in that the relative homogeneity they enjoyed facilitated their cultural and economic cohesiveness. An independent Palestine would have belonged to the latter model, as it developed in Egypt and Tunisia, and not to the more intractable cases of Iraq and Lebanon.

By the turn of the twenty-first century the political map of the world has consolidated in such a way that there are only a few instances left where a state's nation building process is as yet unfinished or a nation has been denied its right to sovereignty. One of these cases, and possibly the cruelest and most distressing one, is Palestine. Palestine has as yet never been allowed to take its rightful place as a sovereign nation among the nations of the world and as an independent state among all the other Middle Eastern Arab states that achieved independence in the last century, the tiny emirates along the shores of the Persian Gulf included. Instead, an immigrant settler society took over nearly all of the land, expelled most of the indigenous population, set up their own state and proclaimed its independence.

The present geo-political reality—whereby Israel stands for Palestine and which most of the western world seems to accept as normal—not only runs contrary to the history of the country but also totally ignores the political rights of the native Palestinian population, who after all make up the vast majority (counted together with the refugee communities, twice as many Palestinians live inside Palestine's borders—Israel, the West Bank and Gaza—than Israeli Jews). One of the major reasons why the conflict continues to rage is the huge gap that exists between how the outside (Western) world views 'reality' in Palestine and how that reality is experienced on the ground by the Palestinians themselves. Any hope that this torn country may one day see reconciliation and peace can only lie in collapsing this gap between 'perceived' and 'lived' reality. As I see it, much depends on successfully countering the ideological and historical distortions that underpin the Zionists' ongoing dispossession of another people.

What I want to do in this article is trace the pattern of continuity we find in the modern history of Palestine (as of the late Ottoman period) and briefly highlight the distinctive economic and political features and cultural cohesiveness that historically mark it out as a geo-political entity of its own. What I am after is a succinct outline of both the political structures as they existed through time and those that were then, at a given moment, offered as alternatives or imposed as dictates. Finally, I will sketch a solution that I and others envision as offering some light at the end of the tunnel.

It is with the appearance on the scene in the nineteenth century of nationalism, the intervention of European colonialism and, directly connected with the two, the decline of the Ottoman Empire that a clearer sense arises of what Palestine meant and stood for in political terms, not only for the people inhabiting the land but also—more fatefully—for those outsiders who had set their eyes on the country. Our first stop, therefore, is the end of the nineteenth century.

Palestine in the Late Ottoman Period

The above is the exact title of a book published in 1986 through my own university (Haifa).[2] In it, more than twenty-five historians, most of them Israeli Jews, set out to reconstruct life in Palestine during the final decades of Ottoman rule. Palestinian historians would have no problem with this definition of the country between the 1850s and the end of the first world war as 'Palestine in the late Ottoman period': administratively divided into three Ottoman provinces, this was the same historical geo-political unit I outlined above as Palestine, and it was overwhelmingly Arab in ethnicity, more than 95 per cent of a total population of (in 1882) half a million.[3] But Palestinian readers would find it bizarre to be told, already in the volume's introduction, that in the late Ottoman period there were *two* communities in Palestine, Jewish and Arab, 'which began aspiring toward national liberation' and that, therefore, both groups were anti-Ottoman: it was 'only natural that much of their protest and grievances be directed against their Ottoman masters.'[4] Any naive reader is likely to get the impression

---

2   David Kushner (ed.), *Palestine in the Late Ottoman Period. Political, Social and Economic Transformation* (Jerusalem: Yad Izhak Ben-Zvi & Leiden: E.J. Brill, 1986)

3   Among them the Jewish community, the ancient *Yishuv*, who considered themselves ethnically Arab; in his *Haifa in the Late Ottoman Period, 1864–1914. A Muslim Town in Transition* (Leiden: E.J. Brill, 1998), Mahmoud Yazbak puts it as follows (p. 212): 'Ottoman Jews nearly all lived in urban centers. Usually few in numbers, they settled within a town's Muslim quarter of which they formed an integral part. When with the Tanzimat they were granted religious autonomy and at the same time given access to positions in the administrative institutions of the Ottoman empire, this further deepened their sense of belonging to the wider Muslim society. It also meant that it was natural for them to address the legal and administrative institutions which that society put at their service.' It was only the few thousand European Jewish settlers, who had begun arriving in Palestine for the first time in 1882, who regarded not just their religion but also their ethnicity as Jewish.

4   Kushner (ed.), *Palestine in the Late Ottoman Period*, p. x.

from this that Palestine during the late Ottoman period and for centuries, if not millennia, before that, meant a country where there were
equal numbers of Jews and Arabs who had the same historical claims
and national vision but who disliked each other and the Ottomans.
Historical fabrication at its fabricating best, of course: in this typical
Zionist narrative of the mid 1980s, Palestine is largely already Israel.
Partition is already in the air.

We need Palestinian scholarship to remind us that even in 1917 the
overwhelming majority of the people in Palestine were Palestinians—by now 600,000—together with a few thousand foreign
Western settlers hoping to colonize the land on behalf of Christian
millenarianism or Jewish nationalism.[5] Indeed, one year later the
British officially called the country Palestine, thus turning it also into a
clear *political* unit. But, at the same time, through the accelerating pace
of foreign dispossession and colonization their imperialist rule encouraged, they also allowed Palestine to be transformed into an historical case study precariously located somewhere between the
annihilated indigenous populations and the liberated colonies that are
Europe's imperialist legacy. It is still there today.

For most of the Ottoman period, Palestine was administratively divided
into the three main sub-districts (*sanjaqs*) of Acre, Nablus and Jerusalem, which culturally and economically were closely connected
through their shared history and traditions.[6] That the people themselves were very much aware of the similarities they had in common

---

5   On the gradual 'opening up' of the 'Holy Land', Europe's penetration of Pal-
    estine during the second half of the nineteenth century, see Alexander Schölch's
    classic study, *Palestine in Transformation, 1856-1882. Studies in Social, Economic
    and Political Development*, translated by William C Young and Michael C.
    Gerrity (Washington, DC: Institute for Palestine Studies, 1993; repr. 2006).
6   See, e.g., Rashid Khalidi, *Palestinian Identity. The Construction of a Modern
    National Consciousness* (New York: Columbia University Press, 1997); Beshara
    Doumani, *Rediscovering Palestine. The Merchants and Peasants of Jabal Nablus,
    1700–1900* (Berkeley: University of California Press, 1995), and Pappé, *A
    Modern History of Palestine. One Land, Two Peoples* (Cambridge: Cambridge
    University Press, 2004), pp. 14-16.

and the internal cohesion these entailed explains why the inhabitants of Jabal Nablus, for example, protested vociferously when the Ottomans in 1858 annexed the Nablus district to the *vilayet* (province) of Beirut. Oppressing the massive protest movement that erupted turned into a bloodbath whereby 3,000 people lost their lives (according to the British consul in Jerusalem; however, he was known to have exaggerated in the past, so the figure may well have been lower). In the final decades of their rule the Ottomans allowed the Arab elites to play a more intensive role in the politics of the country, and before long cities such as Jerusalem, Jaffa, Haifa and Nablus became foci of social and, later, national, unity.[7] As all the Arab lands around Palestine that by now had fallen under the spell of nationalism, Palestinians began to think of their country as a *wataniyya*—a geo-political locality—within a wider *qawmiyya*—the pan-Arab sphere of belonging.

When they took over in 1918, the British did not halt this process, nor did the political structure they imposed collide with the cohesiveness and uniqueness of the indigenous population, as it would do in Iraq. But they also laid the groundwork for the emergence of a different 'Palestine', a dispossessed Palestine, where the Palestinians themselves would be robbed of their land and the country itself would be turned into 'Israel'.

One Palestine, Complete

This, too, is the title of a book by a Zionist historian, Tom Segev.[8] And here too, no Palestinian historiographer would have any objection. But

7   See, e.g., Butrus Abu-Manneh, 'The Rise and fall of the Sanjack of Jerusalem in the Late 19th Century', in G. Ben-Dor (ed.), *The Palestinians and the Middle East Conflict. Studies in their History, Sociology and Politics* (Ramat Gan: Turtledove, 1979), pp. 21-32, reprinted in Ilan Pappé (ed.), *The Israel/Palestine Question* (London and New York: Routledge, 1999), pp. 41-51.
8   Tom Segev, *One Palestine, Complete. Jews and Arabs under the British Mandate* (New York: Henry Holt & Co., 2000). The reference here is to the document the High Commissioner, Herbert Samuel, was made to sign when the British army handed power over to the civil authorities in 1920: 'Received from Major-General Sir Louis J. Bols K.C.B.—One Palestine, Complete' (p. 155).

Segev's English title is misleading: the original Hebrew is sub-titled *Eretz Israel in the Mandatory Period* and nothing could be more typically Zionist than that. Writes Segev: 'Outsiders began to flock to the country by the end of the [19th] century, and it then seemed to awake from its Levantine stupor' (pp. 1–2). His 'One Palestine' is thus also a fabrication: a foreign occupation that Segev wants us to believe was a highly civilized regime that made it possible for the native population to live in relative peace and prosperity—and 'native' here includes the by then still less than the seven or eight per cent of Zionist settlers and colonialists who had been making their way into the country since the 1890s.

Segev is right in one thing: Palestine became more 'complete' because the British continued where the Ottoman reformers had left off when their empire collapsed and welded the three Ottoman sub-districts into 'one country'. As this largely corresponded to the ethnic, cultural and religious fabric on the ground, the move had the acclaim of the local population and met little or no resistance, unlike the unrest that accompanied the making of Iraq, where the British 'unified' three disparate communities—Kurds, Shiites and Sunnis—into the new Iraqi nation state. By 1923 the borders of the new unitary state had been finalized and Mandatory Palestine was a reality.

But it was Palestine's tragedy that as it crystallized as a typical Arab nation state, the political borders the British put in place simultaneously enabled the Zionists to define in concrete geographical terms what they meant by *Eretz Yisrael* (the 'Land of Israel').

In those early years of the British Mandate and incipient Zionist presence, Palestine's indigenous political elites saw their country in terms of a unitary state on the road to independence and democracy, as Iraq and neighbouring Transjordan, and of course Syria and Lebanon under the French.[9] That is, for the majority of the Palestinian lead-

9   Actually, at the time the Arab political elites still envisioned the future of the country more in pan-Arab than Palestinian terms. But the balance of forces on the ground quickly undermined the dream of a pan-Arab entity stretching from Morocco to Iran and dashed even less ambitious plans such as creating a Greater Syria out of the eastern Mediterranean countries (the former Arab Ottoman provinces that made up Bilad al-Sham).

ership and, one assumes, for the population at large as well, Palestine was the national homeland of the Palestinians, a homeland that naturally—because historically—stretched from the Jordan to the Mediterranean. And none of them thought there was any need to stake out a specific claim to this country that was theirs—until they found themselves challenged over 'ownership' by a foreign nationalist movement. Not surprisingly, their first steps onto the diplomatic stage in the global post-1918 political arena were both hesitant and ineffective, especially when seen next to the smoothly operating Europe-grown Zionist movement with its rapidly expanding power base in the US.

The Mandate system promised the new nation states in the Middle East independence and, under the guidance of the League of Nations, was to lead them towards a future based on principles of democracy and self-determination. Ostensibly, this meant that even with their leaders' lack of experience, the Palestinians should have obtained what was rightfully, i.e., democratically, theirs since they obviously formed the vast majority in the country. But the Mandatory charter also incorporated, wholesale, the 1917 Balfour Declaration and, with it, Britain's promise to secure a homeland for the Jews in Palestine. This ran counter to and, in the end, actually thwarted the rights of the Palestinians to *their* homeland. In other words, at the same time that the British declared Palestine 'complete', they introduced the seeds of the country's dismemberment.[10]

10 Nothing illustrates this better than the fact that the first 7 articles of the Mandate Charter are almost exclusively concerned with the establishment of a 'national home for the Jews':
Art. 2: 'The Mandatory shall be responsible for placing the country under such political, administrative and economic conditions as will secure the establishment of the Jewish national home, as laid down in the preamble [...].'
Art. 4: 'An appropriate Jewish agency shall be recognized as a public body for the purpose of advising and co-operating with the Administration of Palestine in such economic, social and other matters as may affect the establishment of the Jewish national home and the interests of the Jewish population in Palestine, and [...] to assist and take part in the development of the county. The Zionist organisation [...] shall be recognised as such agency. It shall take steps in consultation with His

Early eruptions of violence led London to rethink its policy and, in 1928, fresh diplomatic insights coalesced into what we might call the first significant peace initiative to be launched. In a country into which the Zionist settlers were now making steady inroads but where the overwhelming majority of the population (85 per cent by now) remained Palestinian, the British must have felt triumphant when they succeeded in persuading the Executive Committee of the Palestine National Congress—the de-facto government of the Palestinians—to agree to share the country with the Jewish newcomers. It also may explain why, until 1937, the British continued to visualize the future of Palestine as one shared by Arabs and Jews within the one-state paradigm. This meant building an independent state on the basis of parity in the three branches of the executive, legislative and judiciary. Since in this concept Palestine remained at bottom a unitary state, the Palestinian leadership went along with it, in a show of unity rare for a polity generally divided by clannish cleavages of prestige and ancestry.[11]

It would also have been an opportune moment for the two communities to try to co-exist within a political structure acceptable to

Britannic Majesty's Government to secure the co-operation of all Jews who are willing to assist in the establishment of the Jewish national home.'
Art. 5: 'The Mandatory shall be responsible for seeing that no Palestine territory shall be ceded or leased to, or in any way placed under the control of, the Government of any foreign Power.'
Art. 6: 'The Administration of Palestine [...] shall facilitate Jewish immigration under suitable conditions and shall encourage, in co-operation with the Jewish agency referred to in Article 4, close settlement by Jews on the land, including State lands and waste lands not required for public purposes.'
Art. 7: 'The Administration of Palestine shall be responsible for enacting a nationality law. There shall be included in this law provisions framed so as to facilitate the acquisition of Palestinian citizenship by Jews who take up their permanent residence in Palestine.'
And although the Jews made up barely 7.5 per cent of the total population of 800,000, Art. 22 stated: 'English, Arabic and Hebrew shall be the official language of Palestine. Any statement or inscription in Arabic on stamps or money in Palestine shall be repeated in Hebrew, and any statement or inscription in Hebrew shall be repeated in Arabic.'
11 See Pappé, *A History of Modern Palestine*, pp. 86-87.

both. But the Zionist leadership saw things differently and it refused to be part of such a solution. Typically—and this would be a recurrent behaviour—as long as their leading figures thought the Palestinians would refuse the idea, the official Zionist position was that they were indeed ready to support parity. But the moment the intelligence unit of the Jewish Agency reported that the Palestinian side was coming around to accepting the British offer, the Zionists instantly reversed their stance and said they rejected the idea of parity out of hand. Instead, they proposed an alternative solution: the partitioning of Palestine into two political units.[12] The Zionists wanted partition since they counted on the 'historical conditions' (David Ben-Gurion) this would create to enable them to annex to the Jewish state they were planning as much of the territory of Palestine as possible but with as few of its indigenous population as possible.

When two decades later, in the wake of the British decision to leave Palestine in February 1947, the future of Palestine came up for discussion once more in the international arena, it was the Zionist leadership that set the agenda, although it only represented the country's Jewish settlers who still, two years after the end of the second world war, formed only a 37 per-cent minority in the country.

Responsibility for solving the looming conflict in Palestine after British withdrawal was with the United Nations, which appointed a Special Committee on Palestine (UNSCOP). Not only did its members prove highly inexperienced, they also acted more or less within a vacuum into which the Zionist leadership stepped with ease and confidence.[13] In May 1947, the Jewish Agency provided UNSCOP with a map that envisioned a Jewish state extending over 80 per cent of Palestine—more or less the very same territory Israel under Ben-Gu-

---

12   Ibid.
13   On UNSCOP and how, prompted by the Jewish Agency, it manoeuvered the UN towards a pro-Zionist solution which then, on 29 November 1947, led to the General Assembly's Partition Resolution (181), see Ilan Pappé, *The Making of the Arab-Israeli Conflict, 1947-51* (London and New York: I. B. Tauris, 1992), pp. 16-46.

rion would in fact occupy a year later. UNSCOP members did think this was a bit of an exaggeration, but UN Resolution 181 none the less handed over as much as 55 per cent of Palestine to the Jewish state it called for. That the Palestinians rejected the plan did not surprise anyone as they had been opposed to the partitioning (read: giving away) of their land ever since 1918, while the Zionists' endorsement of it was foretold—partition, as we saw, was the solution they favoured for the 'possibilities' it opened up. In the eyes of the international policeman this incongruence seemed a solid enough basis for peace to take hold in the Holy Land. But, of course, imposing the will of one side on the other can hardly be called a fair, let alone democratic, decision. Rather than bringing reconciliation and peace to what by now was an already deeply torn country, UN Resolution 181 triggered violence on an unprecedented scale in the history of modern Palestine.[14]

Palestine Partitioned: 1947–1967

As the Palestinians had rejected the Zionist—and now UN backed—idea of dividing up the country into two states, the Zionist leadership decided it was time for unilateral action and again pulled out the map they had presented UNSCOP with in May 1947. This map showed unambiguously which parts of Palestine they coveted for their future Jewish state. Ostensibly, there was one problem: within the 80 per cent of Palestinian territory they had marked out Jews formed a minority of about 40 per cent (660,000 Jews vs. one million Palestinians). But this was seen as a passable hurdle. Ever since they had set up their Zionist project in Palestine the leaders of the *Yishuv* had been prepared for such an eventuality: the purely Jewish state they wanted would come about through the forcible transfer of the entire indigenous population. Thus, on 10 March 1948, the Zionist leadership put the final touches to 'Plan Dalet', the notorious blueprint that

14 Cf. Pappé, *A Modern History of Palestine*, esp. pp. 123-141.

detailed the ethnic cleansing by Jewish forces of all the areas of Palestine it wanted to see incorporated in their future Jewish State.

When, within five days after the 1948 war had erupted, it realized that the partition plan proved more a recipe for bloodshed than a programme for peace, the international community made one more attempt to try to get the two sides together and find a peaceful solution. A Swedish diplomat, Count Folke Bernadotte, became the first of a long line of outside mediators in the history of the post-mandatory conflict. The two proposals he came up with also partitioned the country into two states, the difference between them being that in the second Arab Palestine was no longer independent but would be annexed to Transjordan. However, both proposals unequivocally demanded the unconditional repatriation of Palestinian refugees as a precondition for peace. Bernadotte remained ambivalent about Jerusalem: it was to become the Arab capital in the first proposal but in the second the city was set aside as an international 'corpus separatum'. But, again, he clearly located the refugees and Jerusalem at the heart of the conflict: the two were inseparable and only a comprehensive and just solution would do.[15]

Bernadotte was assassinated on 17 September 1948 by Jewish extremists. The Palestine Conciliation Commission the UN appointed to replace him pursued the same policy as he had and saw any future solution as resting on three tiers: (1) the partition of the land into two states—not according to the map of Partition Resolution 181 but consonant with the demographic distribution of Jews and Palestinians; (2) the internationalization of Jerusalem, and (3) the unconditional return of the refugees to their homes. This was endorsed by the UN General Assembly in Resolution 194 of 1 December 1948. While during the UN peace conference in Lausanne that followed in May 1949 the Arab countries and the Palestinian leadership agreed to accept these three principles as a basis for negotiations, Israel's intransigent David Ben-Gurion and his government made sure the proposal was

---

15 Ilan Amitzur, *Bernadotte in Palestine 1948: A Study in Contemporary Humanitarian Knight-errantry* (London: Macmillan, 1989).

dead and buried by the summer of that year. At first, the US Administration made some noise rebuking Israel for its stance and exerted some economic pressure, but the Jewish lobby in the United States soon succeeded in re-orientating US policy firmly onto pro-Israeli tracks, where of course it remains until today.[16]

Palestine was not 'partitioned' in 1948: it was *destroyed* and most of its people were *expelled*.[17] And it is Israel's refusal to acknowledge responsibility for the ethnic cleansing it perpetrated and the destruction it wrought and then to seek reconciliation with its victims that have kindled the conflict ever since.[18]

In the late 1950s we see the Palestine Liberation Organization (PLO) emerging as the embodiment of the Palestinian struggle for return, restitution and re-construction. But, as we know with hindsight, this was never to be a particular successful struggle. The international community and the regional Arab powers soon ignored the refugees, with only Gamal Abd al-Nasser ready to adopt their cause and forcing the Arab League to show at least a modicum of concern for their plight. As the Arab states' ill-fated manoeuvers in June 1967 showed, the result was neither enough nor very efficient.

It is in these years, with the PLO phoenix hatching (1948–1967), that we find a more systematic conceptualization of the one-state idea emerging among Palestinians. Intellectuals writing in the paper *Filastinuna* ('Our Palestine') envisaged a secular democratic state as the only viable solution for the Palestine—or, for that matter, Zionist—problem. Still, when

16 See Pappé, *The Making of the Arab-Israeli Conflict*, pp. 203-243.
17 See Ilan Pappé, *The Ethnic Cleansing of Palestine* (London: Oneworld Publications, 2006), in which I adopt the paradigm of ethnic cleansing as the a-priori basis for the narrative of 1948—i.e, it is not that when they created their nation-state, the Zionists waged a war that 'tragically but inevitably' led to the expulsion of most of the indigenous population, but the other way round: the main goal was the ethnic cleansing of all of Palestine that they coveted for their new state and the war was then waged as a cover.
18 See, e.g., my 'Fear, Victimhood, Self and Other', in this volume.

carefully read their articles show that, instead of focussing on actual political models, the 'Palestinian entity' that in their eyes was to trigger the rebirth of the nationalist movement had no clear contours nor were its political structures set out in any concrete way.[19] The debate centred mainly on a pan-Arabist stance that opposed what they called separatism from the *qawmi* (the pan-Arabist version of nationalism) future in the name of a Palestinian *wataniyya* (nation-state territorialism).

Neither was the nature of a future Palestinian entity seriously discussed in the regional or international arenas during the 1950s and 60s. There seemed to have been a lull in the peace efforts, although some schemes were thrown up in the air, among them the Anglo-American Alpha programme and the Johnston plan.[20] These and other, more esoteric initiatives, almost all American, introduced a rather business-like element into the approach to the conflict. That is, they all combined a great belief in partition to safeguard the security interests of Israel and its Arab neighbours with a total disregard for the Palestinians as partners for peace. The Palestinians appear in these schemes only as refugees, their fate played out as another economic aspect of America's Cold War against the Soviet Union. In other words, the solution for them would come from a 'Marshal plan' for the Middle East: American aid to the area in order to help improve the standard of living as the best means of containing Soviet encroachment. This could most effectively be achieved by resettling the refugees in other Arab countries to serve as cheap labour for their development. But, of course, separating them from their roots and moving them further away from their homeland also was an attempt to distance the expelled indigenous Palestinians from Israel's borders and so excise them from that country's collective memory and obliterate them from the world's consciousness.[21] Although the PLO put up enough resistance to en-

---

19 Helena Cobban, *The PLO* (Cambridge: Cambridge University Press, 1984), pp. 28-29.

20 Avi Shlaim, *The Iron Wall; Israel and the Arab World* (London and New York: W. W. Norton and Company, 2000), pp. 109-110.

21 Cf. Nur Masalha, '"Dis/solving" the Palestinian Refugee Problem', in this volume.

courage Arab regimes to leave the refugees—whom they mainly saw as a destabilizing factor—in their transit camps, the fact that the PLO was associated with the Soviet Union pushed the Palestinians, wherever they were, off the agenda in any future Pax Americana.

The Demise of Partition, 1967–2000

In June 1967, all of Palestine became 'Israel'. The new geo-political reality created by Israel's occupation of the West Bank and the Gaza Strip meant that a new peace process had to get rolling. The UN took the initiative, but was soon replaced again by American 'peacemakers'. These early architects of a Pax Americana for the Middle East did have some original ideas of their own, but as these were invariably rejected out of hand by the Israelis, they never made it beyond the drawing board. Before long, the mechanism of American brokerage had become a proxy for Israeli 'peace plans'. At the centre of Israel's perception of a solution were three conditions: first, Israel was to be absolved from any responsibility for 'creating the Arab refugee problem', Israel's euphemism for the ethnic cleansing it perpetrated in 1948[22]—the issue was banned from appearing on any future peace agenda; second, negotiations for peace would only concern the future of the territories Israel had occupied in 1967, i.e., the West Bank and the Gaza Strip; and third, the fate of the Palestinian minority in Israel was to be kept out of any comprehensive settlement for the conflict. What this meant was that Israel insisted it could continue to occupy 80 per cent of Palestine and that more than 50 per cent of the Palestinians themselves would be excluded from all future efforts to achieve peace in the land of Palestine.

Israel's formula was accepted unconditionally by the US and sold to the rest of the world as the best offer in town. At the heart of it stood

22 Thus the title of Benny Morris's 1988 study, *The Birth of the Palestinian Refugee Problem, 1947-1949* (Cambridge: Cambridge University Press, 2nd ed., 2004), as though this was a 'natural' process.

an equation, produced by the Israeli peace camp and enthusiastically marketed by the Americans, of 'Territories for Peace'. This is a rather strange equation, if you stop to think about it, because on one side you have a quantitative and measurable variable that is easily grasped and outlined, on the other, an airy and abstract notion difficult to conceptualize or even illustrate in any fixed or concrete form. Less bizarre perhaps as a working basis for bilateral peace between Israel and its Arab neighbours, it operated quite well for a while in the case of Egypt and Jordan. But even here it produced only a 'cold peace' as it prevented a comprehensive solution to the Palestine question. Because, as it so clearly continued to deny them their rights, what had this equation to offer the ultimate victims of the 1948 war?

However, the architects of the Oslo Accords, in the early 1990s, seemed to think it was fair enough and so re-packaged and then re-sold the 'Territories for Peace' formula as merchandize of their own provenance. Hollow concepts, such as 'Israeli recognition' of the PLO and 'autonomy' for the Palestinians, were meant to corroborate Oslo's equally business-like approach to pushing through a solution. Amidst the display of a dramatic discourse of peace, Oslo was presented as the making of a two-state solution, whereas the reality on the ground was effectively that of one state, 78 per cent of which made up of Israel 'proper' and the remaining 22 per cent directly ruled by Israel through its military occupation.[23]

I am not underestimating the progress made in Oslo, but I also claim that one should not for a moment let out of sight the circumstances under which the accords came about: these make clear why it was such a colossal failure. Dramatic changes in the global and regional balance of power following the demise of the USSR, together with an Israeli 'willingness' to replace the Hashemites of Jordan with the PLO as a partner for peace, opened the way to an even more duplicitous version

23 See Ilan Pappé, 'Breaking the Mirror—Oslo and After', in Haim Gordon (ed.), *Looking Back at the June 1967 War* (Westport, CT, and London: Praeger, 1999), pp. 95-112.

of the 'Territories for Peace' formula. Oslo, then, is the ultimate celebration of the idea of partition: not just of territories, but of everything else that is visible and quantifiable. Because of Oslo it became possible to talk 'legitimately' about further dividing the only non-Jewish parts of post-1948 Palestine—the remaining 22 per cent of the country—between an Israel that already had the other 78 per cent and a future 'autonomous' Palestinian entity. Because of Oslo it became conceivable that within these 22 per cent left of historical Palestine the Jewish settlements (that according to international law are totally illegitimate) could be further divided into 78 per cent under Israeli control and 22 per cent under the Oslo-created Palestinian Authority. Similarly, most of the water resources would go to Israel, most of the areas around Jerusalem would remain in Israeli hands, and so on. For the Palestinians, the quid pro quo—'peace'—meant they would end up with a stateless Palestinian 'state' robbed of any say in matters of its own defense, foreign or economic policies—an 'autonomous' Bantustan much like or, as we now know, a good deal worse even than those the white supremacist Apartheid regime had created in South Africa. As for the Right of Return, according to the Israeli interpretation of Oslo—which is the only one that counts—the Palestinians had better forget about and erase it. It was this Israeli notion of a solution that in the summer of 2000 was presented at Camp David to the world at large as Israel's 'most generous offer'.

The Palestinians had been led to believe that the summit at Camp David would produce the final stages in the Israeli withdrawal from the West Bank and the Gaza Strip (according to UN SC Resolutions 242 and 338) and prepare the ground for new negotiations over a final settlement on the basis of UN Resolution 194—the return of the refugees, the internationalization of Jerusalem and a full sovereign Palestinian state. Even the US had voted in favour of this resolution at the time and continued to re-iterate its support ever since.

However, the Israeli Left, in power again in 1999, saw the Camp David summit as a fitting stage from which to dictate to the Palestinians *their* concept of a solution: Israel should be allowed to *maximize* the divisibility of the *visible* layers of the conflict (retreating from 90 per cent of the Occupied Territories, taking down 20 per cent of the Jewish settlements there, retaining 50 per cent of Jerusalem) while the Palestinians should *stop claiming* their stake in the *invisible* layers: no Right of Return, no full sovereign Palestinian state, and no solution for the Palestinian minority in Israel. After Camp David, for the Israelis an 'acceptable' solution meant that as long as the Palestinian refused to surrender to the Israeli diktat, Israel would be entitled to continue discriminating against them and occupying and exiling them. Whether or not triggered by Ariel Sharon violating the Muslim sanctuary of Haram al-Sharif that month, the second Intifada broke out in September 2000 and, despite the most brutal attempts at oppression fully sanctioned after 9/11 by the obscene rhetoric and sophisticated military hardware coming out of Washington, is still going on as I write these lines.

During the first four years of the second Intifada 'Territories for Peace' was totally absent from the peace talks. In early October 2000, Palestinians in Israel held non-violent protest demonstrations in a number of villages and towns in solidarity with their co-nationalists in the Occupied Territories, calling for the de-Zionization of the Jewish state (i.e., for Israel as the state of *all* its citizens).[24] It spurred West Bankers to demand that Muslim and Christian Jerusalem remain Palestinian, propelled desperate Gazans to take up arms against the continuing Israeli oppression and united Palestinian refugees around the world in their demand for their Right of Return. What this second Intifada has made abundantly clear is that for the Palestinians the end of occupation can only be a pre-condition for peace, never peace itself. The Israeli peace camp, we were told by its 'gurus', felt insulted in October 2000, not by a government shooting at its own citizens, but by Israeli Palestinians showing solidarity with Palestinians under Israeli oppression, and rushed to embrace the version of events spouted by

24 It was during these peaceful demonstrations that the Israeli security service, using live ammunition and rubber-coated steel bullets and employing strategically placed snipers, killed 13 unarmed Palestinian young men, thus causing the Intifada to spill over into Israel itself.

Israel's prime minister at the time, Ehud Barak, during the Camp David summit. As Barak told the world, the Israeli leadership (Labour) had gone as far as it could on the equation of 'Territories for Peace' by offering the Palestinians most of the land Israeli holds occupied since 1967, but the Palestinians had been 'stupid enough' to reject Israel's 'generous' offer.

While Barak's version was endorsed by the United States, not in the least to help US President Clinton save face, several European governments and public figures expressed doubts as to how true it was. They were right, of course. This 'generous-offer' narrative spelled out very clearly what final settlement Israel's political camp had in mind: that the Palestinians acknowledge the Zionist narrative of the 1948 war as exclusively right and valid; that Israel carried no responsibility whatsoever for the making of the refugee problem, and that the Palestinian minority in Israel—twenty per cent of Israel's population—did not form part of the solution to the conflict. These three demands were predictable as they only re-iterated the diktats Israel had put on the table earlier. But Barak wanted more: the Palestinians had to acquiesce in the new reality Israel was rapidly constructing in the Greater Jerusalem area and throughout the West Bank. In other words, a 'final' peace settlement was one in which the world would recognize as forever Jewish the settlement belt that now encircles Jerusalem and those settlements planted in the heart of Palestinian cities on the West Bank, notably Nablus and al-Khalil (Hebron). Thus, as we know today, it was 'final' also in the sense that it was guaranteed to put an end to a feasible independent Palestinian state.

This Israeli diktat showed up again in the guise of a peace process in 2004, this time under the auspices of the so-called Quartet—a 'new' body composed of some of the most senior UN, US, European and Russian diplomats. The 'Road Map' they came up with proved a blatant international endorsement of Israel's idea of how best to divide the Occupied Territories between the Jewish state and a future Palestinian entity, of which even Israeli prime minister Ariel Sharon (who won the elections of 2001 and 2003) said he didn't mind if people called it a 'state'. It was when the two sides failed to make headway—for the same reasons they had failed to reach agreement during the previous 36 years of Israeli occupation, i.e., the Palestinian refusal to acquiesce in Israel's theft of their country—that Sharon decided to offer his own version of the Road Map: a unilateral Israeli withdrawal from the Gaza Strip and the taking down of four tiny 'outpost' settlements in the north of the West Bank. The Quartet wanted the Gaza 'disengagement' to be part of the Map, a first step towards its implementation.[25] Propelled by an Israeli consensus that anyway already regards half of the West Bank (the big settlements blocs and Greater Jerusalem) as an integral part of Israel in a future solution that entirely excludes the Right of Return for the refugees, Sharon again didn't care one way or the other. In effect, if Ehud Olmert (as Sharon's successor in 2006), backed by the political centre in Israel, gets his way, the result will be the implementation of a one-state solution that encompasses Israel and, on a vastly shrunken West Bank, a Palestinian Bantustan. The world will no doubt hail this as the two-state solution Israel has been telling them would bring peace.

Partition as an Obstacle to Peace

What the historical perspective I sketched above unequivocally shows is that insisting on focussing peace efforts on the territories Israel has held occupied since the June 1967 war—the 22 per cent that remain of historical Palestine—has only led and can only lead to total failure. None of the Israeli offers that promised an Israeli withdrawal from most of the Occupied Territories (starting with Oslo, through Camp David 2000, the Ayalon–Nusseibah initiative, the Road Map and the 2004 Geneva Initiative) has succeeded in eliciting a Palestinian response agreeing that any of them could lead to a meaningful end to the conflict. The reason for this is simple: these offers all empty the concept

---

25 'Disengagement' is, of course, Zionist newspeak meant to circumvent the use of such terms as 'end of occupation' and to sidestep the obligations incumbent upon Israel as the occupying power according to international law.

of statehood from the accepted and conventional contents we have come to associate it with especially after the end of the second world war. Israel's 'peace' offers, without exception, impose debilitating limits on the Palestinians' chances and abilities to create their own independence in those 22 per cent of Palestine as they allow Israel to perpetuate its hold over the security, foreign and economic matters of this future mini-state on the West Bank, as is so blatantly the case in the Gaza Strip from which it officially withdraw in August 2005. Moreover, this mini-state structure offers no solution to the refugee question, as it totally ignores the Palestinians' internationally recognized Right of Return. Its political structure has no relevance either to the fate of the 1.4 million Palestinians who live inside Israel, where since 1948 they have been subjected to formal and informal Apartheid policies. And finally, as the creeping but inescapable annexation by Israel of most of East Jerusalem has been tolerated by the international community for so long now, any two-state solution is likely to leave much of Jerusalem in Israeli hands and to forestall the possibility of the Palestinians ever having a proper capital there.

To put us on the road towards a *genuine* solution to these four problems—a Palestinian Bantustan, the refugees, the Palestinians within Israel, and East Jerusalem—we need a peace effort that will succeed in breaking the false mirrors Israel has put up to mislead the world and the fraudulent frames it has used to entrench its occupation. Two things need to happen. Israel needs to be brought to acknowledge its full legal and moral responsibility for the 1948 Nakba, and we need a political structure that will differ from the current one in that it will encompass all the areas that made up Mandatory Palestine. The two are interconnected in that they require Israel, and the world at large, to recognize the gross imparity that is built into this conflict. The process of reconciliation can only start once Israel has acknowledged the ethnic cleansing it committed in Palestine in 1948 and accepts to be held accountable for it. I have written elsewhere on the various mechanisms we need to have in place to make that process possible.[26] Here I would

26 Ilan Pappé, 'Fear, Victimhood, Self and Other', in this volume.

like to associate the end of the conflict with the question of what political structure ought to accompany such a process and eventually may lead to a solution. I use the term 'accompany' on purpose as I view mediation and reconciliation between Israel and its Palestinian victims only as a pre-condition, a first stage that will have to come way before any appropriate political structure can finally be arrived at.

Visions of a One-State Solution:
New Buds on the Ancient Olive Tree

At present, for most Jews in Israel even the mere thought of this way forward is totally anathema, and large numbers of Palestinian West Bankers are equally dead set against it. But in the long run it may well be, for better or for worse, the only game in town. And there are hopeful signs as some among those who have always ardently supported the two-state idea are beginning to recognize the stark reality. Recoiling in disbelief at the outcome of Israeli Prime Minister Sharon's visit to Washington in May 2004, Mustafa Barghouti wrote in *Al-Ahram*:

> If Sharon is to be left unchecked by a president fearful of his re-election prospects and unwilling to provoke his Jewish and right-wing Christian constituencies, then the two-state solution is dead. As with the refugees, the principle of settling the future of Jerusalem by mutual negotiation will be lost. Jerusalem will never again be part of an independent Palestine. The only remaining option is a single state.[27]

27 Mustafa Barghouti, 'Sharon's Nightmare', *Al-Ahram Weekly* 690 (13-19 May 2004); earlier Barghouti writes: 'As Sharon stood in the White House listening to President Bush's declaration of support for his disengagement plan, he visibly swelled with triumph. At a stroke, the president had swept aside decades of American diplomacy, all international laws forbidding the acquisition of land by conquest, and numerous UN resolutions regarding the rights of Palestinian refugees and the illegal status of Israel's settlements in the West Bank. [...] The fatal

In Israel, two long-time comrades of Barghouti in the struggle for the two-state solution had come to a similar conclusion the year before.[28] For Haim Hanegbi the single state has become the one just solution, while Meron Benvenisti, less generously, claims it is by now unfortunately the only *feasible* way out, given the unhindered expansion by Israel of Jewish settlements in the Occupied Territories, the refusal of any Israeli government to massively withdraw Jewish settlers from there, and the demographic growth of the Palestinian population inside Israel. Still, what they advocate is the bi-national model, a kind of a consensual federation between two national entities sharing the executive, legislative and constitutional authorities between them on the basis of parity. Even among the more veteran advocates, who prefer the idea of a secular democratic state for all its citizens, some would regard this bi-national structure as the more practical one, to begin with.[29] As Tony Judt put it three years ago in a *New York Review of Books* article, in this way it will be easier to win over those who have grown disillusioned with the chances of a two-state solution:

blow he has been seeking to deal the fragile peace process had at last been struck. The right of return had been revoked, the status of the West Bank's largest settlements secured. Construction of his wall could continue expropriating Palestinian land and destroying the physical possibility of a Palestinian state, while the American president was assured it remained a merely temporary measure. Troops could be redeployed from Gaza while maintaining total control of the strip's air, land and sea access, its water, imports and electricity. *In short, the final enslavement of the Palestinian people could begin, and all with an American seal of approval.* Yet in years to come, Sharon may find that this moment of imagined triumph in fact marked the day his worst nightmares began to come true. Just as President Bush has reversed years of American policy in Israel and Palestine, so his statement must denote a fundamental shift in the strategy of the Palestinian struggle' (emphasis added).

28 Haim Hanegbi and Meron Benvenisti, in *Ha'aretz*, 8 August 2003.
29 A similar argument was made by two Israeli academics, As'ad Ghanem, who is Palestinian, and Sarah Ozacky-Lazar, who is Jewish, in their article 'The Status of the Palestinians in Israel in an Era of Peace: Part of the Problem but not Part of the Solution', *Israel Affairs* 9/1-2 (Autumn/Winter 2003), pp. 263-289.

The time has come to think the unthinkable. The two-state solution—the core of the Oslo process and the present 'road map'—is probably already doomed. With every passing year we are postponing an inevitable, harder choice that only the far right and far left have so far acknowledged, each for its own reasons. The true alternative facing the Middle East in coming years will be between an ethnically cleansed Greater Israel and a single, integrated, bi-national state of Jews and Arabs, Israelis and Palestinians.[30]

The local and global powers that be—whether in politics, the economy or the media—continue to put all their energies behind trying to consolidate in Palestine a two-state solution, each according to their own understanding. The political elite in Israel wants to see a structure that is guaranteed to have Palestine shrink into oblivion, the Quartet naively claims that it could convince Israel to allow the Palestinians to have a mini-state stretching over 15 per cent of what used to be Palestine, and this Bantustan also seems to satisfy the Arab regimes that are lying prostrate within the American sphere of influence.

Given that this is the local, regional and global balance of power, can we still hope for a political structure to surface that will reflect the history, geography, culture and demography of Palestine in a way that is both compellingly just and realistically possible? As Tony Judt concludes his plea for an alternative: 'A bi-national state in the Middle East would require the emergence, among Jews and Arabs alike, of a new political class. The very idea is an unpromising mix of realism and utopia, hardly an auspicious place to begin. But the alternatives are far, far worse.'[31]

---

30 Tony Judt, 'Israel: The Alternative', *NYRB*, 23 October 2003; Judt adds: 'That is indeed how the hard-liners in Sharon's cabinet see the choice; and that is why they anticipate the removal of the Arabs as the ineluctable condition for the survival of a Jewish state. But what if there were no place in the world today for a "Jewish state"? What if the bi-national solution were not just increasingly likely, but actually a desirable outcome [i.e, also for Jews]?'

31 Ibid.

It is obviously too early to go into any detail about what such a political structure would look like. No doubt the two models of a secular state and a bi-national one will continue to compete in the theoretical discussions on what should replace the two-state option. But what I see as paramount is a joint historiographical effort that will help us re-construct the past along non-ethnocentric, polyphonic lines and embrace the suffering of those whom have been victimized by the structures of evil in the land in a more reflective and humanistic way, as in effect we set out to do in this volume. But this historiographical endeavour can never be merely academic, as it should aim at a de-colonized, de-nationalized and de-gendered reconstruction of Palestine's history. Salvaging the silenced voices from the past means to give their deprived narratives a clear voice today so they can sound a clarion call for a different, better future.

In the meantime, to sketch how exactly to move from the historical de-construction of the past to the re-construction for this more humane and just future remains, of course, an almost impossible task. The comparative lessons we can draw from history are not very encouraging. More useful, therefore, and more immediately urgent is the deconstruction of the present political power structure in Israel as it continues to wield its destructive control over the life of Palestine's past, present and future generations. Here, too, the prospects are at first sight not very encouraging, as this power structure feeds off an international system generated by people interested in perpetuating rather than transforming the present reality.

Four processes are currently at play, globally and locally, that we need to look at more closely in order to assess what chances there are for a new reality to emerge in Palestine. The four are intertwined in a dialectical relationship likely to impact the reality on the ground only when activated as a whole.

The first of these is the entrenched Israeli occupation policy and the backing it enjoys of such global powers as the American military-industrial complex, Christian Zionists and the pro-Zionist Jewish lobbies around the world. Left unchallenged and unabated, Israel will continue to destroy Palestine in the name of the two-state solution, ensuring what it narrowly failed to achieve in 1948: control over as great an area of Palestine as possible with as few Palestinians as possible.

The second process is the growing resentment Israel's policies are evoking among Arabs and Muslims in the Third World. So far, we have seen this anger erupting in the actions of certain extremist fanatical groups only—quickly branded as terrorist acts in the West, such attacks tend to have a boomerang effect and thus feed and benefit the first trend. But, of course, the deeper it becomes, the more this resentment can grow into a legitimate and thus far more effective movement forcefully countering Israel and its policies.

The third process is the incipient fundamental change we can detect in Western public opinion and in the way civil society (for want of a better term) reacts in Europe and, who knows, even the United States. An opinion poll in July 2005 showed that only 14 per cent of Europeans were at that point 'sympathetic towards' Israel and 'agreed with' the Israeli position (vs. 42 per cent among Americans), and these percentages appear to get smaller by the day. Given such statistics, we can see why there is a mushrooming of boycott, divestment and sanction campaigns against Israel reminiscent of the way the anti-Apartheid movement started out in the 1960s.

And, finally, as the fourth factor, there is the cautious emanation at the grass-roots level of de-segregated spaces of co-existence, on the basis of full parity, within areas in Israel itself where Palestinians and Jews live in physical proximity, such as the Galilee. We can see this in the joint kindergartens and schools that have sprung up, but it is also slowly beginning to pervade the business sector and the judicial and municipal fields. Again, it is too early to assess the significance of the phenomenon—right now it is no more than a drop in the ocean of segregation ordained from above. But, together with the growing impact of the other three processes I outlined, these small cocoons may yet develop into, first, a refuge for people who want to live differently from the inhuman reality around them and then also into a model for a future one-state Palestine, a state for all its citizens, free and sovereign, democratic and independent.

After Gaza

Jamil Hilal and Ilan Pappé

Much has changed in the Israeli-Palestinian conflict since we finalized the first draft of this volume halfway the second *intifada*, but much also has remained the same. If after more than forty years of Israeli oppression, colonization and dispossession we thought we could cautiously point to some positive developments, these were quickly swept aside by the negative, violent course that events have taken since. As it is, the deterioration we are witnessing in the first decade of the twenty-first century has proven worse than anything we have seen before. Inevitably it has also undermined the overall Israeli-Palestinian dialogue and disrupted the various ongoing academic encounters between Israelis and Palestinians. PALISAD too ceased to exist as an active forum for joint periodic discussions in Ramallah and Jerusalem, although we continue to meet individually at various venues around the world and some of us occasionally publish together, hopeful of course that at some point in the future we will be able to resume our dialogue.

What stands out among the changes that we see happening is the horrendous escalation in the violence of Israel's military's actions against the Palestinian people, and then also the Lebanese. First Israel re-invaded and re-occupied the entire West Bank, followed by the Apartheid/Segregation Wall it started constructing in 2003. Then came the attack on Southern Lebanon and Beirut in 2006 and, in the winter of 2008–2009, the onslaught on the Gaza Strip. This went hand in hand with the ever more ruthless policy of dispossession and destruction Israel is directing today at Palestinians in other areas, especially in the Greater Jerusalem region and inside 1967-Israel.

In this volume we discussed and analyzed the main ideologies and strategies that undergird Zionism's quest for the unchallenged domination of Palestine and that have been pushing successive Israeli governments in their drive for political and military hegemony throughout the Eastern Mediterranean and even beyond, as its current threat of Iran illustrates. Thus it comes as no surprise that as their main pretext to 'justify' the intensification of the IDF's violence Israel points to the increasing political power and popular support Islamic groups in the region have been gaining, such as Hamas, the Islamic resistance movement in the Occupied Territories, Hezbollah in Lebanon and the Islamic Movement active inside 1967-Israel itself. It also remains a fact that before 2006 regional states and even local Palestinian movements seemed less and less willing to confront Israel's domination or capable to resist it, giving Israeli policy makers the impression that their overall aggressive strategy was paying off. The Israelis were especially satisfied with the way things were going in the West Bank and the Gaza Strip, as the second *intifada* seemed to have petered out around the year 2005: the matrix of walls, electric fences, checkpoints, colonial settlements, 'Jews-only' bypass roads and military bases that now covers the entire West Bank had seemingly succeeded in making it 'pacified' territory. It was, of course, also in Israel's favour that Mahmoud Abbas, now in charge of the Palestinian National Authority, was known for his commitment to 'negotiations' as the only viable strategy to end the conflict.

The situation in the Gaza Strip was different. Here Israel faced determined resistance, as the Hamas movement—like Hezbollah before it in Lebanon—refused to do Israel's bidding. Recall Israel's 'targeted' assassination on 22 March 2004 of the wheelchair-bound Shaykh Ahmad Yasin, Hamas's founder and spiritual symbol, and less than four weeks later of his successor, Dr. 'Abd al-'Aziz Rantisi. For the then Israeli prime minister, Ariel Sharon, and the main political class of those days who are even more dominantly at the centre of Israeli politics today —Ehud Barak, Shimon Peres, Zipi Livni and Benjamin Netanyahu—the solution to the 'Palestine problem' seemed to lie in ensuring total control over the Gaza Strip from the outside and simultaneously, following the South-African Apartheid model, continuing to carve up the West Bank into a number of separated and thus manageable Bantustans, surrounded by ever-expanding hostile Jewish colonial settlements and segregated by Israel's serpentine Apartheid Wall.

In 2005 the Gaza Strip became the main locus of Palestinian resistance as the Israeli army stepped up their operations against Hamas
and the population at large. A handicap proved to be the isolated
Jewish settlers' colony in the Strip, Gush Katif, vulnerable anyway as a
relatively easy target from time to time for Palestinian resistance
fighters. Both factors were behind Sharon's strategic decision in the
summer of 2005 to take the Gush Katif settlers out, a decision that was
not very difficult to make also because Gaza has always been a headache
for Israeli leaders and, unlike the West Bank, has never been realistically considered for annexation: the Gaza Strip's population density is
among the highest in the world and of its 1.5 million inhabitants about
75 per cent are refugees. It was Yitzhak Rabin, after all, who years
earlier had said he would like to see Gaza sink into the sea.

The pull-out decision was also calculated to reap Israel an added
international bonus: it was marketed to the world at large as the end
result of a bitter internal feud between the government of Ariel Sharon
and the country's colonial-settler movement, stage-managed to call up
the spectre of a Jewish civil war. A gullible West duly hailed Sharon as a
courageous peace maker for the way he had acted, considering also that
there had been 'no one to talk to on the Palestinian side', the perennial
Israeli lie that Sharon this time used to marginalize and isolate Arafat.

But things did not turn out the way Sharon and his entourage had
expected. The pull-out was followed by Hamas taking full internal control
of the Strip, first through its democratic victory in the parliamentary
elections in January 2006, and then by pre-emptively upstaging Fatah,
who had been planning to re-seize control in an allegedly US-backed coup.
Israel's response was immediate and came in the form of a total economic
blockade on the Strip, demanding the West follow suit—which it sadly
did. Hamas responded by firing crude home-made missiles at the small
town of Sderot, less than a mile across the border (Sderot was originally
founded in 1951 on lands that had belonged to the village of Najd whose
people Jewish forces had ethnically cleansed on 13 May 1948). Israel
brought in its air force, artillery and naval gunships in what it claimed was
an effort to silence 'the launching sites of these missiles', but in effect
seizing upon them as a pretext to targeting people and buildings anywhere
and everywhere throughout the entire Gaza Strip.

Utterly defenceless, Gazans were subjected repeatedly throughout 2006 to shelling by Israeli tanks, attacks from the air and the sea and violent IDF incursions. With Israel's unexpected defeat in Southern Lebanon by the guerrilla forces of Hezbollah in the summer of that same year, the Israeli army began escalating its brutal actions against the Strip, where it knew it would face little or no resistance and people had nowhere to flee. As Israel's policy turned more and more genocidal, reactions to it by Hamas proved more and more desperate. The noticeable barbarization of Israeli military actions can partly be explained by the frustration of Israel's generals at the humiliating defeat by Hezbollah in Lebanon (televised worldwide by Arab satellite stations): after briefly licking its wounds, the army urgently needed to demonstrate that its superiority had remained unchallenged and that its deterrence capability was intact, factors the army generals broadcast as representing the pivotal 'safeguards' for the Jewish state's survival in a 'hostile' world. With George W. Bush still in the White House, the Islamist character of both Hamas and Hezbollah and their—totally fictitious—association with al-Qaida were enough for Israel to portray the country as spearheading the global war on terror in the Gaza Strip. The US administration followed this up by 'justifying' the killing in Gaza by Israel of innocent women and small babies (a practice not alien to the US forces in Iraq and Afghanistan) as part of the Western crusade against fundamentalist Islam. Had not US Secretary of State Condoleezza Rice portrayed the violence Israel had unleashed against Southern Lebanon and Beirut as 'the birth pangs of a new Middle East'?!

But if not already under George W. Bush, definitely in the post-Bush era the myth that Israel was fighting global Jihaddism and Islamic fundamentalism in Gaza was losing its credibility. Israel swiftly supplanted it with a new lie in 2007: Gaza was a terrorist base of Muslims determined to destroy the Jewish state. Israel's recipe for Palestinians to be 'de-terrorized', so to speak, was for them to agree to spend their lives totally encircled by Israeli barbed wire, walls and warships, with the supply of goods and the movement of people in an out of the Strip depending on the political choice the Gazan population would make. Continuing support for Hamas would mean economic strangulation and physical starvation until they changed their mind and dropped that ideological inclination. If they accepted the kind of politics Israel wanted them to adopt, the prospect would be communal survival but without basic civil and national, let alone human rights—i.e., their fate would be the same as that of the West Bank Palestinians. In other words, Israel's 'choice' for the Gazans was either to be locked up in Bantustans that similarly already segregated people on the West Bank, or to spend the rest of their lives incarcerated in the maximum security jail that we now know the Gaza Strip would effectively become.

The ghettoized people of Gaza were given one year, 2008, to make up their mind. They ignored both options as they continued to support the resistance and refused to succumb to Israel's attempts at strangulation. The Israeli reaction came on 27 December 2008 and lasted for three weeks: by 21 January 2009 1400 Palestinians, if not more, had been massacred, and four times that number injured, many of them maimed for the rest of their lives. Gaza became the killing fields for the most sophisticated and lethal kinds of modern weaponry, including some the international community has clearly outlawed while defining their employment as a war crime, as the Goldstone report confirmed in the autumn of 2009.

The vast majority of Israeli Jews agreed with their political and military elite that 'tough' military policies were the best way forward and felt vindicated by Israel's onslaught on Gaza: not only did Operation 'Cast Lead' have almost unanimous support, most Jews in Israel felt reassured by the way the killing seemed to make up in their minds for the disastrous performance of their army in Lebanon in 2006. A policy so transparent in its naked brutality and simultaneously so un-controversial in its acceptance among the country's Jewish population could not fail to impact the option of the Palestinians inside 1967-Israel. Over the years segregation policies, racist laws, arbitrary house demolitions, and a spatial policy of demographic strangulation have combined to perpetually undermine the already precarious existence of the million and a half Palestinians who are citizens of the state of Israel. When voicing public criticism they have always been keen to shield themselves by adroitly using the democratic means the state puts at their disposal. However, this time theirs was the only criticism sounded from within: it spelled their total de-legitimization in the eyes of Israel's

Jewish majority public. It was this public mood and the official strategy that took advantage of it which are behind Israel's incremental ethnic cleansing policies in the greater Jerusalem area and in the south of Israel, against the Bedouin population there.

Fragmented geographically since 1948 and in the twenty-first century politically divided as never before, the Palestinian people did not need the last four or five years to draw realistic conclusions about their continuing abysmal situation and the absence of hope. And yet, we see two new features of political and public life appearing during these years that point to a regained sense of *sumud.* The first is the total rejection of any dialogue with Israelis, official or unofficial, as the utter futility of any such dialogue is by now inescapably obvious. The second is a newly discovered determination to continue the struggle despite the dismal reality on the ground and the almost certain knowledge that Israel is bound to make things even worse. Here we find two strategies emerging. The first has been armed resistance of a kind, together with increasingly developing civil resistance and grass-roots social movements in confronting Israel's racist policies, the Apartheid Wall and the Jewish colonial settlers; the other is the call for international support of the Boycott, Divestment and Sanctions (BDS) campaign or, less specifically, for any kind of political or cultural pressure on and the cessation of all formal and informal contact with Israel as the occupier.

The call for the BDS campaign comes from a broad spectrum of people and bodies: NGOs and civil society institutions in the Occupied Territories, the Palestinian exilic communities abroad and in the refugee camps, and the 1948 Palestinians. In many ways it was spearheaded by Palestinian academics and was then later endorsed by almost all Palestinian academic institutions and, gradually, most civil society institutions. As we write in our introduction, the campaign was making waves when we held our last PALISAD meetings, dividing the debate at that time not along national lines, but according to personal views, with all Palestinian members but only some of the Israelis fully behind the initiative. If the construction of the Apartheid Wall was by then gradually forcing us to discontinue our meetings, it now seems that the reluctance to renew the dialogue also already reflected the dark mood that has emerged as dominant in these last few years.

With the futility exposed of any kind of contacts between Israelis and Palestinians not based on reciprocity, where do we go from here? Clearly, joint academic action today requires a common political agenda together with new goals and broader horizons. A unique development has been the recent opening of the Centre for Palestine Studies at Exeter University in the UK, headed by Ilan Pappé. The Centre is the first of its kind in Europe and heralds the rectification of long scholarly neglect of, and Western academic disregard for Palestine. Significant too are current projects by Palestinian and mainly anti-Zionist Israeli academics on Palestinian oral testimonies, highlighting their legitimacy as an historical source. Other groups are exploring the visionary and practical aspects of the Palestinian Right of Return as enshrined in United Nations GA Resolution 194, in an attempt to move beyond political sloganeering and generate tangible results. More than ever it is clear today that the 1993 Oslo Accords, ostensibly geared to bring peace to the country, have resulted in the exact opposite: the number of Jewish colonial settlers in the West Bank has trebled (to 500,000, with East Jerusalem), Israel's Apartheid regime is consolidating the West Bank's bantustanization and Israel now 'manages' the Gaza Strip as the world's largest open-air prison. By its own actions Israel has knowingly undermined the viability of an independent Palestinian state 'side by side Israel'. Here the more pronounced political agenda we mentioned above is inspiring growing scholarly and public attention for the one-state solution as the only alternative to end the violence and to enable both peoples to live in peace. This is where the quest for bridging narratives that had given PALISAD its first impetus comes back into play. As Mahmoud Darwish tells us in his 2002 poem 'The State of Siege' (our translation):

A country at the break of dawn
we won't disagree about
the martyrs' share of the land
here all are equal
spreading the grass like a mattress
for us to get along together!

Contributors

Ehud Adiv was born and raised in a Marxist kibbutz. As a parachutist in the war of 1967 he 'discovered' the Palestinian people. By then his kibbutz had moved towards a rightwing nationalist position so he left it and went to study at Haifa University (1970–1972). After a long break as a political activist with and on behalf of the Palestinians (for which he spent time in an Israeli jail), Adiv resumed his academic career. His knowledge of Arabic and his long experience with the Palestinians stood him in good stead during his Middle East studies at Tel Aviv University and later at the Department of Sociology and Politics, Birkbeck College, University of London. The Israeli-Palestinian conflict is also at the heart of his PhD thesis. Adiv continues to be involved, on both academic and political levels, in the fate and future of Palestine. Since 1998, he teaches political theories at Israel's Open University.

Musa Budeiri lives in Israeli-ruled Jerusalem and teaches Political Science at the Institute of Area Studies, Al-Quds University, Jerusalem.

Uri Davis is an anthropologist born in Jerusalem in 1943. He has been at the forefront of the defence of human rights, notably Palestinian rights, since 1965 and has pioneered critical research on Zionism and Israel since the mid-1970s. He has published extensively in these fields, including *Israel: An Apartheid State* (1987 & 1990; abridged ed. 2001); *Citizenship and the State: Comparative Study of Citizenship Legislation in Israel, Jordan, Palestine, Syria and Lebanon* (1997); *Citizenship and the State in the Middle East: Approaches and Applications* (co-ed., 2000) and most recently *Apartheid Israel: Possibilities for the Struggle Within* (2003).

Dr Davis is a member of the Middle East Regional Committee of the international journal *Citizenship Studies*, Honorary Research Fellow at the Institute of Arab & Islamic Studies (IAIS), University of Exeter, and Honorary Research Fellow at the Institute for Middle Eastern & Islamic Studies (IMEIS), University of Durham; Chairperson of AL-BEIT: Association for the Defence of Human Rights in Israel, and MAIAP: Movement Against Israeli Apartheid in Palestine; founding member and Senior Director for Legal and Political Affairs, Mosaic Communities: Multinational Housing Cooperative in Israel, and Observer-Member of the Palestine National Council (PNC).

Lev (Luis) Grinberg is a Senior Lecturer in Political Economy and Sociology in the Department of Behavioral Sciences at Ben-Gurion University, Israel, where during 1998–2003 he was Director of the Humphrey Institute for Social Research. In 1974 he founded the Jewish-Arab student movement 'Campus' and he was the first spokesperson of the Refusers movement 'Yesh Gvul' (1982). His fields of special interest are the Zionist Labour Movement and the Israeli-Palestinian Conflict.

Among his books are *Split Corporatism in Israel* (1991), *The Histadrut Above All* (Hebrew, 1993) and *Contested Memory: Myth, Nation and Democracy* (Hebrew, 2000). His articles include 'Imagined Democracy in Israel', 'The Israeli-Palestinian Peace in the eyes of the "Left"', 'A Historical Slip of the Tongue' and 'The Unwanted Bride: the Language Misery of the Occupation Resistance'. Some of the columns he contributed as a publicist: 'The Arrogance of Occupation', 'Israel's State Terrorism', 'The Busharon Global War', 'Trapped by the USA', 'Lessons from Israel on Preemptive Wars' and 'Symbolic Genocide'.

Rema Hammami is Professor of Anthropology at Birzeit University, Ramallah, where she is Head of the Programme for Women's Studies. She has written extensively on gender, civil society and politics in Palestine and is co-editor of *Analytical Studies of Political and Social Issues in Palestine* (in Arabic). Besides numerous articles, she published *Labour and Economy: Gender Segmentation in Palestinian Economic Life* (1997) which appeared in both English and Arabic.

Jamil Hilal is a Palestinian sociologist who lives and works in Ramallah since 1995. He is an Associate Senior Research Fellow at Muwatin, the Palestinian Institution for the Study of Democracy (Ramallah) and a Senior Researcher at the Law Institute and at the Institute of Women's Studies at Birzeit University, and he is on the steering committee of the University's Development Study Programme.

Hilal has contributed extensively to studies on poverty among Palestinians, especially *The Palestine Poverty Report* (English and Arabic, 1998). He further published *Israel's Economic Strategy vis-à-vis the Middle East* (Arabic, 1996), *The Palestinian Political System since Oslo* (Arabic, 1998) and *The Formation of the Palestinian Elite* (Arabic, 2002). He co-authored a study on customary law in Palestine (published by Birzeit's Law Institute in 2006). Hilal co-edits the *Review of Women Studies* published by the Institute of Women Studies and he is on the editorial board of the *Journal of Palestine Studies* (published in Beirut). He is a member of the Palestine National Council.

Nur Masalha is a Senior Lecturer and Director of the MA Programme in Religion and Conflict, St Mary's College, University of Surrey, UK. He is the author of several books on Palestine and Israel, including *Expulsion of the Palestinians: The Concept of "Transfer" in Zionist Political Thought (1882–1948)* (1992), *A Land Without a People: Israel, Transfer and the Palestinians (1945–1996)* (1997), *Imperial Israel and the Palestinians: The Politics of Expansion* (2000) and *The Bible and Zionism: Invented Traditions, Archaeology and Post-Colonialism in Palestine-Israel* (2007). Masalha is the editor of *Holy Land Studies: A Multidisciplinary Journal*, published by Edinburgh University Press.

Issam Nassar is Professor of History at al-Quds University and Associate Director of the Institute of Jerusalem Studies, Jerusalem. He is a member of the editorial board of the *Jerusalem Quarterly* and of *Comparative Studies of South Asia, Africa and the Middle East.* Among his many publications are *Photographing Jerusalem: The Image of the City in Nineteenth-Century Photography* (1997), and *European Portrayals of Jerusalem: Religious Fascinations and Colonialist Imaginations* (2006).

Ilan Pappé, formerly a Senior Lecturer at the Department of Political Science, Haifa University, currently holds a Chair in the Department of History at the University of Exeter, where he also heads the Centre for Palestine Studies. He has written extensively on the history and politics of the modern Middle East and stands out for his revisionist history of Israel and Zionism. Among his books are *Britain and the Arab-Israeli Conflict* (1988), *The Making of the Arab-Israeli Conflict* (1994, repr. 2004), *The Israel/Palestine Question* (ed.; 1999) and *A History of Modern Palestine, One Land, Two Peoples* (2004, 2nd ed. 2006). In October 2006 he published *The Ethnic Cleansing of Palestine*, an uncompromising deconstruction of the Zionist narrative of '1948', in which he shows how the Zionists used the war in Palestine as a cover for the systematic expulsion of the indigenous population and the destruction of over 500 Palestinian villages and urban centres in their drive for the conquest of Palestine.

Dan Rabinowitz holds a PhD in Social Anthropology from Cambridge University and is Professor of Anthropology at Tel-Aviv University. His scholarly books include *Shakespeare in the Jungle* (1987, an edited collection), *Overlooking Nazareth* (1997), *Anthropology and the Palestinians* (1998), and *Coffins on our Shoulders* (2005). An edited collection, *Mixed Towns, Trapped Communities*, came out in 2007 and a book on The Trans-Israel Highway is forthcoming. He is a regular contributor to the op-ed page of *Ha'aretz* and Chairman of Life and Environment, the umbrella organization of environmental NGOs in Israel.

Salim Tamari is Professor of Sociology at Birzeit University, Ramallah, and Director of the Institute of Jerusalem Studies, Jerusalem. He publishes extensively on Palestinian history and society, especially on Jerusalem and refugee issues. Among his books are *Palestinian Refugee Negotiations: From Madrid to Oslo II (Final Status Issues)* (1996) and *Reinterpreting the Historical Records: The Uses of Palestinian Refugee Archives for Social Science Research and Policy Analysis* (2001). He is the editor of *Jerusalem 1948. The Arab Neighborhoods and their Fate in the War* (1999, 2nd ed. 2002) and (with Issam Nassar) *Ottoman Jersualem* (2003).

Oren Yiftachel is Professor of Geography and Public Policy at Ben-Gurion University of the Negev, Beer-Sheva, Israel. He has taught at Curtin University, Australia, the Technion, Israel, the University of Pennsylvania, Columbia University, UC Berkeley in the USA and at the University of Venice, Italy. He was a research fellow at RMIT, Melbourne, the US Institute of Peace, Washington DC; and the Van Leer Institute, Jerusalem.

Yiftachel is the founding editor of the journal *Hagar/Hajer: Studies in Culture Politics and Identities,* and serves on the editorial board of *Planning Theory* (essay editor), *Society and Space, IJMES, MERIP, Urban Studies, Journal of Planning Literature,* and *Social and Cultural Geography.* He currently works on three main research projects: the spatial transformation of Israel/Palestine; the development of ethnocratic regimes; and the various shades of the 'grey city'.

Among his books are *Planning as Control: Policy and Resistance in a Divided Society* (1995); *Ethnic Frontiers and Peripheries* (co-edited with A. Meir, 1998); *The Power of Planning* (co-edited with David Hedgcock, Jo Little & Ian Alexander, 2002); *Israelis in Conflict* (co-editor, 2004). His *Ethnocracy: Land and Identity Politics in Israel/Palestine* appeared in 2006 with University of Pennsylvania Press.

Moshe Zuckermann, born in Tel-Aviv, lived in Frankfurt/M, Germany, from 1960 until 1970, when he returned to Israel. His primary fields of interest are sociology, political science and general history. Since 1990, he teaches history and philosophy of the social and cultural sciences at the Cohn Institute for the History and Philosophy of Science and Ideas, Tel Aviv University. During 2000–2005 he headed the Institute for German History there. Zuckermann publishes *inter alia* on the history and philosophy of the social and cultural sciences, the Frankfurt School, aesthetic theory and sociology of art, and the impact of the Holocaust on the political cultures of Israel and Germany.

Index